3_

8

HOW WE WIN
THE CIVIL WAR

ALSO BY STEVE PHILLIPS

Brown Is the New White:
How the Demographic Revolution Has Created
a New American Majority

HOW WE WIN THE CIVIL WAR

Securing a Multiracial Democracy and
Ending White Supremacy for Good

Steve Phillips

THE
NEW
PRESS

NEW YORK
LONDON

Published in the United States by The New Press, New York, 2022

Distributed by Two Rivers Distribution

ISBN 978-1-62079-676-0 (hc)
ISBN 978-1-62097-689-0 (ebook)

CIP data is available

The New Press publishes books that promote and enrich public discussion and understanding of the issues vital to our democracy and to a more equitable world. These books are made possible by the enthusiasm of our readers; the support of a committed group of donors, large and small; the collaboration of our many partners in the independent media and the not-for-profit sector; booksellers, who often hand-sell New Press books; librarians; and above all by our authors.

www.thenewpress.com

Composition by dix!
This book was set in Scala

Printed in the United States of America

To Susan: the reality of cancer forces one to a more spiritual place of contemplating life, meaning, and legacy. That reflection has fueled my work on this book to try to make it a lasting legacy for both of us. What I wrote in the dedication of my first book is even truer today—"without Susan none of this would have been possible," and by "this" I mean pretty much anything meaningful I've accomplished in the past thirty years.

To the writers who've gone before: You were my muse in writing this book and I hope I've adequately honored and carried on the tradition.

To the folks who have done the work, are doing the work, and want to do the work: This is a love letter to all of you. On behalf of a grateful world, I thank you.

CONTENTS

AUTHOR'S NOTE

A word about names and capitalization in this book: As I wrote in my first book, *Brown Is the New White*, "Names matter to people who have battled discrimination and oppression." Society and my thinking have continued to evolve, and I wanted to say a few things about my choices on these matters so that there is no misunderstanding.

First is the question of referring to individuals by first names or last names. In a world steeped in racism and sexism, disrespect historically has often been conveyed by using someone's first name and denying that person the dignity of being referred to by their last name. There is a reason why Sidney Poitier's character in *In the Heat of the Night* reacts with an indignant response to being called "Virgil," a scene that has resonated so deeply with so many for so long. To this day, fifty-five years later, I can still see, hear, and relate to Poitier saying with seething rage, "They call me Mr. Tibbs!" So, I absolutely get why referring to people by their first names may be construed as a sign of disrespect.

In this book, I do use, upon second reference, the first names of some of the key people featured—Stacey Abrams, Tram Nguyen, and others—and I do so for a couple reasons. First, a big part of the problem in the progressive movement is a lack of personal connection to those doing the most important on-the-ground work. Many people dismiss and undervalue leaders who don't look the traditional, strong-straight-cis-gendered-white-male-leader part. This results in those leaders being marginalized rather than embraced, centered, and looked to for guidance. I want readers to feel the warmth that I feel for these essential national leaders and develop the connection with them that they deserve. I have gotten to know many of these leaders over the years, and I call them by their first names personally, so hopefully my connection can extend to the reader. With some key leaders, I do use their last names, but that's just because I don't know them as well, and it would feel presumptuous to assume I can be on a first-name basis with them in my book.

Second, there is the issue of how to write out the words describing people in particular groups in this color-conscious country. In this book I use uppercase "B" for Black people and lowercase "w" for white people. In *Brown Is the New White*, I explained that not only was I capitalizing "Black," but I was offended by the fact that most publications still spell Black with a lowercase "b." The professor Lori Tharps wrote a whole essay in the *New York Times* titled "The Case for Black with a Capital B," and her argument remains completely on point today. She wrote, "The New York Times and Associated Press stylebooks continue to insist on black with a lowercase b. Ironically, The Associated Press also decrees that the proper names of 'nationalities, peoples, races, tribes' should be capitalized. What are Black people, then?"[1]

Previously, I capitalized "white" while admitting that, "when it comes to the descendants of Europe, I am frankly more ambivalent about capitalizing 'White.' " And I cited the writer Touré, who argued, "I don't believe that whiteness merits the same treatment [as capitalizing Black]. Most American whites think of themselves as Italian-American or Jewish or otherwise."[2] In addition to endorsing Touré's point, I am no longer capitalizing "white" because white nationalism has become so powerful that I don't want to lend even an ounce of indirect support to the belief that whiteness is a sufficiently distinctive grouping meriting a formal title, characterization, and uppercase letter.

The evolution of our language on these matters is ongoing, uneven, and incomplete, and when quoting others, I have accordingly left original usage—that is, either capitalization or lowercase spelling—in place. Ultimately, I am mindful of and have never forgotten the words of my friend Bill King, who was president of the Stanford Black Student Union in the 1980s when the debate was bubbling up about using the phrase "African American." During a BSU meeting where people were debating which label to use, an exasperated Bill said, "I wish we could just figure out if we're Africans, or Blacks, or African Americans so that we can get on with dealing with being oppressed Africans or Blacks or African Americans or whatever." Or, as the comedian Dick Gregory said, the civil rights movement got so hung up on "Black" that it never got around to "Power." Not wanting to replicate that error, let us now turn the page to the question of how to build the power to finally win the Civil War.

HOW WE WIN
THE CIVIL WAR

INTRODUCTION

A Choice Between Democracy and Whiteness

I decided to reach out to a friend, Taylor Branch, the esteemed historian of the civil rights movement, to hear his thoughts. He was translating this through the lens of Martin Luther King, Jr.'s thirteen-year campaign for social justice. . . . "So the real question would be," he said finally, "if people were given the choice between democracy and whiteness, how many would choose whiteness?"

We let that settle in the air, neither of us willing to hazard a guess to that one.
—Isabel Wilkerson, *Caste: The Origins of Our Discontents*

Families frequently take trips to our nation's capital. It is common to see parents with their children in Washington, DC, visiting the iconic institutions of the country's democracy. Shortly after the Christmas holidays in 2020, Lisa, a fifty-seven-year-old white woman who worked as a nurse in Georgia, decided to make the ten-hour drive from Tennessee to DC with her son, Eric, a white thirty-year-old Nashville resident. On Monday, January 4, 2021, they arrived in DC and checked in at the Grand Hyatt Hotel, five blocks from the White House and three blocks from Ford's Theater, where Abraham Lincoln was assassinated days after the end of the Civil War.[1]

On Wednesday, mother and son made their way to the National Mall, a 1.8-mile stretch of land that encompasses grassy fields, a reflecting pool that is more than two thousand feet long, and gravel paths for walking or running. At one end of the Mall sits the Lincoln Memorial, the monument honoring the president who won the Civil War and the site where Martin Luther King Jr. delivered his historic 1963 "I Have a Dream" speech to 250,000 people and a national television audience. At the other end is the United States Capitol, the building where

Congress convenes and where presidents are sworn into office. A stroll from one end of the Mall to the other takes a visitor past the White House, the Washington Monument, the National Gallery of Art, and various Smithsonian museums, including the National Museum of African American History and Culture. Perhaps more than any other two-mile stretch of terrain in this country, the National Mall represents and celebrates the essence of democracy in America.

As Lisa and Eric walked across the grass toward the Capitol, the United States Congress and Vice President Mike Pence were engaged in the last step in the country's democratic process—affirming the votes of the American people and certifying Joe Biden as the winner of the election (an outcome that had been confirmed by the top elections officials in all fifty states, Republicans and Democrats alike).

When Lisa and Eric entered the Mall on January 6 and turned toward the Capitol, Lisa was wearing jeans, a plaid flannel shirt, glasses, and a red Make America Great Again ski cap. She was also wearing a bulletproof vest. Her son Eric had on a baseball cap, a long-sleeve shirt with a military fatigues pattern, and matching pants. He also had a bulletproof vest matching one his mother was wearing.[2] The two met up with and joined thousands of other people who were angry that Donald Trump had come out on the losing end of America's democratic process. As the crowd grew increasingly unruly and confrontational, Lisa and her son reveled in the conflict.

Many people tried to breach the barricades protecting the country's elected representatives from the restive mob, and Lisa egged on the protesters. One person who had tried to enter the building came back to the crowd and reported that a "tear gas package was thrown in the Congress." The crowd cheered. The man further shared that "Congress is shut down."

Lisa laughed and said, "Oh, my God. That is one of my best days to know that they got tear-gassed." By "they," Lisa meant the country's democratically elected representatives.

The man continued to elaborate on his confrontation with the law enforcement officials who were protecting the members of Congress, saying, "I got maced, and I punched two of them in the face."

"Good," Lisa responded. "While everyone else was on the couch, you guys were training and getting ready."[3]

Not long after Lisa commended the man who had punched two police officers in the face, the crowd turned completely violent, tore down the barricades protecting the citadel of democracy, and surged to the building's entrance. Fearing for the safety and lives of the people they were sworn to protect, the Capitol Police evacuated the vice president and all the members of Congress. Multiple media outlets have recounted the details of the violence of the insurrection.

The *New York Times* account conveyed that "one officer lost the tip of his right index finger. Others were smashed in the head with baseball bats, flag poles and pipes. Another lost consciousness after rioters used a metal barrier to push her into stairs as they tried to reach the Capitol steps during the assault."[4] DC Metropolitan Police Officer Michael Fanone "was pulled into the crowd, beaten with a flagpole and repeatedly tased with his own Taser," CNN reported. In addition, "rioters stole his badge and grabbed at his service gun. When rioters said they should 'kill him with his own gun,' Fanone pleaded with the mob and told them, 'I have kids.' " Fanone "lost consciousness, suffered a heart attack and was hospitalized after the clashes."[5] Video coverage of the attack shows Officer Daniel Hodges "crushed in a doorway between a massive press of rioters and the police line, writhing and screaming in pain. The video shows one of the rioters grabbing at Hodges' helmet and trying to rip it off."[6]

Sgt. Aquilino Gonell "was beaten with a flagpole. . . . His hand was sliced open." A CNN article published seven months after the attack revealed that Gonell "still has a vivid memory of what he faced: of the pepper spray that forced him and other officers from the front line, of the American flag poles, rocks and even guardrails pried from the inaugural stage that were used to attack officers, and of the struggle to keep the flood of insurrectionists from forcing their way through the door he was guarding." Gonell shared, "I bled, I sweat and I fought to prevent those people coming in through that entrance. . . . We literally were fighting inch by inch. . . . And I could hear them, 'We're going to shoot you. We're going to kill you. You're choosing your paycheck over the country. You're a disgrace. You're a traitor.' "[7] All told, 140 police officers were injured defending democracy that day, and four officers died by suicide in the days and weeks after the attack.[8]

After the police finally regained control of the Capitol, Lisa and Eric left the building and headed back to their hotel. The next day, as they loaded their car and prepared for the long drive back to Nashville, they took the time to talk to a reporter from the *Sunday Times* of London and shared their motivations for participating in the unprecedented and violent effort to block the peaceful transfer of power. As Lisa put it, "The left has everything: the media, organisations, the government. We have to organise if we're going to fight back and be heard." Lisa also shared that "a violent revolution has long been on the cards thanks to last year's racial justice protests, anti-police riots and 'unnecessary' coronavirus lockdowns." With tears in her eyes—and apparently while eating a hot dog—Lisa defiantly declared, "I'd rather die as a 57-year-old woman than live under oppression. I'd rather die and would rather fight." [9] Like mother, like son, Eric extended the military metaphor, saying, "We wanted to show that we're willing to rise up, band together and fight if necessary. Same as our forefathers, who established this country in 1776." [10] And with that, mother and son climbed into the car and set off on the road trip back home, their family trip to the nation's capital complete. Four days later, the police located and arrested Eric back in Nashville. When federal agents searched his home, they found fifteen firearms, "including an assault rifle, a sniper rifle with a tripod, pistols, shotguns and hundreds of rounds of ammunition." [11]

Lisa and her son certainly did not choose democracy on that January day. They chose to try to disrupt and destroy democracy. And they were not alone. The Insurrection Index, an online database, has more than one thousand entries of people who participated in the attempted coup of the U.S. government—nurses like Lisa, bartenders like Eric, and also elected officials, students, teachers, businesspeople. [12] One wealthy man, also from Tennessee, invited his friends to travel on his private jet to the insurrection in the capital. An article in *Vanity Fair* noted, "A murmur began to bubble among Memphis's lily white country-club elite. *Did you hear John Dobbs flew his buddies to the capital on his private jet?*" [13]

While the insurrectionists did not choose democracy, many of them did choose whiteness. As Nicole Austin-Hillery, executive director of the U.S. Program at Human Rights Watch, wrote in a blog post with her colleague Victoria Strang on the anniversary of the attack, "There is power in truth, and the truth about the January 6, 2021 attack on the US Capitol is this: racism and a fear of growing diversity in the United States was at the heart of the violence. While then-President Donald Trump encouraged demonstrators to retake the nation under the guise of halting certification of the 2020 election results, racism was in the roots of, and remains embedded in, this movement."[14] The *Washington Post* ran an extensive analysis of the participants in the insurrection and the symbols they carried, finding that "assembled in the crowd were a range of far-right groups, including self-described militias, white nationalists, and sundry conspiracists and agitators."[15]

The Black police officers who defended the leaders overseeing the democratic process of certifying the election that day have confirmed the prevalence of racism among the insurrectionists. In his testimony before the House Select Committee to Investigate the January 6th Attack, U.S. Capitol Officer Harry Dunn said, "One woman in a pink 'MAGA' shirt yelled, 'You hear that, guys, this nigger voted for Joe Biden!' Then the crowd, perhaps around twenty people, joined in, screaming 'Boo! Fucking Nigger!' " Dunn added that his fellow Black officers experienced similar treatment, and he told the committee that "one officer told me he had never, in his entire forty years of life, been called a 'nigger' to his face, and that that streak ended on January 6. Yet another black officer later told me had been confronted by insurrectionists inside the Capitol, who told him to 'Put your gun down and we'll show you what kind of nigger you really are!' "[16]

It was in November of 2018 that Taylor Branch framed the chilling question for Isabel Wilkerson: "If people were given the choice between democracy and whiteness, how many would choose whiteness?" Just over two years later, a proudly pro-white president who had lost a free and fair election incited his followers to march on the Capitol and stop democracy in its tracks. With the Confederate flag flying in their midst, they descended on the citadel of democracy, beat police officers over the head with flagpoles, and hunted down the country's elected officials, with many in the mob yelling racist slurs.

As horrifying, tragic, and deadly as the 2020 post-election attempted coup was, it was not the first time a large percentage of the American people chose whiteness over democracy in the wake of an election whose outcome they did not like.

———

When Abraham Lincoln was elected in 1860 on a platform that de-
nounced the slave trade as "a burning shame to our country," cries of
outrage echoed across the country. Newspapers warned that "Lincoln
intends to use every means to instigate revolt among the slaves. . . .
[They will] cut the throat of every white man, [and] distribute the white
females among the negroes."[17] Defenders of slavery plotted to murder
Lincoln before he could even take office. In the weeks following the
1860 election, state legislatures voted to secede from the rest of the
country because, as the South Carolina secession resolution said, "a
geographical line has been drawn across the Union, and all the States
north of that line have united in the election of a man to the high office
of President of the United States, whose opinions and purposes are hostile to slavery."[18] Five states quickly followed suit, and before Lincoln
could take the Oath of Office, they all came together in the Congress of
the Confederacy, where they unequivocally rejected the outcome of the
democratic process and unapologetically chose whiteness.

Confederate vice president Alexander H. Stephens made it quite
clear that not only were the Southern states rejecting the democratic
outcome of the election of the country to which they belonged, but that
they were enthusiastically choosing whiteness. In his 1861 "Cornerstone Speech," he forthrightly explained that the Confederate government's "foundations are laid, its cornerstone rests, upon the great
truth that the negro is not equal to the white man; that slavery subor-
dination to the superior race is his natural and normal condition."[19]
Three weeks later, in that century's post-election paroxysm of anti-
democratic feelings, the losing side embraced violence, death, and destruction, and went on to wage the nation's bloodiest war—a four-year
war in which 2 percent of the country's population killed one another
(the modern-day equivalent of 7 million people being killed).[20]

As will be shown in the pages of this book, Americans have consistently underestimated the political appeal of whiteness. Lincoln and
his allies were taken by surprise at the ferocity of the opposition to
his election in 1860. In the 1924 presidential election, neither political
party could muster the votes at their respective conventions to pass a
resolution condemning the Ku Klux Klan. In 1948, South Carolina native son Strom Thurmond ran a third-party presidential bid as the head
of the proudly pro-segregationist Dixiecrat Party and won four states

outright. Twenty years later, proud white segregationist Alabama governor George Wallace mounted his own third-party presidential bid
in 1968, quintupling the Dixiecrat vote share, winning five states and
securing 13.5 percent of the national popular vote (the equivalent of
22 million votes in the 2020 election). In 1990, twenty-two years after
Wallace's candidacy, former Ku Klux Klan grand wizard David Duke
shocked the political establishment in his run to become the U.S. senator of Louisiana, winning 43.5 percent of the vote and displaying far
greater vote-getting power than anyone wanted to admit.

And then came Trump. Trump rocketed to the head of the pack
of Republican presidential candidates in 2015 after spewing racist vit-
riol including demonizing Mexicans and Muslims. The media and
public once again underestimated the appeal of white resentment,
with nationally syndicated columnist Ann McFeatters expressing the
sentiments of many Americans in 2015 with a piece titled, "Relax,
Folks: Trump Won't Win, and America Will Remain Great." In that
column, McFeatters wrote what most hoped and believed, namely that
"[Trump] cannot be elected president in a general election because he
is losing women and independent voters by a 2-to-1 margin. In the end,
the majority of Republican voters will not nominate an angry white
male bigot who has publicly, insistently said awful things about immigrants, women, minorities and, basically, anyone who isn't rich and
intolerant like he is."[21] Welp. Not only did Trump win, but after four
years of incompetence, racism, misogyny, and impeachment, he received 11 million *more* votes than he did in 2016—garnering the support of 74 million Americans.

Writer Ta-Nehisi Coates brilliantly stripped away any pretense regarding the painful reality that when choosing Trump, many, many
people were choosing whiteness. In a 2017 essay in *The Atlantic*,
Coates went to the heart of the matter:

> The triumph of Trump's campaign of bigotry presented the
> problematic spectacle of an American president succeeding
> at best in spite of his racism and possibly even because of it.
> Trump removed the questions of racism from the euphemis-
> tic and plausibly deniable to the realm of the overt and freely
> claimed. This presented the country's thinking class with a

dilemma. It simply could not be that Hillary Clinton was correct when she asserted that a large group of Americans was endorsing a president because of bigotry. The implications—that
systemic bigotry is still central to our politics, that the country is
susceptible to that bigotry, that the salt-of-the-earth Americans
whom we lionize in our culture and politics are not so different
from those same Americans who grin back at us in lynching
photos . . . are just too dark.[22]

In 2021, four years after writing that *Atlantic* article—after an entire Trump administration and an outright insurrection and attempted
coup—Coates reflected on the racial wreckage of the Trump administration, writing a follow-up article titled, "Donald Trump Is Out. Are
We Ready to Talk About How He Got In?" In that piece, Coates offered his customary trenchant observations that define the moment
in which we find ourselves, writing, "It is still deeply challenging for
so many people to accept the reality of what has happened—that a
country has been captured by the worst of its history, while millions of
Americans cheered this on."[23]

In 2020 and 2021, millions of Americans chose whiteness wrapped
up in a proudly white nationalist white man in America's White House.
Never in the history of the country has the losing side sought to block
the certification process of a national election, but Donald Trump rallied his supporters to do just that. And yet, as of January 2022, a full
year after the insurrection, nearly 70 percent of Republicans wanted
Trump to run for president again in 2024.[24] It is not hyperbole to say
that the political power of whiteness in this country has grown steadily,
if not exponentially.

————

Despite the mountain of evidence that the battle still rages over
whether this is fundamentally a white nation or a multiracial democracy, too few Democrats and progressives recognize the seriousness of the fight we're in, and, if they do, they are too timid and
fearful to speak the truths that need to be spoken. As *Washington
Post* columnist Perry Bacon warned in 2021, "In basically every major institution in America, there are powerful figures who I doubt

voted for Donald Trump but nonetheless play down the radicalism of the Republican Party, belittle those who speak honestly about it or otherwise act in ways that make it harder to combat that radicalism. That needs to change. Americans desperately need leaders and institutions that are fully grappling with Republicans' dangerous anti-democratic drift." [25]

Although Joe Biden, to his credit, launched his presidential campaign with a condemnation of the 2017 white nationalist march in Charlottesville, Virginia, that turned violent and deadly, calling it "a moment of truth for the country," we have heard little from Biden or many Democrats about said moment of truth since then. The fact that the Biden administration let the voting rights fight languish for a year while it pursued the tantalizing talisman of bipartisan support for the infrastructure bill spoke volumes about its flawed assessment of this historical moment. In the minds of too many in the White House and Capitol Hill, political success depends more on wooing white voters and trying to assuage their fears than it does on tapping and unleashing the energy of the millions of people of color who are rapidly changing the composition of this country.

Even more alarming is that many in the Democratic Party and progressive movement leadership believe that it is a losing battle to challenge voters to embrace the concept that America is a multiracial democracy and not a white nationalist country. Fearing the political costs and consequences—and shockingly unable to count or use a spreadsheet to quantify the electoral power of the demographic revolution—they continue to run away from the central issue. And they do this to disastrous consequences, as was seen in the 2021 Virginia gubernatorial election—in the state that was the literal capital of the Confederacy—when Republican nominee Glenn Youngkin was able to unlock the code of white racial anxiety and thereby boost voter turnout by chanting the words "critical race theory," scaring whites into believing that the realities of racism and our nation's racist history might be taught in the state's schools. Meanwhile, Democratic nominee Terry McAuliffe was unable or unwilling, or both, to aggressively define the fight and wage the battle. There were no condemnations of white supremacy, proclamations that taking on racism was a moment of truth, or affirmations of his intent to champion racial justice and equality. And he lost. In a state Biden had won handily just twelve months earlier.

One of the biggest impediments to progress in this moment is the Democratic consultant class, which, for the most part, has little experience with or understanding of how racism actually works in America. Despite the overarching victories of 2020 that ousted Trump and flipped the U.S. Senate, unaccountable yet influential consultants continue to cherry-pick and misinterpret data about the 2020 election, overlook the real results, and offer a course of action that is like leading lambs to a McAuliffe-like slaughter. Even after the victories in 2020 in the formerly red states of Georgia and Arizona—states with large and growing communities of color—Democrats remain reluctant to define and engage the actual fight we're facing. A fight characterized by the battle for justice, equality, and inclusion by people of color and their allies, on the one hand, and by a virulent, fear-based white backlash on the other.

Data scientist David Shor is a leading proponent of what has come to be known as "popularism," a school of thought described by *New York Times* columnist Ezra Klein as the belief that "Democrats should do a lot of polling to figure out which of their views are popular and which are not popular, and then they should talk about the popular stuff and shut up about the unpopular stuff."[26] For a data geek, Shor's math is surprisingly off, and as of this writing in May of 2022, he had yet to reconcile his assertion that the Democratic Party is losing support among people of color with the fact that Democrats across the board significantly increased the number of votes they received from people of color. Most dangerous is that Shor and his cohort are prescribing a course of action that would be politically fatal in that it would reduce the enthusiasm of voters of color, who are the most reliable Democratic voters and the fastest-growing segment of the population.

At root—although they are reluctant to say this explicitly—the popularists advise that Democrats abandon and distance themselves from the issues that most affect people of color—issues such as the racial wealth gap, reimagining policing and public safety, and immigration reform. These are the realities that directly flow from the fact that our opponents are and have been waging a war to keep this nation a white-dominated one for more than a century. What they are offering with their popularist prescriptions is analogous to Lincoln had he tried to rally support in 1864—in the middle of the Civil War—by focusing exclusively on tariffs on agricultural goods while carefully avoiding talking about the unpopular, harsh reality of slavery. (To his credit, Lincoln's platform did emphatically assert that "slavery was the cause, and now constitutes the strength of this Rebellion," and it went on to "demand [slavery's] utter and complete extirpation from the soil of the Republic".)[27]

To be sure, such ambivalence about equality is nothing new. There were plenty of David Shors in Lincoln's time. One such proponent of post–Civil War popularism was Union general Charles Wainwright, who lamented that Lincoln was under the influence of a small number of abolitionist political leaders "who had negro on the brain."[28] One enterprising artist even created a drawing of Black people curled into the shape of a top hat sitting on Lincoln's head.[29] Lincoln himself was racked with indecision and vacillation, even going so far as tasking General Benjamin Butler with running the numbers on what it would cost to ship Black folks back to Africa.[30] One hundred years later, John F. Kennedy and Lyndon B. Johnson both tried to get the civil rights leaders to tone down their protests and slow down their march toward freedom, with LBJ telling Dr. King in late 1964 that pushing for a voting rights bill was "just not the wise and the politically expedient thing to do" (sound familiar?).[31]

Given the truly existential nature of the fight before us and the fundamental failure of those in positions of power to recognize and properly respond to the moment, I had to write this book. When The New Press first approached me in mid-2020 about writing another book, I told them I was thinking about using the Civil War framework as a theoretical construct to explain contemporary U.S. politics. Then white nationalists carrying the Confederate flag stormed the Capitol wearing sweatshirts actually inscribed with the words "MAGA: Civil War January 6, 2021."

———

The purpose of this book is twofold. First, I am trying to sound the alarm that our opponents are engaged in a continuation of the Civil War, have just recently tried to destroy democracy and move us into fascism, and are actively at work to do it again. Second, I aim to help illuminate the path to victory by putting the places that have successfully flipped from red to blue under the microscope to understand how these states and regions—and the key leaders and organizations there—succeeded and what lessons they offer for the coming months and years. The book is accordingly divided into two parts. Part I focuses on how the Civil War never ended, and the Confederates soldier on, to this day. Part II shows how we win. Then, in the epilogue, I offer a glimpse of the kind of society that could be possible once we win the war.

PART I: THE CIVIL WAR NEVER ENDED

Winning a war requires that you first recognize that you are in a war. Paul Revere, eighteenth-century Revolutionary War hero, is famously said to have ridden through town warning, "The British are coming! The British are coming!" as the British army steadily advanced. The early warning gave the Americans notice to prepare and was critical to success in the first battles of the Revolutionary War. Imagine if Revere had instead ambled down the street saying, "We're going to invite the British to dinner and see if we can reach a bipartisan agreement. Sinema and Manchin are bringing clam chowder." I don't mean to be flip about this (well, maybe a little), but the stakes are actually deadly serious. The ideological, philosophical, and, in some cases, actual descendants of the Confederates are waging an unrelenting, not infrequently violent, war to keep what was once a white nationalist country from becoming a multiracial democracy.

This fight has raged for 157 years—starting just days after the supposed end of the Civil War—and it has been fought following a remarkably consistent set of strategies and tactics, what I call the Confederate Battle Plan. This Battle Plan is multidimensional and has proved highly effective. It has five core components. While the sequence and deployment of the elements has occasionally varied, the presence and power of all five elements has been a constant:

- **Never Give an Inch**—Responding to a lost election by turning to violence, taking up arms and killing hundreds of thousands of your fellow countrymen is obviously the most extreme example of never giving an inch in the fight to preserve white supremacy, but there are others. From fighting tooth and tail to block the Constitutional amendments banning slavery and guaranteeing racial equality, all the way up to the years-long, relentless, still-ongoing efforts to undermine Obamacare and its promise of health care for all, the keepers of the Confederate cause have never given one inch in conceding ground to those working to establish a multiracial democracy.

- **Ruthlessly Rewrite the Laws**—Every time the Confederates have lost, they have quickly and ruthlessly turned to the task of rewriting the laws so that they don't lose again. The purpose of these laws has consistently been to preserve white power and suppress the potential political consequences of allowing all members of the racially diverse population to participate in elections.

- **Distort Public Opinion**—Most people don't actively support fascism, white supremacy, or racism. As a result, the keepers of the Confederate cause have worked assiduously to recast and redefine their fight in a more palatable light. Over the decades, this whitewashing of white supremacy has been accomplished through varied mechanisms distorting public opinion, including books, plays, movies, songs, monuments, and now cable news and social media.

- **Silently Sanction Terrorism**—Starting just days after the 1865 Confederate surrender in Appomattox, Virginia, white nationalists have continued their efforts through the use of bloody, violent domestic terrorism, and their goal has always been to preserve white power by preventing people of color from voting. At every step of the way, while the terrorism has done its part to block democracy and protect whiteness, more mainstream Confederate leaders have silently—and sometimes not so silently—sanctioned the activities of the white domestic terrorists.

- **Play the Long Game**—Contrary to the more comforting notion that racism and white supremacy are the result of ignorance and inadequate education, the post–Civil War fight has been defined by great sophistication and shrewdness in devising and following strategies that have long-term, multi-generational impact.

From the 1800s to the twenty-first century, smart and savvy deals were struck and decisions made that weakened the march toward the multiracial makeover of America, and we are still dealing with the fallout from that long game.

PART II: HOW WE WIN

Part II of this book shows how we win. Trump is no longer president, and the Democrats took control of Congress after the 2020 elections because of the political transformation of the places that were once the cornerstones of the Confederacy. Georgia, Arizona, Virginia, San Diego, California, and Harris County, Texas, are all sizable and important regions where the political balance of power has been upended over the past decade. The story of the metamorphosis of those regions offers vital instruction and also inspiration for how to win.

In achieving those wins, progressives have also deployed a common Battle Plan. Chapter 6 distills and explains the core components of what I call the Liberation Battle Plan. Chapters 7 through 11 are case studies of how each state or region managed to achieve the wins it did. The commonalities in each story are notable, and collectively they provide a curriculum for how to win this Civil War. That these places, groups, and leaders have had such success provides hope and evidence that it is indeed possible.

In looking at the success stories, several important themes emerge, none more important than that, to win, we have to reorient our thinking about what leaders look like. Pretty much all Democrats and progressives now agree that Stacey Abrams is an important and effective political leader in this country (after her work resulted in Democrats winning the two U.S. Senate seats in Georgia that flipped control of the Congress). But I know for a fact that she faced remarkable resistance and received minimal support in her work. Even Biden inadvertently admitted on election night 2020 that he was shocked he won Georgia, saying in his election night speech, "That's not one we expected"—a reflection of how little investment his campaign made in that pivotal state.

A big part of the reason that the movement was slow to support Stacey is that she doesn't look like what we have traditionally thought leaders look like. As she said in an interview on Oprah's OWN network, "I ran for governor as a sturdy woman with natural hair and a gap between my teeth. . . . I haven't had a perm since 1995. I like who I am, and because I knew I was the best person for the job, I wasn't going to wait until Weight Watchers or Jenny Craig turned me into the 'after' picture."[32] Even with minimal resources and inadequate support, she persevered, following the Liberation Battle Plan of developing data-driven plans, building strong civic engagement organizations, and playing the long game. The results have been staggering. When Stacey and I spoke in early 2021 after the newly Democratic Congress passed the Covid relief package, I joked, "You took that $10,000 we helped you raise in 2012, and you've turned it into $2 trillion for the American people?" She replied, "I like to provide return on investment."

The returns that Georgia's political revolution has yielded are just a down payment on what is possible in the coming years, and that's because the success is not just about Stacey. In each of the states that are being transformed, there are leaders like Stacey, but they don't look like the traditional white male model of intelligence and competence. They are mainly women, mostly people of color, immensely awesome, and—most importantly—highly effective. This is not just about feel-good efforts to foster diversity and inclusion; it's about winning a war. There are people who have actually won and are winning now. If we want to win, we will find them, back them, invest in them, lift them up, and follow them to victory.

———

While the historical record is sobering, there is also ample reason to hope. When faced with the choice between democracy and whiteness, many white people have, in fact, done the right thing. Some have even risked and given their lives in that struggle.

Heather Heyer had likely never heard of Viola Liuzzo, but now their names are forever linked as two white women who stood up against white nationalism and made the ultimate sacrifice in the process. Liuzzo was a thirty-nine-year-old Detroit housewife and mother of five children who was so moved by the urgency of the civil rights movement that she got in her car and drove from Michigan to Alabama to volunteer to help out with the voting rights marches taking place in March 1965. Upon the completion of the successful Selma to Montgomery march, she helped drive people back to Selma, a distance of fifty-four miles. After she had dropped off some marchers, a car of Klansmen drove up next to her and saw that she was in a car with a Black man, Leroy Moton. They aimed their guns at Liuzzo, then shot and killed her (the bullets missed Moton, who survived the attack). Liuzzo's death shocked the nation and captured the conscience of the country, lending momentum to the movement to pass the Voting Rights Act of 1965.[33]

Fifty-two years after Liuzzo's murder, Heyer protested the 2017 white supremacist rally in Charlottesville and was killed by an angry young white man (see chapter 5). It was her death that motivated Biden to invoke Charlottesville in his campaign kickoff ad. Heyer, like Liuzzo, gave her life for a cause and a movement that did succeed in defeating those who were working furiously to make America white again.

The very fact that Trump is not president, and Democrats currently control Congress is proof that we can win.

Georgia has been the epicenter of this country's Civil War for centuries. It is where Union general William T. Sherman broke the will of the Confederate army toward the end of the Civil War in his famous March to the Sea. It is where *Gone with the Wind* is set. It was the birthplace of Martin Luther King Jr. and his base of operations for many years. It is where Stacey Abrams has done the work blazing the path and expanding the electorate, making Biden's win possible. And it is the state where King's successor as pastor of Ebenezer Baptist Church, Raphael Warnock, won election to the Senate, flipping control of that entire body to the Democrats. It is a shining case study in how to win, but it is by no means the only one. Arizona, Texas, Florida, North Carolina, Virginia, and other states are also places where we are poised to win.

If we first recognize that we are *in* a war, and then learn the lessons and follow the lead of those who have shown they know how to prevail, we can definitely win the Civil War, secure a multiracial democracy, and end white supremacy for good. For the good of *all.*

Part I

We Are Still in a Civil War

Part I

1

The Confederacy: From Surrender to Success

Most Confederate leaders expected imprisonment, confiscation, perhaps even banishment. Expecting the worst, they were willing to give up many things in order to keep some. If there was ever a moment for imposing a lasting solution to the American racial problem, this was it. But the North dawdled and the moment passed. When the Confederates realized that the North was divided and unsure, hope returned. And with hope came a revival of the spirit of rebellion. . . . This was one of the greatest political blunders in American history.

—Lerone Bennett Jr., *Black Power U.S.A.: The Human Side of Reconstruction, 1867–1877*

General Robert E. Lee had surrendered, but Lewis Powell was having none of it. Lee, commander of the Confederate army, ostensibly ended the four-year Civil War by formally surrendering control of his troops to General Ulysses S. Grant on April 9, 1865, after the battle of Appomattox in Virginia.

Just five days later, at 9:30 p.m., Powell left his Washington, DC, home with a gun, a knife, and a plan to murder the secretary of state, William Seward.[1]

Eight blocks away, shortly after 10:00 p.m. that night, the third act of the play *Our American Cousin* was just beginning at Ford's Theater. The play was a big hit and was revered in its time as "the funniest thing in the world."[2] Twenty-first-century theater critic Robert Viagas described it as a "portrait of a clash of cultures between the hoity-toity British and their country bumpkin distant American cousin who had somehow managed to inherit the family estate. The same vein of humor would later be mined in many movies and TV shows, notably 'The Beverly Hillbillies.' "[3] One big fan of the show was Abraham Lincoln, president of the United States and the architect of the war that defeated the Confederacy and forced General Lee to surrender.

While Powell was making his way to Seward's home, his friend and collaborator John Wilkes Booth slipped into Ford's Theater and made his way upstairs to the box where President Lincoln was enjoying the performance. Booth was a well-known actor whose presence at the theater was familiar and aroused no suspicions. He was also a man of strong political opinions. In a letter drafted six months before the surrender at Appomattox, Booth wrote, "This country was formed for the white, not for the black man. And looking upon African Slavery from the same stand-point held by the noble framers of our constitution. I for one, have ever considered it one of the greatest blessings (both for themselves and us,) that God has ever bestowed upon a favored nation."[4]

Three days before heading to Ford's Theater with his gun, Booth had been among the crowd gathered outside the White House to hear Lincoln give his first post-Appomattox speech. When the president expressed support for extending the franchise to Black people, Booth turned to a friend and said that what Lincoln was proposing "means nigger citizenship." He went on to add, "That is the last speech he will ever make."[5] True to his word, on the night of April 14, 1865, Booth evaded Lincoln's security, made his way to the second floor of the theater, drew his revolver, and shot the president of the United States in the back of the head.

Powell, carrying out his part in the carefully coordinated conspiracy, gained entry into Secretary of State Seward's home by tricking Seward's staff and family into believing he was bringing needed medicine. Once inside the residence, Powell made his way into the cabinet secretary's bedroom and stabbed him in the face. (Seward survived even though "the large bowie knife [had] plunged into his neck and face, severing his cheek so badly that 'the flap hung loose on his neck.' ")[6]

The violent events of that one week in April 1865 encapsulate and illustrate the dynamics that would shape the next 157 years of this country. On Sunday, the South surrendered. By the end of the week, supporters of the Confederacy had murdered the president of the United States of America (the first assassination in U.S. history).

The Civil War may have technically ended, but the fighting never stopped. Over the ensuing decades, those who believe that America is first and foremost a white nation ferociously fought on, taking their fight to every aspect of society, and they did so by following a battle plan—a "Confederate Battle Plan"—that continues to dominate our politics in the third decade of the twenty-first century.

NEVER GIVE AN INCH

Donald Trump was not the first white American leader to refuse to accept the facts of defeat, and his determination to never give an inch was simply the latest example in a long line of resistance that has been carried out since the 1800s by the leaders of the same regions and demographic groups that formed the core of Trump's power base. After losing at the polls, Trump continued fighting by filing lawsuits, sending mendacious tweets, and giving incendiary speeches, including one that incited a violent mob to storm the U.S. Capitol—with members of the mob proudly carrying Confederate flags.

For the participants in the original Civil War, their refusal to give an inch took the form of continuing to shoot and kill their opponents.

Lee surrendered on April 9, 1865, but recalcitrant Southerners fought on for months. In addition to murdering President Lincoln, they turned their weapons and bullets on the young men in the Union army working to defend what Lincoln described in the Gettysburg Address as a "nation, conceived in liberty, and dedicated to the proposition that 'all men are created equal.' " Those who believed that all people were *not* created equal resisted every step toward racial equality, and they did so by any means necessary.

———

John Salmon "Rip" Ford embodied the archetypal white Texan, living a life of swashbuckling adventure. After serving two years as a soldier, he became a practicing physician, got elected to the Texas State Legislature, and then purchased a newspaper. Imbued with confidence and leadership, Ford became a prominent colonel in the Confederate army.[7] His enthusiasm for taking up arms, risking his life for the Confederate cause, and directing Southern men to shoot and kill hundreds of their formerly fellow Americans stemmed from his determination that he would never capitulate to "a mongrel force of Abolitionists, negroes, plundering Mexicans, and perfidious renegades . . . [who would] murder and rob with impunity"—a constellation of people also known as the army of the United States of America.[8]

Despite the formal surrender of his Confederate higher-ups thirty-five days earlier, Ford directed his troops to continue the bloodshed. On May 13, 1865—five full weeks after Appomattox—he rallied a band of three hundred men to resist the advancing Union army coming to Texas to enforce the terms of surrender. Over the course of two days of hostilities on the Rio Grande River, Ford's forces killed 114 Union soldiers.[9]

Custodians of Texas history have looked kindly on the man whose crowning life achievement consisted of orchestrating the violent deaths of dozens, if not hundreds, of Americans as he worked to defend a system that kept Black people in chattel slavery. In 2008—the same year a Black man was elected president of the United States—the Texas Military Forces Museum inducted Rip Ford into their Hall of Honor, stating: "Ford waged a bold campaign that recaptured all the Rio Grande Valley and exiled Union troops to Brazos Island just off the coast. When Federal forces advanced onto the mainland in May of 1865, Ford orchestrated their defeat at Palmetto Ranch, winning the last battle of the Civil War."[10]

Although the Ford-led fight is widely considered the "last battle of the Civil War," James Waddell clearly didn't get the April 1865 memo that surrender was the order of the day. Waddell had viewed his duty as waging war for the Confederate cause on the high seas, having in 1864 retrofitted a former British merchant ship—christened the Confederate States ship *Shenandoah*—into a wartime vessel with cannons, ammunition, and the ability to attack, cripple, and destroy other ships, especially those flying the United States flag.

Although Waddell eventually learned that Robert E. Lee had surrendered (he was given copies of newspapers with the news two months after Appomattox), he drew greater inspiration from the exhortation of Jefferson Davis, deposed president of the Confederate States of America, who defiantly declared in the same newspapers announcing Lee's surrender that "the war would be carried on with renewed vigor." Waddell and his troops did in fact carry on with renewed vigor, continuing to capture American ships for several more months.[11]

Nearly one hundred years after Waddell's efforts darting around the waters off the East Coast, shooting and killing and capturing people onboard ships loyal to the government working to abolish slavery, that same U.S. government honored Waddell by naming a missile destroyer after him. The U.S.S. *Waddell* was commissioned in 1964 and participated in the Vietnam War in the 1960s with a focus on the Mekong Delta region (the same region, as will be seen in chapter 9, where Tai Nguyen, the father of current Virginia leader Tram Nguyen, escorted U.S. ships like the *Waddell* up and down the river before Mr. Nguyen was captured by North Vietnamese troops and sent to a reeducation camp in 1975).[12] The *Waddell* commissioning ceremony was attended by top government officials, including several rear admirals, the wife of a United States senator, a military band, and a chaplain. The program for the event included a letter from the U.S. chief of naval operations extolling "the exemplary record of Lieutenant James Iredell Waddell who . . . courageously commanded the Confederate Navy Ship *Shenandoah* during the Civil War." (One wonders whether commanders of Nazi ships are lauded in contemporary times for their exemplary records and courageous guidance of ships of Aryan supremacy).[13]

Ultimately, on November 2, 1865, superior U.S. government military power prevailed in stopping Waddell and his *Shenandoah*, thus ending the formal armed hostilities portion of the Civil War, and forcing the South to relent in the fight to preserve its preferred form of Black human bondage.

While the surrender of the *Shenandoah* is viewed by historians as the last official surrender by the Confederate forces, the practice of Confederates never giving an inch was just getting started.

———

How would you like to go down in history for having stood up in the United States Congress to speak against the abolition of slavery? Especially if you weren't even a slaveholder yourself? And yet, that is exactly what one of New York's leading politicians did in 1864. John Pruyn, a distinguished New York businessman, lawyer, husband, father, and congressman, spoke out in Congress against the Thirteenth Amendment—the amendment mandating that slavery shall not exist in the United States. Pruyn bemoaned the inordinate amount of attention being paid to "questions of social reform in the condition of the slave population of the South."[14] In his view, the presidential preoccupation with matters of equality was doing great damage, not the least of which was inflicting discomfort on the *slaveholders*, "alienating . . . the friends of the Union in those States and embarrassing their return to their allegiance."[15] Pruyn was not alone in believing that Congress should pay more attention to the "discomfort" that emancipation caused to the slaveholders than to the moral imperative of definitively ending slavery itself.

Although many blanched at the thought of enshrining equality in the nation's governing document, some of America's leaders did work to make sure that the cause for which so much blood was spilled—ending the enslavement of African Americans—became firmly spelled out in the country's Constitution. To accomplish that objective, congressional leaders put forth and ultimately passed three amendments to America's governing document. But it wasn't easy.

Boiled down to their essence, the post–Civil War constitutional amendments held that Black people could not be enslaved (Thirteenth Amendment, ratified in 1865), discriminated against (Fourteenth Amendment, 1868), or denied the right to vote (Fifteenth Amendment, 1870). These policies faced opposition from dozens of members of the U.S. Congress, and, in the case of the Fourteenth and Fifteenth amendments, even the U.S. president. And much of the opposition came from states that were NOT part of the Confederacy. Yes, you read that right. Black folks' supposed *allies* hemmed and hawed when it came time to put a prohibition on slavery and racial discrimination in the U.S. Constitution. As renowned Harvard scholar Henry Louis Gates Jr. put it in his 2019 book, *Stony the Road*, "Reconstruction revealed a fact that had been true but not always acknowledged even before the Civil War: that it was entirely possible for many in the country, even some abolitionists, to detest slavery to the extent that they would be willing to die for its abolition, yet at the same time to detest the enslaved and the formerly enslaved with equal passion."[16]

In 1864, Congressman Pruyn was joined in opposition to the

Thirteenth Amendment by sixty-five of his congressional colleagues, blocking the House of Representatives from securing the two-thirds vote necessary to pass the measure.[17] Bear in mind that, having seceded from the country, no representatives of the Confederate states were even in Congress at that time, and yet the House of Representatives *still* couldn't pass an amendment outlawing slavery. It would take another year and a half before the amendment would pass and become incorporated into the country's founding document (although no official Confederates remained in Congress, many slaveholders and slavery sympathizers stuck around, as the *Washington Post* noted in its database on members of Congress who held slaves, finding that "more than 20 percent of the members who remained in Congress as the country fought the Civil War over slavery were current or former slaveholders").[18]

Even after narrow passage in Congress, the journey to get the necessary ratification for the Thirteen Amendment by two-thirds of the states was uncertain and uneven at best. It was only when Congress made ratification of the amendment an explicit condition of readmittance to the Union (and the financial benefits to the economically ravaged Southern states that that would entail) that a sufficient number of states went on record saying that enslaving human beings was wrong. Once Congress secured the necessary two-thirds of the states to ratify, the other third of the states took their own sweet time expressing opposition to slavery. Mississippi did not ratify the Thirteenth Amendment until 1995.[19] That means that when Mississippi native Oprah Winfrey was starring in the movie *The Color Purple* in 1985, the state's official position was that Winfrey herself could be held in slavery, placing her in an even worse position than her character Sofia. (It kind of puts a whole new light on the character Sofia saying, "All my life I had to fight.")

And that was just the road to pass an amendment to end slavery, not even to grant any rights to people once they were liberated from bondage. For those efforts—the amendments to ban discrimination and guarantee the right to vote—the fighting took longer than the Civil War itself, dragging on for nearly five years after Lee's surrender at Appomattox.

———

The intensity of the refusal to give an inch in the fight over the enslavement of Black people was just a tepid prelude to what would follow.
The next frontier in the fight over the *extent* of freedom and equality
assured to Americans with Black skin was the battle over equal protection of the laws. Again, what was at stake was a seemingly simple
proposition: the laws of a state should apply equally to all its people,
regardless of skin color. As was the case with the Thirteenth Amendment, however, the battle over codifying equality was ferocious, fre-
netic, and long-lasting, with the Confederates and their allies never
giving an inch.

Before attempting another amendment to the Constitution, supporters of Black equality tried to go the easier route of simply passing a
bill through Congress. Opposition to that bill—the Civil Rights Act—
stretched from local Confederate officials in the South all the way to the
White House. In fact, President Andrew Johnson—elevated to power
as a result of Booth's determination to stop "nigger citizenship"—fully
validated the hopes that inspired the actor to shoot Lincoln dead. While
some historians suggest that he believed he was redressing the worst of
the Confederate excesses and violations (such as sedition and treason),
Johnson nevertheless used the full force of his office and platform to
stand side by side with the white supremacists of the day, quite literally
working to stop niggers from becoming citizens. Johnson, who had
been reported to have said, "This is a country for white men, and, by
God, as long as I am president it shall be a government for white men,"
worked strenuously to oppose the racial equality legislation.[20]

In 1866 Johnson vetoed the Civil Rights Act, and he did so with
gusto, offering public arguments that tapped into sentiments of white
victimhood that have echoed across the centuries. In his veto message, Johnson wrote, "The distinction of race and color is by the bill
made to operate in favor of the colored and against the white race."[21]
Fortunately, his enthusiasm for white nationalism was not backed up
by commensurate political skill, and he ultimately failed in his efforts.

Although Johnson's veto of the Civil Rights Act was overridden by
Congress—the first override of a presidential veto in U.S. history—
proponents of the bill could now clearly see the precarious position of
the rights they sought to codify. What was established with the stroke
of a pen could just as easily be taken away. They realized they needed

something more permanent, and so, in an effort to solidify the rights that people had literally just finished fighting and dying for, they proposed to place core protections in the U.S. Constitution in the form of the Fourteenth Amendment, which embedded the equal protection guarantees of the Civil Rights Act of 1866 in the country's charter document.

You would have thought, by the reaction, that they were proposing the very destruction of America itself. The first two attempts to pass the Fourteenth Amendment failed to attract enough votes for it to be passed by Congress. Again, this was in a Congress without any members from the Confederate states. After several months during which seventy proposals were hashed over (that's seven-zero), the amendment ensuring equality finally made it out of Congress in mid-1866 (more than a year after the surrender at Appomattox).[22] It would take another two years before the requisite number of states ratified the amendment, and, again, that only occurred because ratification was an explicit condition for each Confederate state to be readmitted to the country.

Having begrudgingly determined that Black people should not be bought and sold and that they were entitled to the equal protection of all the laws, Congress next had to take on the question whether, in a purported democracy, citizens of a darker hue could also cast ballots and vote like their white brethren. As was the case with its predecessor amendments, the Fifteenth Amendment is pretty straightforward, stating simply that "the right of citizens of the United States to vote shall not be denied or abridged by the United States or by any State on account of race, color, or previous condition of servitude." Basically, don't deny someone the right to vote because of their race or color. The Confederates and their successors have been resisting that proposition for 157 years (and counting).

Chief among the opponents of giving Black people the right to vote was, again, President Andrew Johnson. In his Third Annual Message to Congress in 1867 (the equivalent of the modern-day State of the Union address, with the exception that it was written), Johnson did not mince white supremacist words:

The subjugation of the States to Negro domination would be worse than the military despotism under which they are now suffering. . . . It is the glory of white men to know that they have had these qualities in sufficient measure to build upon this continent a great political fabric and to preserve its stability for more than ninety years. . . . It must be acknowledged that in the progress of nations Negroes have shown less capacity for government than any other race of people.[23]

In reflecting on the seventeenth president's remarks, the historian Gates wrote: "[Johnson's] aversion to black suffrage was as deep as his aversion to the idea of the fundamental equality of black people with white people. . . . [He] marshaled the central tenets of white supremacist beliefs in an all-out effort to prevent black men from voting."[24] It took another three years after Johnson's ode to "the glory of white men" before the Fifteenth Amendment was ratified.

Even ostensible allies of Black folks were wishy-washy on protecting the right to vote. Ulysses S. Grant commanded the army that defeated the Confederacy, and then ascended to the presidency in 1868, as a member of Lincoln's Republican, anti-slavery, Party. According to the historian Eric Foner, in private, in 1870, "Grant told the Cabinet that, on reflection, the Fifteenth Amendment had been a mistake: 'It had done the Negro no good, and had been a hindrance to the South, and by no means a political advantage to the North.' "[25]

And those were just the fights in Washington, DC. While resisting changes to the federal Constitution, Confederates were also feverishly following another key part of the Confederate Battle Plan—rewriting state laws to restore Confederate power and entrench white supremacy.

RUTHLESSLY REWRITE THE LAWS

The post–Civil War ruthless rewriting of laws took place in three sequential periods:

- Black Codes (1865–66)[26]
- Redemption (mid-1870s to mid-1890s)
- Restoration (1890–1908)[27]

The essential thrust of these waves of postwar legislative warfare was to retain as much of the slave-labor economic relationships as possible (the Black Codes), undermine the democratic reforms of Reconstruction that extended the franchise to African American men (Redemption), and then straight up defy the constitutional voting rights mandate set up by the Fifteenth Amendment—as if the South hadn't lost the Civil War at all (Restoration). Confederates have never suffered from a paucity of ambition or vision.

———

Being a slaveholder was a sweet gig. Not having to work is nice. It's why it's so hard to come back home after a vacation, especially if it's been at a nice hotel or even a resort. It's great to have somebody else cook your food, clean your room, bring you whatever you want as soon as you pick up the phone and call the front desk. You don't want that bliss to end. Being a slaveholder must have been like being on vacation all the time. In the way that children whine or cry at having to leave vacation, slaveholders wanted to maintain the gravy train of free Black labor—figuratively wailing like Scarlett O'Hara in *Gone with the Wind*, "Where shall I go? What shall I do?" The answer was to pass as many laws as possible to keep things the way they were.

In his book *Black Power U.S.A.: The Human Side of Reconstruction, 1867–1877*, historian Lerone Bennett Jr. described the Confederate mindset animating the actions of the era immediately following the supposed surrender at Appomattox. "Although most Southern whites agreed reluctantly that black people no longer belonged to individual white men," he wrote, "most Southern whites still believed that black people in general belonged to white people in general."[28] The Black Codes enacted in the months following the formal cessation of fighting translated that sentiment into laws and legislation.

Faced with the fact that they could no longer enjoy the unfettered use of human beings in chains, the Confederates regrouped, retreated, and rethought how to perpetuate the essence of slavery—the free use of Black labor for white benefit. In the period immediately following the Civil War, several Confederate cities and states began to draft new laws for Black people—Black Codes—that could accomplish these ends. Florida governor William Marvin, appointed by President

Johnson in 1865 to facilitate the state's reentry to the Union, captured the spirit and intention of these laws when he said that the best course of action would be for African Americans to return to the plantations, work hard, and "call your old Master—'Master.' "[29]

In his 1988 book *Reconstruction*, Foner described the Black Code laws and their purpose as follows:

> Virtually from the moment the Civil War ended, the search began for legal means of subordinating a volatile black population that regarded economic independence as a corollary of freedom and the old labor discipline as a badge of slavery. Many localities in the summer of 1865 adopted ordinances limiting black freedom of movement, prescribing severe penalties for vagrancy, and restricting blacks' right to rent or purchase real estate and engage in skilled urban jobs.[30]

Don't sleep on the phrase "purchase real estate" in Foner's description. Modern-day conservatives—and even too many liberals—promote the view that Black people are poor because they lack the necessary skills, training, or character to get good jobs or run businesses that can generate wealth. What Foner showed, however, is that as soon as the Civil War ended, Confederates got busy writing laws in 1865 *barring African Americans from purchasing real estate.* Homeownership and the attendant appreciation of property values is a key way that many Americans—especially white Americans—have created wealth for themselves and their families, and African Americans were barred *by law* from participating in that wealth-generating enterprise almost from the moment the shooting stopped in the Civil War. Today, the country still has a Grand Canyon–sized racial wealth gap, with the average white family having eight times the assets of the average Black family.

I am a witness to the power of how homeownership can alter a family's economic and life trajectory. In 1964, ninety-nine years after the end of the Civil War, the white family that owned the house at 2637 Dartmoor Road in Cleveland Heights, Ohio, wouldn't sell that house to my parents because they were Black. We eventually got the home after a white civil rights lawyer, Byron Krantz, purchased it for my family and deeded it over to us, and my mother later used the accumulated equity to pay for my tuition to private school, which gave me contacts, connections, and skills that opened the doors to economic opportunity and success. Most Black folks have not been so lucky.

In addition to their economic impact, the ruthlessly rewritten laws that were the Black Codes also foreshadowed the role of the criminal justice system in maintaining control and suppression of descendants of Africa in America. There is a loophole in the Thirteenth Amendment that has been exploited by Confederates for more than a century now. In her brilliant documentary film *13th*, Ava DuVernay depicts how the constitutional ban on slavery has a six-word exception—"except as a punishment for crime"—that has enabled a continuation of the control of Black bodies and labor since the days of the Civil War. Columbia professor Jelani Cobb explains in *13th*, "When we think about slavery, it was an economic system. The demise of slavery at the end of the Civil War left the Southern economy in tatters. . . . How do you rebuild your economy? The Thirteenth amendment loophole was immediately exploited."[31]

The Black Codes were essentially an attempt to make the North surrender its victory after the South supposedly surrendered the fight. For the North, the Black Codes were a bridge too far too soon for a nation that had just waged a bloody multiyear war to end slavery. As W.E.B. Du Bois described it in his book *Black Reconstruction in America*, the severity of the Southern Black Codes stirred the conscience of "the ordinary everyday people of the North . . . who, without any personal affection for the Negro or real knowledge of him, nevertheless were convinced that Negroes were human, and that Negro slavery was wrong; and that whatever freedom might mean, it certainly did not mean reënslavement under another name."[32] The determination to enforce the equality for which a war had been fought resulted in the rejection of the Black Codes, passage of constitutional amendments, and formalization of Reconstruction—the first faltering step toward making America a true multiracial democracy.

———

The Redemption period—the mid-1870s to the mid-1890s—was a direct and immediate backlash to Reconstruction. For a brief historical moment during the Reconstruction era, from 1863 to 1877, America tried to create a society that was not based on white supremacy. Coming out of the Civil War, the nation grappled with the political, economic, social, and moral rebuilding of the country. During this period, the government created programs and laws to bring millions of formerly enslaved people into the fabric of society. Schools were created, hospitals established, and racial barriers removed from voting and running for office. In her revolutionary journalistic endeavor, *The 1619 Project*, Nikole Hannah-Jones described Reconstruction as follows:

> Led by black activists and a Republican Party pushed left by the blatant recalcitrance of white Southerners, the years directly after slavery saw the greatest expansion of human and civil rights this nation would ever see. . . .
>
> The South, for the first time in the history of this country, began to resemble a democracy, with black Americans elected to local, state and federal offices. Some 16 black men served in Congress—including Hiram Revels of Mississippi, who became the first black man elected to the Senate. (Demonstrating just how brief this period would be, Revels, along with Blanche Bruce, would go from being the first black man elected to the last for nearly a hundred years, until Edward Brooke of Massachusetts took office in 1967.) More than 600 black men served in Southern state legislatures and hundreds more in local positions.[33]

The short shining moment of democracy didn't last long. Reconstruction was betrayed by Northern allies, abandoned by the federal government, and destroyed by determined Confederates working to reestablish their power and dominance. Once Reconstruction was undermined and overthrown, those who pined for the good old days of enjoying free Black labor were quick to rush in and ruthlessly rewrite the laws to accomplish with words what they had failed to achieve with bullets—the restoration and perpetuation of white supremacy in America—working swiftly to make America great again. The Black Codes of the 1860s were just a dress rehearsal for the sweeping revisions made possible once the Union withdrew troops from the South (in 1877) and turned the region back to its white nationalist leaders.

At its core, the Confederate's Redemption phase focused on resisting and undermining as many of the pro-democracy measures put in place after the Civil War as possible. African Americans at the time made up a large percentage of the population in several Southern states—the *majority* of people in Mississippi and South Carolina—and the civil rights bills and Fifteenth Amendment threatened to fundamentally transform the political balance of power. The Redemption Era sought to stop that from happening. In *Struggle for Mastery*, Michael Perman describes the essence of the period, writing, "For fifteen to twenty years . . . [Southern] Democrats had to acknowledge the continuing existence of the electoral system established during Reconstruction and somehow work within it. But they never accepted it . . . [or] accorded it legitimacy, just as they had never sanctioned the governments run by the Republicans during Reconstruction. Instead, they manipulated and subverted the system without actually eliminating it."[34]

To understand what manipulating and subverting the system looked like during the Redemption period, one need only take a look at the example of Edward McCrady and the Eight Box Law.

Some legislators apply their intellect, energy, and creativity to the task of meeting their constituents' needs—things like public safety, transportation, and taxes. For much of his time in the legislature, that is exactly what nineteenth-century South Carolina attorney and politician Edward McCrady did. But then Black folks got free, and McCrady had more pressing concerns than the welfare of his constituents. He had to do everything he could to preserve white power by making it as difficult as possible for Black people to vote. McCrady devised the diabolical—and diabolically effective—scheme known as the "Eight Box Law." Walter Edgar, emeritus history professor at the University of South Carolina, described the law as follows:

> The Eight Box Law of 1882 was an election law designed to ensure white supremacy in South Carolina without violating the Fifteenth Amendment—which barred states from depriving their citizens of the vote on the basis of race. The law provided for separate ballot boxes for each of the eight offices, including, state senator, state representative, congressman, governor, and

other statewide offices. Any ballot cast in an incorrect box was disallowed. Election managers were required to read the labels to illiterate voters—enabling election officials to read them correctly to white voters and incorrectly to black voters. This was not a violation of federal law and would be difficult to prove in court. In just six years, the Eight Box Law reduced the number of black voters from 58,000 to 14,000.[35]

When viewed through the lens of history, we see that the 2021 fusillade of voter suppression legislation, consisting of hundreds of voter suppression bills being introduced across the country, was not the first time Confederates worked to manipulate the system to dilute the political power of people of color.

The third and most far-reaching phase of the ruthless rewriting was the Restoration period (from 1890 to about 1908—or, I guess one could plausibly argue, until 2022). While Redemption involved undermining and resisting the new legal requirements of the constitutional amendments, Restoration gave a states' rights statutory middle finger to the federal government and allowed Confederates to simply rewrite entire state constitutions to restore white people to the positions of prominence and power that they had enjoyed before the Confederate surrender at Appomattox. Carol Anderson described in detail the process during that period in her book, *One Person, No Vote*, writing, "They devised ways to meet the letter of the law while doing an absolute slash-and-burn through its spirit." Anderson illustrated the slash-and-burn approach by focusing on the 1890 activities in Mississippi:

> The Magnolia State passed the Mississippi Plan, a dizzying array of poll taxes, literacy tests, understanding clauses, newfangled voter registration rules, and "good character" clauses— all intentionally racially discriminatory but dressed up in the genteel garb of bringing "integrity" to the voting booth. This feigned legal innocence was legislative evil genius.
> Virginia representative Carter Glass, like so many others, swooned at the thought of bringing the Mississippi Plan to his

own state, especially after he saw how well it had worked. He rushed to champion a bill in the legislature that would "eliminate the darkey as a political factor . . . in less than five years." Glass . . . planned not to "deprive a single white man of the ballot, but [to] inevitably cut from the existing electorate four-fifths of the Negro voters" in Virginia.[36]

Pay careful attention to that word "integrity." It is getting as much use in the 2020s by modern-day Confederates passing voter suppression laws in the states of the old Confederacy as it did when the original Confederates reestablished white power across the South in the 1890s.

The Redemption period rewriting was so thorough, so scientifically designed to disenfranchise Black people, so ruthlessly effective that it lasted nearly a hundred years, until another revolution, another movement, and a different, more supportive president named Johnson (Lyndon B. Johnson) put the full force of the federal government behind trying to again—and again against great resistance—establish a multiracial democracy in America's Southern states.

DISTORT PUBLIC OPINION

Wars are not just fought on battlefields with guns and bullets. They are also fought with words, ideas, images, and information. Or disinformation, as the case may be. Especially when the truth of the cause is so ugly that it violates fundamental human values, moral codes, and social norms. In that situation, it becomes particularly important to distort reality, shape public opinion, and rewrite history. Beginning a tradition that has continued down through the years to Donald Trump and his contemporary imitators, that is exactly what the Confederates did in the days, weeks, months, and years after Appomattox.

The Confederates' post–Civil War national disinformation campaign was sophisticated, multidimensional, and far-reaching, and it had multiple objectives. First, it sought to undermine popular support for Reconstruction and the steps toward building a multiracial democracy that were instituted in the 1860s and 1870s. Second, more globally, it recast and sanitized the entire white nationalist movement that had led to the bloody and treasonous Civil War. And third, it paved the path for the lenient treatment of the traitors to the country, creating a glide path for the Confederates to recapture control of the South.

———

Any effective public information campaign requires strong and simple branding. "White Nationalism Forever" wasn't terribly catchy, and you couldn't dance to it. What sounded better—and what endured for decades—was the phrase "The Lost Cause."

Leading the way in this massive act of national revisionism was a man named Edward Pollard, described by Professor Gates as "a strategic genius in this war of symbols and interpretation."[37] Pollard was well equipped to rebrand violent and bloody white supremacy. An experienced journalist at Virginia's *Richmond Examiner*, one of the key newspapers in the capital of the Confederacy, he honed his writing chops by penning such tomes as a pre–Civil War 1859 work titled *Black Diamonds Gathered in the Darkey Homes of the South*, a book that advocated for the resumption of the slave trade.

When the Civil War technically ended and Robert E. Lee surrendered, Pollard started his quest to reserve power and privilege for white people in America. In the months after Appomattox, Pollard literally rewrote history, line by line and page by page, publishing the 530-page book *The Lost Cause: A New Southern History of the War of the Confederates*, in 1866. Two years later, he completed his seminal work, *The Lost Cause Regained*. Gates distilled the core messages of the Pollard ideology:

> The Lost Cause myth that Pollard promoted developed along two overlapping lines. First, its advocates argued, the Civil War was not an act of treason but rather a revolt against an overreaching federal government, in which the Confederates lost but fought with courage and honor. In this sense, they viewed the Civil War as similar to the American Revolution, with Robert E. Lee as George Washington in a gray uniform. Second, slavery did not cause the war.[38]

It is difficult to overstate the reach, sweep, and endurance of the Pollard whitewashing of white supremacy. Twenty-first century historian Jon Meacham wrote as recently as 2020 that "no other American title of 1866 is shaping the nation in the way Pollard's is even now." Meacham went on to explain, "In our own time, the debates over Confederate memorials and the resistance in many quarters of white America, especially in the South, to address slavery, segregation and systemic racism can in part be understood by encounters with the literature of the Lost Cause and the history of the way many white Americans have chosen to see the Civil War and its aftermath."[39]

Pollard was not the only person to pick up his pen to put down lies. Much as Trump has taken to perpetuating the Big Lie about his 2020 electoral loss, Jefferson Davis, president of the Confederacy, also used his post-presidency years to try to rewrite history with his autobiography. Davis's twisting of the truth spills across nearly 1,400 pages in two volumes of what historian David Blight says "may be the longest and most self-righteous legal brief on behalf of a failed political movement ever done by an American." Blight's 2001 book *Race and Reunion* dissects the Confederate president's racist revisionism:

> Jefferson Davis set the tone for the diehards' historical interpretation. In private and public utterances, Davis's fierce defense of state rights doctrine and secession, his incessant pleas for "Southern honor," and his mystical conception of the Confederacy gave ideological fuel to diehards. It was forever a "misnomer to apply the term 'Rebellion' to the Confederacy," Davis wrote in 1874. "Sovereigns cannot rebel."[40]

The reach of Pollard, Davis, and their compatriots was captured by University of Vermont professor James Loewen in his book *Lies Across America: What Our Historic Sites Get Wrong*. In a 2015 *Washington Post* column, Loewen wrote, "The Confederates won with the pen (and the noose) what they could not win on the battlefield: the cause of white supremacy and the dominant understanding of what the war was all about."[41] As Jon Meacham put it in his 2020 *New York Times* column, "To recall that the war had been about what Lincoln had called a 'new birth of freedom' meant acknowledging the nation's failings on race. So white Americans decided to recall something else."[42]

———

The most effective propaganda campaigns extend beyond serious books seeking to make somber and sober points. To truly affect public opinion, it's also helpful to influence the art and culture that moves people and makes them laugh. Here, the Confederates did their work with great effectiveness, even enlisting perhaps unwitting allies such as Mark Twain.

While the country's political leaders were debating what rights to extend to Black people, Mark Twain was working on a novel. Lauded as the "greatest humorist the United States has produced," in a *New York Times* obituary, Twain was revered by luminaries such as William Faulkner, who called him "the first truly American writer." During the heyday of the Black Codes, Redemption Era, and attacks on Reconstruction, Twain was drafting *Adventures of Huckleberry Finn*, what many consider to be the greatest book of all time. It is also a book with more than two hundred utterances of the word "nigger." It is a book with classic dialogue such as "Good gracious! anybody hurt?" "No'm. Killed a nigger." [43]

It kind of makes it hard to marshal public support for constitutional amendments for Black equality when many of the people in the country are kicking back with a book in which its protagonist says that "nobody" was hurt; only a nigger was killed. If you're not a person, why would you need civil rights laws to protect you? Why would you need enforcement of equality? Why would you need protection of your right to vote? Those things are reserved for non-niggers, the people we worry about being hurt.

In addition to laughter being a core part of cognitive reorientation, another key part of reshaping public opinion was through song. While you couldn't dance to a song called "White Nationalism Forever," Americans for many years now have certainly been tapping their toes and belting out the words to the catchy tune "Dixie."

Popularized in the years immediately before the Civil War, "Dixie" involves a Black person in the North singing the following wistful lyrics about the land where Black people were brought and held in bondage:

I wish I was in the land of cotton, old times there are not forgotten,
Look away, look away, look away, Dixie Land.

In Dixie Land where I was born in, early on a frosty mornin',
Look away, look away, look away, Dixie Land.

Then I wish I was in Dixie, hooray! hooray!
In Dixie Land I'll take my stand to live and die in Dixie,
Away, away, away down South in Dixie,
Away, away, away down South in Dixie.

"Dixie" was created in 1859 as part of a minstrel show in New York. Minstrelsy—men, usually white men, in blackface, imitating happy, enslaved African Americans—was once one of the most popular art forms in the United States. The song grew to great popularity during the prelude to the Civil War in the 1850s, and it was explicitly and intentionally promoted in opposition to the pre–Civil War abolitionist movement. Ultimately, "Dixie" was embraced and elevated as the song of the Confederate cause, and "received an unofficial endorsement when it was played at President of the Confederacy Jefferson Davis's inauguration in February 1861."[44] The terms "Dixie" and "Dixieland" came to mean the segregationist South. (As discussed later in chapter 2, in 1948 the white nationalist, segregationist presidential campaign of Strom Thurmond was conducted under the banner of a political party known as "the Dixiecrats.")

As African Americans and their allies worked to refashion a nation that had been firmly conceived and rooted in white nationalism, they had to contend with significant competition for the attention of the American mind. In the years after the Civil War, when people finished reading Pollard's *The Lost Cause Regained* and chuckling 219 times at each use of the word "nigger" in *Adventures of Huckleberry Finn*, they could wrap up a pleasant evening by breaking into a rousing rendition of "Dixie."

In addition to national attention shifting and laws being ruthlessly rewritten, another aspect of the Confederate Battle Plan was also being developed and deployed, to deadly effect. What they could not accomplish politically by rewriting the laws and molding minds, Confederates achieved by cowardly creeping around in robes, hoods, and masks that shielded their identity while they reloaded their guns and put bullets in Black people's bodies and ropes around their necks.

SILENTLY SANCTION TERRORISM

Although the Ku Klux Klan is rightly reviled today and seen by main-stream society as a disreputable fringe group of unrepresentative racist radicals, the organization has not always had such pariah status. Critical to understanding the strategic role of entities such as the Klan (they were not the only white domestic terrorist organization) is examining *who* created these groups and *when*.

Christmas is a time for family, fellowship, and, for the religiously inclined, reflections on the birth of Christ. Families gather, sing songs, and often attend church, where the minister reminds them of the teachings of the Bible such as "Love your neighbor" and "Thou shall not kill." In the South, the first Christmas after the end of the Civil War was a bit different.

Mere months after the surrender at Appomattox, half a dozen Southern young white men gathered in Pulaski, Tennessee, in December 1865 to discuss what to do with their lives in the wake of the failed Civil War. These six former Confederate war veterans—good Christians all, no doubt—decided to create an organization they would call the Ku Klux Klan.[45] This Christmas-time creation would become a group that would coordinate the activities of white men who would put on white robes and hoods and then ride throughout the South seizing Black men, putting nooses around their necks, throwing the ropes of the nooses over elevated tree branches, and then pulling on the ropes so that the Black men were suspended in the air, with the nooses slowly choking the breath and life out of their bodies. These lynchings usually occurred at night. In the silent night, the holy night, when all was calm, and all was bright. Holy infant, so tender and mild. Indeed.

While the KKK grew somewhat organically, the lack of structure and discipline diminished its effectiveness in terms of wreaking the desired terror and havoc. Seeking to whip the operation into the kind of shape where its members could more efficiently and systematically whip Black human beings until their backs were bloodied and raw, the organization turned to Nathan Bedford Forrest, an expert on protecting slavery and transforming aggrieved, fearful, and resentful white men into armed and violent killing machines.

In the years immediately preceding the Civil War, Forrest took out an ad in his local Memphis, Tennessee, newspaper announcing his products and services. The ad read, "Forrest and Maples, slave dealers . . . have constantly on hand the best selected assortment of field hands, house servants, & mechanics, at their Negro Mart." The ad went on to helpfully suggest that "persons wishing to purchase are invited to examine their stock before purchasing elsewhere." [46]

Forrest proved his bona fides in using violence to defend white supremacy as a leading general during the Civil War. In that role, he presided over the 1864 Battle at Fort Pillow on the Mississippi River in Henning, Tennessee—a battle described as "the most famous atrocity of the nation's bloodiest war." [47] Upon prevailing in that particular fight, the Confederates refused to take the surviving Black soldiers as prisoners of war and proceeded to summarily execute them. One of the Confederate soldiers under Forrest's command wrote a letter to his sisters immediately afterward in which he recounted the massacre:

> The slaughter was awful. Words cannot describe the scene. The poor deluded negros would run up to our men fall on their knees and with uplifted hands scream for mercy but they were ordered to their feet and then shot down. The white [sic] men fared but little better. The fort turned out to be a great slaughter pen. Blood, human blood stood about in pools and brains could have been gathered up in any quantity. I with several others tried to stop the butchery and at one time had partially succeeded but Gen. Forrest ordered them shot down like dogs and the carnage continued. [48]

All of this made Forrest the perfect person to head up a nascent white terrorist organization. [49] The founders of the KKK turned to Forrest in 1867 and convinced him to become the organization's first grand wizard. [50] He did not disappoint. History professor Jonathan Bryant summarized Forrest's impact as follows:

> Freedmen's Bureau agents reported 336 cases of murder or assault with intent to kill on freedmen across the state [of Georgia] from January 1 through November 15 of 1868. . . . In Columbia County armed Klansmen not only intimidated voters but even

cowed federal soldiers sent to guard the polling place. Not surprisingly, while 1,222 votes had been cast in Columbia County for Republican governor Rufus Bullock in April, only one vote was cast for Republican presidential candidate Ulysses Grant in November 1868. Similar political terrorism and control of the polling places help account for Georgia's quick "redemption" and return to conservative white Democratic control by late 1871.[51]

For all of this murder and mayhem, Forrest has been embraced, elevated, and cherished in our country for more than a century. As we will see in chapter 3, up until July 2021, a bust honoring Forrest remained in a position of prominence and prestige in the Tennessee State Capitol building, and, as of the publication of this book, prominent Southern organizations are still selling Forrest memorabilia such as ink pens and bars of soap.

———

The scale of white domestic terrorism was so extensive that in 1871 the United States Congress conducted an extensive investigation that consisted of holding hearings and gathering testimony for months. The findings of that inquiry were compiled into a thirteen-volume report in 1872 that included pages and pages of testimony such as this account to Congress by a Mississippi Black resident in 1871, which also features follow-up questions from a congressman:

> There was one negro whipped by this same body of men that came to my plantation, on an adjoining plantation. It was a man named Rife Hickman. He was taken out before the party visited my plantation. They took him out and whipped him very severely; he did not recover so as to work for two or three weeks. Rife Hickman was living on a plantation belonging to Dr. Cheatham.
>
> QUESTION: Is it your opinion that these outrages are committed with a view of controlling the political action of the blacks there?

ANSWER: I think so. I could see no other object in pursuing that course. It has succeeded in accomplishing that result.

QUESTION. Did the Negroes there abstain from voting, or
vote with the democrats?

ANSWER: Yes, sir. I do not know what this election will
show, but I think it will show that they either have stayed away
from the polls or have voted with the [Confederate] democrats
entirely. I know in the portion of the county where I am ac-
quainted the colored people will not attempt at all to go to the
polls; they have told me so. They have said that they did not feel
safe in voting, and, under the circumstances, I advised them to
that end.[52]

From testimony such as the above, the congressional committee
conducting the hearings on Klan activity learned that in Louisiana
alone, "2000 persons were killed, wounded and otherwise in the state
within a few weeks prior to the [1868] presidential election."[53] *Two
thousand people killed or wounded.* Within "a few weeks." Assuming "a
few" is roughly four weeks, that breaks down to five hundred people
killed or wounded every week. Seventy-one per day. Three per hour.
Just in one state.

Throughout the decades, the sanctioning of white domestic terrorism has usually been silent, but it has not always been so. Consider the
Minority Report to the same 1871 congressional hearings, written in
large part by U.S. senator Francis Blair of Missouri:

> The atrocious measures by which millions of white people have
> been put at the mercy of the semi-barbarous negroes of the
> South, and the vilest of the white people, both from the North
> and South, who have been constituted the leaders of this black
> horde, are now sought to be justified and defended by defam-
> ing the people upon whom this unspeakable outrage had been
> committed.[54]

While thousands of Black people were being killed, this distinguished member of Congress was worried about "the atrocious

measures" that white people had to endure. Blair had previously run for vice president in 1868 with the slogan, "This is a White Man's Country; Let White Men Rule." (And that's the same Blair family whose name graces Blair House, also known as the President's Guest House, located next door to the White House and where today many foreign dignitaries stay; it's where Joe Biden stayed the night before being sworn in as president.)[55]

Nathan Bedford Forrest was not the only white nationalist terrorist during his time, and the KKK was not the only such organization. In their book *Ku Klux Klan: Its Origin, Growth and Disbandment*, John C. Lester and D. L. Wilson point out that "there were several other very important ones, such as the White Brotherhood, the White League, the Pale Faces, the Constitutional Union Guards, and . . . the Knights of the White Camelia."[56]

Ever since the earliest hours in the aftermath of Appomattox, the Confederates' intention has been clear. For the next thirty years, underlying it all—all the legislation, speeches, and books—was the core currency of war: bloodshed. The clearest proof that the South never surrendered and continued to wage the Civil War is that they continued to wage a violent and bloody Civil War, long after the supposed cessation of armed hostilities.

PLAY THE LONG GAME

Georgia senator John Brown Gordon understood the long game. An attorney, slaveholder, plantation owner, respected commander in the Confederate army, and reputed head of the Georgia Ku Klux Klan, Gordon made a bid for statewide office in 1868, three years after the end of the Civil War and in the early years of Reconstruction. Since the electorate was no longer all-white, and Black folks were able to vote in those years immediately following the war, Gordon was defeated at the polls. After that setback, as the KKK and other domestic terrorists attacked African Americans daring to attempt to vote, Gordon's electoral prospects improved, and he won election to the U.S. Senate five years later, in 1873.[57]

In Washington, Gordon was a leader of the Southern whites who were watching, waiting, and biding their time in hope of seizing an opening to restore white people to power in the Confederate states. Their moment presented itself in the closing decades of the nineteenth century, with the election of 1876; and they were ready.

Holding the office of president of the United States is a tantalizing honor, and most of the Confederates had their eyes on that prize in the closely contested 1876 presidential race. The results were super close, with the candidate of the Party of Lincoln—Rutherford B. Hayes—apparently falling short to then New York governor and friend of the Confederacy Samuel Tilden. With the election outcome hanging in the balance, the outcome in a handful of states remained undetermined. The post-election slugfest was eerily similar to the 2020 attempted coup by Trump, during which Trump's supporters tried to intimidate local elections officials. In the 1876 conflict, Confederates brought their guns to the canvassing boards to try to stop the counting of votes once their candidate was in the lead.

The fight played out for months, with no clear resolution in sight, and as Inauguration Day approached—with the attendant deadline for electoral votes to be certified by Congress—something had to give. Many Confederates fiercely fought to affect the results so that their guy could win the White House, with some proclaiming "Tilden or Civil War."[58] But while many were focused on the immediate fight, Senator Gordon had his eye on the long game.

Gordon knew that the most important objective wasn't which white man got to live in the White House. The cause of the Confederacy was political power for white supremacy as a system and way of life. If that could be achieved, the Lost Cause might be found after all.

As the election of 1876 stretched into the post-election controversy of 1877, Gordon developed a plan. A veteran of the Civil War, Gordon had been wounded in the war and also watched his own brother writhe in agony on the battlefield as blood poured out of him. He knew what was at stake, and he understood that if they kept their eyes on the prize of power—removing Northern troops from the South so that they could then ruthlessly rewrite laws and silently or not so silently sanction white terrorism—then the Confederacy could be resurrected. In his calculation, conceding one term of the presidency in 1877 to the

Party of Lincoln was a small price to pay for the prospect of decades of white Confederate control in the South.

With the clarity of that perspective, Gordon helped broker one of the most consequential and shameful deals in U.S. history. It was a compromise on the order of the Founding Fathers' 1776 capitulation to slaveholders that caused them to strike the anti-slavery passages from the Declaration of Independence.

Clear-eyed that real power lay at the state and local level, Gordon convinced the Confederates to surrender the shiny bauble of the White House for the bricks and mortar of restoring white supremacy throughout much of America.[59] As one party official accurately put it at the time, "I think the policy of the new administration will be to conciliate the white men of the South. Carpetbaggers to the rear, and niggers take care of yourselves." [60]

The essence of the Hayes-Tilden compromise was as simple as it was deadly. In exchange for conceding the fight for the White House, the Confederates would receive control of their states once again. The government troops that had been holding white terrorists at bay and enforcing some modicum of multiracial democracy would be withdrawn. The result, as Lerone Bennett Jr. wrote, was the "funeral of democracy." [61]

And so, just like that, in a hotel room in Washington, DC, Georgia senator John Brown Gordon brokered the 1877 deal that essentially turned control of the South back to the Confederates, allowing them to win what they had lost on the battlefield. Hayes was sworn in weeks later, and he lived up to his end of the deal, methodically withdrawing federal troops from Southern states.

With all obstacles removed, the once-vanquished white Southerners moved throughout the region with the fury and force of a conquering army. Which, in essence, they were. The results were as tragic as they were predictable. Foner recounts the political and moral carnage:

> [African Americans] found themselves enmeshed in a seamless web of oppression, whose interwoven economic, political, and social strands all reinforced one another. In illiteracy, malnutrition, inadequate housing, and a host of other burdens, blacks

paid the highest price for the end of Reconstruction and the stagnation of the Southern economy.[62]

By the end of the nineteenth century, the job was done. Jefferson Davis was not president of the Confederacy, but most of what he and his allies had fought for had been accomplished. For the foreseeable future, the South no longer needed to fight. They'd won the fight. They now just needed to govern their white man's land, and that they did, for most of the entire twentieth century.

2

The Twentieth Century, Part One:
50 Years, One Battle Plan

After endless blood and gold had flowed to sweep human bondage away . . .
not a single Southern legislature stood ready to admit a Negro, under any
conditions, to the polls; not a single Southern legislature believed free Negro
labor was possible without a system of restrictions that took all its freedom
away; there was scarcely a white man in the South who did not honestly
regard Emancipation as a crime, and its practical nullification as a duty. . . .
The problem of the Twentieth Century is the problem of the color-line.

—W.E.B. Du Bois, *The Souls of Black Folk*, 1903

Drapetomania was first discovered by Dr. Samuel Cartwright in 1851.[1] Cartwright developed his medical knowledge and scientific understanding as a student at the University of Pennsylvania's School of Medicine, an Ivy League institution that is the oldest medical school in the country, a place of higher learning whose alumni include some of the most distinguished scientists in the country, including multiple Nobel laureates. After medical school, Cartwright practiced in several states and served as a surgeon under General Andrew Jackson before Jackson became president.[2]

In keeping with the long-standing tradition of sharing important medical discoveries with other practitioners in the field, Cartwright published a paper in *DeBow's Review*, a prominent Southern publication that described itself as "a monthly industrial and literary journal." Each issue of DeBow's had hundreds of pages of articles on such topics as commerce, agriculture, sugar, cotton, tobacco, and manufacturing. Cartwright's seminal exposition ran on page sixty-four of Volume 11, after an article on how much weight a road of wooden planks could bear and right before an article on the amount of U.S. cotton available to ship to Great Britain. The title of the Cartwright piece was, "Diseases and Peculiarities of the Negro Race," and here is how he described the peculiar disease of drapetomania:

> DRAPETOMANIA, OR THE DISEASE CAUSING NEGROES TO RUN AWAY.
>
> It is unknown to our medical authorities, although its diagnostic symptom, the absconding from service, is well known to our planters and overseers. . . . If the white man attempts to oppose the Deity's will, by trying to make the negro anything else than "the submissive knee-bender," (which the Almighty declared he should be,) by trying to raise him to a level with himself, or by putting himself on an equality with the negro . . . the negro will run away; but if he keeps him in the position that we learn from the Scriptures he was intended to occupy, that is, the position of submission . . . the negro is spell-bound, and cannot run away.

While serious, the affliction was considered curable "with the advantages of proper medical advice, strictly followed." Such advice included the insight that, "according to my experience, the 'genu flexit'—the awe and reverence, must be exacted from them, or they will despise their masters, become rude and ungovernable, and run away." To prevent the running away, Cartwright shared the lessons learned of those who had successfully prevented an outbreak of the malady: "When sulky and dissatisfied without cause, the experience of those on the line and elsewhere, was decidedly in favor of whipping them out of it, as a preventive measure against absconding, or other bad conduct. It was called whipping the devil out of them." [3]

———

Most Black people in America have, in fact, suffered from drapetomania—starting from the moment they were snatched from the shores of Africa, placed in chains, and herded onto ships for a perilous multi-month journey to America that only some would survive, and continuing up through the current Black Lives Matter movement. Descendants of Africa in America have shown by word and deed the persistence articulated by Harriet Tubman in describing the tenacity required to continue along the Underground Railroad, traveling from the shackles of the South to freedom in the North: "If you are tired, keep going; if you are scared, keep going; if you are hungry, keep going; if you want to taste freedom, keep going." [4]

As drapetomania surged throughout Black America and was passed down from generation to generation, Confederates had to be vigilant in their efforts to preserve the power and privileges of white people. Aspirations for racial equality were viewed as inherently revolutionary and dangerous to a system rooted in Black oppression and exploitation. As James Baldwin wrote in *The Fire Next Time*, "Try to imagine how you would feel if you woke up one morning to find the sun shining and all the stars aflame. You would be frightened because it is out of the order of nature. Any upheaval in the universe is terrifying because it so profoundly attacks one's sense of one's own reality." For whites watching Blacks get free, Baldwin observed, "heaven and earth are shaken to their foundations." [5] And as the cause of white nationalism extended to seeking to subjugate other non-white peoples, they discovered that drapetomania was not confined to African Americans. The vast majority of people of color have consistently demonstrated that they are also determined to fight for freedom, justice, and equality.

While the Confederate cause of restoring much of the pre–Civil War order of things was largely complete by the beginning of the twentieth century, the ever-present press for racial equality by people of color required constant monitoring and suppressing from those who had been restored to power. And even the slightest threat to the status quo required swift and savage retaliation.

The twentieth-century successors to, and heirs of, the original Confederates are legion—presidents, senators, governors, judges, lawyers, media moguls, philanthropists, conservative think tank leaders, and plenty of plain ol' regular people too—and they have followed a very similar Battle Plan to the one used by the original Confederate leaders in the immediate aftermath of the Civil War. While they would innovate and adapt to changing times and conditions, the core components of the Battle Plan guided Confederate conduct throughout the entire twentieth century.

NEVER GIVE AN INCH

In order to understand the dynamics of twenty-first-century American politics, it is critical to examine how the racial loyalties of the country's political parties underwent a slow but steady transformation in the twentieth century.

In the decades leading up to and after the Civil War, the relative relationship of the parties to white nationalism was as clear as the statement by 1860 Democratic presidential nominee Stephen Douglas, who, running against Abraham Lincoln, unequivocally asserted that "I hold that this government was made on the white basis, by white men, for the benefit of white men and their posterity forever, and should be administered by white men and none others." [6] Republicans, on the other hand, were formed as the anti-slavery party, oversaw the successful conduct of a civil war that ended slavery, and nominated a man who became president and signed the Emancipation Proclamation. The Democratic Party of the time had opposed all that stuff, so the positions of the parties were pretty obvious at the beginning of the twentieth century. But then things started to change, and over the course of several decades—one lifetime—our nation's political parties underwent a fundamental racial realignment.

What propelled that realignment was the determination of Southern whites—who were originally almost all Democrats—to never give an inch in the fight to preserve white power.

In the early twentieth century, the racial identity of the political parties became less "black and white" for two reasons. First, Black folks, seeing the writing on the wall with the restoration of the Confederates to power in the Southern states, fled the South and headed North. Isabel Wilkerson's brilliant book, *The Warmth of Other Suns*, described this significantly overlooked and underappreciated period of history as follows:

> From the early years of the twentieth century to well past its middle age, nearly every black family in the American South, which meant nearly every black family in America, had a

decision to make. There were sharecroppers losing at settle-
ment. Typists wanting to work in an office. Yard boys scared
that a single gesture near the planter's wife could leave them
hanging from an oak tree. . . .

Over the course of six decades, some six million black southerners left the land of their forefathers and fanned out across
the country for an uncertain existence in nearly every other corner of America. The Great Migration would become a turning
point in history. It would transform urban America and recast
the social and political order of every city it touched.[7]

My own grandparents, Arenzia Cochran and Fannie Hutchins,
traveled from Mississippi and Alabama to Cleveland during World
War I, and that is how I came to grow up in Northeast Ohio (and become a lifelong Cleveland sports fan, but that tale of decades of hard-
ship is another story for another time).

As cities across the North got Blacker, the political calculus for winning elections began to change. Whereas politics had formerly been
contests among white people, now candidates had to contend for the
support of African Americans, who were making up ever-increasing
shares of city populations.

While the Great Migration was taking place, a second major development occurred—the Great Depression, followed by the New Deal
programs designed to address the severity of the economic suffering
from the Depression. African Americans, as America's original working people, resonated with the policy agenda of President Franklin
Roosevelt, a Democrat, and, for the first time since shots were fired by
white Democrats at Fort Sumter, launching the Civil War, meaningful numbers of African Americans started supporting the Democratic
Party.

In his book *The Politics of Civil Rights in the Truman Administration*, William Berman explored how newly diverse Northern urban
areas saw significant numbers of African Americans take the unprecedented step of supporting the Democratic Party in response to Roosevelt's New Deal policies. As the number of Black voters in the North
grew in the 1930s, some Northern Democrats responded by pushing

for civil rights legislation, a move which Berman says "was bitterly resented, and actively opposed, by congressmen from the South."[8]

By the end of World War II, things were reaching a boiling point.

During the Second World War, Black soldiers went overseas to risk and, in many cases, give their lives on behalf of the interests of the United States. After the war, in 1945, these soldiers returned home to a country as racist as they had left it—many of them encountering the same kinds of racial violence that had been practiced against African Americans for centuries. While none of this was new to Black America, President Harry S. Truman, a Democrat, was both shocked and moved to act, saying, "My stomach turned over when I learned that Negro soldiers, just back from overseas, were being dumped out of army trucks in Mississippi and beaten. Whatever my inclinations as a native of Missouri might have been, as President I know this is bad. I shall fight to end evils like this."[9]

True to his word, Truman created the "President's Committee on Civil Rights," and he instructed it to investigate racial discrimination in America and bring him recommendations to redress the problems. Armed with findings from the committee, Truman leaned into the political and symbolic power of his position as president to call for change in the form of civil rights legislation. Some have speculated that Truman was also making a play for Black votes in Northern states, betting that African Americans could provide the margin of difference in closely contested states in the 1948 presidential election. If true, it is certainly the kind of political play that has completely fallen out of favor among Democrats in the twenty-first century.

On February 2, 1948, Truman took what has been described as a "great political risk by presenting a daring civil rights speech to a joint session of Congress."[10] In that speech, he urged Congress to, among other things, pass a law making it illegal to put ropes around the necks of human beings and hang them from trees until the breath was squeezed from their bodies.[11]

This was not what Southern Democrats expected of the political party that had seceded from the Union and waged a war to defend slavery. Not after spilling blood and losing limbs and going through all the trouble to destroy Reconstruction, rewrite state constitutions, sanction the rise of white domestic terrorism, and work day and night to restore white supremacy in the Confederate states.

Georgia senator Richard Russell typified the outrage of the twentieth-century Confederates, saying that Truman's suggestions represented "a vicious and unwarranted attack" that threatened to "destroy segregation and compel intermingling and miscegenation of the races in the South." (One of the U.S. Senate office buildings, by the way—where all of the Senators in Congress have their offices—is, as of early 2022, named the Russell Senate Office Building.)[12]

————

Many Southern politicians shared Senator Russell's sentiments and saw Truman's proposed incursions toward equality, however incremental, as an existential threat that justified a withering response. Accordingly, they set out to destroy the national Democratic Party by mounting a third-party candidacy. Weeks after Truman announced his proposals, several Southern governors got together—in a form of a "Confederacy," if you will—and decided to launch an all-out political assault on the Democratic Party in an attempt to divide the vote and defeat the incumbent president.[13] Their champion of choice was Strom Thurmond, who was governor of South Carolina at the time and would later go on to become a U.S. Senator (the predecessor to current senator Lindsey Graham).

No single individual personified the Confederate cause in the twentieth century more than Thurmond, a man whose life lasted the entirety of the century, stretching from his birth in 1902 to his death 101 years later in 2003. Thurmond served in the U.S. Senate and wielded massive political influence for nearly fifty years, the third-longest-serving senator ever.

Thurmond was already a leading figure in U.S. politics by mid-century. Born the same year that several Southern states were ratifying state constitutions designed to disenfranchise Black voters, he quickly established himself in South Carolina as a man with a bright future, becoming a military officer, lawyer, and judge before entering politics and winning the office of governor in 1946. Seen by many as a respected family man (he had five children, including one, much-later recognized, mixed-race daughter from Thurmond's impregnating—if not raping—the teenaged family housekeeper), Thurmond commanded respect across the political spectrum and was a rising political star.[14]

The constellation of Confederate governors, united in opposition to Truman's racial equality agenda, moved quickly to make their mark. In short order, they pulled together a convention and formed a new political party, the States' Rights Democratic Party—colloquially referred to as the "Dixiecrats"—to champion the purported Lost Cause of defending white rights. Thurmond was their choice to be their standard-bearer in the 1948 presidential election. The Dixiecrats' mission was clearly spelled out in the platform on which Thurmond ran that year:

> We stand for the segregation of the races and the racial integrity of each race; the constitutional right to choose one's associates; to accept private employment without governmental interference, and to earn one's living in any lawful way. We oppose the elimination of segregation, the repeal of miscegenation statutes, the control of private employment by Federal bureaucrats called for by the misnamed civil rights program.[15]

On the campaign stump, Thurmond channeled the white fear, resentment, and rage that has animated U.S. politics for centuries. In a July 1948 speech that could just as easily have been given during the actual Civil War, he told a cheering crowd, "I want to tell you, ladies and gentlemen, that there's not enough troops in the army to force the Southern people to break down segregation and admit the nigger race into our theaters, into our swimming pools, into our homes, and into our churches!"[16]

The anticipated strength of the Dixiecrat campaign is the little-known backstory to the iconic November 3, 1948, photo of President Truman holding up a newspaper with the incorrect headline "Dewey Defeats Truman." The reason that the media thought that Republican nominee Thomas Dewey, then governor of New York, *would* defeat Truman is that the Confederate states were aggressively working to woo Democratic voters, thereby weakening the coalition that had previously provided majority support to Democratic presidential candidates.

The Dixiecrat crusade was an early, pre-Trump test run of the white nationalist vote in America, gauging its size, scale, and electoral significance. Thurmond's ticket won four states outright and secured 11 percent of the vote in the states they contested.[17] In elections where the outcome is decided by just a few percentage points, a bloc of voters representing 11 percent of the electorate is more than enough to get the attention of candidates and elected officials (if a third-party candidacy had received 11 percent of the vote in 2020, that would have amounted to 17 million votes, more than twice the margin of difference between Biden and Trump).

Although the Dixiecrats fell short in their specific objective of denying Truman a second term, the aftershocks of their political earthquake reverberated across the country and across the century. Thurmond biographer Joseph Crespino described the lasting significance of the Dixiecrat candidacy:

> Thurmond was the first southerner in the postwar period to bring together on a regional scale the visceral politics of white supremacy with southern business and industrial opposition to the New Deal. . . . Thurmond now had filing cabinets full of speeches and press releases that blended the regional language of states' rights—the old-fashioned southern way of speaking in a dignified voice about the necessity of white supremacy— with inchoate themes of antistatism and anticommunism. . . . Much was lost in trying to translate white supremacist rage into abstract conservative principle. Yet it would be refined and improved by Thurmond and others in the years to come.[18]

The pro-segregation Dixiecrat campaign elevated Thurmond's stature and propelled him from being governor of a small state (albeit the state where the Civil War started) to the highest precincts of power in the country as a U.S. senator in the nation's capital. Once ensconced in the Senate, Thurmond did all he could to never give an inch in the fight to preserve white supremacy and block racial justice. Most notably, he filibustered the Civil Rights Act of 1957, standing and speaking in opposition to racial equality for twenty-four hours and eighteen minutes, a record for the longest filibuster that stands to this day. From his perch of power in the Senate and with his influential platform, Thurmond championed the Confederate cause for another forty-seven years.

RUTHLESSLY REWRITE THE LAWS

Ruthlessly rewriting the laws to benefit white power did not just take place in Southern state Capitol buildings where state legislatures met. Courts and the judicial branch got in on the act too. Although drafting legislation is supposedly left to the legislative branch of the government, judges all the way up to the U.S. Supreme Court also contributed mightily to the Confederate cause by narrowly reinterpreting and restricting the few racial justice laws that had managed to make it onto the books.

The work of undermining racial justice legislation in the courts gathered momentum after the rough road of passing post–Civil War constitutional amendments for equality. Once the amendments were ratified, judges—white men in black robes—quickly set about limiting the reach of the words that had been written into the country's top governing document. The most notorious of these cases was the 1896 *Plessy v. Ferguson* case, where the court grudgingly admitted that the Fourteenth Amendment existed but then, in what is generally regarded as one of the most disgraceful decisions in Supreme Court history, quickly limited the impact of the law by claiming that racial segregation was perfectly fine so long as the separate facilities were "equal."

Much less known than *Plessy*, but in the same spirit of Confederate rewriting, restricting, and reducing the scope of pro-equality laws, are the white primary cases. It sounds ridiculous today to even recount this, but the law of the land as interpreted by the top court in the country made it perfectly permissible for states to restrict participation in primary elections just to white people. In *One Person, No Vote*, Carol Anderson explains how this judicially sanctioned nonsense came about:

> First, because the South was a one-party region, whoever won in the spring would certainly be the victor in November. As long as the all-important and decisive primary was a whites-only affair, the results would be foreordained. And second, in 1921 the U.S.

Supreme Court had ruled in *Newberry v. United States* that the federal government, and, thus, the U.S. Constitution itself, had no authority over the conduct of primary elections in the states. With no federal interference and a hermetically sealed party system, the white primary became a masterful way to "emasculate politically the entire body of Negro voter." . . . And then a paper-thin aura of legality was achieved because blacks were welcome to vote in the irrelevant and perfunctory general election.[19]

With racial discrimination working so efficiently, starting in 1890 and continuing into the early twentieth century, at least eight states— Louisiana, North Carolina, Virginia, Florida, Alabama, South Carolina, Mississippi, and Texas—embraced and implemented the white primary trick as an elegant solution to the problem of potential Black political power. The most tenacious adherents of this practice were in Texas. Despite having one of its white primary schemes rejected by the Supreme Court in a unanimous 1927 decision, where the authors of the majority opinion held that "it seems to us hard to imagine a more direct and obvious infringement of the Fourteenth [Amendment]," the creative Confederates in the Lone Star state went back to the drawing board—the white board, if you will—and ruthlessly rewrote their voter suppression legislation.[20] As Anderson wrote, "the shenanigans continued." Such shenanigans included the following:

South Carolina decided to maintain the white primary while at the same time purging its books of all election laws. The rationale was simple: With nothing written down, there was nothing that the courts could find in violation of the Fourteenth or Fifteenth Amendments. Not to be outdone, Texas offered up yet another scheme, this one with a pre-primary in the guise of the all-white, private Jaybird Democratic Association, that would then feed into the Democratic primary without any official machinery involved—no election laws, public funding, or certification by the party.[21]

It wasn't until 1953—thirty years after Texas Democrats first formalized their racist electoral invention—that the Supreme Court, in the *Terry v. Adams* case, ultimately issued a decision sufficiently ironclad that it closed the door on any further creative attempts to use white primaries as a vehicle to circumvent, subvert, and essentially, ruthlessly rewrite the Fifteenth Amendment of the Constitution. As Anderson wrote, the court issued a decision finding "that the scheme in whatever guise was unconstitutional, and, with that, finally and completely driving a stake through the heart of the white primary." [22]

The white primaries were just one of many methods used to rewrite rules and undermine the principles written into the Constitution. In a 2021 *Washington Post* article, journalist Gillian Brockell succinctly summarized the pillars of early twentieth-century voter suppression:

- **Poll Taxes**—Nearly every Southern state instituted poll taxes during the Jim Crow era. . . . The tax disproportionately excluded Black voters. Plus, a lot of these laws required the tax be paid well before voting day and to produce multiple receipts, extra steps that made voting even harder.
- **Literacy Tests**—In Mississippi, the county clerk would demand a passage to be read from the state constitution and then decide if the prospective voter passed. Black voters were required to read dense, difficult sections; White voters, easier ones.
- **Grandfather Clauses**—Lawmakers argued that since poll taxes and literacy tests could also prevent White people from registering to vote, the laws were not racist. But by adding "grandfather" clauses, exempting anyone whose grandfather could vote from taxes and tests, poor or illiterate Whites had a way around the law. [23]

The battery of voter suppression legislation passed in 2021 in states with growing numbers of people of color is simply part of a long and proud tradition of racists ruthlessly revising any laws that could conceivably diminish white power.

DISTORT PUBLIC OPINION

Racism is not a good look. It's why people go to such great lengths to avoid being tagged with the label. Even avowed twenty-first-century leaders of the Ku Klux Klan, like Chris Barker of the Loyal White

Knights of the KKK (an organization whose website said in 2021, "Our goal is to help restore America to a White Christian nation, founded on God's word"), have gone on national television as recently as 2017 to assert that they are not racist.[24] The image is so bad that the white supremacist movement quite consciously rebranded itself to, as one reformed racist put it, "give people a space to say racist ideas in a more explicit, proud, confident way."[25] So many people have responded over the years to exposure of their racist acts or statements with plaintive "I'm not racist" pleas that writer Ta-Nehisi Coates was compelled to ask in a 2008 article, "Who does a guy have to lynch around here to get called a racist?"[26]

It is not an accident that America has widespread national ignorance and amnesia when it comes to white supremacy and Confederate power in America. The *Washington Post* podcast *Post Reports* produced an episode in 2020 on one of the most violent anti-Black attacks in U.S. history—the 1921 Tulsa race massacre. During those riots, hundreds of African Americans were killed by the town's whites, and, in a neighborhood of economically prosperous Black folk, 1,250 homes were burned and razed. Despite the enormity of that carnage, few people in this country know that it even happened. As explained by reporter Michele Norris on that podcast episode, "It's hard to put [the details] together because the history was expunged. There was actually a concerted effort to erase the history. . . . For years, newspaper archives were removed. Police logs were removed. So it's been very hard for historians to go back and piece together what happened."[27]

This distortion of public opinion remains relevant today because downplaying the history of white supremacy in America affects contemporary attitudes, public opinion, and political will to make the country more fair, equal, and just. Where there is no understanding of shameful national tragedies, there is no shame. And when there is no shame, there is no action (the authors of the 2021 anti–"critical race theory" legislation understand this reality all too well). Suppose that the national consensus was that either the Holocaust did not happen (and there is in fact a whole Holocaust deniers' movement), or that if it did, it was the Jews' fault, and it was, on balance, probably good for them anyway (perhaps by introducing discipline and structure into their days?).

The impact of history on present behavior and future outcomes was highlighted for me during a conversation several years ago with a woman from Germany. Konstanze Frischen is a white woman with a unique perspective on racism. She grew up in Germany and moved to the United States as an adult to help lead Ashoka, a national nonprofit organization that supports social entrepreneurs. When she came to this country, she wanted to make Ashoka more relevant to the cause of racial justice, and we met to discuss what steps it could take. I'll always remember her reflection on the challenge. "In Germany, there is a national sense of shame about the Holocaust," she said, adding, "Here in the United States, there is no shame."

Given the centrality, significance, and century-long ramifications of whitewashing the Confederate fight to preserve and extend white supremacy in America, it is worth spending a little time exploring how we got here.

———

Shaping and distorting public opinion has been a pillar of Confederate strategy, and slaveholders and their descendants have mastered the communications and opinion-shaping tools of whatever time they lived in. In the nineteenth century it was newspapers, magazines, books, and live theater. In the early twentieth century a newfangled technology emerged of moving pictures and feature films, and the Confederates quickly turned this tool to their advantage as well.

There are a few things to know about the 1915 movie *The Birth of a Nation*. It was the first film ever screened at the White House, with President Woodrow Wilson, born and raised in the Confederate South, reportedly thoroughly enjoying the cinematic accomplishment. It is one of the most profitable movies ever made, having brought in nearly $2 billion in inflation-adjusted dollars.[28] Upon the death of its director D.W. Griffith in 1948, the film critic at *The Nation* magazine reflected on Griffith's signature achievement, writing, "To watch his work is like being witness to the beginning of melody, or the first conscious use of the lever or the wheel; the emergence, coordination, and first eloquence of language; the birth of an art: and to realize that this is all the work of one man."[29] Pretty impressive. Oh, also, its original title was *The Clansman*. As in Ku Klux Klansman.

The silent, black-and-white film about the virtues of white Confederates captured the imagination of much of white America. The rapturous adulation and giddiness that flowed in California upon the movie's premiere was described in a 2021 article in the *California Supreme Court Historical Society Review*:

> On Monday, February 8, 1915, a capacity crowd filled Clune's Auditorium . . . in downtown Los Angeles for the world premiere of D. W. Griffith's monumental three-hour silent film *Birth of a Nation*. There was a 40-piece orchestra, live chorus and female ushers dressed in post–Civil War costumes. Among the approximately 3,000 theatergoers were Governor Hiram Johnson and L.A. City Council members. . . .
>
> The reviews were extravagant: the "biggest drama ever filmed" (*L.A. Times*) and "thrilling to the last degree" (*L.A. Express*). The *L.A. Herald*'s Guy Prince lauded the "awe-inspiring" "immenseness" of the 12-reel picture, and the "moments of intense excitement that the mere repeating sends the chills on a marathon in our spinal region."[30]

The film *Birth of a Nation* is based on a novel, *The Clansman*, by Thomas Dixon, a man described as "the great-granddaddy of white nationalism" in a 2019 *Washington Post* op-ed by Diane Roberts, a professor specializing in Southern culture. Roberts went on to offer further important context of the man whose content helped shape the minds of a nation:

> Dixon was once hugely famous, a celebrity preacher and writer of lurid novels that sold in the millions, despite their frankly awful prose. . . . Offended by a stage version of Harriet Beecher Stowe's "Uncle Tom's Cabin," he started writing novels to defend the white South and argue that ex-slaves were savages who had no place in America. . . . *The Birth of a Nation* revived white supremacist rage, which had lain somewhat dormant since the passage of Jim Crow laws at the end of the 19th century. . . . It also inspired the resuscitation of the Ku Klux Klan, which Dixon depicted as a bunch of chivalrous white gentlemen.[31]

One person who eagerly consumed the messages and mythology of Thomas Dixon at that time was a white teenage girl in Georgia named Margaret Mitchell. Mitchell organized her friends to perform dramatic readings of Dixon's play, also titled *The Clansman*, and she later wrote him a gushing letter stating, "I was practically raised on your books, and love them very much." [32]

Not only did Mitchell grow up reading Dixon's works, but she also learned at the knee of family members who lived the white nationalist reality that she had only experienced through books. She recounted listening to her relatives talk nostalgically about the days of the Confederacy, and the Lost Cause narrative sunk deep into her young imagination. [33] Properly imbued and inspired by Dixon's pro-Klan propaganda, Mitchell put pen to paper herself and extended the pro-Confederate cultural universe by writing the book *Gone with the Wind*, which was first published in 1936.

In terms of cultural popularity and widespread impact on public opinion about the Confederate South, *Gone with the Wind* picked up where *Birth of a Nation* left off. Twenty-four years after President Wilson settled in, perhaps with popcorn, to watch the celebration of a white nationalist terrorist organization, the entertainment industry spent massive resources turning the best-selling novel *Gone with the Wind* into another cinematic tour de force that would paint a pretty picture—in full color this time—of the bondage and brutality that was slavery in America. With the power of Hollywood magic, the movie *Gone with the Wind* transformed murderous traitors into dashing leading men and attractive leading ladies.

Gone with the Wind's release was a crowning achievement for the Confederacy. The contemporary writer Therese Oneill captured the sweeping nature of the historical spectacle as follows:

Over a million people poured into Atlanta just to be in the festive atmosphere of the premiere [the state's *entire population* was 4 million people at the time]. The Governor of Georgia declared the day of the premiere a state holiday, and the mayor of Atlanta organized three days of parades and parties. Citizens took to the streets in hoop skirts and top hats, celebrating what was to them the faded glory of their homeland. Tickets were scalped at $200 a head [roughly $3,000 in 2022 money]. Attendees of the premiere included the Vanderbilts, the Rockefellers, the Astors, J.P. Morgan, and all the Governors of what used to be the Confederacy.[34]

In 1976—thirty-seven years after its initial release in theaters—*Gone with the Wind* made its broadcast television debut on NBC and smashed all pre-existing records for popularity as nearly half of all the households in the country tuned in.[35] Two years later, in 1978, CBS paid the then-largest license fee in history for the right to air the movie on television for the subsequent two decades.[36]

As the success of *Birth of a Nation* and *Gone with the Wind* showed, winning hearts and minds through popular culture could be quite effective. Nonetheless, although impactful, films and other forms of entertainment were also financially risky and subject to competition from other creators who had books and movies of their own that were contesting for people's attention. In America's classrooms, however, there was much less competition and far fewer distractions for those seeking to mold the minds of the country's children.

———

Propaganda efforts typically tend to focus on changing the opinions of people, but what if you can shape their thinking before they've formed many opinions at all? That's why "Get 'em while they're young" is an advertising adage applied by marketers from cigarette makers to cereal companies to computer manufacturers. Done well, you can create a customer base that will be loyal to your product or cause for decades.

Confederates and their descendants have not let pass the opportunity to indoctrinate, at scale, America's children, and they have performed this task exceedingly well. The full picture of these twentieth-century efforts is only now, in the early twenty-first century, becoming clear.

In the wake of the national racial reckoning after the 2020 murder of George Floyd by a white police officer in Minnesota, several Southern newspapers turned the microscope on their own states and examined the nature and extent of ongoing efforts to sanitize the history of white supremacy. Among their many troubling findings was what they discovered about the work and impact of one particular organization. That organization, the United Daughters of the Confederacy (UDC), "spent decades shaping and reshaping textbooks to put a strong emphasis on Lost Cause views of the Civil War and Reconstruction, glorifying the white supremacist foundations of the Confederacy and providing justification for racial segregation and Jim Crow laws."[37]

One hundred years before the contemporary crackdown by today's Confederate political leaders on schools educating students about the truth of this country's racial history, Southern white women helped lead the charge to shape the young, malleable minds of the region's children. In her book *Dixie's Daughters: The United Daughters of the Confederacy and the Preservation of Confederate Culture*, historian Karen Cox describes the strategic significance that the defenders of the Confederacy attached to indoctrinating the region's children:

> [The UDC] joined male Confederate organizations in a campaign to eradicate "unsuitable" textbooks from southern classrooms, and they established their own textbook and education committees for that purpose. . . . They planned Confederate commemorative activities for students, often at the invitation of principals and school superintendents, and they sponsored essay contests to encourage public school children to learn about the Confederacy and its heroes. . . .
>
> Members believed that if white children were properly instructed, they would become "living monuments" to the Confederacy. Unlike marble statues, these children served as future defenders of the "sacred principles" for which their Confederate ancestors had died—namely, states' rights and the preservation of white supremacy.[38]

While children were the "living monuments," dead monuments were also critical to the champions of the Confederacy, and the UDC was one of the driving forces behind the erection of some 450 monuments, markers, buildings, and other commemoratives to the Confederate cause.[39]

Those—and many other—monuments have come to public attention in recent years.

Over the past decade or so, when enough unarmed Black people have been killed by cops to gain the attention of the mainstream media, questions get raised about the appropriateness of having statues and monuments honoring Confederate leaders littering the American landscape . To be more precise, I should say statues and monuments honoring *white supremacist murderers* littering the American landscape. The Southern Poverty Law Center estimates that there are more than two thousand such monuments across the country (in a country with only fifty states, that's a lot of racist statues).[40]

In the debates over taking down the monuments, the larger, far more illuminating question that rarely gets asked is, "What are they doing there in the first place?"

Mitch Landrieu offered an eloquent answer to this question in 2017. A moderate white Democrat, Landrieu belongs to a family with a prominent history in New Orleans politics and government; his father served as mayor of New Orleans in the 1970s, and his sister won election to the U.S. Senate three times. Landrieu himself became mayor of New Orleans in 2010. After many years of debate and delay about what to do about the prominent statues, Landrieu distinguished himself from other timid leaders of the time when he decided in 2017 to just go ahead and take the statues down.

In a landmark speech (landmark because so few white leaders have had a similar level of clarity and courage), Landrieu powerfully explained the strategic significance of these monuments to the "Distort Public Opinion" part of the Confederate Battle Plan:

> The Robert E. Lee, Jefferson Davis, and P.G.T. Beauregard statues were not erected just to honor these men, but as part of the movement which became known as The Cult of the Lost Cause. . . . This "cult" had one goal—through monuments and through other means—to rewrite history to hide the truth, which is that the Confederacy was on the wrong side of humanity.
>
> First erected over 166 years after the founding of our city and 19 years after the end of the Civil War, the monuments that

we took down were meant to rebrand the history of our city and the ideals of a defeated Confederacy. It is self-evident that these men did not fight for the United States of America. They fought against it. They may have been warriors, but in this cause they were not patriots.

These statues are not just stone and metal. They are not just innocent remembrances of a benign history. These monuments purposefully celebrate a fictional, sanitized Confederacy; ignoring the death, ignoring the enslavement, and the terror that it actually stood for. After the Civil War, these statues were a part of that terrorism as much as a burning cross on someone's lawn; they were erected purposefully to send a strong message to all who walked in their shadows about who was still in charge in this city.[41]

Public spaces are supposed to be for everybody. Pleasant places where people can walk, mingle, enjoy the society in which they live and dream, and perhaps think of a better future. What these monuments have done is poison our public spaces. For decades. Rather than being a place where people of color can enjoy themselves as equal members of society, they become reminders of injustice, inequality, and racism. Rather than being places where whites can find common cause with citizens of color, they become a reaffirmation of the supposed superiority of white people. And so they have had to—and still must—come down.

SILENTLY SANCTION TERRORISM

Did you ever stop to think about where members of the KKK get their robes? It turns out that in 1924, businesses such as the Martin Manufacturing Company in Lancaster, Ohio, ran ads in *The Fiery Cross*—"America's Leading Klan Publication"—offering the opportunity to, Avon-like, make money by selling Klan Robe Bags.[42] The ads ran in the same newspaper where you could find articles about stopping the immigration of Chinese people into America and critiques of the policy proposals of Catholic school board members, all interspersed with placements for Hunter's Point barbecue sandwiches and J.J. Hasseld Choice Meats. Racists gotta eat too.

Companies advertised in the Klan's newspaper because at the dawn of the twentieth-century, the KKK, and its white nationalist worldview, were powerful and respectable forces in America.

We have a good idea of just how powerful and respectable they were because of the excellent 2011 scholarship of Harvard professor Roland Fryer, who, along with Steven Levitt of the University of Chicago, published a fascinating study of the early twentieth-century Klan. Their paper, "Hatred and Profits: Under the Hood of the Ku Klux Klan," is one of the most detailed and methodologically rich analyses of Klan operations and influence in the mid-1920s, when the organization was at the height of its influence. Freyer and Levitt managed to get their hands on a whole bunch of internal Klan documents of the secretive organization as a result of myriad unusual developments: "In one case Klan headquarters was burglarized and the stolen files dropped off at a police station; in another case old records were found years later stored in an attic."[43]

Through those data sets, which included robe order forms, applications for membership, and dues ledgers, they were able to identify more than 55,000 specific Klan members in seven states. They then cross-referenced those names with available public records data in specific counties to fill out the qualitative picture of the characteristics of Klan members (regarding whether they were married, homeowners, etc.). And then, on top of all that, they did some fancy statistical modeling to extrapolate and estimate the overall size and scale of Klan membership to create a truly compelling picture of just who belonged to the white nationalist terrorist organization.

On the basis of their research, Fryer and Levitt roughly affirmed prior estimates that national Klan membership in the 1920s was in the neighborhood of 2 to 4 million people—2 percent to 5 percent of the entire adult population. (Their research revealed that in Indiana alone, for which they had the most extensive records of specific members, 18.4 percent of all adults belonged to the KKK.) That breadth of membership is the equivalent of there being 13 million adult Klan members in 2022. And bear in mind that those are just dues-paying, robe-buying members, each one of whom likely talked to and influenced other family, friends, neighbors, and children, extending their influence to millions more people.

The 1920s Klan was so big that between earning income from

dues, selling goods such as "swords, Bibles, helmets," and providing services such as dry-cleaning and life insurance, the organization "conservatively generated annual revenues from all sources of at least $25 million—equivalent to $300 million in current (2012) dollars." [44]

The reach of the KKK extended far beyond stereotypical images of tattooed bikers in bars; it attracted support from the highest precincts of power in the country. In her book *The Second Coming of the KKK*, historian Linda Gordon was able to quantify Klan "members elected to high offices: sixteen senators, scores of congressmen (the Klan claimed seventy-five), and eleven governors, pretty much equally divided between Democrats and Republicans." [45]

Whatever the specific number of people who held secret membership in the Klan, the public influence and political power were plain for all to see.

By the 1920s, as the Klan was riding high from the smashing success of its promotional film, *Birth of a Nation*, and reveling in reclaimed Confederate power and influence, the sanctioning of white terrorism was not so silent. Offered the opportunity to condemn the Klan, the top political leaders and presidential candidates of both parties shrank from the call to speak out against murder, terrorism, and violent attacks on Black people.

At the 1924 Republican National Convention, a few delegates did try to get the party to go on the record as opposing the efforts of groups associated with white domestic terrorism. The proposed resolution did not go over well, as described in a 2018 *Washington Post* article:

> [The KKK's] imperial wizard, Hiram W. Evans, first descended on Cleveland, where Republicans had gathered to nominate Calvin Coolidge. There, about 60 Klan leaders and lobbyists prevailed upon party officials to smother a resolution condemning the Klan before it ever went to a floor vote, a move called a "brilliant victory" by The Fiery Cross, a Klan newspaper in Indianapolis that also described the Republican convention as having a "real, genuine Klan atmosphere." [46]

On the other side of the political aisle, a month later, some delegates to the Democratic National Convention introduced their own resolution to condemn the Klan. There, the Democratic Party showed that it too could cower to the Klan and sanction domestic terrorism.

At that 1924 Democratic Convention, the Klan flexed its political power in truly historic fashion. Normally, the political battle over who a party will select as its presidential nominee is settled before the convention begins. Most recently, this was the case in 2016 when Hillary Clinton and Bernie Sanders battled down the stretch of the primary election season, and a similar protracted contest played out in 2008 when Barack Obama bested Clinton. In both cases, while the race was strenuously fought, the determination of who would be the party's nominee was resolved before the convention.

Historically, in the few cases where a political party's nomination fight resulted in a contested convention, there were never more than two or three rounds of voting.[47] In 1924, *it took 103 attempts* before the convention could select a nominee.[48] The reason it was so difficult to reach agreement was that the front-runner, then New York governor Al Smith, was a Catholic, and the Ku Klux Klan didn't want a Catholic in the White House.[49]

A key player in the Democratic Convention drama was William Pattangall, a man known for his sense of humor. The lawyer and writer had made a name for himself by writing biting satire skewering political corruption in his home state of Maine. He wrote a regular column called "The Meddybemps Letters," in which he penned fictional missives making fun of state politicians with lines such as, "I took a little walk around town . . . and ran into a young man named Burrill who was in the last legislature and didn't seem to realize it was anything to be ashamed of, because he spoke of it openly."[50] One thing that Pattangall did not find amusing was the lynching of Black people.

Thinking that others might share his sentiment, Pattangall proposed to his fellow delegates at the 1924 Democratic Convention that they pass a resolution going on record condemning the Klan. The backlash was ferocious. Not only was the convention divided about the amendment, but state delegations were also internally divided between pro- and anti-Klan members. Soon delegates were pushing and shoving on the floor of the convention. The governors of Kentucky and Colorado reportedly got into fistfights with other convention attendees as they struggled to keep their state banners out of the hands of anti-Klan delegates. (You read that right: the governors of Kentucky and Colorado wanted the banners for their states to be held by Klan *supporters* at the Democratic National Convention, and they physically fought with those who disagreed with them.)[51] Even such revered Democratic politicians as three-time presidential nominee William Jennings Bryan, exalted for his populist and fiery "Cross of Gold" speech, could not muster the courage to explicitly criticize the organization that lit actual fire to crosses as part of their terroristic repertoire.[52]

The *New York Times* offered a detailed contemporaneous description of the intensity—and ultimate failure—of the battle to condemn the Klan at the Democratic National Convention. The battle raged for five straight hours:

> The effort to get the name of the Ku Klux Klan into the platform resulted in one of the most entertaining evenings that have been seen in recent national conventions. There was, to begin with, two hours of oratory for and against the proposal, which was closed for the defense—that is, for the majority of the Resolutions Committee who did not want to name the Klan—by William Jennings Bryan, who spoke with his old-time fire and enthusiasm and very nearly with his old-time success.
>
> In the course of the argument Mr. Moir tried to knock a man who was raising a point of order off a chair and was restrained by a police captain and several patrolmen. . . . When [Pattangall] got down to his added paragraph and the religious freedom plank and read, "We condemn secret political societies—" there was an uproarious outburst from galleries and floor, the buzzing of rattles, whistles, shouts and cheers.[53]

Pattangall's measure to condemn the Ku Klux Klan failed to pass the 1924 Democratic National Convention.

Unrestrained by public condemnation, lynchings rapidly spread as a tool of violence and terrorism across the country. In her book

Raising Racists, Kristina DuRocher captures the commonality of lynching in Southern culture in the early twentieth century. DuRocher opens her book with this sentence: "In 1935, a white family traveled to a field in Fort Lauderdale, Florida, to pose for a commemorative photograph with the corpse of African American Rubin Stacy." Mr. Stacy was a homeless tenant farmer who had been lynched after he was arrested for frightening "a white woman when he approached her to ask for food." [54] DuRocher then further illuminates the sentiments of the day by describing an NAACP official's interaction with some white children who were walking to school near where a recent lynching had occurred, writing, "The girls eagerly told him about their attendance at the lynching . . . almost as joyously as though the memory were of Christmas morning or the circus," with [one girl] interjecting about the "fun we had burning the niggers." [55]

Notably, few people were ever arrested and prosecuted for hanging Black men from trees. A detailed study of American lynchings in 1933 found that "of the tens of thousands of lynchers and onlookers, the latter not guiltless, only forty-nine were indicted and only four have been sentenced." [56]

Rubin Stacy was just one of thousands of Black Americans lynched in the first half of the twentieth century. To help educate the modern-day American public about the true nature, history, and reality of white domestic terror in America, the Equal Justice Initiative, the organization created by renowned civil rights lawyer Bryan Stevenson, has created an interactive map listing the people lynched and the counties where they were killed. In some cases, the EJI site has videos with audio recordings summarizing the details of many of the murders. It's a powerful recounting, and that's the point. [57]

As the number of Black bodies hanging from trees increased, not surprisingly the number of Black people attempting to cast ballots decreased. The whole point of the terrorism was to protect white political power from the consequences of America becoming a multiracial democracy where people of all races could vote. As Mississippi senator Theodore Bilbo enthusiastically advised his supporters in 1946, "the best way to keep the nigger from voting . . . [was to] do it the night before the election. . . . If any nigger tries to organize to vote, use the tar and feathers and don't forget the matches."[58]

Carol Anderson succinctly summarized how "black political power evaporated in a hail of gunfire and flames" as unbridled white domestic terrorism was allowed to run unchecked in the first half of the twentieth century:

> The tools of Jim Crow disfranchisement worked all too well. In 1867, the percentage of African American adults registered to vote in Mississippi was 66.9 percent; by 1955, it was 4.3 percent. Between 1954 and 1962, only eight Black people in all of Claiborne County had managed to come through Mississippi's gauntlet. Those vote-chilling numbers scarred the southern electoral landscape. Five counties in Alabama had zero to less than 2 percent of African Americans registered. In Georgia, "less than 10% of the age-eligible African Americans were registered in 1962" in thirty counties with significant Black populations. In fact, four entire counties had fewer than ten nonwhites registered.[59]

The terror extended beyond those placing the ropes around necks. Many more were complicit. When Martin Luther King wrote in his "Letter from a Birmingham Jail" that "we will have to repent in this generation not merely for the hateful words and actions of the bad people but for the appalling silence of the good people," he was not just speaking in the abstract. Public displays of oppression and murder of Black folks in the South were as common and accepted as attendance at a high school play or football game. In 2018—*2018*, not 1918—Mississippi's sitting senator, Cindy Hyde-Smith, revealed the resilience of this mindset with her folksy affirmation of her friendship with a cattle rancher who endorsed her campaign. Hyde-Smith was so pleased with his support, she said, "If he invited me to a public hanging, I'd be on the front row."[60] Because *that's what people did*—invited their friends to public hangings of Black people. For entertainment.

David Oshinsky, in his book *Worse Than Slavery*, describes how

people in positions of authority regularly silently sanctioned white domestic terrorism. "What made mob violence so terrifying in Jim Crow
Mississippi," Oshinsky wrote, "was the virtual absence of opposition.
Local sheriffs often encouraged it, grand juries never brought indict-
ments, and coroners simply reported 'dead at the hands of parties unknown.' White ministers avoided the subject because it made their
congregations 'uncomfortable.' Not a single white editor in Mississippi
found the courage to condemn lynching without qualification in the
years between 1900 and World War I." [61]

Speaking of the crimes of the complicit, sociologist Arthur F. Raper
pulled back the curtain on them to astonishing effect in his 1933 book
The Tragedy of Lynching. Over the course of two years, Raper coordinated the work of a research team that visited the scenes of twenty-
one lynchings that occurred in 1930 and published the findings in his
book. "What were the cops doing?" you might wonder about the behavior of those responsible for preventing violence and murder. Raper's study conveyed their mindset by sharing a quote from a Southern
sheriff, who asked, "Do you think I'm going to risk my life protecting
a nigger?" Oshinsky added, "In most cases the sheriff and his deputies
merely stood by while the mob did its work, and later reported that the
mob had taken them by surprise." [62]

There is a comforting, yet entirely incorrect, belief that time alone
brings change—what Martin Luther King described as "the strangely
irrational notion that there is something in the very flow of time that
will inevitably cure all ills." [63] The cold hard truth is that the record of
the first half of the twentieth century is the bloody, painful proof of
the neutrality of time. White domestic terror ran rampant across this
country for decades.

PLAY THE LONG GAME

In the first half of the twentieth century, Confederates didn't need to
play the long game as much because their efforts at the end of the
previous century were so effective that the benefits yielded results for
more than fifty years. But drapetomania is a powerful force—people
of color kept fighting for freedom. And as the twentieth-century civil

rights movement started to make meaningful changes in American politics and society in the second half of the century, the Confederate forces would need to deploy all aspects of the Confederate Battle Plan in their desperate attempt to hold back the tide of change that was crashing across the country.

3

The Twentieth Century, Part Two:
50 More Years, Same Battle Plan

If I were standing at the beginning of time, with the possibility of taking a kind of general and panoramic view of the whole of human history up to now, and the Almighty said to me, "Martin Luther King, which age would you like to live in?" . . . I would turn to the Almighty, and say, "If you allow me to live just a few years in the second half of the 20th century, I will be happy."

Something is happening in our world. The masses of people are rising up. And wherever they are assembled today, whether they are in Johannesburg, South Africa; Nairobi, Kenya; Accra, Ghana; New York City; Atlanta, Georgia; Jackson, Mississippi; or Memphis, Tennessee—the cry is always the same: "We want to be free."

—Martin Luther King Jr's last speech, "I've Been
to the Mountaintop," April 3, 1968

The second half of the twentieth century was shaped by the cresting power, strength, and success of the civil rights movement. The reach and reverberations of that movement shook the foundations of the entire nation, and evidence of the masses of people rising up was everywhere:

- In 1955, a Black seamstress named Rosa Parks stood up to injustice by sitting down on a bus in Montgomery, Alabama;
- In 1963, hundreds of thousands of people came to Washington, DC, for the March on Washington for Jobs and Freedom and heard Dr. King articulate the aspirations of the movement and share his dream with the world;

- Cesar Chavez, Dolores Huerta, and the United Farm Workers helped organize a years-long, highly successful international grape boycott in the late 1960s;
- LaNada War Jack and dozens of Native American student activists reclaimed "the land known as Alcatraz Island in the name of all American Indians by right of discovery" and occupied it for eighteen months in 1969 and 1970;[1] and
- Fred Korematsu and the movement for redress and reparations in the 1970s and 1980s fought to right the wrongs of the World War II incarceration of Japanese Americans that saw the United States government round up more than 120,000 United States citizens and ship them off to concentration camps.

In the words of an essay by Bernice Johnson Reagon, founder of the civil rights musical ensemble Sweet Honey in the Rock, "The Civil Rights Movement was a borning struggle, breaking new ground and laying the foundation for ever-widening segments of the society to call for fundamental rights and human dignity. Few forces have created as many ripples that crossed racial, class and social lines as did the Civil Rights Movement."[2]

As we will see in part II of this book, those ripples have extended all the way into the twenty-first century and up to the present day, as leaders who learned from the civil rights movement have gone on to create coalitions and organizations that have played pivotal roles in flipping control of formerly Confederate states, helping to wrest the highest seat of power in the United States government from the white nationalists occupying the White House.

In the second half of the twentieth century, it was harder to hide from or deny the far-reaching ramifications of these civil rights–driven movements that sought to restructure a nation built by stolen people working on stolen land. But the Confederates nonetheless did their level best to try to stop, suppress, and slow the ongoing efforts to finally make America a multiracial democracy. They ferociously fought that fight for the rest of the century, and they did so with all of the elements of their tried-and-true Confederate Battle Plan that had served them so well, ever since John Wilkes Booth slipped into Ford's Theater five days after the Confederate army had supposedly surrendered.

NEVER GIVE AN INCH

In the 1990s, I served on the school board in San Francisco, one of the most liberal cities in the country. To address the educational inequities in the district, we proposed closing a low-performing high school and merging it with another school that had exemplary instructional leadership and admirable outcomes in terms of the school's college enrollment rates. The idea was not well received by the parents at the high-performing school. At one raucous school board meeting (the first time I'd been booed in public) a very liberal white parent angrily shouted, "We don't want them here! Send them somewhere else!" Again, that was in lefty, progressive San Francisco in the last decade of the twentieth century. Imagine the sentiments toward integration in the middle of the century in cities and states where people had historically resorted to murdering Americans to preserve slavery and white nationalism.

The Supreme Court's 1954 *Brown v. Board of Education* decision is hailed as a landmark event in America's struggle for racial justice, and rightly so. The unanimous ruling rejected the shameful 1896 *Plessy v. Ferguson* case that upheld racial segregation as constitutional so long as facilities were "separate but equal." The *Brown* decision unequivocally declared that "in the field of public education the doctrine of 'separate but equal' has no place." (It is important to note that the *Brown* decision did nothing to disturb racial segregation *outside* "the field of public education," and it remained perfectly legal for another decade to racially discriminate in hiring, housing, and the rest of American life, right up until the passage of the Civil Rights Act in 1964—the year I was born.)

True to Confederate form, any erosion of white nationalist hegemony demanded a reaction that was vocal, vociferous, and in keeping with never giving an inch in the fight to preserve white power. The NAACP Legal Defense and Education Fund, which spearheaded the litigation that resulted in the *Brown* decision, offers on its website an excellent summary of the Southern response to the decision:

Almost immediately after Chief Justice Earl Warren finished reading the Supreme Court's unanimous opinion in *Brown v.*

Board of Education in the early afternoon of May 17, 1954, Southern white political leaders condemned the decision and vowed to defy it. . . .

On February 25, 1956, Senator Harry Byrd of Virginia issued the call for "Massive Resistance"—a collection of laws passed in response to the *Brown* decision that aggressively tried to forestall and prevent school integration. For instance, the Massive Resistance doctrine included a law that punished any public school that integrated by eliminating its state funds and eventually closing the school.

In addition to legal and legislative resistance, the white population of the southern United States mobilized en masse to nullify the Supreme Court's decree. In states across the South, whites set up private academies to educate their children, at first using public funds to support the attendance of their children in these segregated facilities, until the use of public funds was successfully challenged in court. In other instances, segregationists tried to intimidate black families by threats of violence and economic reprisals against plaintiffs in local cases.[3]

As described by historian Dan Carter, "over ninety percent of the region's congressmen and senators signed the 'Southern Manifesto' drafted by the die-hard Dixiecrat senator Strom Thurmond."[4] While stopping short of calling for secession and the outright shooting and killing of those not enamored of white nationalism, "the declaration called upon whites to unite in an unbroken phalanx of opposition to any changes in the South's racial system."[5]

The Never Give an Inch mindset played out perhaps most starkly in Prince Edward County, Virginia, in 1959. In her book, *Something Must Be Done About Prince Edward County*, journalist Kristen Green described the actions of the leaders of the town in which she grew up, writing, "The county's white leaders responded exactly as they had warned. Defying the new court order, the Prince Edward County Board of Supervisors announced it would eliminate the county's entire education budget, thereby closing all twenty-one white and black public schools." Green elaborated on their rationale, saying, "It was better to abandon schools, county leaders decided, than for white children to sit in a classroom next to black classmates."[6]

After closing the public schools, the white residents of Prince Edward County showed that they were perfectly capable of meeting the needs of those students they actually cared about and sprang into action, organizing a separate, private education system for whites only. *Washington Post* reporter Glenn Frankel recently recounted the painfully poignant first day of class: "On the first day of school in September 1959, 14 buses helped ferry 1,475 white students to the private academy, while 1,700 black children stood and watched."[7] As described by the writer Emily Richmond in a 2014 *Atlantic* article, "black students were left largely to fend for themselves, cobbling together educations in church basements and home-school settings."[8]

Prince Edward County's leaders kept its public schools closed for five full years—*longer than the duration of the Civil War itself.*

Virginia and Prince Edward County were not the only places to never give an inch in the wake of the *Brown* decision. As Green recounted, "Many Southern communities developed two school systems: an underfunded public system mostly attended by black students, and private schools set up for white children. Within a decade, these segregation academies would be an accepted part of the Southern landscape." In quantitative terms, the reach of these segregationist academies was vast. By 1969, just ten years after Prince Edward County's defiance, "three hundred thousand students were enrolled in all-white schools across eleven Southern states . . . only a fraction of which had been open before Brown." (In case you're counting along at home, the number of states that seceded and formed the Confederacy was . . . eleven.)[9]

While whites across the South were digging in and never giving an inch in the face of the constitutional mandate to desegregate their schools, one ambitious Alabama politician was making meticulous mental notes about what worked—and what didn't—in translating white fears, rage, and resentment into votes and political power.

———

Reflecting back on his career, former Alabama governor George Wallace said, "I started off talking about schools and highways and prisons and taxes—and I couldn't make them listen. Then I began talking about niggers—and they stomped the floor."[10] At first, when he was talking about schools and highways, Black folks liked Wallace. As a judge in Alabama in the 1950s, he earned a reputation for relative fairness toward African Americans in his courtroom. Prominent Black civil rights lawyer J.L. Chestnut Jr. noted, "Judge George Wallace was the most liberal judge that I had ever practiced law in front of. He was the first judge in Alabama to call me 'Mister' in a courtroom."[11]

With that track record, Wallace attracted the support of the NAACP in his first run for governor in 1958—three years after Rosa Parks refused to give up her seat on an Alabama bus, sparking the boycott that attracted national attention to a movement whose leadership included a twenty-six-year-old minister named Martin Luther King Jr. During his first, closely fought gubernatorial election, Wallace criticized his opponent, Alabama attorney general John Patterson, for his close ties to the Ku Klux Klan. When challenged to denounce the Klan, Patterson said that the Klan membership included "many fine peace-loving individuals who merely wanted to preserve [white Southerners'] way of life" (offering an answer that Donald Trump would echo fifty-nine years later when he was pressed to condemn the deadly 2017 white supremacist march in Charlottesville, Virginia—see chapter 9).[12]

Wallace, for his part, condemned the Klan, lost the election, and immediately understood the cause of his defeat, telling his campaign team on election night, "Well, boys, no other son-of-a-bitch will ever out-nigger me again."[13]

True to his word, Wallace became a staunch, unapologetic white nationalist, running on a Dixiecrat-like segregationist platform, and riding that energy into the Alabama governor's office four years later, in 1962. Speaking from the portico of the Alabama State Capitol—the very spot where Jefferson Davis had been sworn in as president of the Confederacy 102 years earlier—Wallace gave an inaugural address in which he famously declared, "In the name of the greatest people that have ever trod this earth, I draw the line in the dust and toss the gauntlet before the feet of tyranny, and I say segregation now, segregation tomorrow, segregation forever."[14]

As the state's top elected official, Wallace did everything he could to never give an inch and to resist any encroachment on the privileged place of white people.

Wallace will forever be known as the white politician most visibly opposed to the work of Dr. King, and he worked hard to build his brand in the crucible of the fight to defend white supremacy. Just six months into his term as governor, he famously and in very public fashion literally stood in the way of the efforts to desegregate the University of Alabama by standing in the door of the admissions building, blocking entry to the Black students seeking to enroll. This nationally televised confrontation solidified his Champion of the Confederacy credentials and sent a strong message across the country.

That opening act of never giving an inch in the fight to defend the cause was followed two years later by Wallace exercising his gubernatorial powers to turn loose the force of the state on peaceful protesters seeking to cross the Edmund Pettus Bridge in Selma, Alabama, in March of 1965. It was Wallace's National Guard that precipitated Bloody Sunday by unleashing attack dogs, tear gas, and billy club–wielding cops on horseback to bash the skulls of people such as John Lewis, Amelia Boynton, and other men, women, and children who were operating under the mistaken belief that the Fifteenth Amendment had, in fact, secured their right to vote.

It turns out that being the enemy of the civil rights movement was a powerful political brand to have. Having seen Wallace block school segregation and then unleash the dogs on peaceful Black Americans seeking to vote, millions of Americans concluded in 1968 that such a man would make a great president of the United States. Just as the civil rights legislation proposed by President Truman in 1948 catalyzed several Southern governors to form a segregationist political party and mount the defiant Dixiecrat presidential campaign, so too did the steps in the 1960s toward making America a multiracial democracy precipitate proud segregationist George Wallace's decision to make a run for the White House in 1968.

Looking to maximize the political leverage of aggrieved white people, Wallace sought to win enough states to deny any candidate the number of electoral votes necessary to win outright, forcing the decision to the House of Representatives, where Confederates wielded outsize influence. The same constituency that would later propel Trump

in 2016 to the front of the Republican primary pack—white Southerners and whites outside the South who were animated by racial fear
and resentment—flocked to Wallace, helping him send shock waves
through the national political landscape.

The 1968 election was one of the closest contests in U.S. history,
with Richard Nixon besting Hubert Humphrey by less than 1 percent
of the vote. While Nixon prevailed by a mere 512,000 votes, Wallace
garnered 10 million votes—13.5 percent of all votes cast—and he prevailed in five states outright, a showing notably stronger than that of
Strom Thurmond and the Dixiecrats twenty years earlier. Wallace won
8 percent of the vote *outside* the South, far more than the Dixiecrats'
1 percent showing in non-Southern states in 1948. The potential to
sway the fiercely fought election is shown in the results: in sixteen
states, with 222 electoral votes, Wallace won more votes than Nixon's
margin of victory. Wallace's strong showing nearly accomplished his
objective of effectively nullifying the votes of millions of Americans
and sending the contest to the House of Representatives, where, at a
minimum, he had hoped to extract Hayes-Tilden–like compromises
for the Confederacy, if not actually get handed the literal keys to the
White House.[15]

The through line should not be lost that of the seven original Confederate states who started the bloody war to preserve white supremacy
and Black slavery, five of them—Mississippi, South Carolina, Alabama,
Georgia, and Louisiana—backed third-party, segregationist presidential candidacies in either 1948, 1968, or both (ultimately eleven states
comprised the Confederacy, but it started with seven). Those states
would form the indispensable foundation of Trump's electoral coalition in 2016, and Trump would not have won the White House without
securing the support of those Confederate cornerstone states.

Politicians with national ambitions in the second half of the twentieth century got the message that the Confederates were determined
to hold the line and never give an inch. As Wallace biographer Carter
observed, "George Wallace laid the foundation for the dominance of
the Republican Party in American society through the manipulation
of racial and social issues in the 1960s and 1970s. He was the master teacher, and Richard Nixon and the Republican leadership that
followed were his students."[16] In an interview with historian Herbert

Parmet, Nixon admitted that "we had to move to the right to cut Wallace off at the pass." Or, as Carter put it in his biography of Wallace, "when George Wallace had played his fiddle, the President of the United States had danced Jim Crow." [17]

Alabama newspaper editor John Anderson further connected the dots in his 1998 obituary of Wallace, saying, "His startling appeal to millions of alienated white voters was not lost on Richard Nixon and other Republican strategists. First Nixon, then Ronald Reagan, and then George Herbert Walker Bush successfully adopted toned-down versions of Wallace's anti-busing, anti–federal government platform to pry low- and middle-income whites from the Democratic New Deal coalition." [18]

George Wallace's career and influence offer a profound cautionary tale on multiple levels. Not least of which is a lesson for Democrats who continue to hope and believe—against all the evidence—that simply by highlighting economic issues, they can win support from whites who cling to the Confederate worldview and values. President Joe Biden's decision in the first year of his presidency to prioritize pursuing an infrastructure bill—roads and bridges—over democracy and voting rights protections was just the latest manifestation in the desperate Democratic hope that focusing on highways and schools will boost support among whites. Wallace couldn't have been more clear about what works best in wooing such voters—talking about schools and highways is much less effective than railing against niggers. That's what whips whites into a frenzy of floor stomping and enthusiastic voting for white nationalist candidates.

DISTORT PUBLIC OPINION

In terms of distorting public opinion, Confederates in the second half of the twentieth century kind of had it easy. The heavy lifting of writing books, making movies, and erecting statues to manufacture a fictional white nationalist universe of virtuous slave holders and dangerous darkies had already been done. Gone with the Wind remained one of the most popular books in America into the twenty-first century. Statues of racist murderers polluted the landscape in dozens of states and hundreds of cities for more than a hundred years.

Because the construction of a fictional universe had already been completed, the public opinion distortion work of Confederates in the second half of the twentieth century largely centered on the perpetuation and protection of what had already been created. Perpetuation took the form of continuing to brainwash the impressionable minds of Southern children, and protection consisted of seeking to fight off any attempts to remove the white supremacist public statues poisoning the country's public spaces.

———

When they weren't shutting down school districts so that white children wouldn't have to sit next to Black children, Confederates were busy indoctrinating young white minds with Lost Cause propaganda. As described in the previous chapter, at the beginning of the twentieth century, the United Daughters of the Confederacy was one of the most active organizations zealously monitoring what was being taught in the schools in the South lest any truth about white supremacy seep into the country's classrooms. The UDC's work continued apace throughout the second half of the century, and the scale, scope, and reach of their efforts should not be underestimated. In an article titled "Twisted Sources," the Institute for Southern Studies documented the damage, including a calculation of just how many children were influenced and impacted: "69,706,756. That's how many students were enrolled in the South's public elementary and secondary schools between 1889, when the government began counting students, and 1969, the height of the segregationist Jim Crow era, according to the U.S. Department of Education statistics." [19]

Serving as racial censors who metaphorically install and enforce "whites only" signs on the content allowed into the classroom is bad enough. That has to do with what kinds of information goes into the mind of a child. Even more odd—and more chilling—is the practice of catechisms, as that has to do with what comes out of the mouths of those children.

Encyclopedia Britannica defines a catechism as "a manual of religious instruction usually arranged in the form of questions and answers used to instruct the young, to win converts, and to testify to the faith." [20] Catechisms are most prominent in a religious context where, frequently in question-and-answer format, instruction is provided about the principles and beliefs of the faith. In the Catholic Church, for example, the catechism includes questions such as, "Who created Heaven and Earth?" and "Is the Blessed Virgin Mary truly the Mother of God?"[21]

The way that the UDC utilized catechisms and the statements it required young people to recite were, shall we say, a bit different from the church's approach. *Dixie's Daughter* author Karen Cox explained that an early activity of the UDC was "to establish children's groups known as Children of the Confederacy (CofC)." These CofC chapters proliferated across the South, and the typical practice was to hold monthly meetings where "children studied history and the Confederate catechism (a book of call and response to questions about the 'facts' of the southern past), wrote essays, and sang favorite Confederate songs, such as 'Dixie.' "[22] One early call-and-response routine from a 1904 "UDC Catechism for Children" went like this:

> Q: *What causes led to the War Between the States from 1861 to 1865?*
> A: The disregard, on the part of the States of the North, for the rights of the Southern or slaveholding States.
> Q: *What were these rights?*
> A: The right to regulate their own affairs and to hold slaves as property.
> Q: *How were the slaves treated?*
> A: With great kindness and care in nearly all cases, a cruel master being rare.[23]

Right about now you might be thinking, "Yeah, I hear you, and that kind of racist brain-washing was unfortunate, but that was a long time ago. Lots of folks were pretty racist back then, and things have changed now." And you would be both right and very, *very* wrong. It was a long time ago, but things have not changed.

California State University, Long Beach communications professor Amy Heyse published a 366-page dissertation in 2006 titled, "Teachers of the Lost Cause: The United Daughters of the Confederacy and the Rhetoric of Their Catechisms." In the course of her exhaustive research, Heyse gathered as many versions of the catechisms as she could get her hands on. One such version, "A Confederate Catechism for Southern Children," was republished—and, by logical extension—used by the UDC on the children in their sphere of influence—in and after 1946. That version included the following incantations:

> *Q: What did the North and the South fight about?*
> A: The North would not grant us constitutional rights, nor would they let us alone, the South could no longer submit to the tyranny and oppression of the North, and was obliged to fight.
> *Q: Was slavery the cause of the war?*
> A: It was one of the issues, but the matter of "States Rights" was the cause of the war.
> *Q: Why is it so important for Southern children to learn these truths?*
> A: Because when the older people pass away, we can take their places, and teach the truth, and be proud of our Confederate ancestry.
> *Q. Did we kill many Yankees?*
> A: Yes, thousands and thousands of them.[24]

Thousands and thousands of them. At the exact same time that American soldiers were going overseas to fight the white supremacist Nazis in World War II, Southern white children were exhorted to chirp with pride that their forefathers had killed "thousands and thousands" of American soldiers waging a war to end the enslavement of Black people in America.

Professor Heyse also got her hands on a version of the catechism that was being used *in 1999* (inadvertently further proving the point that in trying to temporally pinpoint the work of the Confederacy, simply saying "turn of the century" is inadequate; you have to say *which* century). Like the opening crawl of a Star Wars film, the 1999 version of the catechism begins with a context-setting origin story. However, the UDC's catechism story began not that long ago and not that far away. According to Heyse, the document opens with the following language:

The concept of a Catechism on the History of the Confederate States of America was approved at the UDC Annual General Convention, Washington, D. C. in November 1953. After much research and consultation with noted authors, historians and educators, it was compiled by Mrs. Harry Davis Allen of Memphis, Tennessee in 1954 and first printed in October of that year. After reprints over the past forty years, the material has been updated to speak to the reader of today.[25]

Note the phrases "the reader of today," and "reprints over the past forty years," meaning that the catechism had been used for that entire span of the twentieth century—for forty consecutive years from the 1950s up until 1999. Here is what, at the very end of the twentieth century, the UDC was requiring children to chant:

Q: What causes led to the War Between the States? How was this shown?
A: The disregard of those in power for the rights of the southern states and by the passage of laws annulling the rights of the people [sic] the south.
Q: What were these rights?
The right to regulate their own affairs, one of which was to hold slaves as property.
Q: How were the slaves treated by their owners?
A: The slaves were treated, in most cases, with kindness and care. Many claims of cruelty and abuse were found to be the result of plantation overseers.
Q: What was the feeling of the slaves toward their masters?
A: The slaves, for the most part, were faithful and devoted. Usually ready and willing to serve their masters.[26]

That's the *nineteen ninety-nine* version of the catechism. The casual nature of the tone of the document can obscure the fundamentally white nationalist and inhumane essence of the catechism. Without batting an eye or expressing an ounce of shame, for more than a hundred years, the UDC has been affirming the appropriateness of holding human beings "as property." The implications of that mindset are quite literally chilling.

And just in case you've held out hope to this point that the UDC might have abandoned its cult-like indoctrination of young people in more recent years, I'm sorry to have to disappoint you. As I type these words in May of 2022, the UDC website prominently displays a category called "Children of the Confederacy," and within that category's drop-down menu is a link to a page on catechisms with a picture of what sure looks like the 1999 version of the catechism. On that webpage, it is quite clear that the Confederate indoctrination methodology is alive and well, with the 2022 Catechism page stating the following: "Catechisms are a part of the culture and history of the CofC. *Members are encouraged to recite basic beliefs and elements of Confederate history* [emphasis added]. Children compete at all levels to display excellence." [27]

———

If the organization's name—the United Daughters of the Confederacy—had you worried that it was letting the men off the hook, you need not be concerned. The UDC has a sibling organization, the Sons of Confederate Veterans (SCV), and it has conducted similar activities—organizing white men, indoctrinating white boys, and defending white nationalist murderer monuments. On its website, the SCV says it was organized in 1896, and "continues to serve as a historical, patriotic, and non-political organization dedicated to ensuring that a true history of the 1861-1865 period is preserved." And by "true history," they of course mean false history.

As of late 2021, the SCV still published a bimonthly magazine, *Confederate Veteran*. The April 2021 edition of the magazine opens with a letter from editor-in-chief Frank B. Powell III that says, "Lincoln was a Marxist and a Communist before being a Marxist and a Communist were popular." [28] The letter does not go on to elaborate whether those supposed Marxist sympathies made it any less of a crime and tragedy that Confederate supporter John Wilkes Booth assassinated the president of the United States.

Many Americans believe, incorrectly, that racism and white nationalism are unfortunate but archaic relics of a bygone era. They persist

to this day, however, and a big part of the reason that white nationalism won't just disappear and die is that highly organized and fanatical
modern-day Confederates are working day and night to make sure that
the Lost Cause of the Confederacy never in fact gets lost. The United
Daughters of the Confederacy and the Sons of Confederate Veterans
are Exhibits A and B of that tenacity and endurance.

Far from fading in significance, the UDC sure looks like it's here
to stay, fanning the flames of Confederate fantasy, filling the heads
of innocent children with white nationalist nonsense, preserving the
towering bronze tributes to white nationalist murderers. Its website
indicates that it has Children of the Confederacy chapters—the group-
ings where the catechisms regularly reverberate—in eighteen states
and the District of Columbia. In a speech at the end of the twentieth
century, then president general of the UDC, June Murray Wells, estimated there were around 25,000 members across 700 chapters in
thirty-two states.[29]

A review of publicly available data filed by the UDC with the Internal Revenue Service affirms that there are at least 759 UDC chapters,
which cumulatively list more than $10 million in assets and an $8 million investment portfolio. As of 2019, they were still awarding scholarships every year to students, bestowing their largesse in that year on
eighty-nine students—young leaders who are presumably proficient
in the pro–white nationalist catechism.[30]

As for the men, the SCV has 738 different active affiliated entities—
a reach, size, and scale similar to that of the UDC. The largest SCV
chapter reported nearly $2 million in revenue in 2018 and $13 million
in assets.[31] The SCV has an online store where, as of May 2022, you
could purchase, among many other items, Confederate flag–themed
clothing, barbecue grills, coolers, wireless headphones, yo-yos for children, and books such as *Was Jefferson Davis Right?* and *ReKilling Lincoln*
(supposedly exposing "the little-known dark side of America's sixteenth
president.")[32] If you don't want to go through the hassle of ordering online, you can just pick up the phone and call SCV to order your Confederate white nationalist merchandise by dialing 1-800-My-Dixie. You
will be greeted by a message saying, "God Bless Dixie" and prompted to
press 6 for sales and merchandise. I kid you not.[33]

Seeding the minds of children with racist, white nationalist, violence-glorifying lies and having them ask hopefully, "Did we kill many Yankees?" can, not surprisingly, result in racist, white nationalist acts of violence when those children become adults. Writing in the *New York Times* in 2017, Cox described the lasting impact of the UDC's mis-education of children, those whom they called "citizens of tomorrow":

> Those "citizens of tomorrow," who drank from the cup of history brewed by the U.D.C. for generations, became the "living monuments" that Southern white women sought to build. In the 1950s and '60s, they were segregationists who hoisted the Confederate battle flag with talk of defending states' rights and who denounced federal intervention into their affairs. They were members of the White Citizens' Councils who spoke of "states' rights and racial integrity." And they were individuals like Senators James O. Eastland and Strom Thurmond and Birmingham's infamous commissioner of public safety, Eugene Connor, known as Bull. They were also people like Byron De La Beckwith, who assassinated Medgar Evers in 1963.[34]

It is important to realize that the UDC and SCV are not the most extreme fringe of the white supremacist ecosystem in this country. And that is precisely why they have been so dangerous. They've mainstreamed white nationalism in ways that are far more insidious—and far more effective—than explicit white power appeals.

———

There is no example that better illuminates how the glorification of white nationalist murderers remained acceptable for so long than the story of Nathan Bedford Forrest's bust in the Tennessee State Capitol. As discussed in chapter 1, Forrest, a slave trader and leading general during the Civil War, was a white supremacist mass murderer. And up until July 2021, there was a three-thousand-pound bronze bust in the Tennessee State Capitol honoring this man who was also the first grand wizard of the Ku Klux Klan. The saga of the homages to Forrest lasted for most of the second half of the twentieth century and well into the twenty-first.

In the early 1970s, nearly a hundred years after Forrest died, the owners of a tourist destination called Travellers Rest Plantation decided to partner up with those who believed that what Tennessee needed was for the state Capitol to prominently display a bust of the former leader of the white domestic terrorists (that "plantation" in the name means just what it says—a place where white people held Black people in chains and chattel slavery).[35] Today they hold weddings on that plantation. Its website describes the location: "A true gem nestled just a few miles outside of the hustle and bustle of downtown, Historic Travellers Rest is the venue to say 'I do!' with its rich history and idyllic grounds."

For the Sons of Confederate Veterans, Travellers Rest was also the perfect spot to say, "I *do* think the state's governing building should have a prominent public display honoring the leader of the KKK." It was at Travellers Rest that they launched their 1973 fundraising drive to pay for the bust by putting up a portrait of the KKK mass murderer at the former slavery site turned wedding venue. Members of the public were encouraged to purchase 24-by-30-inch full-color prints of the grand wizard's portrait to help raise funds for the creation of the bust.[36] (As of April 2022, you could still buy the portrait from the SCV website for $25, "plus $7.50 for postage and handling.")[37]

Tennessee's political leaders of the 1970s were delighted to throw their weight behind the Confederate cause of the 1860s, and the state legislature overwhelmingly passed a resolution calling for the creation of a Nathan Bedford Forrest bust. The legislative authors of the resolution were apparently not so busy dealing with the state's challenges of education, health care, and economic opportunity that they couldn't include Martha Stewart–esque Capitol decorating instructions such as, "There is an empty niche on the second floor of the state capitol which would be appropriate for the display of a bust of General Forrest."[38] With the fundraising for the bust sufficient to commission an artist, the bust was created, and in 1978 it was placed in that very second-floor niche in the state Capitol.

African American leaders called the Forrest bust "an insult to all Blacks." Undaunted and undeterred, the modern-day Confederates in Tennessee defended and protected the bust—and the white supremacist message it sent to members of the public—for decades. In 1979, Black community leaders met with Governor Lamar Alexander and urged him to take action, but he threw up his hands, said it was an issue for the legislature, and besides, the bust wasn't so bad anyway. In 1980, members of the KKK, wearing robes and hoods, held a press conference in front of the bust of their former grand wizard. In 2015, after a white nationalist, Confederate flag–flying young white man murdered nine Black church members in South Carolina at a Bible study, the Tennessee state legislature took action. The action? Ruthlessly rewriting the law to make it harder to remove statues or monuments in the state—requiring a two-thirds vote from the Tennessee Historical Commission instead of a simple majority.[39]

Finally, in 2021—nearly forty-three years after the bust was installed and a year after the international racial reckoning in the wake of the murder of George Floyd—the Forrest bust was removed from the Tennessee State Capitol.[40] Even getting to that point required dealing with Confederates never giving an inch and seeking to rewrite the rules. Earlier that year, in March, after the state historical commission voted 25 to 1 to remove the Forrest bust, State Senator Joey Hensley—a member of the Sons of Confederate Veterans—put forward a bill to remove all of the members the offending commission.[41]

While the bust was ultimately removed, the cause endures. As of May 2022, the Sons of Confederate Veterans were still selling General Forrest Homemade Soap (for the low, low price of $10)—"Scents include Bay Leaf & Tobacco or Leather, Dirt, & Tobacco. Please specify upon purchase," according to the website.[42]

Tennessee was not the only Capitol building with public monuments to Confederate leaders. The U.S. Capitol, as of early 2022, still had a dozen full-size monuments of racist, white supremacist traitors standing proudly, defiantly, in the rotunda of the country's governing building.[43] By law, each state is allotted space in the Capitol for two statues of people from its state, and in the first half the twentieth century, the Confederates did what they do, rushing the homages to traitors into the main legislative building of the nation that they'd betrayed.

RUTHLESSLY REWRITE THE LAWS

From the time of the redrafted state constitutions in the 1890s that restored white Confederates to power, a wide array of disenfranchisement measures spread across the decades of the twentieth century and across the states of the old Confederacy. As discussed in the previous chapter, Black voter participation plummeted throughout the first half of the twentieth century, and it took the toil, sweat, and, yes, blood of many people in the second half of the century to bring about a moment and a movement to create the Voting Rights Act of 1965, which served to take a wrecking ball to the traditional pillars of voter suppression. Not surprisingly, Confederates responded to the Voting Rights Act the way they have responded to every perceived threat to white nationalist power.

Historically, when Confederates have lacked the votes or political power to actually rewrite the rules, they typically fall back to the position of ridiculously reinterpreting pro-equality laws in ways that would preserve as much white power as possible. "Sure the country waged a long, brutal Civil War to end slavery and then, with great difficulty, passed three constitutional amendments to enforce racial equality, but," Confederates in the courts and executive branch said, "those amendments don't apply in *this* situation. Or that one. Or that one over there." In fact, in the minds of Confederates tasked with interpreting and implementing pro-equality laws, it's been hard to find *any* actual situations where the civil rights laws are relevant and applicable. Yes, the Fourteenth Amendment required equal protection of everybody in a state, but that didn't apply to laws sanctioning "whites only" restrictions on trains and buses. Yes, the Fifteenth Amendment said you can't deny the right to vote on the basis of color, but that doesn't apply to Texas's whites-only Democratic primaries. Yes, Jimmie Lee Jackson, James Reeb, and Viola Liuzzo gave their lives in the fight to get Congress to pass the Voting Rights Act in 1965, but . . . well, you get the picture.

Confederates often talk a good game about "limited government," respecting settled law, and the importance of judges not being "activists." In the case of one of the most important pro-equality pieces of legislation in the history of the country, however—the Voting Rights Act of 1965—Confederates in both the courts and the executive branch have gleefully joined in a double-barreled assault on this core protection of a fragile multiracial democracy.

Long before he became chief justice of the United States Supreme Court in 1986, William Rehnquist was an unapologetic defender of one of the court's most racist decisions. In 1952, Rehnquist was fresh out of law school and working as a clerk for Supreme Court Justice Robert Jackson when the court first heard oral arguments in the *Brown v. Board* case. During this clerkship, young Mr. Rehnquist wrote a memo to his fellow clerks laying out his defense of the 1896 *Plessy v. Ferguson* "separate but equal" case that held that state-mandated segregation laws did not violate the equal protection clause of the Fourteenth Amendment. Ari Berman's book *Give Us the Ballot* provides the background:

> In 1952, as a twenty-eight-year-old clerk to Justice Robert Jackson, Rehnquist had written an explosive memo as the Court prepared to hear the first round of arguments in *Brown v. Board of Education*. "I realize that it is an unpopular and unhumanitarian position, for which I have been excoriated by 'liberal' colleagues, but I think *Plessy v. Ferguson* was right and should be reaffirmed," Rehnquist wrote.[44]

Far from such views and actions damaging his career prospects, Rehnquist went on to himself become a member of the Supreme Court in 1972 and then chief justice of the court for nearly two decades, from 1986 to 2005, presiding over the very same body whose landmark 1896 racist decision he'd earlier eagerly embraced. From his position of power and ideological influence, Rehnquist took on the task of molding the mind of an eager young protege named John Roberts, who, as a twenty-five-year-old Harvard Law grad, clerked for Justice Rehnquist from 1980 to 1981.

John Roberts did not—and does not—like the Voting Rights Act. For nearly his entire adult life, he has worked to weaken, undermine, and roll back the most powerful provisions of the legislation that finally ushered in democracy in America. The Voting Rights Act of 1965, for the first time in nearly one hundred years, put real teeth and power behind efforts to stamp out the kinds of racist disenfranchisement schemes that had maintained white political power throughout the South since the end of Reconstruction. Recognizing the resilience of racists and their ability to reinvent themselves and refashion their laws, the act required states with histories of voter suppression to clear all their subsequent voting laws with the U.S. Department of Justice (in fact, the Justice Department itself was created in 1870 specifically to fight Confederate voter suppression and intimidation of African Americans).[45]

The impact of the implementation of the Voting Rights Act was nothing short of revolutionary. With the doors to democracy finally opened to voters of all races and the white domestic terrorists kept at bay, African American voter participation soared. Prior to the act's passage, just one-quarter of eligible Black voters were registered to vote in the South. By 1968 the number had increased to 62 percent.[46] In states such as Mississippi, the percentage of African Americans who were registered to vote surged from 6.7 percent in 1964 to 59 percent in 1968.[47] It is not hyperbole to state that the Voting Rights Act—"written in blood before it was signed in ink," as Jesse Jackson has said—finally made America a democracy—175 years after the adoption of the Constitution.

But, as with all things racial justice, this could not stand in a country where Confederates continued to wield power and influence. Encouraged and emboldened by the whites-first mentality of his mentor Justice Rehnquist, Roberts brought his white grievance mindset to his job in the Justice Department of President Ronald Reagan in 1981. Setting up shop in the ostensibly pro–civil rights agency after Reagan was swept into the White House with overwhelming Confederate support, Roberts went to work ruthlessly reinterpreting and restricting the reach of the Voting Rights Act. As Berman explains in detail in *Give Us the Ballot*, "The Department of Justice became the nerve center of the Reagan revolution, the most intellectually vibrant and ideologically conservative agency of the federal government." Roberts wrote to a friend early in his tenure at the agency, "This is an exciting time to be at the Justice Department. . . . So much that has been taken for granted for so long is being seriously reconsidered."[48]

Seriously reconsidering settled law is not something professed conservatives are supposed to do. That is usually the province of radicals. But waging a violent and bloody civil war to defend white supremacy was nothing if not radical, and John Roberts was more than willing to carry on that radical Confederate tradition by working from within to rewrite, restrict, and undermine the civil rights laws that so many people had sacrificed to create. Working as a special assistant to the U.S. attorney general, Roberts actively and aggressively sought to weaken the critical Section 2 of the Act, which prohibited state and local governments from creating voting laws that result in racial discrimination. During his time in the Justice Department, Roberts wrote more than twenty-five memos proposing to make it harder to challenge discriminatory local voting laws.[49]

Two decades after toiling for the Confederate cause in the bowels of the bureaucracy under Reagan, attorney Roberts ascended to the most powerful position on the highest court in the land in 2005. He did not disappoint. As chief justice of the Supreme Court, Roberts authored an opinion cutting the heart out of the essential enforcement mechanism of the Voting Rights Act. In that 2013 case, *Shelby County v. Holder*, Roberts joined his colleagues in writing a decision that, in its efforts to whitewash history, could take its place alongside Pollard's nineteenth-century book *The Lost Cause*, D.W. Griffith's *Birth of a Nation*, and Margaret Mitchell's *Gone with the Wind*.

On the fiftieth anniversary of the Bloody Sunday march that helped lead to the passage of the sweeping 1965 voting rights legislation, the *New York Times Magazine*, in 2015, published an extensive summary of Roberts's opinion and the long train of attacks on the seminal law over the prior decades:

> Chief Justice John Roberts Jr., writing for the majority [in Shelby], declared that the Voting Rights Act had done its job, and it was time to move on. Republican state legislators proceeded with a new round of even more restrictive voting laws. All of these seemingly sudden changes were a result of a little-known part of the American civil rights story. It involves a largely Republican countermovement of ideologues and partisan operatives who, from the moment the Voting Rights Act became law, methodically set out to undercut or dismantle its most important requirements.[50]

The assault on the Voting Rights Act at the end of the twentieth century mirrored the attacks on the Fourteenth and Fifteenth

Amendments at the end of the nineteenth century. For an entire century, Confederates relentlessly and ruthlessly rewrote and reinterpreted any rules or laws that dared to rein in the power and influence of white people in America.

Those hundred years of resistance were not restricted to the legislative and judicial arenas. Another part of the Confederate Battle Plan that has endured for more than a century is the practice of murdering people who are working to make America a multiracial democracy.

SILENTLY SANCTION TERRORISM

Mississippi is the Blackest state in America (38 percent of its population is Black, according to the 2020 Census).[51] It has been that way for a long time, because the state's rich black soil was so great for growing the white cotton that many, many Black hands were needed to pick it in order to make many white people wealthy. As Harvard professor Sven Beckert wrote in his book *Empire of Cotton*, "New cotton fields sprouted in the sediment-rich lands along the banks of the Mississippi . . . and by the end of the 1830s, Mississippi already produced more cotton than any other southern state."[52]

This cotton-picking state of affairs was just fine for Confederates until Black folk got free. By that point, in the 1860s, slavery had grown so rapidly that the *majority of people* in Mississippi were Black.[53] So, of course, the prospect of African Americans voting in Mississippi was terrifying. So terrifying that many white people sanctioned the use of white domestic terrorism to block Black voting.

For a long time, terrorism and the ruthlessly rewritten state constitution of 1890 worked well to preserve the political balance of power that had prevailed during the heyday of the plantations. But in the 1950s and 1960s, Black Mississippians were loudly proclaiming, "We want to be free." And since Mississippi was still the Blackest state in America in the early 1960s (42 percent Black), this latest push for freedom, justice, and multiracial democracy had to be resisted by any means necessary.[54] And resist they did, with the able assistance of Samuel Bowers Jr.

———

Few families better exemplify the multigenerational tenacity of American white domestic terrorism than the Bowers family.

Great Grandpa Bowers, E.J. Bowers Sr., was a Confederate soldier in Mississippi who, in the admiring words of his great-grandson Sam, "lynched every Yankee soldier that he got his hands on during the Civil War."[55] After Robert E. Lee surrendered at Appomattox in 1865, the Bowers family fought on, keeping the cause alive.

Mississippi's post–Civil War voter suppression and destruction of democracy enabled Great Grandpa Bowers's son, E.J. Bowers Jr., to run for Congress with minimal competition in 1902. No African Americans were allowed to run, leaving the field to mediocre white men, and, accordingly, mediocre white man Bowers Jr. won his election to the House of Representatives. When he got to Washington, Congressman Bowers forcefully championed the Confederate cause of elevating whites and keeping down Blacks, saying during a 1904 speech to Congress:

> More than a decade of negro denomination and misrule has taught us in that severest but most valuable of school—experience—that he is not fitted for government, and should therefore, so far as possible within the constitutional limits, be eliminated as a political factor, and, speaking for myself, I thank God that the constitutional convention of Mississippi swept the circle of expedients, within the field of permissible action under the limitations of the Federal Constitution, to obstruct the exercise of the franchise by the negro race. . . . The restriction of suffrage in Mississippi was the wisest statesmanship ever exhibited in that proud Commonwealth.[56]

That distinguished politician passed on many important lessons to future generations of his family, most notably to his grandson, Samuel H. Bowers Jr., whose exploits spanned most of the twentieth century during his eighty-two years on this planet (1924–2006). Reflecting on the formative influences in his life, Sam proudly pointed to his grandpa E.J. Jr., "at whose knee, I received a goodly portion of my education."[57]

Inspired and educated by his Confederate ancestors' teachings and example, Sam Bowers would go on to lead the extralegal white terrorist wing of the Confederates in the 1960s. Much like his great-grandfather lynching Yankee soldiers who were trying to end slavery, Sam Bowers focused his time, talent, and energy on killing people who were trying to help Black people vote.

In 1964, civil rights activists from across the country prepared to come to Mississippi for a major voter registration drive in what was called "Freedom Summer." The white leaders of the state in the 1960s were no more enamored of the concept of multiracial democracy than their predecessors were a century earlier when they voted to secede from and go to war with the United States. Seeing democracy as a threat, the Mississippi state legislature in 1964 prepared for Freedom Summer by authorizing the hiring of hundreds of additional state troopers "to deter any summer 'invasion' by Northern students." The mayor of Jackson, Mississippi, announced his city was making plans to be able to arrest and incarcerate 25,000 prisoners.[58]

Seeing the prospect of Black people voting as an existential threat to white supremacy in Mississippi, Sam Bowers wanted the domestic terrorist troops to step up their game. Believing that the existing white terrorist organization, the Ku Klux Klan, was insufficiently violent, forceful, or bloodthirsty, Bowers created a new group, the White Knights of the Ku Klux Klan. The *New York Times* described the White Knights as "an organization that defined itself in its unhesitating willingness to use violence." The new operation, founded in early 1964, with Bowers as its "imperial wizard," had an estimated ten thousand members at its peak, and "the F.B.I. attributed nine murders and 300 beatings, burnings and bombings to Mr. Bowers and the group."[59]

Among the many people who participated in Freedom Summer's voter registration activities were James Chaney, an African American man from Meridian, Mississippi, and Michael Schwerner and Andrew Goodman, two white New Yorkers. In the summer of 1964, Bowers orchestrated the abduction and murder of these three young men.

The search for the bodies of Goodman, Schwerner, and Chaney riveted the attention of the nation in the summer of 1964 as volunteers scoured Mississippi fields and rivers looking for the activists. Their bodies were eventually found on August 4, 1964, in Neshoba County, Mississippi. The entire ordeal carried significant symbolic meaning about the struggle for racial justice in America, and national outrage about the case generated the political will to pass the Civil Rights Act of 1964.

The symbolism cut both ways, however, and law enforcement officials in Mississippi sent the strongest possible signal about their silently sanctioning terrorism, as they showed no interest in seeking out the murderers. Bowers was never arrested by local authorities, and it took a massive investigation by *federal* authorities who interviewed more than one thousand Mississippians to amass the evidence to bring charges against Bowers and his fellow terrorists.[60] Bowers only served six years for those murders, and he wasn't locked away for life until he was convicted of the killing of Vernon Dahmer—another 1960s murder designed to stop Black people from voting.

At age fifty-eight, Vernon F. Dahmer Sr. was the head of the local NAACP and a champion of voting rights in Mississippi. A successful businessman, Dahmer helped pay the poll taxes for people wanting to participate in the democratic process, and he used his grocery store as a site for registering African Americans to vote. In 1966, two years after getting away with killing Chaney, Schwerner, and Goodman, and one year after passage of the Voting Rights Act, Sam Bowers got his goons and guns and went to work in the way domestic terrorists do. The *New York Times* described what happened: "Mr. Bowers sent two carloads of Klansmen with 12 gallons of gasoline, white hoods, and shotguns to the Dahmer house near Hattiesburg, Miss., on a cold January night. The burning gasoline was tossed into the house; Mr. Dahmer, whose lungs were seared, held attackers at bay so his family could escape, then died later in the arms of his wife."[61]

It was only in 1998—twenty-two years after Dahmer's murder—that the Mississippi attorney general Mike Moore, who, notably, had been elected with significant Black support, brought charges against Bowers. That was after five failed attempts at conviction in the 1970s. Bowers was finally found guilty, sentenced to life, and died in prison in 2006.

The high-profile nature of the murders of Chaney, Schwerner, and Goodman, coupled with the defiance and silent sanctioning of white terrorism by local authorities, established Neshoba County, Mississippi, as a prominent symbolic location in the fight to defend white supremacy in the South. That symbolism was not lost on a future Republican nominee for president of the United States of America.

PLAY THE LONG GAME

It's not every day that a presidential campaign gets launched at the site of the murder of civil rights activists, and to have that campaign, in essence, find common cause with the killers. But that's what happened in 1980 when Ronald Reagan kicked off his general election campaign at the Neshoba County Fair.[62] The appearance of the soon-to-be president of the United States was the culmination of a multi-decade "long game" of transforming the erstwhile anti-slavery Party of Lincoln into the home of white racial grievance in the closing decades of the twentieth century and the opening decades of the current century.

But let's back up a moment.

———

To recap, Republicans used to be the pro-Black party, and Democrats were the party of white racial fear and resentment. A big part of the reason the Republican Party was even formed in the first place was its opposition to slavery. Although it is far too little discussed in U.S. history discourse, it was Republican nominee Abraham Lincoln's 1860 election that prompted the Southern states to band together, form a treason caucus, secede from the Union, and wage a violent and bloody multiyear war to try to preserve the privilege of holding Black bodies in bondage. Just *six weeks* after Lincoln's election, South Carolina voted to secede, followed in short order by its Confederate kin in the cotton states of Mississippi, Florida, Alabama, Georgia, Louisiana, and Texas. Georgia delayed its treasonous declaration until January of the new year, a fact that was apparently much appreciated by the state's social elite, as author Margaret Mitchell illustrated in *Gone with the Wind* when Scarlett O'Hara said, "I'm mighty glad Georgia waited till after Christmas before it seceded or it would have ruined the Christmas parties, too."[63]

After the destruction of Reconstruction and the Hayes-Tilden Compromise of 1877 that withdrew Union troops from the South, white Democrats—Confederates—controlled Southern politics, and

Republicans were ostracized and marginalized as outsiders, Northerners, Yankees, and carpetbaggers. And that was pretty much the state of politics in America for the next hundred years. The most ardent white nationalists were all Democrats. If a political leader dared utter a word of support for equality and lack of fealty to white nationalism, a political hailstorm would rain down on them in the form of third-party candidacies designed to split the white vote and weaken the national Democratic Party. Strom Thurmond and George Wallace were Democrats.

But Black people are drapetomaniacs, and they kept upsetting the setup by, you know, marching and demonstrating and pointing out pesky details standing in the way of white power such as the Fourteenth and Fifteenth Amendments to the United States Constitution. With each incremental step toward equality, white Southerners resisted and rebelled. One hundred years after the Civil War supposedly ended, as Southern whites grappled with the nonviolent revolution of the civil rights movement, they responded by once again leaving their longtime political home. Except this time, instead of leaving the Union, they left the Democratic Party.

For its part, the Republican Party—the Party of Lincoln, the party of racial equality and opposition to slavery—was, by the 1960s, ready to receive these white defectors, Confederate mindsets and all. How that transformation occurred is the result of a political long game. A long game spearheaded by the white leaders of the state that spearheaded the creation of the Confederacy—South Carolina, the site of Fort Sumter, where white nationalists first formally fired bullets to defend their right to hold people in slavery. The birthplace of Strom Thurmond and his chief political strategist Harry Dent, a key architect of the Southern Strategy.

Harry S. Dent Sr. was a Southern Baptist deacon who didn't drink or smoke. Married to his wife Betty for fifty-six years, he was the father of five children.[64] He was also a shrewd political operative and long-time aide and close political adviser to Senator Thurmond. Together, Dent and Thurmond helped orchestrate the Southern Strategy that wooed worried white Southerners away from their historic home in the Democratic Party.

As the walls of white electoral exclusivity slowly crumbled and

America inexorably inched toward becoming a multiracial democracy, Dent could read the writing on those walls. He realized that the Confederates' once-solid hold on the Democratic Party was imperiled, especially as more Black people began to participate in politics, despite the best efforts of Bowers and the other voter suppression terrorists.[65]

―――――

In the second half of the twentieth century, the civil rights movement increasingly gained strength and power—perhaps most dramatically conveyed by President Lyndon Johnson, with his strong Southern drawl, telling a nationally televised audience in 1965 that when it came to Black civil rights, "their struggle must become our struggle too. . . . It is not only Blacks who must overcome, but we must all overcome." And then, substantively and symbolically Johnson wrapped his arms around the cause, embracing the movement's slogan and telling the world, "We *shall* overcome."

Those words, and the subsequent legislation behind it to protect the right to vote and finally remove the whites-only signs from the country's voting booths, clearly conveyed that Confederates were no longer welcome in or in control of the Democratic Party. As wayward white voters started to search for a new political home, Harry Dent and Strom Thurmond held open the door and waved them into the Republican Party. That was the genesis of the Southern Strategy.

White nationalist South Carolinians don't tend to stand idly by when their white power is threatened. Channeling his secessionist forefathers who left the Union weeks after Lincoln's election, Strom Thurmond publicly left—seceded from, if you will—the Democratic Party and joined the Republican Party sixty days after Democratic president Lyndon Johnson signed the 1964 Civil Rights Act. Thurmond and Dent spent the next several years doing everything in their power to bring the rest of the Southern whites with them. The year 1968 was a pivotal point in that effort.

Ideologically, politically, and racially, Strom Thurmond should have backed George Wallace's 1968 third-party presidential bid. Wallace, like Thurmond had twenty years earlier, was giving a political middle finger to a party that had gone from electing as president Jefferson Davis, murderer of Black people and the troops who sought to bring about their equality, to having what sure seemed to be a nigger-lover in the White House spouting the "We shall overcome" chorus of the civil rights anthem. Something had to give, and, as discussed earlier, Wallace sought to punish the Democrats by dividing the Democratic vote the way Thurmond and the Dixiecrats did in 1948.

But Dent and Thurmond were beyond making statements and spitting in the eye of more powerful forces. They wanted real power for themselves and their cause, and they were prepared to play a long game to get it. Much as their predecessors had orchestrated events a hundred years earlier in the decades immediately after the Civil War, Dent and Thurmond sought to replicate the model of striking a savvy deal in a presidential election as a way to build long-term Confederate power. Their first vehicle was Richard Nixon.

As discussed in chapter 1, the Confederates had struck a strategic deal back in 1877 in which they conceded that their preferred person would relinquish his claim on the White House in exchange for turning control of the Confederate states back to the white nationalists. In Atlanta, Georgia, in 1968, at the height of the civil rights movement and the threat it represented to white power, Dent and Thurmond struck a similar deal with Republican Richard Nixon.[66] They would forgo backing the true Confederate champion, Wallace, and throw their support behind Nixon in exchange for Nixon looking the other way as the white nationalists reconsolidated their power in the former slaveholding states.

During that 1968 campaign, segregationist Thurmond used his white supremacist street cred to spread the word to whites across the South that their new best friend was the Republican Party. Traveling indefatigably from state to state, Thurmond talked up Nixon's candidacy to whites across the South.[67] As Angie Maxwell and Todd Shields write in *The Long Southern Strategy: How Chasing White Voters in the South Changed American Politics*, "Thurmond traded his endorsement and campaign support for Nixon's 'benign neglect' of civil rights enforcement," and he vouched for Nixon's anti–civil rights bona fides, telling white Southerners, "He has promised that he won't enforce either the Civil Rights or the Voting Rights Acts. Stick with him." [68]

All of it worked exactly as they had hoped. Wallace was weakened, Nixon won the election, and then, like Rutherford B. Hayes in the 1870s, Nixon delivered on his promise of making sure the federal government did not stand in the way of white power. One immediate example occurred with the Supreme Court, where Chief Justice Earl Warren—architect of the *Brown v. Board of Education* decision—announced his retirement that same election year of 1968. President Johnson put forward Homer Thornberry to replace Warren on the court, and he also proposed to elevate the liberal court member Abe Fortas to the role of Chief Justice. Strom Thurmond immediately went to work, offering a Confederate example that Mitch McConnell would expertly follow after the death of Justice Antonin Scalia in 2016. Thurmond blocked both Thornberry and Fortas, effectively delaying any action until Nixon became president, at which time Nixon appointed Warren Burger, someone far more sympathetic to the Confederate cause.

The pace of the white Southern exodus from the Democratic Party briefly slowed in the early 1970s in the wake of the Watergate scandal that drove Nixon from office. (Notably, Nixon's deal to ice out Wallace came back to bite him in the posterior when Wallace refused Nixon's request to use his influence with an Alabama senator who could have helped Nixon stave off impeachment.)[69] After Nixon's resignation in 1974, the Southern Strategy was further stalled by Georgia Democratic governor Jimmy Carter's 1976 presidential campaign. Carter's Southern roots and the cultural connection symbolized by his strong Southern accent kept many white voters in the Democratic fold. But even Carter did not win majority support among whites (exit polls show Carter receiving 48 percent of the white vote, a figure no Democratic presidential nominee has surpassed since).[70] After four years in office, as Carter's poll numbers shrank, so did the number of whites in the Democratic Party, and the stage was set for the curtain to really rise on the Republicans' Southern Strategy. All they needed was an actor to take center stage.

———

Ronald Reagan became famous in the 1940s and 1950s as an actor who appeared in dozens of Hollywood movies. More than anything, he learned how to play a part and deliver his lines, and those skills prepared him well for a career in politics. Playing the role of stern white leader alarmed by racial unrest after the Watts neighborhood riots in 1965 in Los Angeles, Reagan was elected governor of California in 1966 (see chapter 10). From that high political office, he twice ran for president, in 1968 and 1976, falling short both times. By 1980, he decided to run again, and this time, he was determined to do whatever was necessary to win.

In 1980, Reagan finally secured the Republican nomination for president, and he needed white voters to stomp the floor if he wanted to win the White House. Fully appreciating the implications of a Southern white exodus from the Democratic Party, Reagan went all in to expedite that exodus. Most memorably, he shamelessly and unapologetically embraced the symbolism of linking arms with the white Confederates of Mississippi in the place most famous for the murder of Chaney, Schwerner, and Goodman. Looking back on Reagan's campaign launch, *New York Times* columnist Bob Herbert, in a 2007 column, stripped away any non-racist pretense surrounding both the decision to go to Neshoba County and its centrality in sealing the long game of the Southern Strategy. As Herbert wrote:

> The campaign debuted at the Neshoba County Fair in front of a white and, at times, raucous crowd of perhaps 10,000, chanting: "We want Reagan! We want Reagan!" Reagan was the first presidential candidate ever to appear at the fair, and he knew exactly what he was doing when he told that crowd, "I believe in states' rights."
>
> Everybody watching the 1980 campaign knew what Reagan was signaling at the fair. Whites and blacks, Democrats and Republicans—they all knew. The news media knew. The race haters and the people appalled by racial hatred knew. And Reagan knew. He was tapping out the code. It was understood that when politicians started chirping about "states' rights" to white people in places like Neshoba County they were saying that when it comes down to you and the blacks, we're with you.[71]

Twelve years after Thurmond and Nixon struck their 1968 deal that set the Southern Strategy in motion, Reagan closed the sale, winning over whites and sending Carter's share of the white vote plummeting to just 36 percent of the Caucasian constituency.[72] Once elected to office, Reagan put in place a wide array of people committed to continuing to support the Confederate cause well into the twenty-first century. Future Supreme Court chief justice John Roberts was just one example.

The arc of the long game was cogently captured by Maxwell and Shields in their book *The Long Southern Strategy*:

> Initially, the GOP acted on the advice of Senator Barry Goldwater of Arizona who, in a speech following Richard Nixon's loss to Democratic candidate John F. Kennedy in 1960, told fellow Republican leaders, "We're not going to get the Negro vote as a bloc in 1964 and 1968, so we ought to go hunting where the ducks are." To do so, the GOP decided to capitalize on white racial angst, which was not in short supply in the South. . . .
>
> The Long Southern Strategy targeted white southerners who felt alienated from, angry at, and resentful of the policies that granted equality and sought to level the playing field for all of these groups. . . . The Southern political landscape is red now, but it did not turn red with one brushstroke.[73]

The policy goals had been accomplished. And white Southerners had, again, successfully seceded from the political unit that impeded their dream of fostering and protecting white nationalism, or, as they preferred to put it, their way of life.

—————

The larger tale of the twentieth century is that while the Confederates soldiered on, the drapetomaniacs and their allies also fought on. The civil rights movement gave Lyndon Johnson the political power to pass the Voting Rights Act and the Immigration and Nationality Act (ending the century-old whites-only immigration practices of this country). Those two pieces of sweeping legislation brought millions of people of color into the electorate. So many people of color, in fact, that in a nation that had held Black people in slavery and fought a brutal war over whether to continue holding them in slavery, a Black man was elected president of the United States. The Confederate Battle Plan would be used against him as well.

4

Fear of a Black President

Sir, we are concerned that ultimately at the end of the day, if you are fortunate enough to get the Democratic nomination, fortunate to become President of the United States, will you pull a bait-and-switch, sir, and enslave the white race? Is that your plan? And, if it is your plan, be honest. Tell us now.

—Jon Stewart, interview with then U.S. senator and presidential candidate Barack Obama, *The Daily Show*, April 21, 2008

For millions of white people, television host and comedian Jon Stewart's joking question to Barack Obama wasn't so funny. In fact, it touched on their deepest fear—that the demographic transformation of America would lead to cataclysmic changes in the country's culture and their own lives.

It is a fear that began centuries ago and continues to this day. Decades before the United States of America was even a thing, the white people of the South passed "Slave Laws" to put their basest biases and anxieties into legislation and policies. South Carolina's leaders were so concerned about the "safety and security of the People" of the state that they adopted a series of measures in 1712 explicitly designed to control the behavior of "Negroes and other slaves [who] are of barbarous, wild, savage natures."[1] The preamble to the South Carolina Slave Code explained that the rationale for the legislation stemmed from the need to "restrain the disorders, rapines and inhumanity, to which [Negroes] are naturally prone and inclined."[2]

In the years immediately after the Civil War, many white people were certainly in their feelings about the ascendance of African Americans to positions of power. Journalist James Shepherd Pike traveled to South Carolina in 1873, at the height of Reconstruction, to document what he saw. Hs findings were published in a book, *The Prostrate State: South Carolina Under Negro Government*. Chapter 1 of Pike's book has the rather lengthy, though certainly descriptive title of, "A Black Parliament—Humiliation of the Whites—Society bottom-side up—An Extraordinary Spectacle."[3] After venturing to the state Capitol building, Pike found a degree of Black empowerment that shocked his Caucasian sensibilities:

> The Speaker is black, the Clerk is black, the door-keepers are black, the little pages are black, the chairman of the Ways and Means is black, and the chaplain is coal-black. . . . It is the dregs of the population habilitated in the robes of their intelligent predecessors, and asserting over them the rule of ignorance and corruption, through the inexorable machinery of a majority of numbers. It is barbarism overwhelming civilization by physical force. It is the slave rioting in the halls of his master, and putting that master under his feet.[4]

This irrational yet ubiquitous fear of Black people has coursed through the veins of this country across the centuries. From the seventeenth- and eighteenth-century slave codes, to the bloody rebellion of the Civil War itself, to the race massacre in Tulsa, Oklahoma, in 1921, to Strom Thurmond's 1948 warning about the government forcing nigger integration of swimming pools, to the 1955 lynching of Emmett Till in Mississippi for supposedly looking at a white woman the wrong way, to Samuel Bowers' 1960s Mississippi murders of Chaney, Schwerner, Goodman, and Dahmer, to the owners of the home at 2637 Dartmoor Road in Cleveland Heights, Ohio, refusing to sell their house to my parents in 1964 because they were Black, to millions of Americans voting for proud segregationist George Wallace for president in 1968, the fear that Jon Stewart joked about is real, deep-seated, and long-lasting. Viewed against this historical backdrop, it is not surprising that many white Americans in 2007 and 2008 watched the ascension of a Black man to the White House with great trepidation.

Chicago—Obama's political hometown—offered a chilling preview of what was to come in terms of white fear of Black political power. In 1983, African American Harold Washington, a Democrat,

ran for the office of mayor and narrowly defeated his Republican opponent. Washington rode to victory on the strength of historically high
voter turnout and near universal support from Black people in a city
deeply divided by race (an estimated 82 percent of African Americans
cast ballots, 97 percent of them for Washington).[5] Washington's campaign electrified Black America and helped motivate Chicagoan Jesse
Jackson to mount his 1984 Rainbow Coalition presidential campaign.
I was a freshman in college at the time, and I still remember the gleam
in the eye of an African American upperclassman telling me about the
results of the election. White Chicagoans, however, were not so happy.

Bear in mind that, as a practical political matter, there are no Republicans in Chicago. The city has not elected a Republican mayor
since 1927, and in the election previous to 1983, the Republican received just 16 percent of the vote.[6] But when a Black man won the
Democratic nomination, that Democratic domination vanished as
hundreds of thousands of white voters flocked to the candidacy of the
Republican nominee, Bernard Epton, who was largely unknown, essentially unqualified, but—most importantly—white.

Leanita McClain, the first Black editorial writer for the *Chicago Tribune* (and, at age thirty-two, the youngest), wrote a raw and searing
column describing the fear she witnessed among her white co-workers
and other people she thought were friends as they grappled with the
prospect of a Black man ascending to the Windy City's top position for
the first time in history:

> I have been unprepared for the silence with which my white col-
> leagues greeted Washington's nomination. I've been crushed
> by their inability to share the excitement of one of "us" making
> it into power. . . . No one in this town had talked about anything
> but the election for weeks. But suddenly the morning after
> the primary, whites could not find enough other things to talk
> about, if they talked at all. Not just the most bigoted of bigots,
> but all whites, even the more open-minded of my fellow jour-
> nalists. Even the standard niceties took on a different quality.
> Their "good mornings" had the tenor of death rattles, not just
> the usual pre-coffee hoarseness. There was that forced quality,
> an awkwardness, an end to spontaneity, even fear in the eyes of

people who had never thought about me one way or the other before. . . .

Whites were out of their wits with plain wet-your-pants fear. Happy black people can only mean unhappy white people in this town. . . . Filthy literature littered the city streets like the propaganda air blitzes of World War II. The subway would be renamed "Soul Train." The elevators in City Hall would be removed because blacks would prefer to change floors by swinging from the cables. Flyers proclaiming the new city of "Chicongo," with crossed drumsticks as the city seal, were tacked to police station bulletin boards.[7]

The intensity of the white backlash in Chicago was so widespread and so intense—the title of her essay on the election was "How Chicago Taught Me How to Hate Whites"—that it added to a sense of fundamental betrayal and anguish that contributed to McClain's taking her own life the year after Washington was elected mayor. In what she referred to as a "generic suicide note," McClain wrote, "Do not try to pull me back into this world. I will never live long enough to see my people free anyway."[8]

———

1983 was not that long ago. Barack Obama had just graduated from Columbia University. Joe Biden had been a senator for a dozen years. And that freak-out was just over one African American becoming mayor of one city. Imagine the psychological and emotional reverberations of a Black man becoming the most powerful person on the planet. As Isabel Wilkerson wrote in *Caste*, "The greatest departure from the script of the American caste system was the election of an African-American to the highest office in the land. History has shown that there would be consequences to this disruption of the social order, and there were."[9]

When Obama took office in 2009, the fields of racial resentment had already been plowed by generations of Confederates, and the soil of racial fear was ready for planting. Politically, Confederate descendants saw Obama's election as an inflection point similar to Reconstruction in the 1860s and the civil rights movement of the 1960s. To avoid the kind of spectacle Pike found in South Carolina in 1873, where white society lay "prostrate in the dust, ruled over by this strange conglomerate, gathered from the ranks of its own servile population," twenty-first-century Confederates needed to immediately oppose the African American president of the United States and the multiracial New American Majority that had propelled him into office.[10] And oppose him they did, virtually from the day Obama was sworn into office in 2009, unleashing the same tried and trusted five-part Battle Plan that had served Confederates so well since the end of the Civil War.

NEVER GIVE AN INCH

Tennessee has been the site of significant levels of sacrifice made by Confederates and their successors as they dug in their heels and never gave an inch in the fight to preserve white supremacy. As discussed previously, one of the state's favorite sons is Nathan Bedford Forrest, confederate general and first grand wizard of the Ku Klux Klan. Forrest was part of the military leadership command that suffered catastrophic defeat in 1864 on a battlefield just outside Nashville during the Battle of Franklin. Seven thousand young white men lost their lives on that battlefield, in what historians James Lee McDonough and Thomas Connelly called a "bloody holocaust [that was a] massive slaughter and the death-knell of a once mighty army." [11]

One hundred and forty-five years later, with a Black man in the White House seeking to advance public policies that would benefit people of all races, the resolve of the descendants of the Confederates to hold the line for white nationalism in places like Tennessee remained rock solid, up to and including the willingness to sacrifice one's life.

In his book *Dying of Whiteness*, Dr. Jonathan Metzl recounts the story of one such twenty-first-century Confederate casualty. "Trevor" (Metzl changed names to protect identities) was a forty-one-year-old white man in Tennessee who faced debilitating pain from liver inflammation and hepatitis. When Metzl met Trevor in 2016 in Nashville—near the site of the Battle of Franklin—Trevor appeared yellow with jaundice and ambled with the help of a walker to alleviate the pain he felt in his stomach and legs. Metzl went on to place Trevor's plight in its larger political context:

As it turned out, debates raged in Tennessee around the same time about the state's participation in the Affordable Care Act and the related expansion of Medicaid coverage. Had Trevor lived a simple thirty-nine-minute drive away in neighboring Kentucky, he might have topped the list of candidates for expensive medications called polymerase inhibitors, a life-saving liver transplant, or other forms of treatment and support. Kentucky adopted the ACA and began the expansion in 2013, while Tennessee's legislature repeatedly blocked Obama-era health care reforms.[12]

When asked about the actions of his state's leaders—the Confederate "generals" of the 2010s, the men and women who staunchly protected the bust of Forrest in the state's highest governmental building—Trevor defiantly declared his support for the cause of resisting anything having to do with the programs championed by a Black president. "We don't need any more government in our lives," he told Metzl. "And in any case, no way I want my tax dollars paying for Mexicans or welfare queens." As for his own fate, Trevor, mirroring the resolve of the young white men in the 1860s who charged into battle in Tennessee under General Forrest's exhortations, said, "Ain't no way I would ever support Obamacare or sign up for it. I would rather die."[13]

And die he did, just like thousands of other Tennessee white men who perished during the Civil War, all of them preferring to give their lives rather than give an inch to a government helmed by a president who believed that people of color were human beings to be embraced and treated as equals.

———

The vigorous opposition to the Affordable Care Act (ACA) is probably the clearest example of the determination and tenacity of twenty-first-century Confederates to never give an inch in the face of efforts by a president who looked like the people who had once been held in chains in this country.

Obama believed, somewhat naively, that congressional Republicans were people of good faith who cared about the quality of life of their constituents, and he bent over backward in an attempt to craft a bipartisan solution to an American health care crisis that had left nearly 50 million people—people of all races and political persuasions—without health insurance.[14] Tactically, Obama squandered the momentum of his political honeymoon by slow-walking the signature proposal of his administration while congressional committee after congressional committee held hearing after hearing on the minutiae and mechanics of how to provide health care to all Americans. After many months of compromise and cajoling and negotiating, Republicans in Congress gave not one inch, and every single one of them voted against the measure. For his book *The Ten Year War*, journalist Jonathan Cohn sat down with Obama to reflect on the fight to pass the ACA, and with the clarity of hindsight, the former president shared that he had miscalculated. As Cohn recalls, "the regret looming large in his mind was a failure to anticipate the intensity of GOP opposition."[15]

Blocking passage of public policies that benefit people of color (even if those same policies also benefit white people) had become par for the course for Republicans in the 1990s and 2000s. As such, opposition to enacting universal health care legislation is historically less revealing than the post-passage crusade to undermine, repeal, resist, and ultimately try to destroy any effort to allow low-income Americans to receive health care and medical treatment. In the immediate months and years after passage of the ACA, contemporary Confederates waged a multi-front, multi-dimensional attack on Obamacare. As Cohn notes, "The Republican assault on the Affordable Care Act began officially on March 23, 2010, the same day Obama signed the law and possibly while the ink on his signature was still drying."[16]

One front of the fighting took place in the courts. Law professors Abbe R. Gluck, Mark Regan, and Erica Turret wrote a law review article in 2020 documenting the unrelenting war on the policy designed to keep people healthy and alive, identifying nearly two thousand different legal challenges to the ACA from the day the law was enacted, March 23, 2010, until April 2020. The professors call Obamacare "the most challenged statute in American history," meaning none of the forty-three previous—and white—presidents had received treatment like this.[17]

A well-funded army of lawyers worked in close partnership with the attorneys general of former Confederate states to file wave after wave of lawsuits seeking to have judges who were ostensibly opposed to judicial activism actively affirm arguments that would gut or kill the ACA. Seven challenges came before the U.S. Supreme Court, with the fate of health care coverage of millions of Americans constantly in peril and judicial jeopardy. To capture the landscape and establish a historical record, Gluck, Regan, and Turret provided an overview to the nature of the legal attacks (which continued even after Obama had left office), writing, "The main groups of cases can be roughly divided into three categories: cases involving the insurers the ACA relies on, cases about the ACA's new civil rights protections (including its contraception protections), and cases challenging the Trump Administration's efforts to weaken the law. There are also hundreds of other cases on a wide range of topics." [18]

A second front was in Congress. The ink did dry on Obama's signature on the bill, but only barely before Republicans in Congress voted more than seventy times to repeal or alter America's health care law. [19]

The third front, as is frequently the case in geographically far-flung wars, was retrenchment and resistance at the state and local levels. Particularly telling and illuminating has been the resistance to expanding Medicaid, as provided for in the ACA.

Most political leaders, especially those working with insufficient resources to meet the needs of their constituents (which is just about all political leaders), don't turn down free money that will benefit the people in their state. But when it came to a government program informally known by the name of the Black president, such rational behavior went out the window. The ACA provided federal funding to states so that more people could receive health care coverage under the federal Medicaid program. Pretty sweet if you're an elected official wanting to meet your constituents' needs. Pretty important in terms of public policy and public health, to say nothing of basic morality and compassion.

But, when waging a civil war, there will be casualties, and when it came to fighting Obamacare, the needs and lives of some of the residents of the Confederate states would have to be sacrificed for the cause. These Obama opponents, these leaders of states with long traditions of resolute resistance to any steps toward equality, did not just refuse to extend coverage to their own state's poor people and go about their days. No, they vigilantly, and often viciously, fought and sabotaged and undermined any efforts and any person who dared suggest that poor people anywhere in the country should have health care coverage.

As of May 2021, 2 million people in twelve states were eligible to receive health care coverage, but, in the same way that former governor of Alabama George Wallace stood in the schoolhouse door in 1963 to oppose racial integration of the University of Alabama, these governors metaphorically stood in front of hospital doors and health clinics, continuing the tradition of barring universal access to public services, whether they be the buses of Montgomery, the colleges of Alabama, or the hospitals of Southern states.

Notably, but not surprisingly, the overwhelming majority of the opposition against the ACA has come from the former Confederate states, the Dixiecrat states, the states that Strom Thurmond and George Wallace won in their white nationalist presidential campaigns. Obama senior adviser David Axelrod summarized the oppositional mindset in his 2015 memoir, writing that many white Americans thought "health reform was just another giveaway to poor black people at their expense."[20]

Few people have studied the health care war longer than Jonathan Cohn, and in reflecting on his twenty years of writing about that fight, he correctly concludes that the ACA struggle is a case study in the battle for progressive change and offers lessons for all progressives:

> If the champions of [other progressive] causes hope to succeed, they need to learn from the Ten Year War [for health care] and adapt. The task starts with grasping the true nature of the opposition. The operating theory of the Affordable Care Act, both how to pass it and then how to implement it, was that adopting some conservative ideas would secure at least some buy-in from Republicans. But Republicans are more oppositional and more ideologically extreme than at any point in modern U.S. history. . . .
>
> It means that opposition will be as tribal as it is substantive, based less on the merits of arguments and more on who

is making them. It's hard to escape the conclusion that for the most intense Obamacare critics, it was the "Obama" part more than the "care" they found so objectionable, whether because of partisan identity, race, or both.[21]

If there's one thing U.S. history has shown, it's that whenever there's been a policy proposal to give something to people of color, whether it be freedom from slavery, the right to vote, or access to health care, that proposal has been met with unrelenting resistance from Confederates—even, as in Tennessee Trevor's case, being willing to die. Never giving an inch.

RUTHLESSLY REWRITE THE LAWS

Imagine walking into Starbucks, ordering your beverage of choice, proceeding to the cashier, and then being challenged by the barista to prove you are who you say you are. Imagine further that you state your first and last name but the barista again challenges you, asking what your middle initial is and then demands to see a form of photo ID that lists your name and middle initial exactly as you just said it. And, to complete the analogy, imagine further that at the Starbucks stores in communities of color you had to stand in line for three to four hours before you could receive your coffee, but in stores in white communities you could breeze in and out with a refreshing drink in hand in mere minutes.

These examples are and sound ridiculous because businesses actually want to complete transactions with their customers. They don't erect absurd obstacles that stand in the way of those interactions. In our capitalist country, there are few, if any, matters more important than making money. Consumerism and consumption are king, and the process to help people spend money has been streamlined and refined so that in the vast majority of cases, any person can quickly and efficiently conduct the act of purchasing with the most convenience and fewest obstacles possible. And while there is in fact identity theft and credit card fraud, the technology exists to prevent those crimes from becoming widespread. You can go into almost any store in the country, pull out a credit card or your phone, and complete a financial transaction, and the company is operating on a high level of confidence that you are who you say you are.

When it comes to voting, however, it is another story entirely. In a country with a multi-century history of systemic racism and oppression, manifested by numerous impediments to voting and unrelenting efforts to suppress the votes of people of color, there is little interest in making participating in our democracy as easy as participating in our consumer economy. Quite the contrary. In a nation where their share of the population pie is steadily shrinking, today's Confederates do everything they can to make voting as difficult as possible in order to "eliminate the darkey as a political factor," as Virginia state legislator Carter Glass put it so plainly back in 1890.

———

Almost immediately after Obama won the White House in 2008, the clear consensus from Republicans from coast to coast was that they couldn't let that happen again. Within months of a Black man riding into the White House at the head of a wave of new voters who spanned the population spectrum in terms of race, ethnicity, class, age, gender, and orientation, the Confederate states and their ideological counterparts across the country set about ruthlessly rewriting laws to suppress the vote once again.[22]

Among the primary suppression weapons deployed after Obama was elected were voter ID laws that require a person to provide some form of official identification before they are allowed to vote. These laws are the modern-day equivalent of the poll tax, literacy test, and Eight Box Law—ostensibly neutral legislation that has the desired effect of reducing the number of votes of people of color (today thirty-five states have some sort of voter ID requirement).

We know the point of these measures because in 2012 the top Republican in the Pennsylvania legislature at the time accidentally slipped up and spoke the truth. During Obama's reelection campaign, Pennsylvania was, as it always is, a closely contested battleground state, and the Republican-controlled legislature had passed a voter ID law. Mike Turzai, Republican majority leader of the Pennsylvania House of Representatives, let the cat out of the bag at a Republican state committee meeting by saying that the state's voter identification law was "going to allow [Republican presidential candidate] Governor Romney to win Pennsylvania."[23]

In the years immediately following Obama's election, as documented by Ari Berman in *Give Us the Ballot*, "395 new voting restrictions were introduced in 49 states from 2011 to 2015"—legislation designed to restrict the ranks of people of color voting and to do it in ways that would have a lasting, suppressive effect.[24]

————

The prize for the most aggressive and blatant display of ruthlessly rewriting laws to suppress voters in the Obama era goes to the great state of North Carolina, a state Obama won in 2008 by a scant 0.4 percent—14,177 votes (his closest margin of victory in any state). That outcome was such an affront to the Confederates in the Tar Heel state that they embarked on a ruthless and relentless voter suppression–driven power grab, with the clear and ultimately explicit objective of suppressing Black votes to secure white power.

No one did more to try to thwart America's first Black president and to advance the Confederate cause in North Carolina than Art Pope.

There's an old joke that goes, "You know how I became a millionaire? I opened up a lemonade stand, and the first day I sold two glasses of lemonade. On the second day, I sold four glasses. On the third day, my rich uncle died and left me a million dollars." That's basically how Art Pope got rich (minus the lemonade stand). Pope, like Donald Trump, was wealthy because his father had become wealthy. Pope's dad operated a series of five-and-dime stores similar to Woolworth's in the 1950s and 1960s. It is not known whether Pope's stores, Variety Wholesalers, practiced racial segregation in the same way as the stores that became the target of sit-ins and protests in North Carolina in 1960. What is known is that Pope used his father's fortune to continue the Confederate cause during the Obama years.

Pope grew up in Fuquay-Varina, North Carolina, thirty minutes south of Raleigh (Varina was the name of the wife of Jefferson Davis, president of the Confederate States of America).[25] In an early embrace of the Confederate tactic of sanctioning white terrorism, Pope, as a college student at the University of North Carolina at Chapel Hill in 1975, filed a formal complaint against a Black student group because they protested the presence on campus of David Duke, former grand wizard of the Ku Klux Klan.[26] With little understanding of or apparent regard for the chilling effect of terrorism on those being targeted, Pope cast his lot early with those doing the terrorizing. His "explanation" was that Duke's right to foment terror, carefully cloaked in the more anodyne words "free speech," was more important than the impact of his actions.

After college, when he came into the family fortune, Pope almost single-handedly underwrote the efforts to flip control of the North Carolina state legislature so that Republicans would have a working majority to rewrite any law they liked. Pope, his family, and his business entities spent more than $2 million targeting twenty-two state legislative races in North Carolina in 2010, the first election year in which a Black man was president of the United States.[27] In one race alone, Pope and his affiliated entities spent hundreds of thousands of dollars in a single small district, defeating a Democratic incumbent, who lost by just 161 votes.[28] As a result of the massive infusion of conservative spending, Republicans took control of the state legislature for the first time since 1870, five years after the end of the Civil War, when, in a cruel historical twist of fate, the Republicans of that era briefly held power during Reconstruction because they were the *anti*-Confederate party.

Much like their Confederate ancestors in an earlier century, the Pope-backed politicians joined in a Black voter suppression orgy that was brazen and audacious. They not only passed voter ID laws, but threw themselves into ruthlessly redrawing legislative districts in such an unapologetically racist fashion that it took the breath away of the judge who threw out their pro-white legislative maps.

Loretta Biggs, the first Black woman ever appointed as a federal judge in North Carolina, knew racial discrimination when she saw it.[29] Reviewing the state's voter ID law in 2019, she noted that "North Carolina has a sordid history of racial discrimination and voter suppression stretching back to the time of slavery, through the era of Jim Crow, and, crucially, continuing up to the present day." In the new voter ID law, conceived in the years following Obama's election, Biggs found that the North Carolina legislature had "used racial data to target minority voters with 'surgical precision.' "[30]

Rewriting laws and redrawing maps were just part of the multi-dimensional Battle Plan deployed against America's first Black president and the movement and people that propelled him to power. The other parts of that plan were also vigorously utilized to undermine and obstruct anything associated with Barack Hussein Obama.

DISTORT PUBLIC OPINION

The Voting Rights Act of 1965 exists, in large part, because the events of Bloody Sunday were caught on camera. On March 7, 1965, as John Lewis, Martin Luther King Jr., Amelia Boynton, and so many other movement activists crossed the Edmund Pettus Bridge, Alabama state troopers, under the direction of Governor George Wallace, unleashed tear gas, billy clubs, and horses as they beat and attacked the peaceful people who just wanted the right to vote.

Members of the media recorded the savagery on their cameras, and then the film was driven fifty miles from Selma to Montgomery, where it was put on an airplane to Atlanta, the closest major airport. After the one-hour flight to Atlanta, the footage was transferred to a bigger airplane and flown to New York City, where the major news stations broadcast their shows. By nine p.m. Eastern time that evening, the footage was loaded into the system. ABC—one of the three networks that existed at the time—broke into the television program *Judgment at Nuremberg*, which was being watched by 48 million people—one-quarter of the entire U.S. population—and aired the Bloody Sunday footage for fifteen minutes straight, riveting the nation and galvanizing public sentiment behind the cause of voting rights.[31] As Taylor Branch observed in his seminal civil rights trilogy, *America in the King Years*, for "forty-eight million unsuspecting viewers transferred from the mystery of Holocaust atrocities nestled among good Germans to real-life scenes of flying truncheons on Pettus Bridge . . . the Nuremberg interruption struck with the force of instant historical icon."[32]

What would have been the impact on national public opinion if one of the three networks had access to the footage but failed to acknowledge that Bloody Sunday even happened? Or acknowledged that it happened but claimed that all of the violence was caused by the peaceful marchers? That is the world in which Barack Obama tried to govern, dealing most prominently and problematically with a network called Fox News.

For most of American history, politicians in general and presidents in particular have had to contend with the media and convince them of the merits of their actions and proposals. Civil rights groups and organizations of color have had the additional burden of trying to convince largely white institutions and opinion leaders of the importance of their concerns and issues. It wasn't until Barack Obama was elected, however, that an entirely alternative and fact-free world could be created and maintained by certain members of the media, and Fox News was one of the chief perpetrators of this new alternate reality.

With the ascent of Fox News, not only was there a billionaire-backed major television network utterly opposed to everything Obama proposed, but one that also saw and exploited the potential to distort public opinion by stoking racial fears, anxieties, and prejudices through ubiquitous and unrelenting misinformation.

———

On August 14, 1961, Barack Obama's parents placed a birth announcement in the *Honolulu Star-Bulletin* stating the following: "Mr. and Mrs. Barack H. Obama, 6085 Kalanianaole Highway, son, August 4." No one disputes the fact that that announcement appeared in the actual 1961 edition of that newspaper in Honolulu, Hawaii. Even Donald Trump does not dispute this. Yet, millions of Americans came to believe that Obama was not born in the United States (and, so we're clear, Hawaii is and was part of the United States of America). The leaders of this effort, eventually known as the "birther movement," claimed that Obama's birth certificate was forged and that he was actually born in Kenya (the childhood home of Obama's father).

The eagerness with which people willingly suspended disbelief becomes clear when you pause for a moment to consider the facts that are undisputed. Notably, no one disagrees that Obama was in fact born on the date of August 4, 1961. What the birthers argue and believe is that he wasn't born in the United States. To arrive at that conclusion, you would have to believe that, in between changing diapers and caring for a ten-day-old infant, two young college students began to devise an enormous conspiracy to deceive the world about the true birthplace of their son on the off chance that forty-seven years later he might grow up to run for president of the United States. To follow the conspiracy theory to its logical conclusion, if Obama was in fact born in Kenya, then his parents—while living in Africa—somehow, years before the internet was invented, managed to get a tiny announcement placed in a Hawaii newspaper.

The ease with which fiction replaced fact is, at first glance, remarkable, until you pause to reflect on the success of the Lost Cause propaganda effort that has bamboozled millions of people into believing the opposite of the truth about the Civil War.

The birth certificate controversy offered Trump a test run of the public opinion distortion machinery that he would deploy to impactful and deadly effect in subsequent years. Starting in 2011, when he was flirting with a presidential bid to oppose Obama's reelection, Trump became the most prominent proponent of the idea that the sitting president of the United States was not born in America. And if Obama wasn't born in America, the unstated but deeply felt logic went, then he was therefore an illegitimate president—a convenient justification for opposing, resisting, and defying a Black president. *It's not his skin color, it's just that he's not actually an American.* Trump trumpeted the lie for years, using the coverage of and reaction to it as his own personal laboratory for refining the right mixture of words, assertions, and provocative statements to maximize attention and attract passionate support from the many millions of people who didn't like the fact that a Black man was in the White House.

The fact and manner in which Trump and Fox News and other elements of the Confederate media and communications complex perpetrated the lie laid bare the power of the reality distortion infrastructure with which Obama had to contend.

Fox News had (and continues to have) a massive twenty-four-hour platform to shape public opinion and propagate lies that feed on and inflame racial prejudices. This disinformation machine was a powerful force that solidified opposition to Obama. It also paved the path for the election of Trump. By the last year of Obama's presidency, in 2016, *72 percent of registered Republicans believed that Obama was not born in the United States.*[33]

The "birthers" also questioned the first Black president's faith as another way of undermining his authority. Barack Obama is a Christian man, married in and a years-long parishioner of a Christian church. By August of 2010, according to a Pew Research Center poll, one in every five Americans—and nearly one-third of all Republicans—believed Obama was Muslim.[34] This was not just some idle curiosity and speculation about the specific form of worship of the president. As I noted in *Brown Is the New White*:

> Because of 9/11, the word "terrorist" has often become associated—if not used interchangeably—with "Muslim," "Islam," and "Arab" in the American mind-set. The conflating of religion and terrorism (something that doesn't happen, for some reason, when Christians commit terrorist acts) reached the point where, in 2015, leading Republican candidates for president were saying unapologetically that a Muslim should not be allowed to become president of the United States.[35]

What was at issue was not a birth certificate, but the legitimacy of the president of the United States. As Adam Serwer wrote in *The Atlantic* in 2020, "Birtherism is the baseless conjecture that the 44th president of the United States not only was born abroad and was therefore ineligible for the presidency, but also was a secret Muslim planning to undermine America from within. It is the combination of these two elements that transformed birtherism from mere false speculation about Obama's birth to a statement of values about who belongs in America, and who does not."[36]

The othering of Barack Obama was not simply a tool of political obstruction and opposition from modern-day Confederates seeking to throw sand in the gears of a government run by a Black man. It was a strategy within a larger plan of dominance. A necessary first step to justify the oppression of a group of people is to establish the "otherness" of that group. Once that has been accomplished, racist resistance, slavery, segregation, economic exploitation, and domestic terrorism become more acceptable to broad sectors of the population. The fear of a Black president and the propagation of his otherness stretched far beyond the ballot box to the dark corners of society where white domestic terrorists in America gathered, plotted, and planned.

SILENTLY SANCTION TERRORISM

"I was just doing my job." That's how Daryl Johnson, a balding, unassuming middle-aged white man, described the report he put together in 2008 for the Republican president George Bush and his presidential administration.[37] Johnson grew up in overwhelmingly white Idaho, graduated from the Mormon college Brigham Young, and moved to Washington to help keep America safe in a dangerous world by working as a counter-terrorism analyst for the U.S. Army.[38] Part of that work involved drafting a report, titled *Rightwing Extremism: Current Economic and Political Climate Fueling Resurgence in Radicalization and Recruitment*. The report highlighted an alarming surge in concern among white domestic terrorists about the possible election of Barack Obama.

Johnson is the kind of government bureaucrat that conservative elected officials have historically embraced and celebrated. During his years in Washington, DC, he studied and became an expert on terrorist threats to the country, moving up the ranks in the government agency that was supposed to help protect America, ultimately becoming a senior intelligence analyst in the Department of Homeland Security in the years after the September 11th terrorist attack on the United States. As an analyst, he oversaw a team that monitored the activities of extremists, terrorists, and others who would do harm to the country he loves.

In 2007, Johnson saw tangible signs of growing fear of a Black president and escalating organizing among white supremacists. He described his findings as follows:

In January of 2007, Capitol Police tipped us off that Barack Obama, a senator from Illinois, was going to announce his candidacy for president. We all knew that was going to be the worst-case scenario for white supremacists. They said it would be the low point in America when you had "a black" occupy the White House—that was kind of in their literature.

When he won the Democratic nomination, we started seeing white supremacist groups lashing out and threatening him.
That, coupled with the housing bubble bursting in '08, left a
lot of people underwater financially—they started looking for
scapegoats for their problems.[39]

As Obama's candidacy took off, so too did the dangers and threats.
Looking back on the rise of domestic terrorism in the United States,
the *New York Times* recounted in 2019 just how fear of a Black president played out in the darkest corners of America's white supremacist
community:

> Former law enforcement officials say white supremacists were
> energized by the 2008 election. On social media they discussed
> the possibility of a race war should Mr. Obama become presi-
> dent. Hate crimes peaked that year in October, according to the
> National Archive of Criminal Justice Data, when his election
> seemed assured.
>
> And traffic to white nationalist websites like Stormfront
> increased after the election, said Derek Black, a former white
> supremacist whose father founded Stormfront. Mr. Black, who
> has left the movement, said that having a black president moti-
> vated new recruits to join.[40]

Over in the Department of Homeland Security (DHS), Johnson
meticulously documented the threat in order to inform his law enforcement colleagues across the country. He drafted a report that went
through twenty-three revisions, was vetted at multiple levels of government, and was coordinated with the FBI. The DHS report clearly
identified the threat posed by "domestic rightwing terrorists . . . that
have capitalized on the election of the first African American president, and are focusing their efforts to recruit new members, mobilize existing supporters, and broaden their scope and appeal through
propaganda."[41]

One example of the hypocrisy of Confederates when it comes to
talking tough about terrorism can be found in the doublespeak of former vice president Mike Pence. A potential 2024 presidential candidate

(as of this writing), Pence has tried to build a profile and brand as someone tough on terrorism—just so long as the suspected terrorists are not white. As a member of Congress in the Obama era, Pence helped lead the movement to defund and dismantle the domestic antiterrorism work of the U.S. intelligence agencies. As DHS's Johnson explained, after Republicans, including Pence, grilled DHS Secretary Janet Napolitano over the origins of Johnson's report flagging white domestic terrorists as a threat, "work related to violent right-wing extremism was halted. Law enforcement training also stopped. My unit was disbanded. And, one-by-one, my team of analysts left for other employment. By 2010, there were no intelligence analysts at DHS working domestic terrorism threats."[42]

The attack on Johnson's report and the defunding of the domestic terrorism watchdog work gave license to those working to restore white supremacy in America, and their numbers grew accordingly. As the *New York Times* wrote in 2019, "A decade later, there is clear evidence that violence by white extremists is an undeniable and intensifying problem."[43]

What an obscure white bureaucrat learned is that protecting white people from criticism about the prevalence of racism and white supremacy was far more important to many elected officials than protecting a Black president of the United States. In this way, by essentially sweeping the problem under the rug and looking the other way, lawmakers silently sanctioned terrorism, contributing to a climate of extremism that would erupt in multiple domestic terrorist attacks during the presidency of the white man who replaced Barack Obama in America's White House.

PLAY THE LONG GAME

Jeff Nesbit was just looking for a job. Having worked in the White House as the communications director for then vice president Dan Quayle, a Republican, Nesbit found himself unemployed and trying to find work in Bill Clinton's Washington, DC, in 1993. Like many White House alumni, he turned to consulting, offering strategic communication services to clients and companies interested in increasing their effectiveness in the nation's capital. One of his first clients was an innocuously named organization called Citizens for a Sound Economy. Little did Nesbit know at the time that he'd stumbled into working for what was essentially a front group for two of the richest people in the world—billionaires Charles and David Koch.[44] The Koch brothers would go on to bankroll the faux grassroots Tea Party movement in 2009 that would tap into and channel the modern-day Confederates' fear of a Black president into a persistent, highly agitated opposition that spent considerable time and energy working to intimidate members of Congress and block and constrain the agenda and policies of the Obama-Biden administration.

Owners of the oil industry conglomerate Koch Industries, Charles and David Koch were each worth billions of dollars when Obama became president.[45] They had been on an ideological mission to influence and shape U.S. politics ever since David Koch ran for vice president on the Libertarian Party's ticket in 1980. And, in a lesson progressive donors could learn from, the brothers have been putting their money where their ideological mouths are, spending hundreds of millions over the past forty years to influence public policy and build public support for limited government and lower taxes.[46] Journalist Jane Mayer details much of their work in her landmark book *Dark Money*:

> Given the size of their fortunes, Charles and David Koch automatically had extraordinary influence. But for many years, they had magnified their reach further by joining forces with a small and intensely ideological group of like-minded political allies, many of whose personal fortunes were also unfathomably large. . . .
>
> The Kochs waged a long and remarkable battle of ideas. They subsidized networks of seemingly unconnected think tanks and academic programs and spawned advocacy groups to make their arguments in the national political debate. They hired lobbyists to push their interests in Congress and operatives to create synthetic grassroots groups to give their movement political momentum on the ground. In addition, they financed legal groups and judicial junkets to press their cases in the courts. Eventually, they added to this a private political machine that rivaled, and threatened to subsume, the Republican

Party. Much of this activism was cloaked in secrecy and presented as philanthropy, leaving almost no money trail that the public could trace. But cumulatively it formed, as one of their operatives boasted in 2015, a "fully integrated network." [47]

That fully integrated network helped advance the lawsuits that never gave an inch on Obamacare and supported the Confederates in Congress opposed to all things Obama. Although the Kochs' focus has largely been on their economic ideas and agenda, they have frequently played with fire by stoking the racial resentments and fears that have fueled U.S. politics for centuries. Those fires became much more widespread after Obama's election, and they erupted into a full-scale conflagration with the election and presidency of Donald Trump.

It turns out that it is very easy to rile white people up to oppose the government when the head of that government is a Black man. And as Strom Thurmond and George Wallace showed, racial rage can pick up on and be harnessed via nonracial cues and codes. In many ways, the opposition to Obama was a twenty-first-century sprouting of the twentieth-century seeds planted by Confederates such as Thurmond, whose life work, as biographer Joseph Crespino wrote, involved "trying to translate white supremacist rage into abstract conservative principle." [48]

The Tea Party sprang up immediately after Obama's election. Members rallied support in opposition to Obama's agenda, especially health care reform. More importantly, they struck political fear in the hearts of members of Congress who needed courage to pass policies such as the Affordable Care Act. In town hall meetings across the country in 2009, members of Congress cringed at the gatherings where angry white people showed up to shout and complain about policy reforms that, while benefiting everybody, might actually also help some "undeserving" people of color and hence they were against it. Alex Isenstadt captured the chaos in a 2009 piece in *Politico*, writing, "On the eve of the August recess, members are reporting meetings that have gone terribly awry, marked by angry, sign-carrying mobs and disruptive behavior. In at least one case, a congressman has stopped holding town hall events because the situation has spiraled so far out of control." [49]

Behind it all were the funders of Jeff Nesbit's new job. As the *New*

York Times wrote in 2013 after the Tea Party and their Confederate con-
spirators in Congress precipitated a government shutdown in the year
after Obama's reelection:

> The current budget brinkmanship is just the latest develop-
> ment in a well-financed, broad-based assault on the health law,
> Mr. Obama's signature legislative initiative. Groups like Tea
> Party Patriots, Americans for Prosperity and FreedomWorks
> are all immersed in the fight, as is Club for Growth, a business-
> backed nonprofit organization. . . .
>   The billionaire Koch brothers, Charles and David, have
> been deeply involved with financing the overall effort. A group
> linked to the Kochs, Freedom Partners Chamber of Commerce,
> disbursed more than $200 million last year to nonprofit orga-
> nizations involved in the fight. Included was $5 million to Gen-
> eration Opportunity, which created a buzz last month with an
> Internet advertisement showing a menacing Uncle Sam figure
> popping up between a woman's legs during a gynecological
> exam.[50]

Although white mainstream media executives and journalists were
reluctant or unable to see the racial dynamics at play, ample academic
research has affirmed the salience of race and racism in the Tea Party's
reaction to Obama (as if the protesters waving signs saying, "Where's
the birth certificate?" weren't enough of a clue). In his book *America Is
Not Post-Racial*, the scholar Algernon Austin shares the results from
his exhaustive quantitative and qualitative analysis, finding that "there
are 25 million Obama Haters in America, more than 90% of whom
identify as Republicans or as Republican-leaning. Obama Haters are
people who do not merely disapprove of the job President Obama is doing; they are angry and afraid at the thought of him. . . . Many Haters
see whites as an oppressed minority group in the United States."[51]

The Koch brothers have disavowed any racist motives associated
with their prodigious funding, but I'm sure that in the nineteenth century many business leaders claimed they only supported slavery because the profits from the cotton were so irresistible, not because they
liked the whipping of the Black backs of the people picking the cotton.

The Kochs knew they needed popular support for their agenda: limiting the size and power of government. They agitated people to support that agenda, which would, by the way, result in restraining the ability of government to deal with inequality and injustice. Their long game of methodically funding anti-government ideas merged nicely with the long game of preserving white power and privilege. One of the most impactful results of their spending was the growth and proliferation of widespread opposition to the Obama administration.

As with a person who lights a campfire that becomes a raging forest fire, the Tea Party movement the Kochs helped create subsequently swept into office a white nationalist fascist named Donald John Trump. Reflecting on that unexpected outcome, Charles Koch wrote in his 2020 book *Believe in People*, "Boy, did we screw up. What a mess!"[52] Oops.

5

Make America White Again

To Trump, whiteness is neither notional nor symbolic but is the very core of his power. . . . One hopes that after four years of brown children in cages; of attempts to invalidate the will of Black voters in Philadelphia, Atlanta, and Detroit; of hearing Trump tell congresswomen of color to go back where they came from; of claims that Joe Biden would turn Minnesota into "a refugee camp"; of his constant invocations of "the Chinese virus," we can now safely conclude that Trump believes in a world where white people are—or should be—on top.

—Ta-Nehisi Coates, January 2021

More than anything else, Donald Trump revealed the political power of white supremacy. You can do nearly anything—*anything*—and it will still be excused by the majority of white voters so long as you are fighting for white people. Early in his presidential campaign, Trump discovered to his joy and amazement that, "I could stand in the middle of Fifth Avenue and shoot somebody, and I wouldn't lose any voters. It's, like, incredible."

New York University history professor Tim Naftali wrote a lengthy piece in *The Atlantic* in 2021 outlining how "Donald Trump is the worst president America has ever had." [1] The human toll alone was catastrophic. The dismissive response to a global pandemic contributed to the U.S. death toll being much greater than it needed to be. Hundreds of thousands of people died needlessly while their president simply shrugged, saying famously in an August 2020 interview, "They are dying. That's true. It is what it is." [2] As Naftali wrote, "In the face of a devastating pandemic, he was grossly derelict, unable or unwilling to marshal the requisite resources to save lives while actively encouraging public behavior that spread the disease." [3]

Trump's presidency was also defined by levels of naked racism and white nationalism not seen in the White House since President Woodrow Wilson settled in to watch *Birth of a Nation* in the East Room in 1915. I commissioned a report, *The Trump Administration's Record of Racism*, that documented close to three hundred specific examples of racist statements and actions made and committed by the Trump administration in just the first two years in office.[4] As Ta-Nehisi Coates wrote in 2017, "In Trump, white supremacists see one of their own."[5]

How did Americans respond to Trump's racism, cruelty, and incompetence? Eleven million *more* people voted for him in 2020 than did so in 2016. That electoral stamp of approval was not about satisfaction with his administration's excellent navigation of the country's challenges. It was fundamentally about his unabashed leadership of the modern-day, pro-white Confederate crusade.

Isabel Wilkerson opens the first chapter of *Caste* with a story about the deadly consequences that occurred in Siberia in 2016 when a long-buried, infected carcass was brought to the surface, unleashing poisonous toxins of anthrax into the atmosphere, sickening and killing people. The title of that chapter is "The Afterlife of Pathogens," and Wilkerson deftly analogizes the poisonous virus in Siberia to what Trump unearthed in America, saying "the anthrax, like the reactivation of the human pathogens of hatred and tribalism in this evolving century, had never died. It lay in wait, sleeping, until extreme circumstances brought it to the surface and back to life."[6]

Wilkerson's analysis could not be more accurate. The lasting consequence of the Trump era is that the worst instincts of the worst people have been validated from the highest precincts of power and prestige. Unapologetic white supremacy has been unleashed into the environment, there are limited options for an effective vaccine against this "virus," and battling it is the imperative of the hour. Newly empowered, emboldened, and entrenched, Confederates in the Trump era gleefully let loose the full arsenal of the Confederate Battle Plan, and we will be fighting the fallout from those battles for at least the rest of the decade.

NEVER GIVE AN INCH

The last time white people were this mad about losing an election, they plotted to kill the president-elect before he could be sworn in. Before Abraham Lincoln even stepped foot in the White House as president, the Confederates had planned a pre-inaugural, ultimately unsuccessful, assassination attempt as the soon-to-be president was en route to the Capitol, a conspiracy known as the Baltimore Plot.[7]

One hundred sixty years later, despite losing the presidential election, Trump used his final months in office to orchestrate a historic assault on the very foundation of American democracy—the peaceful transfer of power. A *New York Times* article described the weeks immediately following the November 2020 election as

> 77 days [where] the forces of disorder were summoned and directed by the departing president, who wielded the power derived from his near-infallible status among the party faithful in one final norm-defying act of a reality-denying presidency. . . . With each passing day the lie grew, finally managing to do what the political process and the courts would not: upend the peaceful transfer of power that for 224 years had been the bedrock of American democracy.[8]

Looked at through the prism of history, Trump's bloody insurrection of January 6, 2021, really isn't that surprising. We've been here before. And if we needed any clearer illustration of the unbroken continuity of the Civil War, and never giving an inch in that war, it was dramatically displayed when a mob that included men carrying Confederate flags and wearing sweatshirts emblazoned with the words "MAGA: Civil War January 6, 2021" stormed the Capitol to protest a democratic outcome that they hated as much as the original Confederates had hated the election of Lincoln and his anti-slavery agenda.[9]

———

Many people smirked, winked, and rolled their eyes when Trump launched his attempt to stay in power after Election Day, and many more laughed at the buffoonish cast of characters carrying out the assault on democracy. Most memorably, Trump attorney Rudy Giuliani held a November 7, 2020, press conference about an impending lawsuit challenging the election results in Pennsylvania. Trump excitedly tweeted: "Lawyers Press Conference at Four Seasons, Philadelphia. 11:00 A.M.," only to delete that tweet and replace it minutes later with corrected information stating, "Lawyer's Press Conference at Four Season's Landscaping, Philadelphia. Enjoy!"

Four Seasons Total Landscaping is not a posh hotel in downtown Philadelphia, the kind of locale one would expect attorneys for the president of the United States to frequent. No, Four Seasons Total Landscaping is what its name suggests—a landscaping company that offers its lawn care services in all four seasons of the year. It is located ten miles outside downtown Philadelphia, across the street from a crematorium, next to Big Joe's Roofing, and just down the street from Fantasy Island Adult Bookstore where the sign outside advertises DVDs, lotions, novelty gifts, and viewing booths.[10]

The Four Seasons debacle epitomized the incompetence of the election-undermining effort, leading comedian and co-founder of Crooked Media Jon Lovett to produce a November 2020 episode called "Coup Clutz Clan" on his podcast *Lovett or Leave It*. In a show of the store owners' sense of humor and marketing savvy, they started selling sweatshirts emblazoned with the words "Make America Rake Again!"[11] But there were certainly similar screwups in the conduct of the actual Civil War, and while the Trump team's level of incompetence was laughable, the subject matter was deadly serious. When we view these events with dispassion and from a proper distance, it is absolutely clear that in late 2020 and January 2021 we witnessed an attempt to overthrow the elected government of the United States of America.

Tellingly, the strategic focus of Trump's post-election insurrection tracked the psychology of the defenders of the original Confederacy. The primary targets of Trump's attacks and recount strategy—where he and his allies pushed to invalidate votes and perpetuate the lie of "voter fraud"—were Black-run cities and counties. This was a tactic straight out of the playbook used to undermine the Reconstruction states during the 1870s.

When African Americans moved from the cotton fields to the

corridors of power during Reconstruction, the Confederate line of attack was to lob false allegations of incompetence and corruption at those governments that were run by or included African Americans in positions of leadership. As just one illustrative example, Harvard professor Henry Louis Gates Jr. cites a 1902 novel by Joel Chandler Harris, *Gabriel Tolliver: A Story of Reconstruction*, that features a fictional narrator who describes the Black-run Georgia Constitutional Convention, what Harris refers to as "the mongrel convention." The book's narrator, sounding almost like Trump's mendacious, fantasy-spewing attorneys after Election Day, observed, "No safeguard whatever was thrown around the ballot-box, and it was the remembrance of this initial and overwhelming combination of fraud and corruption that induced the whites, at a later day, to stuff the ballot-boxes and suppress the votes of the ignorant." [12]

In the days immediately following the election it was almost like Trump was reading from Harris's novel when he stated, "Detroit and Philadelphia are known as two of the most corrupt political places anywhere in our country—easily. They cannot be responsible for engineering the outcome of a presidential race." [13] In Philadelphia, people of color make up 65 percent of the population; Detroit's population is 90 percent people of color, 78 percent Black. [14]

As if that constellation of Black cities wasn't sufficient for racist slander from Trump's team, in the days after the 2020 election former Speaker of the House Republican Newt Gingrich chimed in by adding a few more Black-run cities as convenient punching bags, saying, of Trump's overwhelmingly white supporters: "I think as they watch Joe Biden's Democratic Party steal the election in Philadelphia, steal the election in Atlanta, steal the election in Milwaukee, I think the more information that comes out, the greater the rage is going to be." [15] Atlanta's population is 62 percent people of color (51 percent Black). In Milwaukee, the population is 65 percent people of color (39 percent Black). [16]

———

Sometimes judges can speak truths more plainly than others do. Appointed to lifetime terms to shield them from political repercussions of their actions, federal judges have greater freedom to articulate the anger and outrage that a situation calls for. In the wake of the attempted coup, a number of judges did speak out forcefully, and their words are a lasting record of the seriousness of what transpired as Trump's team of modern-day Confederates refused to give a political, legal, or logical inch in their determined quest to overturn the results of the country's presidential election.

For an arena such as the law, where nuance and muted language are the norm, Judge Linda Parker, an African American woman who sits on the bench in the U.S. District Court for the Eastern District of Michigan, wrote an opinion dismissing Trump's claim in language that was nothing short of a legal smackdown:

> The right to vote is among the most sacred rights of our democracy and, in turn, uniquely defines us as Americans. The struggle to achieve the right to vote is one that has been both hard fought and cherished throughout our country's history. Local, state, and federal elections give voice to this right through the ballot. And elections that count each vote celebrate and secure this cherished right.
>
> These principles are the bedrock of American democracy and are widely revered as being woven into the fabric of this country. . . . [Trump's Michigan supporters] seek relief that is stunning in its scope and breathtaking in its reach. If granted, the relief would disenfranchise the votes of the more than 5.5 million Michigan citizens who, with dignity, hope, and a promise of a voice, participated in the 2020 General Election. . . .
>
> This lawsuit seems to be less about achieving the relief Plaintiffs seek—as much of that relief is beyond the power of this Court—and more about the impact of their allegations on People's faith in the democratic process and their trust in our government. Plaintiffs ask this Court to ignore the orderly statutory scheme established to challenge elections and to ignore the will of millions of voters. This, the Court cannot, and will not, do.
>
> The People have spoken.[17]

Judge Parker would go on a few months later to issue sanctions—judicial discipline—against nine of Trump's lawyers, finding that "this case was never about fraud. It was about undermining the people's faith in our democracy and debasing the judicial process to do so." [18]

In addition to the psychological and emotional toll of beating back the coup attempt, there was a considerable financial one as well. All told, the American people had to pay more than half a billion dollars after the election to defend democracy in America. In 2021, *Washington Post* reporters Toluse Olorunnipa and Michelle Ye Hee Lee conducted a detailed analysis of what it cost to defend the democratic transfer of power. They arrived at the figure of $519 million, writing, "The expenditures include legal fees prompted by dozens of fruitless lawsuits, enhanced security in response to death threats against poll workers, and costly repairs needed after the Jan. 6 insurrection at the Capitol." The military deployment on and after January 6 made up the largest share of the expenditures, more than $480 million. [19]

———

The continuity and kinship of the modern-day Confederates with their nineteenth-century ancestors is best understood by looking at what happened in the hours immediately after the bloody coup attempt was ultimately suppressed. Many Republican leaders were shaken by what had just transpired, given that the murderous mob had actually come for them. Literally. As the headline of an Associated Press story published on January 9, 2021, succinctly summarized the situation, "Capitol Mob Built Gallows and Chanted 'Hang Mike Pence.' " [20]

A violent attempted coup was a bridge too far for many Republican elected officials, and some Republicans in Congress decided to perform their constitutional duty and affirm and accept the results of the votes of the American people. *But most did not.*

Some of the most hardened contemporary Confederates, despite having almost died themselves at the hands of the marauding masses just hours earlier, nonetheless cast votes on January 6 inside the House chamber to reject the election results from key states, an action that would have had the practical effect of nullifying the election of Joe Biden. Of the 147 members of Congress who voted to overthrow the democracy, the majority of them were from the former slaveholding states. [21]

It took the bloodiest war in the history of this country to suppress the nineteenth-century racist rebellion. The 2020s will witness an ongoing battle over the nature of this nation because these current Confederates also refuse to give an inch. Far from being chastened by the violence and bloodshed that their fear-mongering has engendered, their resolve has been fortified. Nowhere is this more evident than in the velocity and intensity of their work to ruthlessly rewrite the laws in order to restrict democracy, suppress the participation of people of color, and preserve the power of white people. Just as their predecessors had done after Reconstruction, and just as they'd done after the election of America's first Black president.

RUTHLESSLY REWRITE THE LAWS

It turns out that the hundreds of voter suppression laws passed after the election of the first Black president weren't enough to help the South rise again after all. Even in the face of a global pandemic, massive, reality-distorting disinformation, and an attempt to grind the gears of the U.S. Postal Service itself to a halt as a way of thwarting people seeking to avoid pandemic risks by voting by mail, people of color kept coming, voting in record-breaking numbers, and ultimately taking back control of the White House and Congress.

But Confederates are nothing if not tenacious and resilient. So even though they'd lost, again, they turned, again, to the Battle Plan that they always used, and once more set about ruthlessly rewriting the laws that threatened their hold on power. Like a marksman focusing on his intended target, they trained their sights on the laws that make it easier for people to vote. In a post-2020 paroxysm of voter suppression bill-drafting, the states of the old Confederacy passed a torrent of new legislation to accomplish their old-time, long-standing objective: preserve white power by suppressing votes of color.

The speed and efficiency with which they unfolded their democracy-denying agenda was breathtaking. In mere weeks, hundreds of voter suppression bills were introduced in dozens of states. The array of neo-Confederate legislation would have done the actual nineteenth-century Confederates proud. The Brennan Center for Justice, a nonpartisan think tank, tracked the explosion of voter suppression legislation and found that in the first half of 2021, nearly four

hundred bills designed to block access to the ballot box were introduced.[22] As the Brennan analysis concluded, "The United States
is on track to far exceed its most recent period of significant voter
suppression—2011," the period after the election of Obama when "the
country confronted backlash to the election of its first Black president."
Affirming that Confederates are consistent as well as persistent, the
Brennan report states, "Today's attacks on the vote come from similar sources: the racist voter fraud allegations behind the Big Lie and a
desire to prevent future elections from achieving the historic turnout
seen in 2020."[23]

Fortunately, Confederates don't have unfettered control of every
state government, but in the states where there is both a conservative
legislature and a governor willing to sign its bills, things can get ugly.
By June of 2021, seventeen states had enacted twenty-eight new laws to
suppress the vote.[24]

In state after state, the common rationale for the voter suppression
measures has been a vague and unproven allegation of "fraud." Allegations of the sort that Trump threw around liberally with his Big Lie
about why he lost. Allegations that Confederates threw around liberally in undermining Reconstruction. Allegations that are core components of the Confederate Battle Plan in the 2020s.

Not surprisingly, the most restrictive legislation of 2021 has been
passed in the states where the size of the white population is shrinking
fastest. Places like Georgia, Arizona, and Texas. The *New York Times*
described Georgia's law as follows:

> Go page by page through Georgia's new voting law, and one
> takeaway stands above all others: The Republican legislature
> and governor have made a breathtaking assertion of partisan
> power in elections, making absentee voting harder and creating
> restrictions and complications in the wake of narrow losses to
> Democrats. . . . Offering food or water to voters waiting in line
> now risks misdemeanor charges.[25]

One of the most pernicious parts of this recent wave of attacks is the
surgical precision with which the voter suppression bills of 2021 were
crafted. Conservative state legislatures took dead aim at the precise

measures that had been used in 2018 and 2020 to make it easier to vote. In Texas, for example, the legislature outlawed drive-through voting and twenty-four-hour voting, recent innovations in Harris County that contributed to the dramatic rise in ballots cast by people of color in Houston.[26]

In March 2021, Ron Brownstein of *The Atlantic* and CNN, and the Brookings Institution's William Frey offered some of the most trenchant analysis of what lay behind the frantic rush to restrict democracy. "They see the wave of demography coming and they are just trying to hold up a wall and keep it from smashing them in," says Frey. "It's the last bastion of their dominance, and they are doing everything they can."[27] As Brownstein put it, "With their drive to erect new obstacles to voting, particularly across the Sun Belt, Republicans are stacking sandbags against a rising tide of demographic change."[28]

DISTORT PUBLIC OPINION

In December of 2020, many Americans came to believe that Jesse Richard Morgan possessed evidence of widespread voter fraud regarding how the presidential election was stolen from Donald Trump. One of the people who held that belief was Trump himself.

The year before he came to Trump's attention, Morgan tried to poison his wife by sprinkling a dangerous medication onto her pizza. Had she consumed the medication, to which she was allergic, she "would have died," according to 2019 Pennsylvania court papers she filed when she sought a restraining order against her then husband. Years earlier, in 2003, Morgan's mother told a judge that her son had a "long history of drug and alcohol use" dating back to when he was fourteen years old. After Morgan entered but failed to complete a drug treatment program in the early 2000s, Common Pleas Judge Stephen P. Linebaugh complained that Morgan "constantly lied." In 2006, Morgan pleaded guilty to forgery, went to prison, and over the next several years was sent back to prison multiple times for parole violations.[29]

Around the time he tried to poison his wife's pizza, Morgan and his two brothers released a "documentary" film about their personal experiences with paranormal activity and ghost-hunting. The fundraising pitch for their 2019 movie, *The Shadows Amongst Us*, says that all of the brothers "either had extreme paranormal events happen to them or currently have paranormal events happening to them." As for the paranormal experiences of the pizza-poisoning brother, he "has even had some of his footage shown on national television on paranormal shows. He has had ghost teams investigate his property and has been interviewed by 4 different experts on national TV."[30]

Promising that the film "will give you chills . . . because the events in this film are real," the movie shows Morgan recording himself on his Android phone's camera as he prepares to go investigate a noise in the basement ("because my wife doesn't believe me"). As he heads down the stairs, he apparently sees a grainy, dark shadowy figure peer around the corner and look up at him, causing Morgan to drop his camera, utter a string of swear words, and run back upstairs. The ghost-chasing movie was still available on Amazon Prime as of May 2022 ($9.99 to buy and $2.99 to rent; and yes, I downloaded it and watched most of it).

Despite Morgan's obvious lack of credibility, he was nonetheless featured at a December 1, 2020, press conference organized by the Thomas More Society, a nonprofit organization with $10 million in annual revenue that provided legal muscle and support to right-wing causes, including, in this case, a lawsuit to try to throw out the votes of 7 million Pennsylvanians. Morgan, a truck driver for a subcontractor of the U.S. Postal Service, had provided the lawyers with a twenty-eight-page, fairly rambling affidavit in which he alleged that he had encountered "weird" behavior from Post Office higher-ups in October 2020 when he had been tasked with delivering what he believed to be "completed ballots" from Long Island, New York, to Lancaster, Pennsylvania. He decided to contact the lawyers backing Trump's cause when he heard them complaining on television about their impression that in Philadelphia "100,000 votes magically appeared." Morgan believed that the tractor-trailer he used to transport mail may have been the source of that magical appearing act.[31]

The instant amplification of Morgan's story was a modern-day manifestation of the nineteenth-century quote, "A lie will go round the world while truth is pulling its boots on." Writing for the on-line newsletter *The Dispatch*, Khaya Himmelman wrote the following about how Morgan's story helped shape the belief of millions of Americans that the 2020 election had been stolen from Donald Trump:

> Morgan's claim quickly went viral. . . . On December 2, Morgan was interviewed by Lou Dobbs for Fox Business. A clip of that interview has been viewed more than 93,000 times on Lou Dobbs' Facebook page and more than 535,000 times on Twitter. President Trump also tweeted the Lou Dobbs interview as well as a clip of Morgan on Hannity, which has been viewed more than 2 million times.[32]

The *New York Times* also described the rise of Morgan and his story, writing, "The president tweeted out the truck driver's account, which quickly gained 154,000 mentions on Twitter, according to an analysis by Zignal Labs. The driver would appear on Newsmax, Mr. Bannon's 'War Room' and 'Hannity,' among the most-watched programs on cable."[33] At the time he tweeted out Morgan's claims, Trump had nearly 90 million followers on Twitter.

―――

The extent to which millions of American people still believe that the 2020 election was in fact stolen from Trump is remarkable. Except it really isn't. If you stop to think about it, is distorting public opinion about one election that much harder than transforming the complete understanding of a four-year-long Civil War, the bloodiest war in the history of the country? Is Trump's Big Lie that much more far-fetched than the Lost Cause propaganda that's been promoted for more than a hundred years? And, for that matter, isn't Trump's Big Lie actually *part* of the Lost Cause whitewashing of history? The majority of Americans did not back Biden and reject Trump's white nationalist politics, according to Lost Cause logic; the election was stolen.

How did we get here? Ask Adolf Hitler. In his 1925 manifesto *Mein Kampf,* Hitler wrote:

> In the big lie there is always a certain force of credibility; because the broad masses of a nation are always more easily corrupted in the deeper strata of their emotional nature than

consciously or voluntarily; and thus in the primitive simplicity of their minds they more readily fall victims to the big lie than the small lie, since they themselves often tell small lies in little matters but would be ashamed to resort to large-scale falsehoods.

It would never come into their heads to fabricate colossal untruths, and they would not believe others could have the impudence to distort the truth so infamously. Even though the facts which prove this to be so may be brought clearly to their minds, they will still doubt and waver and will continue to think there may be some other explanation.[34]

What Hitler called the "impudence to distort the truth so infamously" is pretty much a summary of the essence of Donald Trump and his presidency. Trump spouts lies with astonishing ease and confidence. In his four years in office, Trump told 30,573 lies (what the *Washington Post* euphemistically called "false or misleading claims").[35] Over the course of a four-year presidency, that's twenty-one lies every single day, basically a lie every single waking hour. In her quest to find the story behind the decision to hold the November 2020 Big Lie press conference at Four Seasons Total Landscaping, *New York* magazine writer Olivia Nuzzi discovered and described the culture of lying that permeated the Trump administration:

Whether it's war and peace or public relations and gardening, sorting out the truth is a complicated endeavor when it relates to Donald Trump. Everyone involved in anything, no matter the size, no matter how stupid, seems to lie as a first resort, or to know very little, or to lie about knowing very little, or to know just enough to send blame in another direction, and the person in that direction seems to lie also, or to know very little, or to lie about knowing very little, but perhaps they have a theory that sends blame someplace else, and over there, too, you will find more liars, more know-nothings, and before long, a whole month will have passed, and you still haven't filed your story about how the president's attorney wound up undermining democracy in a parking lot off I-95 on a strip of cracked pavement in a run-down part of a city that ordinarily would command no consideration from the national political class or the very online public or the equally online mainstream media, which, when forced to look, found lots of reason to laugh.[36]

For a Big Lie to take hold, you need at least two things—a liar and the communication capacity to spread that lie. The alchemy of intermingling those two elements in this period of media and technological development is what makes Trump such an existential threat to this country and the world.

Trump's contempt for truth and his eagerness to distort reality are especially dangerous at this particular point in history given the technological transformation in the ways people get information. In decades past, resentful racists were largely relegated to muttering into their beer in the corners of dark bars or silently seething in their parents' basements. But with the power of the internet, all of these folks can now much more easily find each other. And when the Liar-in-Chief had the means to instantly communicate with and validate the delusions of his followers, who happily lap up the lies and falsehoods that reinforce their view of reality, truth and reality ceased to be terribly relevant to modern American politics.

In the decades after the Civil War, it required years of work and millions of dollars to whitewash history and create the fantasy worlds popularized in blockbuster movies like *Birth of a Nation* and *Gone with the Wind*. Today, all it takes is a tweet, a Facebook post, and a five-minute rant on Fox News, Newsmax, One America News Network, or YouTube.

In the context of a national civil war and in the aftermath of a violent and bloody attempted coup that was organized on social media platforms, every social media company needs to ask if they want more blood on their hands. For this reason, Twitter is to be commended for its decision—prior to Elon Musk possibly buying the company—to permanently ban Trump from its platform, and Facebook must be held to account for why it refuses to take such a similarly strong stand (Facebook has only "suspended" Trump's account for two years, saying it will "assess" where things stand in 2023).[37]

SILENTLY SANCTION TERRORISM

With the rise of Donald Trump, the country's white domestic terrorists are getting the kind of encouragement they haven't enjoyed in
nearly a century. And, tragically, lots of blood has already been spilled
by Trump's sanctioning of domestic terrorism in support of making
America white again. According to Frank Figliuzzi, who worked for
the FBI for twenty-five years and directed all counterespionage across
the government, "never has our nation had a president who served as a
kind of radicalizer-in-chief." Figliuzzi went on to elaborate on Trump's
role in sanctioning terrorism, pointing out that "he has yet to apologize for painting people of color as outsiders and invaders, for calling
for them to be sent back to where they came from, and for asserting
that no humans would want to live in certain American cities. As a
consequence, he has given license to those who feel compelled to eradicate what Mr. Trump himself has called an infestation."[38]

It is not hard to connect the dots between the climate created by
Trump and the subsequent acts of domestic terrorism. In fact, it pretty
much takes a willful act of avoidance to *not* connect the dots.

———

Heather Heyer had not planned to go protest the white supremacist
Unite the Right rally in Charlottesville because she thought it was too
dangerous. It was during the first months of the Trump administration in 2017, and the thirty-two-year-old white paralegal Virginian was
dismayed that large numbers of white supremacists were preparing a
march to protest Virginia governor Ralph Northam's plans to remove
the statue of Confederate general Robert E. Lee. The night before,
hundreds of white nationalists, some holding tiki torches, marched
through the University of Virginia campus. Their chants included
phrases such as "White lives matter," "You will not replace us," and
the Nazi-associated slogan "Blood and Soil."[39] The marchers can also
be clearly seen and heard in a Vice News documentary chanting, "Jews
will not replace us."[40]

Heyer was a white woman with a conscience, and she told her friend
that while she wanted to stand up for what was right, she worried about
violence at the protest. Also, she had a lot on her plate, working as a

bartender and waitress to supplement her income as a paralegal.[41] At the last minute, the call of conscience was too great, and she decided to go ahead and attend the rally as a counter-protester. That decision on a sunny August day would lead to her tragically crossing paths with James Alex Fields Jr.

Fields was a twenty-one-year-old white man who kept pictures of Adolf Hitler beside his bed. At an age when many young people are drawn to sports or music or video games, Fields found comfort in the clutches of white supremacists. On a trip to Auschwitz when he was in high school, he remarked to a friend, "This is where the magic happened."

It is not surprising, then, that Fields was a fan of Robert E. Lee. Holding that worldview and those values, he also gravitated to Donald Trump, in whom he saw, correctly, a modern-day Confederate leader.[42]

Firm in his belief that the fate of white people was at stake, Fields quickly joined his white supremacist brethren in voicing their outrage about the proposed removal of the statue of a white supremacist traitor to the United States. As Heyer and the other peaceful protesters gathered, Fields was incensed, gunned the engine in his car, and accelerated at full speed into the crowd of counter-protesters. His speeding vehicle injured thirty people and struck Heyer in the midsection, tossing her onto the hood and then flinging her several feet away. Heyer was rushed to the hospital where doctors valiantly worked to save her life, but the injuries were too severe, and she died. At thirty-two years of age. Killed by a proud white-nationalist Confederate sympathizer.

On August 15, 2017, the president of the United States was asked about what had happened in Charlottesville and the killing of Heyer. Trump replied that there were "very fine people, on both sides."[43] When pressed two years later on what he meant, Trump clarified that by "very fine people," he meant the individuals who were marching "because they felt very strongly about the monument to Robert E. Lee, a great general."[44] And by "great general," he meant the leading architect of the white supremacist killing of hundreds of thousands of Americans who fought to end slavery.

Fields was not the only domestic terrorist who clearly understood the signals and messages being sent by the white nationalist in the White House.

In early October of 2018, Trump's campaign team was worried that Democrats were going to win enough congressional races to take back control of the House of Representatives, but the advisers thought they had found a clever solution. Quite mindful of the catalytic effect that Trump's demonizing Mexicans had had on his own candidacy when he rocketed to the top of the Republican pack in 2015, "Trump's political team reviewed polling from congressional districts that were competitive. . . . They showed that border protection, safeguarding immigration officers and standing up to illegal immigration resonated with voters there," according to an October 2018 *Politico* article.[45]

Shortly after taking a look at those poll results, Trump "found the perfect opening with a migrant caravan snaking up through Central America toward the U.S. border. . . . And now the president is talking and tweeting nonstop about the caravan, hoping his strategy will pay off in the final two weeks before Election Day," *Politico* reported.[46] The caravan, as the *New York Times* explained at the time, consisted of an estimated 7,000 people, including 2,300 children, made up of "a mix of those who face grave danger in their countries and intend to petition for asylum and those fleeing poverty and unemployment."[47] The U.S. midterm elections were not high on the priority list of people fleeing for their lives.

On Monday, October 22, 2018—two weeks before Election Day—Trump tweeted to his 90 million followers the false statement that the caravan included "criminals and unknown Middle Easterners" seeking to enter the country.[48] The next day, Tuesday, October 23, the Department of Homeland Security piled on, tweeting without evidence that "@DHSgov can confirm that there are individuals within the caravan who are gang members or have significant criminal histories."[49] On Thursday of that week, Secretary of Defense James Mattis ordered eight hundred additional troops to the U.S.-Mexico border to "monitor events" in light of "the migrant caravan heading north through Mexico." Trump had tweeted that morning: "I am bringing out the military for this National Emergency. They will be stopped!"[50]

As the pronouncements from Trump and his administration became increasingly hysterical, a white man in western Pennsylvania was paying close attention.

At the end of that week of fear-mongering—on Friday, October 26, 2018—Robert Bowers, a forty-six-year-old white man living in the Pittsburgh metro area, posted to a right-wing social media platform his belief that the Jewish humanitarian organization Hebrew Immigrant Aid Society (HIAS) was somehow complicit in the bad things Trump said that the caravan was up to. (HIAS had held its annual National Refugee Shabbat the prior week, an occasion dedicated to raising awareness about the plight of refugees.) The next morning, Saturday, October 27, 2018, Bowers posted, "HIAS likes to bring invaders in that kill our people. I can't sit by and watch my people get slaughtered. Screw your optics, I'm going in." [51]

Bowers then grabbed an assault rifle and three semi-automatic pistols, got in his car, and drove across town to the Tree of Life synagogue where morning services were underway. He walked into the Jewish house of worship and proceeded to hunt and shoot people for twenty minutes while shouting anti-Semitic phrases. Eleven people were killed and six were wounded in what became the deadliest attack on Jews in U.S. history.[52]

———

At the exact same time that Trump was escalating the rhetoric and fear in the country by whipping Robert Bowers and other contemporary Confederates into a frenzy about the caravan, Cesar Sayoc was making and mailing bombs to Trump's political opponents. Each day of that same week of October 22, 2018, a bomb was discovered en route to a prominent liberal or Democratic leader. On Monday, a device was discovered at the home of investor and philanthropist George Soros. On Tuesday, a package addressed to Hillary Clinton was intercepted by the Secret Service. On Wednesday, the discovery was of bombs intended for Barack Obama, California representative Maxine Waters, former U.S. attorney general Eric Holder, and former chair of the Democratic National Committee, Florida representative Debbie Wasserman Schultz. On Thursday, two packages were found addressed to Joe Biden. On Friday, it was Sen. Cory Booker, philanthropist and environmentalist Tom Steyer, and then-senator Kamala Harris. At the end of that week of mailing murderous packages, Sayoc was located and arrested; he subsequently pleaded guilty.[53]

In a lengthy 2020 piece in *The Washingtonian*, writer Luke Mullins turned the spotlight on how domestic terrorists like Sayoc became emboldened under Trump. In an article titled "Inside the Mind of the MAGA Bomber, the Trump Superfan Who Tried to Wreak Havoc on the Last National Election," Mullins wrote:

> After Trump the candidate called Mexicans "rapists," Sayoc's own racist views took on a Trumpian flavor. During a 2015 get-together with his former junior-college teammates—Sayoc had been a soccer star before dropping out of college—he alarmed his old friends. "He was saying things like, 'Build a wall to keep all the Mexicans out,' " ex-teammate Eddie Tadlock told the *New York Times*. In 2017, Sayoc took a second job at a pizza shop. His manager, Debra Gureghian, told the *Times* that he spoke admiringly of Adolf Hitler, insisted that Hispanics and African Americans were taking over the world, and—repeating Trump's infamous conspiracy theory—alleged that President Obama wasn't a US citizen.[54]

———

Racist domestic terrorist activity in the age of Trump did not end in 2018. On August 3, 2019, Patrick Crusius, a twenty-one-year-old white man in Dallas, Texas, picked up his AK-47 assault rifle, got into his car, and drove ten hours to the heavily Latino border town of El Paso, Texas, where he proceeded to a local Walmart. Once there, Crusius got out of his car, took his rifle, and shot and killed twenty-two people. He is said to have told the police that he was targeting Mexicans, and almost all of the victims were in fact Latino.

Shortly before the El Paso attack, an essay was posted online that law enforcement authorities believe was written by Crusius to explain his motives.[55] The 2,300-word document begins with the statement, "This attack is a response to the Hispanic invasion of Texas." A *Washington Post* article by Yasmeen Abutaleb describing the contents of the document said that among the "political reasons" listed for the mass murder was Crusius's concern that "the United States will soon become a one-party state run by Democrats because of the growing Hispanic population."[56]

———

Racist domestic terrorist activity did not end in 2019. At the time of the writing of this book in early 2022, the full extent of domestic terrorist involvement in the January 6th insurrection was still not known. While it is certain that that involvement was substantial—the head of the FBI testified before Congress that the assault on the Capitol "is behavior that we, the FBI, view as domestic terrorism"—a full accounting of those events was still being investigated and examined.[57] But there is at least one insurrectionist whose story speaks volumes. That person is Ian Benjamin Rogers.

When FBI agents arrested Rogers on January 15, 2021—Martin Luther King Jr.'s birthday—they seized forty-nine firearms, boxes containing thousands of rounds of ammunition, five pipe bombs, and a multitude of text messages showing "his belief that Donald Trump won the 2020 presidential election . . . [and an] intent to engage in acts of violence himself locally if there was not an organized 'war' to prevent Joe Biden from assuming the presidency." Oh, and Rogers also had an actual "White Privilege Card" made up to look like a credit card. The card had a "WP" logo (for White Privilege) and a sub-heading that read "Trumps Everything," and its "card number" was 0045 0045 0045 0045 (Trump being the 45th president). For cardholder name, it said "Scott Free," and "Member Since Birth" and "Good Thru Death" were the issue and expiration dates.[58]

It is possible, if not likely, that the White Privilege cards were created by people thinking they were a joke—as of May 2022, you could still buy them for $6.99 each on Amazon, where they are described as "perfect motivational gifts for men on any occasion—Birthday Gifts, Christmas Gifts Cards, happy new year, thanksgiving, father's day gifts, wedding, valentines gift or just because."[59] Nothing should give one more pause in making funny ha-ha's about white supremacy, however, than the fact that your joke product might wind up in the hands of a person with forty-nine firearms, thousands of rounds of

ammunition, pipe bombs, and an expressed intention to commit terrorist acts. Confederates are not joking around.

——

Many white journalists in the United States have great reluctance
confronting the reality of white domestic terrorism in America. Julia
Ioffe does not. Born in Russia, her family immigrated to Maryland
when she was a child, but she returned to live and work in Russia as a
young adult. That international experience and exposure is likely what
opened her eyes to the ways in which racist words can create a climate
in which terrorist acts flourish. Writing in the *Washington Post* after
the 2018 Pittsburgh synagogue shooting and comparing Trump's response to that shooting and other domestic terrorist activity to Russian
president Vladimir Putin's tepid response to the 2015 assassination of
opposition leader Boris Nemtsov, Ioffe connected the pertinent dots to
illustrate how a president can silently sanction terrorism:

> The pipe-bomb makers and synagogue shooters and racists
> who mowed a woman down in Charlottesville were never even
> looking for Trump's explicit blessing, because they knew the
> president had allowed bigots like them to go about their busi-
> ness, secure in the knowledge that, like Nemtsov's killers, they
> don't really bother the president, at least not too much. His role
> is just to set the tone. Their role is to do the rest.[60]

The interplay between and alchemy of both approaches toward
domestic terrorism—that of silently and not so silently sanctioning
domestic terrorism was on full display for the entire world to see in late
2020 and January of 2021. During the first presidential debate between
Trump and Biden in September 2020, moderator Chris Wallace (of Fox
News ironically enough, given the question he posed) asked Trump
point blank, "Are you willing, tonight, to condemn white supremacists
and militia groups?" At first Trump hemmed, hawed, demurred, and
deflected, "refusing," as the *New York Times* wrote, "to categorically
denounce white supremacists." [61] As he bobbed and weaved around the
demand to directly condemn the white supremacists, Biden sharpened

the issue and challenged Trump to specifically renounce the Proud Boys.

According to the Anti-Defamation League (ADL), a 109-year-old organization focused on fighting extremism and hate, "The Proud Boys are a right-wing extremist group with a violent agenda. They are primarily misogynistic, Islamophobic, transphobic and anti-immigration. Some members espouse white supremacist and antisemitic ideologies and/or engage with white supremacist groups."[62] National Public Radio did a deep dive on the Proud Boys, including "an examination of hours of interviews and statements" from the group's founders, finding that "in addition to the group's often hateful and discriminatory ideology, violence has always been at the core of the group's identity."[63] The *New York Times* filled in the picture, adding, "The organization, which has maintained links with both overt white supremacists and more mainstream Republicans, has been a vocal—and often violent—supporter of former President Donald J. Trump."[64]

What was Trump's response to the demand that he denounce the violent extremist group with links to white supremacists? With a metaphorical wink and nod and an actual smirk, Trump delivered his nationally televised message—"Proud Boys, stand back and stand by."

His meaning and message were received loud and clear. The *New York Times* described the organization's reaction, writing, "Within minutes, members of the group were posting in private social media channels, calling the president's comments 'historic.' " In one channel dedicated to the Proud Boys on Telegram, a private messaging app, group members called the president's comment a tacit endorsement of their violent tactics. In another message, a member commented that the group was already seeing a spike in "new recruits."[65]

And stand by they did, gearing up for and playing an integral role in the insurrection on January 6, 2021. When the hallmark of democracy hung in the balance, the proud white nationalists went to work trying to block the peaceful transfer of power so they could keep the proudest white boy of all in the most powerful position in the world.

Eleven members of Congress filed a lawsuit to hold Trump and his domestic terrorist allies accountable for the attempted coup, and federal judge Amit Mehta ruled in February 2022 that the lawsuit could proceed. In his order, Judge Mehta wrote, "The court concludes that the Complaints establish a plausible § 1985(1) conspiracy involving President Trump. That civil conspiracy included the Proud Boys, the Oath Keepers, Tarrio [chairman of the Proud Boys], and others who entered the Capitol on January 6th with the intent to disrupt the Certification of the Electoral College vote through force, intimidation, or threats."[66] The Oath Keepers are described by ADL as "a large right-wing anti-government extremist group. . . . [They] explicitly focus on recruiting current and former military members, police officers and first responders."[67] The organization was founded two months after Barack Obama became president of the United States.

All told, Donald Trump's election and presidency represented the kind of glory days for white nationalist terrorists the country had not seen in nearly a hundred years—when, in the 1920s, the country's political parties refused to condemn the Ku Klux Klan while domestic terrorists lynched Black people at a rate of two people per week. By the last year of Trump's presidency, the FBI said that the greatest terrorist threat facing the United States came from white nationalists. FBI Director Christopher Wray testified to this reality at a congressional hearing in September 2020. "Not only is the terror threat diverse—it's unrelenting," Wray said.[68]

The fact that white domestic terrorism remains unrelenting 157 years after the purported end of the Civil War shows just how long of a long game the Confederates are playing.

PLAY THE LONG GAME

The early years of the 2020s find modern-day Confederates at a crossroads in terms of how to best pursue the long game. The two paths are embodied by the careers and trajectories of South Carolina senator Tim Scott and Donald Trump.

Hopefully, Tim Scott doesn't think he's in the U.S. Senate because he's smart. While he surely has some talent and intelligence, the Republican Scott is today South Carolina's U.S. senator because he's Black.

Not too long ago, in 2012, Republicans were worried that white nationalism was a bad brand. There was a brief period of time in 2012 and

2013—after the reelection of America's first Black president—when the Republican Party worried that it was too white (or, at least, that it *looked* too white), and it was during that window, with incumbent Jim DeMint announcing he was stepping down, that a Senate seat became vacant in South Carolina. The decision on DeMint's replacement fell to Governor Nikki Haley. Born to immigrant Indian Punjabi Sikh parents, Haley's birth name is Nimrata Nikki Randhawa. As a woman of color in the Confederate state of South Carolina and the overwhelmingly white Republican Party, Haley has regularly been touted as a rising star who could help her party broaden its appeal.[69] Mindful of the mathematical benefits of such a broadening, Haley turned her attention in 2013 to the task of selecting the state's newest senator.

There were plenty of people with far more experience and qualifications than Scott that Haley could have chosen. Whoever got the nod from Haley in 2013 would have to turn right around and try to win the seat outright in the 2014 statewide elections, and it usually took around seven hundred thousand votes to win such a race in South Carolina. Logically, then, a track record of success in getting a lot of votes should have been a top qualification for the job.

At the time when Haley was weighing her options for whom to appoint, there were eight Republicans who had recently won a statewide election, and she could have picked any of them. There was also a Republican congressman with a dozen years of service whom she could have selected. By contrast, Tim Scott had just finished his first term in Congress and had never run statewide. In fact, he'd spent the bulk of his time in elected office running in and representing teeny, tiny slices of the electorate, first on the Charleston County Council, where he'd received 5,569 votes, and then in the state legislature, where he won his seat with just 3,052 votes.[70]

But what Scott lacked in experience, he more than made up for in melanin. As *Washington Post* reporter Aaron Blake wrote at the time, one of the main reasons Scott became a front-runner for the position was "the premium the Republican Party has placed on diversification since the 2012 election." Blake went on to note the Confederate backdrop for the choice by writing, "This is the state of longtime Sen. Strom Thurmond (R-S.C.), where having a black senator would make a huge historical statement." (He could have also added that South Carolina was the first state where shots were fired in the war to keep Black people enslaved, so that added a bit of historical resonance as well.)[71]

And if you're confused by the race-based decision-making behind appointing Scott to a high position in a party that claims to hate affirmative action, that's entirely understandable. What the selection of Scott showed is that, completely contrary to public perception, it is actually the Republicans who practice promoting unqualified racial minorities when it suits their purposes. (Exhibit A is one Clarence Thomas, associate justice of the U.S. Supreme Court, who, prior to holding his current job, was previously an undistinguished and unremarkable government bureaucrat in the 1980s and then became a very inexperienced federal judge, with barely one year of judicial experience when he was selected to replace African American legal legend Thurgood Marshall on the highest court in the land.)

Similarly hypocritical conduct, behavior, and thinking is playing itself out in the 2022 Georgia U.S. Senate election, where Trump has recruited former University of Georgia football star Herschel Walker, an African American, to run against Senator Raphael Warnock, also African American. On its face, Walker's candidacy makes no sense. He was a football star forty years ago, hadn't even lived in Georgia for a decade (making his home in Texas until launching his Senate bid in 2021), and has had no role in politics or public service suggesting he has even the slightest knowledge or qualifications to serve in the U.S. Senate.[72] But Walker is Black. And so is Warnock. So, he's running. Republicans are not even batting an eye at the hypocrisy and lunacy of Walker's candidacy because contemporary Confederates, in playing the long game, are getting more sophisticated about navigating the tricky terrain of racial politics.

Recognizing the undeniable size and strength of the multiracial New American Majority, the top strategists and leaders in the Republican Party wanted to distance themselves from the politics of raw white racial resentment that have fueled the Confederate movement for more than a century and, more recently, served as the cornerstone of the Southern Strategy that had served the GOP so well prior to the election of Obama. The centerpiece of the rebranding and distancing from the Confederate cause was a document informally known as the "Republican autopsy," officially titled the "Growth and Opportunity

Project" (GOP, like the party's initials). Commissioned by Republican Party chair Reince Priebus in the wake of Obama's 2012 reelection, the autopsy was the result of a high-profile, multi-month, post-election reflection and analysis of why the party had lost two presidential elections in a row.

The 102-page report was written by top Republican leaders such as Ari Fleischer, former press secretary to President George W. Bush, and Henry Barbour, nephew of former Mississippi governor Haley Barbour, and it was released to great fanfare in early 2013, garnering headlines such as "Republican Party: Get Diverse or Face Extinction."[73] At the time, the report was seen by many as the new Republican Long Game. Its essence was a plea to do better by people of color, specifically highlighting the demographic revolution:

> The Republican Party must focus its efforts to earn new supporters and voters in the following demographic communities: Hispanic, Asian and Pacific Islanders, African Americans, Indian Americans, Native Americans, women, and youth. . . . Unless the RNC gets serious about tackling this problem, we will lose future elections; the data demonstrates this.[74]

What that also meant, and what the report made explicit, was the need to tone down the anti-immigrant stuff, specifically: "If Hispanics think we do not want them here, they will close their ears to our policies."

The primary policy recommendation put forward in the autopsy was to relent on the relentless demonization of immigrants and to pursue meaningful immigration reform. The belief that the smart move and correct conservative long game was to champion immigration reform was so strong that Republican Florida senator Marco Rubio, a Latino, bet his political future on that assumption. In 2012, Rubio took the lead on crafting a bipartisan immigration reform proposal that actually came extremely close to becoming law in 2013.

———

While Republicans of color Haley, Scott, and Rubio sought to manifest a modern-day Republican Rainbow Coalition, Donald Trump had a different idea. Unsurprisingly, none of the steps or recommendations to embrace people of color went over well with the most passionate Confederate true believers. In his 2015 book *The Wilderness*, McKay Coppins described the reaction as a "visceral backlash," saying the report's authors "didn't expect their recommendations to be interpreted as a knife-in-back betrayal of their party's base or its founding principles."[75]

Right-wing radio host Rush Limbaugh complained that the party had been "bamboozled." In a tweet Trump asked if the party had a "death wish" with its suggestion of championing immigration reform. Trump then proved his point by not only rejecting the immigration reform recommendation, but running for president on a platform primarily defined by opposition to Mexican immigrants and immigration, electorally crushing "Little Marco," as Trump called Rubio, and his less-Confederate campaign. All of which led *Politico* to publish a piece in 2016 titled "Trump Kills GOP Autopsy."[76]

Over the past several years, some Republicans continued to hold out hope that an electoral repudiation of Trump would validate the "cool it with the Confederacy" talk recommendations of the autopsy, and political analyst Stuart Rothenberg asked in a May 2020 article in *Roll Call*, "Will 2020 be the year the RNC's 'autopsy' was right?"[77] Instead, the opposite has happened, and that reality, what Coates called a country being "captured by the worst of its history, while millions of Americans cheered this on," now defines what will be the biggest battles of at least the next few years, leading up to and through the 2024 presidential election.

Whereas political conventional wisdom once held that white supremacy was bad politics, the surprising strength of Trump's electoral performance in 2020 has fundamentally changed the electoral calculus for the modern-day Confederates. In states with large numbers of people of color, state legislatures passed draconian new laws in 2021 that would have been thought to be electoral suicide a decade ago. From New Jim Crow voter suppression laws to the attacks on so-called critical race theory, where new policies make it a near-fireable offense to even mention racism, to aggressive anti-transgender laws in Texas, to bans on public health measures such as masks and vaccines designed to contain a deadly pandemic, to the horrific anti-choice legislation passed in Texas, to the Supreme Court's decision to overturn *Roe v. Wade*, the attacks have been as unrelenting as a volley of shots from a Confederate army led by Nathan Bedford Forrest.

The reason that legislators have been so emboldened to embark on this new Confederate long game of going all in on white nationalism is because of the surge of Trump voters in 2020. No longer fearing the New American Majority that elected Obama, the prevailing Confederate view is that the old American minority of Confederate whites can win if they just fight hard and long and dirty enough.

Harvard professors Steven Levitsky and Daniel Ziblatt have spent their professional lives studying fragile democracies, and they turned their analytic eyes to the United States in their book *How Democracies Die*, where they examined the threat posed by Trump's authoritarian tendencies. After watching the 2021 Confederate stampede to ruthlessly rewrite laws regarding how our elections occur, they wrote an article in *The Atlantic* in which they seek to sound the loudest possible alarm:

> Republican politicians learned several things in the 2020 election's aftermath. First, Trump's failed campaign to overturn the results revealed a variety of mechanisms that may be exploited in future elections. Second, Republicans discovered that their base would not punish them for attempting to steal an election. To the contrary, they now know that efforts to overturn an election will be rewarded by Republican voters, activists, local and state parties, and many donors.
>
> The 2020 election was, in effect, a dress rehearsal for what might lie ahead. All evidence suggests that if the 2024 election is close, the Republicans will deploy constitutional hardball to challenge or overturn the results in various battleground states. . . . Given the considerable authority that the Constitution grants to state legislatures, the processes of voting, vote counting, and even the selection of electors can easily be subverted for partisan ends.[78]

The contemporary Confederates are not settling for a self-indulgent bacchanalia of pro-white public policies that they feel are part of a long-overdue restoration of the proper place of straight white Christian men in society; they are taking dead aim at democracy itself. In particular, they are laying the groundwork to steal the 2024 election.

———

The 2020 election revealed two profound realities that will shape American politics for the rest of the decade. First, it quantified the size of the constituency for white nationalist politics, and that number is far, far larger than any of us cared to admit. I myself wrote in *Brown Is the New White* in 2016, "Roughly 20–25 percent of the Republican base consists of White voters susceptible to racial demagoguery, and those voters are angry and eager to support a leader who will stand up and fight for the way America used to be."[79] I grossly underestimated that number. While 25 percent might reflect those most rabid about white nationalism, fully 90 percent of Republicans have shown that are at least tolerant of, if not also susceptible to, racial demagoguery. Whatever rationalization people want to make for their votes backing Trump, the hard ugly truth is the number of people who choose whiteness over democracy is tens of millions. Precariously close to an electoral majority.

But that is the second lesson and the urgent, important, and hopeful lesson. As shown by the simple fact that Trump is no longer president, the number of people who are Confederate supporters is NOT a majority. And their ranks are shrinking every day. Despite Trump doing all he could to slow down immigration and speed up deportation, the demographic revolution rolled on, and America is becoming increasingly racially diverse at an even faster clip than originally projected, with people of color now comprising fully 40 percent of the country's population. Add in the meaningful minority of whites who have always supported the vision of this being a multiracial democracy, and that is the New American Majority. The majority that toppled Trump.

Confederates have *always* been a minority, which is why they lost the original Civil War and why the essence of their entire Battle Plan is to destroy, deny, and distort democracy. By contrast, the essence of the New American Majority strategy is expansion of democracy, and Liberators, as I call them, have a Battle Plan too. With the right leaders, organizations, plans, and tenacity, Liberators are winning across the country. They and their stories offer hope and the roadmap for how we win the Civil War.

Part II

How We Win

6

The Liberation Battle Plan

Human misery is the predicted, aforethought consequence of deliberate, deliberated arrangements of power that would distort the whole planet into miserly, personal rights of property belonging to extremely few men and their egotistical and/or avaricious interests.

Ad hoc, loner, protests will not make the difference, will not impose the revolutionary changes such undue suffering demands. I think it is necessary to form or join a well-defined organization that can and will work to destroy the status quo as ruthlessly, as zealously, as non-stop in its momentum, as are the enemy forces surely arrayed against our goals.

—June Jordan, "Declaration of an Independence
I Would Just as Soon Not Have," 1976

Confederates have had to keep fighting—never giving an inch—because people of color have never stopped striving for freedom, justice, and equality. Just as a Confederate Battle Plan has clearly emerged over the past century and a half, so too has a Liberation Battle Plan come into focus.

The Liberation Battle Plan has been honed, refined, and followed to success in the twenty-first century in the states and cities where genocide, slavery, and exploitation of people of color once flourished. Now, many of the same places and groups of people who historically bore the brunt of white nationalist oppression are on the cutting edge of change and of winning the Civil War once and for all and finally ushering in an era of true multiracial democracy and equality. By taking a close look at how those places have prevailed against the Confederates, we can glean critical lessons from their successes. What we find is that the Liberation Battle Plan consists of four indispensable steps:

- Invest in Level 5 Leaders;
- Build Strong Civic Engagement Organizations;
- Develop Detailed, Data-Driven Plans; and
- Play the Long Game.

While the steps do not always unfold in the exact same sequence, when all four steps have been followed in a city, state, or region, we see the most success in terms of turning a state or region from red to blue, or red to purple.

Good ideas and important lessons can be found in unusual places. My own life's journey has led me to read about and study a broad spectrum of human endeavors, from Third World communist movements working to oust European colonialist dictators to capitalist entrepreneurs striving to build companies that could establish market dominance in a specific sector of the economy. When I was in college, I met Kwame Ture (known as Stokely Carmichael when he popularized the phrase "Black Power" in the 1960s), and to this day I recall his 1984 speech at Stanford where he challenged, if not mocked, our intellectual independence by saying, "Socialism—they got you scared of a word." Years later, I spent considerable time refining and utilizing a database program for trading options contracts in the decidedly non-socialist stock market. I have read Mao Tse-Tung's *On Practice* and Burton Malkiel's *A Random Walk Down Wall Street*, and I have found that there are some common components associated with success in both the political realm and the business world. Both sectors involve getting a group of human beings to work together in a disciplined and coordinated fashion to influence political or economic behavior of the public. In illuminating the essential elements of the Liberation Battle Plan, I use examples from both arenas—starting with the story of how Walgreens shifted its focus from selling milkshakes to providing medication such as the drugs my wife takes in her fight against cancer.

INVEST IN LEVEL 5 LEADERS

I did not know that Walgreens was once famous for milkshakes. The story of how one of the largest drugstore chains in the United States *stopped* being famous for milkshakes is an example of Level 5 leadership at work.

The concept of Level 5 leaders was popularized by Jim Collins, author of the book *Good to Great*. Collins has dedicated his professional life to studying why some companies succeed and others don't. Of the 1,435 companies he analyzed, eleven stood out as "great," and all eleven of them had what he calls Level 5 leaders. As Collins explains it, "The term Level 5 refers to the highest level in a hierarchy of executive capabilities that we identified in our research." Levels 1–4 consist of traits such as being a good team member and competent manager.[1] Collins found that Level 5 leaders are different, a cut above, distinctive in some fundamental ways:

> Level 5 leaders display a powerful mixture of personal humility and indomitable will. They're incredibly ambitious, but their ambition is first and foremost for the cause, for the organization and its purpose, not themselves. While Level 5 leaders can come in many personality packages, they are often self-effacing, quiet, reserved, and even shy. Every good-to-great transition in our research began with a Level 5 leader who motivated the enterprise more with inspired standards than inspiring personality.[2]

The Walgreens milkshake story starts with a man named Cork. Charles R. Walgreen III, known to his family and friends as "Cork," was the grandson of the founder of Walgreens and spent his entire adult life working at the company, starting out by stocking shelves in 1958 and rising up to become CEO in 1971.[3] Today, in some cities, like San Francisco where I live, it seems like you can't walk more than a few blocks without passing a Walgreens. Nationally, the company has more than 9,021 stores, and the corporate leaders take pride in the statistic that "78 percent of the U.S. population lives within five miles of a Walgreens."[4]

My wife was diagnosed with brain cancer in 2016, and ever since then, Walgreens has been a regular part of our life. (Nearly every doctor's visit includes the question, "So you use the Walgreens on Sixteenth Street, is that right?") From chemotherapy drugs to steroids that reduce brain inflammation to anti-seizure medication, Walgreens is our pharmacy of choice, and we are not alone, as the company's fundamental purpose today is providing medication for millions of people.

The way that Walgreens went from milkshakes to medications, growing from a small food front store in 1901 in Chicago into the second-largest pharmacy in America and a financial powerhouse generating more than $100 billion in annual revenue, is a testament to Level 5 leadership at a pivotal point in its corporate history.

In its early days, Walgreens included restaurants and soda fountain counters inside its stores. Some parts of the malted milkshake origin story are a bit murky, but everyone pretty much agrees that in 1922 (the same year the electric blender was invented), Walgreens employee Ivar "Pop" Coulson added two scoops of vanilla ice cream—"manufactured in Walgreens' own plant on East 40th Street in Chicago"—to a malted milk drink, and since then the company's profits (and America's waistlines) have never been the same.[5] Walgreens' fledgling operation grew from twenty stores in 1919, a few years before the milkshake invention, to more than five hundred a decade later.[6]

Regarding Cork Walgreen and his Level 5 leadership, the moment of truth came in the early 1980s. Collins offers the account of an executive who was present at the decisive moment:

> After years of dialogue and debate . . . the team had finally reached a watershed point of clarity and understanding: Walgreens' brightest future lay in convenient drugstores, not food service. . . .
>
> Cork said at one of our planning committee meetings, "Okay, now I am going to draw the line in the sand. We are going to be out of the restaurant business completely in five years." At the time, we had over five hundred restaurants. You could have heard a pin drop. He said, "I want to let everybody know the clock is ticking . . ." Six months later, we were at our next planning committee meeting and someone mentioned just in passing that we only had five years to be out of the restaurant business. Cork was not a real vociferous fellow. He sort of tapped on the table and said, "Listen, you have four and a half

years. I said you had five years six months ago. Now you've got
four and a half years."

Collins adds, "Walgreens had, after all, invented the malted milkshake and food service was a long-standing family tradition dating
back to his grandfather." Sometimes strong leaders have to move
past sentimentality, look at the big picture, and make the tough decisions. As Collins explained, "If Walgreens had to fly in the face of
long-standing family tradition in order to focus its resources where it
could be the best in the world (convenient drugstores), Cork would do
it. Quietly, doggedly, simply."[7]

As summarized in Good to Great, Level 5 leadership is "about ferocious resolve, an almost stoic determination to do whatever needs to
be done to make the company great. . . . Level 5 leaders are fanatically
driven, infected with an incurable need to produce results."[8]

In the political and social change sphere, this type of leadership
has also been essential to success, from winning elections to passing
legislation to shifting public attitudes on cultural issues. Northwest-
ern University sociology professor Aldon Morris spent eight years researching the civil rights movement of the 1950s and 1960s, seeking
to understand "how this important movement took root and became a
major force in American society."[9] His research included extensive interviews with key leaders of the movement and careful review of documents, correspondence, and other primary materials. His book Origins
of the Civil Rights Movement is one of the few works that methodically
and scientifically discerned and distilled the lessons learned from that
seminal historical period's key figures, including Rosa Parks, John
Lewis, Joseph Lowery, C.T. Vivian, Ella Baker, and others.

What Morris found that worked for movements of people marching
through the streets is very similar to what Collins discovered in thriv-
ing corporate suites—the presence of effective leaders with indomi-
table will as a necessary condition for success. He described effective
leaders as those who "engage in organization-building, mobilizing,
formulation of tactics and strategy, and articulation of a movement's
purpose and goals to participants and the larger society."[10]

In many ways, this shouldn't be surprising; successful leadership
essentially involves getting a constellation of people to perform at a

high level and to work together with discipline and diligence toward a common goal. In progressive politics, defeating a wealthy, powerful, well-organized, tenacious, and ruthless opponent doesn't happen by accident. Prevailing against such opposition requires leadership, and not just any kind of leadership.

In a lot of ways, what we now call Level 5 leadership is what James Baldwin meant when he described Lorraine Hansberry as a person characterized by "strength dictated by absolutely impersonal ambition: she was not trying to 'make it'—she was trying to keep the faith." [11]

If we look back at the past decade and ahead to the next, the places that have had the most success and show the most promise for leading the charge in finally helping this nation end the Civil War are the ones where there is at least one Level 5 leader, if not more, in key roles in the social change movement and political ecosystem, keeping the faith, doing the work, fanatically driven to produce results, and winning the fights.

BUILD STRONG CIVIC ENGAGEMENT ORGANIZATIONS

In 2007, several months before the Iowa caucuses that catapulted Barack Obama to the front of the Democratic field, his campaign team made a risky strategic bet. They needed money to hire hundreds of staffers in Iowa, but they didn't have the funds in the bank to justify such an expenditure. Up against the massive financial and institutional support that the Clintons commanded as the former first family of the United States, the upstart Obama enterprise was taking a big risk. But his campaign really didn't have much of a choice, and, most importantly, they had a strategic weapon. That weapon was a national civic engagement organization that connected and stitched together the energy and activities of inspired but disparate individuals drawn to his message of hope. Through the campaign's website, Obama for America, people in multiple states and cities could connect to a central organization, and the diffuse expressions of support could be organized and channeled into dollars in the bank, phone calls to potential supporters, and the important, unglamorous, and methodical activities of knocking on doors and making phone calls and making notes of the conversations volunteers were having.

Obama's campaign manager, David Plouffe, described the thinking behind the decision in his book *The Audacity to Win*:

> We made an aggressive gamble and staffed up to huge numbers very quickly. Presidential campaigns usually hire in waves for the caucuses, with most staff brought on toward the end of the campaign when people are beginning to pay closer attention. We took the opposite approach—not an insignificant budget risk at the time—and placed more staff in more communities earlier than any campaign in caucus history. . . .
>
> We had assumed we would be playing catch-up with the Clinton campaign after the first four contests. . . . Now, it was not implausible that we could actually be better funded and organized than the Clinton campaign as we moved deeper into the race.[12]

As inspiring as Senator Obama was, as effective at eliciting emotion through his speeches, as insightful as he was through his books, it would have amounted to little without a strong civic engagement organization at its core. Unorganized people cannot defeat an organized and entrenched and well-financed status quo. Taking down Goliath requires strong civic engagement organizations to translate inspiring messages and images into volunteer energy and hours, and ultimately into votes and power.

June Jordan is one of my two favorite writers of all time (James Baldwin is the other). In a 1976 essay published amid America's Bicentennial celebrations, Jordan turned her talents to describing one of the essential elements of the Liberation Battle Plan—nurturing strong social change and civic engagement organizations. Her essay from which I quote to open this chapter is titled "Declaration of an Independence I Would Just as Soon Not Have," and it eloquently articulates the limitations of acting *without* the support of a powerful and effective organization:

> Well, for a long time I thought it was perfectly fine to be alone as far as political cause was concerned. You wrote poems, free-lance exposé articles, essays proposing remedies, even novels

demonstrating the feasibility of solutions that you ardently trusted as possibilities for activist commitment. Or you hitched onto ad hoc committees against this or that nightmare and, when and if you had the bucks, you made tax-deductible donations of endorsement for whatever public fight seemed to you among the most urgent to be won. What did this yield? I felt pretty good, yes, and comfortable with my conscience. But nothing changed, nothing ever really changed as the result of such loner activity.[13]

Forty-five years after Jordan shared her insights, a team of distinguished scholars turned their analytical gaze to the same question of what it takes to bring about meaningful political change. Hahrie Han, Elizabeth McKenna, and Michelle Oyakawa spent years researching the efforts of advocacy and social change organizations. They distilled their findings into the 2021 book *Prisms of the People*. The book's core purpose is to surface "the strategic choices that leaders ... make in response to uncertain moments that evoke the question, 'What do we do?' "[14]

Their entire book is an illustration and exploration of the centrality of strong civic engagement organizations in the quest to build political power. In case, like me, your recollection of grade school geometry is spotty, a refresher on what exactly a prism is might be helpful to appreciating Han et al.'s findings, and why they use it as the defining metaphor. With apologies to mathematicians everywhere, a prism can be thought of as a cube—yes, you can even envision an ice cube for conceptual purposes. For this example, the way a prism works is that light comes in one end and then is projected out, in an altered form, at the other end. In describing the work and the impact of social change and civic engagement organizations, the authors explain why they chose the prism metaphor:

First, it underscores the transformative power of the organizations in our study to act not as neutral repositories of activism but as vehicles that transform people's activity and engagement into political power. Second, just as tiny prisms can refract light as far as it will travel, the leaders in our study could exert power at a much larger scale than their numbers might suggest, because of their internal organizational designs.[15]

As Han et al. concluded, "Organizations and leadership matter. Meeting the challenge of democracy has always required organizations that can cultivate and channel people's passion and resources through vehicles of collective action and overcome structural segregation to generate a sense of collective belonging."[16]

Morris's study of the civil rights movement also identified what Han et al. found in their work. From his study of the 1960s movement, he uncovered the importance and significance of well-run organizations. In particular, he emphasized the centrality of connection to "mass-based indigenous institutions which provide activists with groups of people who are accustomed to accomplishing goals in an organized manner and with much of the money and labor force capable of being harnessed for political goals."[17]

Strong civic engagement organizations are especially important in mobilizing voters of color because of the country's gargantuan racial wealth gap. As I explored in *Brown Is the New White*, "Since the beginning of U.S. history, people of color were placed in poverty as a group and kept in poverty by government-sanctioned and government-promoted policies (including frequent government inaction in the face of racial discrimination and violence by private actors working to "keep people of color in their place"). Conversely, Whites were lifted up, privileged, and protected as a group."[18] The modern-day manifestation of this historical legacy is that the average white family in America has a net worth of $188,200 while the net worth for a Black family is $24,100. Latino families have a net worth of $36,100.[19]

The racial wealth gap leaves people of color with far fewer resources and options to allow them to interrupt their daily lives—in which they are frequently forced to survive by a slim financial thread—to take the time and effort to vote. From finding child care for their children to getting time off work to navigating transportation obstacles and logistics (especially in big cities), it's just harder for people of color to cast their ballots. In terms of arriving at the destination of a true multiracial democracy where people of all racial backgrounds can participate, it is critical to have vehicles that can navigate the obstacles created by economic inequality, and strong civic engagement organizations are the vehicles that have gotten the job done.

All of the states, counties, and cities that have achieved significant success toward winning the Civil War against Confederates over the past decade have done so in large part because of strong, well-run, highly disciplined organizations working directly with the marginalized communities most in need of political and social change. Two states that are featured as case studies in *Prisms of the People* are also examined in the following chapters in this book: Virginia and Arizona, places where Liberators have fought and won in the face of intense opposition from modern-day Confederates. The transformative power of strong social change organizations has been proven time and again throughout history. Nelson Mandela's courage and leadership in fighting the Confederates of South Africa (who learned many of their racial segregation practices from the United States) would not have changed his country without the organizational apparatus of the African National Congress, the United Democratic Front, and hundreds of other groups. Barack Obama would not have ascended to the White House without the Obama for America organization that deployed thousands of staff and 2.2 million volunteers in cities and states across the country in identifying and mobilizing voters. (McKenna and Han did a deep dive on the significance of the Obama civic engagement operation in their 2014 book *Groundbreakers: How Obama's 2.2 Million Volunteers Transformed Campaigning in America*.)[20] Georgia and Arizona would not have achieved historic, Trump-defeating voter turnout in 2020 without exemplary, state-based, well-run civic engagement organizations.

DEVELOP DETAILED, DATA-DRIVEN PLANS

When I worked in the San Francisco Unified School District in the early 1990s, one of my mentors, Beverly Jimenez, told me that the most powerful person in the district was the man who controlled the bus schedules. For all the grand policy pronouncements and curricular innovations, it was the guy who determined which vehicles picked up which children at what time of day who actually had the greatest impact on the system. If a student is standing on the street corner waiting for the bus, it's kind of hard to provide the latest cutting-edge classroom instruction. And in a district with nearly sixty thousand students at the time, the logistical challenge was enormous, involving hundreds of buses, bus drivers, and pickup points. The need for a detailed, data-driven plan was paramount.

Such was also the case with the Montgomery Bus Boycott. The history books tell a simplistic story of Rosa Parks defying the system and refusing to give up her seat on the bus for a white person, sparking the bus boycott and subsequently smashing racial segregation in the South. The actual boycott was far more complicated and involved far more planning. Far more.

Imagine if you had to take responsibility for figuring out how to make sure your next-door neighbor got to their workplace every day. How far away is that workplace? What time does she or he leave the house in order to arrive on time? How many people in the household need transportation, and will they all fit in one car? It's a challenging proposition, but doable, with some focused attention and planning. Now imagine if you had to take responsibility for coordinating the transportation of the families in ten different households? How about fifty thousand? That was the logistical miracle underlying the success of the Montgomery Bus Boycott, and it would not have happened without a detailed, data-driven plan of where the tens of thousands of Black folks in Montgomery lived, where they needed to go, and who had cars that could provide transportation to replace the people-moving function formerly provided by the racially segregated buses.

We know the names of Rosa Parks and Martin Luther King Jr., but there would have been no success without Jo Ann Robinson and her fellow activists in the Montgomery Women's Political Council (WPC).

Black folks didn't just magically boycott the buses. The success of the boycott depended on getting the word out, and to get the word out to nearly fifty thousand people across the city required meticulous planning and a data-driven knowledge of the transportation needs of the city's African American residents. Remember, this is 1955—long before Facebook, text messaging, and email.

A vast array of very basic questions reveal the absolute strategic genius and data sophistication that underlay the boycott. What day does the boycott begin? How many people do you need to reach? How many

flyers do you need to print? Jo Ann Robinson and her sisters in struggle at the WPC had done the math. She explained their military-like
sophistication and tech-savvy number-crunching in her memoir *The
Montgomery Bus Boycott and the Women Who Started It*:

> We used thirty-five reams of paper at 500 sheets per ream. That
> made 17,500 sheets, cut into thirds, for a total of 52,500 leaflets
> distributed. . . . By 4 A.M. Friday, the sheets had been dupli-
> cated, cut in thirds, and bundled. . . . Everything was done by
> the plan, with perfect timing. By 2 o'clock, thousands of the
> mimeographed handbills had changed hands many times.
> Practically every black man, woman, and child in Montgomery
> knew the plan and was passing the word along. No one knew
> where the notices had come from or who had arranged for their
> circulation, and no one cared. Those who passed them on did so
> efficiently, quietly, and without comment. But deep within the
> heart of every black person was a joy he or she dared not reveal.[21]

That data-driven plan enabled them to get the word out, ensuring
a successful first day of what many thought would be a one-day boycott. Completely lost to history is how long the boycott lasted. Martin
Luther King had consulted with another minister, his college friend
the Rev. T.J. Jemison, for lessons from a bus boycott that Jemison had
helped to organize in Louisiana two years earlier, in 1953. That boycott
had lasted for two weeks until it "fell apart," despite the "herculean
efforts" to master the multiple challenges.[22] That was as long as they
could withstand the ferocity of the opposition (including silent and not
so silent sanctioning of domestic terrorism), and the daunting task of
coordinating a massive amount of logistics to provide transportation
for tens of thousands of people. So, up until that point, two weeks was
considered a stretch goal in terms of the maximum duration of a bus
boycott.

In Montgomery, however, they successfully boycotted the public
bus system for *more than an entire year—thirteen months*. They were
able to orchestrate a logistical pummeling of the racist city leaders
because of an extraordinarily detailed, data-driven plan. Here is how
Robinson described the effort:

Each day some 325 private cars picked up passengers from 43 dispatch stations and 42 pickup stations. The dispatch stations were designated places where workers congregated in the early morning, beginning at 5 A.M., to be taken to work. From 5 A.M. until 10 A.M., dozens of cars left these points every ten minutes for anywhere within the working radius of Montgomery. The dispatch stations included most of the Negro churches, all of the Negro funeral homes, several clubhouses, stores and other key places where business was being conducted and where people went in and out purchasing things, popular corners, and the eight Negro-operated service stations. By ten o'clock in the morning, most of the workers had been dispatched, so casual hourly pickups were scheduled during the rest of the day.[23]

As these examples show, the Montgomery Bus Boycott required far more than one courageous person refusing to give up her seat on the bus and one eloquent minister giving voice to the years of pent-up anger and the righteousness of the cause (although, to be sure, it absolutely required both of those things). To win, to defeat the opposition in the original capital of the Confederacy, required a detailed, data-driven plan.

In all of the case studies in this book, the success of attaining political power has been predicated on an extraordinarily precise and carefully crafted plan that determined how to allocate scarce resources, where to allocate them, and when to make those allocations. By definition, marginalized communities cannot win by simply overwhelming or outspending their opponents. They must carefully assess the lay of the land, make smart decisions about what course of action to take, and then boldly go where the data tells them to go.

PLAY THE LONG GAME

The United Parcel Service (UPS) company started out more than a hundred years ago with two young guys running around Seattle delivering messages for 15¢ per message. Back in 1907, very few people had telephones or cars (the Model T wasn't invented until 1908), so it was a logistical pain to try to communicate with someone if you wanted to reach them faster than by writing a letter. To address that need, nineteen-year-old Jim Casey, UPS's founder, rounded up some of his friends and started a service where "the messengers walked, ran, used one of the bicycles, or took streetcars or horse-drawn carriages and taxis, if necessary" to get the messages to their destination across town.[24] The business was successful and it began to grow over many years into a full-scale package delivery operation with an increasingly large reach, first across the city and then beyond.

Ultimately, the company's leaders realized that if they could conquer the challenges of truly national delivery, that would make them an unparalleled force in American commerce. As his enterprise took shape, Casey wanted to be able to move packages across the country, but the obstacles were enormous, and it took *sixty-eight years* to assemble a coast-to-coast package shipping operation.[25]

Why did it take so long? Most of us, when we see a truck driving on the highway, don't think about what types of license or paperwork is required for the vehicle to deliver its contents from one location to another. It turns out that you can't commercially transport products across state lines without the proper permits, and those permits are hard to get.

UPS didn't accomplish its coast-to-coast transport capacity in one fell swoop. Rather, the company doggedly pursued it, state by state and in some cases city by city, with applications, considerable paperwork and documentation, meetings with attorneys, and state and federal hearings, with occasional appeals, over several decades. The saga is captured in the 2007 book *Big Brown* by journalist and former UPS employee Greg Niemann:

> From 1952 until 1980 the company waged legal battles before regulatory commissions and courts across the nation to secure additional permissions to expand delivery service. Early applications requested only small expansions of territory, either just a particular city or perhaps an entire metropolitan area. Then, emboldened by growing operational success and depending upon regulatory jurisdictions, the company began to request more and larger areas, whole states, and even multistate regions in a single application.

Every service expansion was hard-earned and in many cases came about only after UPS lawyers and executives presented mountains of evidence and hours of testimony, after customers pleaded for service, after local officials made personal appeals. Sometimes letter-writing campaigns by employees and customers were necessary to spur legislators to prompt bureaucrats into action. Each year saw numerous successes, some major, some local, yet all contributing to eventual nationwide service. With each victory, large or small, a bell in the national (now corporate) office rang to celebrate a UPS expansion.[26]

UPS's commitment to the long game has paid off in impressive fashion. Today, the company is the largest courier company in the world, with more than half a million employees facilitating the delivery of 25 million packages a day, a service that generates more than $85 billion in annual revenue.[27]

––––––

In modern-day America, we respect, if not revere, business leaders far more than we do nonprofit or social change leaders. That's a big part of why this chapter uses some examples from corporate America to illustrate the various components of the Liberation Battle Plan. Things are more legit in many people's eyes if they've been developed or applied in the private sector. Over the past thirty years, I've met and worked with many top corporate leaders, philanthropists, and political donors in America, and researching and writing this book has brought to light an interesting and inspiring reality.

Hollywood and the mass media worship entrepreneurs, and articles, movies, and books shower praise on their creativity, innovation, and success. What I did not fully appreciate until trying to tell the stories of the people and groups that are winning the Civil War is that, to a person, they are all entrepreneurs, and successful ones at that. Most of the Level 5 leaders described in the following pages started an organization from scratch and built it up to become a multimillion-dollar powerhouse that is transforming the political balance of power of large, previously Confederate-run, regions of the country. In so doing, they have learned to build and run effective organizations, crunch and analyze data, and sustain their efforts for multiple years, always against great odds. In every single one of the places where Liberators have defeated the Confederates, the work has taken at least a decade of steady, consistent, and tenacious organizing.

As we face the considerable challenges posed by Confederates who never give an inch and are prepared to destroy democracy in order to grab power and protect whiteness, it is imperative that we learn from the people and places where we are winning. No state has been more important than Georgia, and if we want to win in the months and years ahead, we must all humble ourselves in light of the reality that most of the "smart money" was not smart enough to properly identify Georgia as the principal place to invest, and we must learn as much as we can from the leaders and organizations who did the work that brought about the changes that are benefiting so many people across the country and the world. Fortunately, the architects of the Georgia political miracle have been generous in sharing how they built such an impressive political structure.

7

Georgia: "That's Not One We Expected"

Georgians deserved better, so we devised and began executing a 10-year plan to transform Georgia into a battleground state. . . . Years of planning, testing, innovating, sustained investment and organizing yielded the record-breaking results we knew they could and should. . . . The lessons we learned can help other states looking to chart a more competitive future for Democrats and progressives, particularly those in the Sun Belt, where demographic change will precede electoral opportunity.
— Stacey Abrams and Lauren Groh-Wargo, "How to Turn Your Red State Blue," February 11, 2021

Denmark Groover never intended for Verlene Warnock's son to grow up and become a United States senator. A Georgia state representative in the 1950s and 1960s, Groover was a staunch segregationist and a key leader in the Georgia state legislature. I had my own inadvertent encounter with Groover's legacy when, as a college student in the 1980s, I visited Martin Luther King's burial site in Atlanta and was shocked to see the Confederate flag flying over his tomb. Upon closer inspection, it was actually the Georgia state flag, but at that time the bulk of the design of the state flag consisted of the Confederate stars and bars. Georgia was able to officially fly the banner of the racist traitors to our nation because of the passage of a 1956 bill calling for the redesign of the flag as part of the "Massive Resistance" to the Supreme Court's *Brown v. Board of Education* school desegregation decision (see chapter 3). The legislative leaders refashioned the flag so that the Confederate battle emblem was the dominant visible element, and Groover was not shy about their intent, declaring, in defiant opposition to the decision in *Brown*, that "we in Georgia intend to uphold what we stood for, will stand for, and will fight for . . .

anything we in Georgia can do to preserve the memory of the Confederacy is a step forward."[1]

One of the main things Groover stood for and fought for was protecting white power by disenfranchising Black voters. Having himself lost an election in 1958 because of what he perceived as a unified African American vote for his opponent, he set about in 1964 to codify methods of weakening the strength of the Black vote, and his tool of choice was the practice of runoff elections.

Whereas common electoral practice had been the fairly basic and democratic procedure whereby the person with the most votes wins the election, for Groover and the other segregationists that wasn't good enough. Wanting to avoid a scenario where a candidate with strong and unified support from Georgia's Black voters could prevail in a race where the white vote splintered among many candidates, they devised a scheme to ensure that the Black vote would be as diluted as possible.

The arrangement they came up with required a runoff election any time a candidate did not receive 50 percent of the vote—in a state where African Americans composed less than 50 percent of the voters. Warning his colleagues that "the Negroes and the pressure groups and special interests are going to manipulate this State and take charge," Groover championed his runoff voting bill as a way to "prevent the Negro bloc vote from controlling the elections."[2]

For decades, it worked like a charm. From 1964 to 2020, no African American ever won a statewide runoff election in Georgia.[3] The runoff election system was so well received and worked so well to disenfranchise Black voters that, like the spread of the white nationalist state constitutions rewritten in the 1890s and the defunding of public education by several Southern states in tandem with support for private, all-white academies after the 1954 *Brown* decision, it was quickly adopted by other Southern states where the Black vote posed a threat to white power. As of January 2022, ten states in the country had runoff election rules for primary elections, almost all of them in the former Confederacy.[4] Everything was going according to plan. What the plan did not anticipate was Verlene and Jonathan Warnock's son.

While Groover was working in the state Capitol in Atlanta in the

1950s defending white political power against Black people, Verlene Warnock would spend her days walking up and down rows of rich black soil in the fields of Waycross, Georgia, picking white cotton that white people would sell at great profit.[5] She and her husband Jonathan, an army veteran who owned a car restoration business, raised a son, Raphael, who wanted to become a minister. Young Raphael Warnock would in fact attend divinity school and go on to follow in the footsteps of Martin Luther King by becoming the senior pastor of Atlanta's Ebenezer Baptist Church, the same church that was King's religious home and base of operations.

In 2020, in a country with a president as racially inflammatory as George Wallace had been in the 1960s, Reverend Warnock decided to run for the United States Senate, seeking to capture a seat held by Republicans (in fact, the seat Warnock sought had previously been held by John Brown Gordon, architect of the infamous 1877 Hayes-Tilden Compromise that, as discussed in chapter 1, handed power back to the Confederates).

Running in the November 2020 election, Warnock won the most votes—33 percent of all votes—against a large and divided field, including the incumbent senator, Republican Kelly Loeffler (who received 26 percent of the votes). This was the exact scenario envisioned by Groover and for which the runoff election was designed—to prevent a Black candidate from emerging victorious. The Georgia system worked as planned, going to a runoff election two months later, where the advantages of incumbency, wealth, and whiteness had historically redounded to the benefit of white candidates.

But not this time. Warnock and the growing Georgia multiracial electorate prevailed, defeating Loeffler, and, along with the victory of Democrat Jon Ossoff, who was running for Georgia's other seat in the Senate, giving Democrats control of both Senate seats for the first time in decades. Because of the victory in those runoff elections, control of the U.S. Senate flipped to the Democrats, handing them the power to move trillions of dollars toward the kinds of economic and social justice initiatives that the Confederates have worked so hard to eviscerate. (Dr. King's final crusade, for example, was the Poor People's Campaign, and one of Warnock's first votes was to pass a bill that lifted millions of people out of poverty.)[6]

The obstinance of the defenders of the Confederate cause has produced profound unintended consequences and a level of poetic justice that Groover and his colleagues never imagined. Not only did Senators Warnock and Ossoff win their runoff elections and flip control of the entire U.S. Senate, but the fallout from the state flag controversy also sowed the seeds that are growing into an increasingly powerful multiracial electoral force.

It turns out that I was not the only person offended by the Confederate-dominated Georgia state flag in the late 1980s and early 1990s. Led by civil rights leaders and Black state legislators, a movement emerged that demanded the racist Confederate symbol be removed from the state's official flag. During the 1990s, the movement gained strength and momentum, and in 2001 Democrat Roy Barnes, Georgia's powerful governor, joined the cause and succeeded in getting the flag redesigned so that the racist emblem was removed. The backlash from the state's white voters was swift and severe.

A year after removing the Confederate flag insignia from the Georgia state flag, the state's voters removed Barnes from the governor's office, voting him out in what was seen as a shocking upset. Up until that point, Barnes had been considered "one of the most powerful governors in history," earning him the nickname "King Roy."[7] Barnes's defeat was part of the long-running Confederate practice of never giving an inch, and eliminating the actual Confederate flag was certainly a crime meriting the most severe political punishment in the eyes of most of the state's white voters. In 2010, Barnes attempted a political comeback, mounting another bid for the governor's office, but the state's electorate had neither forgotten nor forgiven, and he lost the contest, signaling the end of an era.

The defeat of King Roy created a political vacuum in Georgia Democratic politics in the early years of the twenty-first century. Assessing that landscape and seeing the need for new political leadership, the recently elected state legislator Stacey Abrams stepped forward to become the leader of the Democrats in the Georgia State House. The state—and the country—would never be the same.

INVEST IN LEVEL 5 LEADERS—STACEY ABRAMS

On December 16, 2010, I received an email from my friend Ben Jealous, then president of the national NAACP. In that email, he introduced me to his close friend, a young state legislator in Georgia, and asked me to meet with her. I agreed to find a time to get together, and she sent me a thoughtful response:

> Steve,
>
> Thank you so much for the willingness to meet with me. I would welcome the time and the advice—and I'm willing to travel. We have some good opportunities here in Georgia to create a road map for the South, but it will require careful planning and friends beyond our borders. I appreciate your help.
>
> Take care,
> Stacey
>
> Representative Stacey Abrams
> House Minority Leader
> Georgia General Assembly
> District 84[8]

Stacey's origin story is both completely familiar and entirely unheard of. It is familiar in that she grew up Black in America. As such, she had to navigate the typical obstacles, barriers, and treatment that nearly every African American has experienced. Of particular significance to this saga, she grew up as a dark-skinned Black woman in a working-class family.

Raised mostly in Gulfport, Mississippi, Stacey was one of six kids growing up, and she has said her family was part of what her mother called "the genteel poor," which meant "we had no money, but we watched PBS and read books."[9] Stacey's mother, a college librarian, and her father, a shipyard worker, came of age during the civil rights movement and participated in boycotts and marches. Her mother tried to sit up front on buses and was kicked off. Her father participated in boycotts and was beaten and jailed for his involvement. The Abrams parents raised their children with a "you can be anything" mantra and emphasized education and civic engagement. Stacey remembers how, as a child, family outings included going to the polls. When she was seventeen, she set up her first voter registration table before she could even vote herself.

Like many people of color, much of Stacey's fire and determination were forged through painful experiences at a young age. In Georgia, every high school valedictorian gets invited to the governor's mansion for a reception and celebration, and Stacey was Avondale High School's valedictorian in 1991. She and her parents were excited to join the other students and their families being honored by the governor, but their car wasn't working. Like a lot of Black people over the years, Stacey's family was familiar and comfortable with taking the bus (there's a reason one of the seminal events of the modern civil rights movement was the Montgomery *Bus* Boycott). When the Abrams family arrived at the governor's mansion, in the fancy part of town, they got off the bus and walked up the driveway to the gated entrance where they told the guard their names and that they were there for the reception. Looking at Stacey, her parents, their dark skin, and the bus they got off of, the guard sneered at the family and said, "This is a private event, you don't belong here." Stacey's parents forced the guard to check his list again, and he did in fact find their names and relented on his obstruction. Stacey turned the pain of that encounter into motivational fuel, and she regularly recounts the experience in her speeches, saying:

> I don't remember meeting the governor of Georgia. I don't re-call meeting my fellow valedictorians from 180 school districts. The only clear memory I have of that day was a man standing in front of the most powerful place in Georgia, looking at me and telling me I don't belong. And so I decided twenty-some odd years later to be the person who got to open the gates.[10]

After high school, Stacey went on to graduate from Spelman College, a historically Black college, in Atlanta. From there she traveled to Texas, where she completed a master's degree from the Lyndon B.

Johnson School of Public Affairs at the University of Texas at Austin, followed by three years in New Haven, Connecticut, where she received a JD from Yale University. At age twenty-nine she was appointed the deputy city attorney of Atlanta. In 2006, at the age of thirty-three, she ran for and won her seat in the Georgia State House, rising up to become House minority leader in 2010, the year Roy Barnes lost his comeback gubernatorial bid. For six years, Stacey served as minority leader—the top Democrat in the chamber—until resigning to run for governor in 2018.

———

Isabel Wilkerson writes in *Caste*, "We are all players on a stage that was built long before our ancestors arrived in this land. We are the latest cast in a long-running drama that premiered on this soil in the early seventeenth century." In this play, Wilkerson adds, "For generations, everyone has known who is center stage in the lead. Everyone knows who the hero is, who the supporting characters are, who is the sidekick good for laughs, and who is in shadow . . ."[11]

For most of American history, people who look like Stacey Abrams are more traditionally thought of for roles such as the maid, not the governor. Roles such as the character Mammy, the housekeeper in *Gone with the Wind*, or Aibileen, a domestic worker in *The Help*, a novel adapted into a film about a young white woman and her relationship with two Black maids. They are thought of as the people who clean the houses of the wealthy and powerful. They are not envisioned as the ones who clean up the messes of the Democratic Party and determine who runs the White House.

The unheard-of part of Stacey's story is not only the extent to which she has refused to stay in the roles pre-assigned to people like her, but how successful she has been in tackling whatever task she sets her mind to. She's had ambitions and dreams that are startling for a dark-skinned Black woman from the American South to have. And with a level of success greater than almost any Black woman not named Oprah, Michelle, or Shonda, she has gone about making those dreams a reality. She is a romance novelist who, by the third year of law school, had written her first novel. By the age of thirty-six, she had written eight novels (as someone who has struggled to finish now two books, I remain in awe of that accomplishment alone). She is the author of a *New York Times* No. 1 best-selling legal thriller *While Justice Sleeps*. She has also written two nonfiction books (one a bestseller) and one children's book. She is a tax attorney who worked for an Atlanta law firm early in her career. She started a business at the age of thirty-seven, and it has survived and then flourished to the point where it attracted $30 million in investment in 2021. She's produced two films and appeared on the television show *black-ish*, receiving an Emmy nomination for her performance. In March of 2022, she made a cameo appearance in the Season 4 finale of *Star Trek: Discovery*, playing the role of President of United Earth, saying to Captain Burnham—and all of us—"There's a lot of work to do. Are you ready for that?" [12] And as if all of that weren't enough, in 2021, she was also nominated for a Nobel Peace Prize for her voter protection work, which, in the words of one of the nominators, "follows in Dr. Martin Luther King Jr.'s footsteps in the fight for equality before the law and for civil rights." [13]

When I reflect on Stacey's career, I'm reminded of what Alabama lawyer and voting rights activist Faya Rose Touré said when she came to speak at Stanford in January 1990 (she went by Rose Sanders at the time). Touré had graduated from Harvard Law School and returned to Selma, Alabama, to keep the faith and carry on the work of the civil rights activists from the 1960s. She and her husband Hank, who also graduated from Harvard Law, joined forces with one of the stalwart Black lawyers in Alabama, J.L. Chestnut Jr., and their firm has been a pillar of the civil rights movement in Alabama for decades. (As mentioned in chapter 3, as a young lawyer Chestnut appeared before Judge George Wallace and was treated with respect, back before Wallace discovered the political power of "talking about niggers.") When she came to Stanford, Touré, speaking to a packed auditorium, said with great confidence, conviction, and Southern inflection, "We didn't get into these elite universities because we're smart. If it were just about intelligence, my *momma* would've gotten in a long time ago."

More than thirty years later, I remember that statement like it was yesterday because it so succinctly distilled the Black experience, blew up the myth of meritocracy, and placed the onus for the slow pace of progress where it belongs—on those doing the obstructing. If it were just about talent and intelligence, Touré's mother, my mother, and a long, long line of incredibly smart Black women would have been running this country a long time ago. But Black women do not fit the profile of what talent, intelligence, and leadership looks like.

That is the reason that no state in the country has ever elected a Black woman as governor. It has nothing to do with a paucity of talent, intelligence, or ability and everything to do with what white Americans think governors look like. That is why Stacey's political ascendance is so historic and significant. Her climb has been much, much steeper because, as a Black woman in American, she has had to face myriad additional obstacles including the skepticism of donors who initially weren't supportive, backbiting and jealousy from supposed supporters, and cynicism and hostility from the media and Democratic establishment. The narrowness of Stacey's defeat in the 2018 general election obscured the enormity of the achievement of winning the Democratic gubernatorial primary in the first place. It was in fact, and appropriately so, historic. And, of course, she's not done yet, as she is again running for governor of Georgia in 2022.

The world now knows who Stacey Abrams is and what she is capable of. She is the first Black woman to ever win her party's gubernatorial nomination, was on the short list to be picked as Joe Biden's vice president, may well be the first Black woman governor in America, and is quite possibly a future president. Of greatest consequence to progressive people across the world, she built the operation that flipped the state of Georgia in 2020 and helped save the country from white nationalist fascism. How she accomplished that is the best curriculum possible for anyone wanting to know how to win the Civil War.

———

I met with Stacey in my office in downtown San Francisco in March of 2011, and she had come prepared, providing me with a detailed, multiyear, data-rich, twenty-six-page plan for turning Georgia blue. I have met with a lot of people in politics over the years—including senators, governors, presidential advisers, Fortune 500 CEOs, foundation presidents, and heads of multimillion-dollar organizations—and I had never seen someone with a plan as detailed, data-driven, clear-eyed, and sophisticated as Stacey's. I immediately committed to helping her by raising money, making introductions to key donors and leaders, and trying to elevate her work to receive the attention it deserved.

It was slow going at first. My wife and I contributed $10,000 to her political action committee in 2012, and other donors chipped in close to $43,000, bringing the total for her PAC to $52,870 at a time when other whiter and more connected politicians across the country were raising millions. Georgia was not on the radar, and the experts didn't think Democrats had much chance of winning there anytime soon.

Stacey embodies Level 5 leadership, as applied to the political and social change world. As Collins said of Level 5 leaders, they are "incredibly ambitious, but their ambition is first and foremost for the cause, for the organization and its purpose, not themselves."[14]

For all of the fame that has flowed to her in recent years, one of the most remarkable aspects of Stacey's track record is that she has accomplished much of this work without the platform of an elected office. For the past few years, she's basically been a nonprofit activist who, through talent, determination, brilliance, and force of personality, has upended the national political balance of power.

After her historic and inspiring gubernatorial bid in 2018, Stacey was showered with opportunities and offers. Most notably, then Senate minority leader Chuck Schumer mounted a full-court press to encourage and pressure her to run for the U.S. Senate seat in Georgia. (I know because shortly after the 2018 election, as I was catching the bus home from work, Schumer called to ask me to talk to Stacey about making the Senate bid.) His courtship included selecting Stacey to give the nationally televised Democratic response to the State of the Union address in 2019.

While all of that was flattering and ego-boosting, she didn't just want a job or prominent position; she wanted to make a difference. As Stacey explained in a graduation speech in 2021, "Not receiving the position I wanted did not absolve me from the responsibility to do the work."[15] What "the work" entailed was fighting for democracy, and she took to that task as someone who intimately understood the impact of voter suppression based on what she had encountered in her gubernatorial race.

In Stacey's race against then-sitting secretary of state Brian Kemp, not only was Kemp in the position to oversee the rules and count the votes in his own gubernatorial bid, he also manipulated those rules to improperly purge 340,134 voters from the rolls.[16] Kemp ended up winning that election by 54,723 votes and went on to become the next governor of Georgia (Kemp is up for reelection, and if he survives a primary challenge, he will again face Stacey in November 2022).

Having endured that 2018 political heartbreak, Stacey was uniquely suited to translate the pain of the suppression of Black voters into the power to protect the votes of ordinary Americans across the country as they sought to participate in our fragile democracy. She knew that defending democracy in a country defined by systemic racism requires fierce, protracted, hand-to-hand combat.

I learned of her post-election plans when she called me in November 2018 while I was at my neighborhood Philz Coffee in San Francisco, enjoying my large Ecstatic coffee with extra ice. It was two weeks after the election, and Stacey's campaign was working feverishly to make sure all of the votes were counted, as Kemp sought to secure his slim lead by blocking the tabulation of as many votes from Black neighborhoods as he could (and if you are seeing a pattern here of how Confederates relate to the electoral process, then I have done my job). I took the call, conferenced in my wife, and we discussed next steps. Stacey said that the vote gap she faced, while small (roughly 1 percent of all votes cast), was likely too large to overcome, and she was going to cease her campaign.

Looking ahead to the future, Stacey said she had decided to start a new organization called Fair Fight Action. As she put it in an interview at the time, "I sat shiva for 10 days. Then I started plotting."[17] I'll admit I first scratched my head and wondered, "Is that really the best next step?" We discussed the scenario of continuing to build on the foundation she'd laid in her gubernatorial bid, helping the Democrats win Georgia in the 2020 presidential campaign, and then running for governor again in 2022, but she kept returning to the importance of combating voter suppression as fundamental to Democrats' prospects of winning any of those future races. Her ambition was for the cause, the purpose. Her focus was, as it has always been, on "doing the work."

So, in 2019 she set about doing the work of building Fair Fight Action, an organization that became the critical command center for combating voter suppression all across the country in 2020, the year that the full force of the president of the United States was unleashed to squash voting and civic participation by Democrats, in general, and by people of color, in particular. Stacey's prescience in understanding that that was the fight to fight—two years before the Trump fusillade for fascism—turned out to be an indispensable element of literally saving democracy in America.

Without question, Stacey is a next-level leader who sees all the pieces on the chessboard and can project several moves ahead, but she also understands that social and political change is a collective endeavor. One person, however brilliant, can't overcome the ruthlessness and zealousness of, as June Jordan put it, "the enemy forces surely arrayed against our goals." That collective endeavor does not materialize by accident. It must be built, coordinated, and operated according to a meticulous and detailed plan. As Stacey said in her first email to me in 2011, it takes "careful planning."

Stacey not only had a vision, she also had a plan that would guide the work of strengthening and building the organizational infrastructure capable of defeating a white nationalist president and his army of enablers.

DEVELOP DETAILED, DATA-DRIVEN PLANS

The hallmark of Stacey Abrams's life—and the key to her success—has been careful planning. Her meticulous preparation is now legendary, and she described it in her book *Lead from the Outside*:

> When I was eighteen, I spent an evening in our college computer lab, the fluorescent lights crackling overhead reflecting off the near-green screen. While the few other students there on a weeknight likely toiled over papers, I'd been driven from my dorm room by what felt like an urgent project. In the lab that night, I created a spreadsheet. The Lotus 1-2-3 document laid out my life plans for the next forty years. Seriously. The sheet contained four columns: year, age, job, and tasks. . . . For the next decade, I followed the plans on my spreadsheet.[18]

I crossed paths with the content of the spreadsheet when, at a dinner in Atlanta in May of 2012, Stacey told me, quite matter-of-factly, that she planned to run for governor in 2018—*six years down the road*. Although Stacey's forty-year plan is perhaps an order of magnitude beyond the capacity of most mere mortals, careful, multiyear planning is critical to every fight in this Civil War.

The linchpin of Stacey's plan was increasing the number of people of color who voted in Georgia elections.

———

There have always been a lot of Black people in Georgia. That's what happens when the land is fertile for growing cotton, selling cotton is extraordinarily profitable, and, in preindustrial America, the best and cheapest way to get the fibers from the field to the factory was to make unpaid Black people spend hours in the fields, bent over pulling cotton from the plants in the ground. At the end of the Civil War in 1865, Georgia's Black population accounted for 44 percent of all the state's residents.[19] Despite making up nearly half of the state's people, African Americans were 0 percent of the state's voters. You can see how the civic engagement of African Americans would threaten the state's status quo. Hence the fight that has unfolded over the past 157 years, up to and including Georgia's latest round of voter suppression legislation passed by Republicans in 2021, after the state's massive voter turnout defeated Trump and then elected Democrats Warnock and Ossoff to the U.S. Senate.

The size of the state's Black population was augmented by a significant twenty-first-century "reverse migration" as African Americans returned to the South, the land they'd left a century previously during the early twentieth-century Great Migration. One hundred years later, after America elected a Black president and African American professionals such as filmmaker Tyler Perry and actor Donald Glover showed it was possible to succeed while based in Southern cities like Atlanta, Black folks started coming home. This reverse migration is fundamentally transforming politics in Georgia and, by extension, it is fundamentally transforming politics in the entire country. From 2010 to 2018, seven of the ten counties with the fastest-growing Black populations in the United States were near Atlanta. From 2010 to 2016, the Atlanta area alone gained 251,000 Black people.[20]

From the standpoint of winning elections and building power, the task of increasing the number of Black folks voting sounds simple, and the math, on paper, is inescapable. From 2006 to 2012, Democrats in Georgia regularly lost statewide elections by an average of 230,000 votes, but nearly 1 million African Americans who were eligible to participate each cycle weren't voting.[21]

Politically, the destination was clear but the path was not. Everyone on the progressive side *wanted* to win elections in Georgia and turn the state blue. But beyond performing biennial linguistic gymnastics to try to find the elusive formulation that would convince more white voters to back Democrats, there really wasn't much of a plan. Politicians and their consultants recycled the same tried and untrue tactics year after year, with predictable—and pathetic—results.

It's not that *nobody* knew what to do. As early as the 1980s, Jesse Jackson had described the political potential of registering and mobilizing those ignored and overlooked potential voters; employing a David versus Goliath framework, he called them metaphorical "rocks just laying around."[22] Jesse picked up those rocks and executed that strategy in his Rainbow Coalition presidential runs, winning the Georgia Democratic primary in 1988. The strategic problem over the ensuing thirty years was that the people who traditionally run and fund campaigns—the people former Atlanta mayor Andrew Young once called "smart-ass white boys"—were the ones who didn't know what to do. Stacey Abrams is not a smart-ass white boy, and she had a detailed, data-driven plan.

The carefulness of Stacey's plan was evident in the level of detail in her document. As the leader of the Democrats in the State House, she had meticulously recorded her work relating to all the aspects of governing and power building in her first two years as minority leader (2010–12), showing the increase in the number of bills drafted in 2012 (20, up from just one prior to her tenure), press releases issued (134, up from 10), and town halls held (44, twice as many as the prior session's 20). She had pinpointed the exact number of votes in statewide elections, and the Democratic margin of defeat (the margin was 258,851 in 2010; down from 418,675 in 2006). And she had carefully analyzed the pool of potential voters—the rocks just laying around—identifying 1,041,000 unregistered people of color.

Her plan was rooted in reality and tailored to the specific challenges involved in a long-term effort to transform the state. At that time, in 2012, the gerrymandered maps adopted by the Republican-controlled legislature projected that Democrats would win just 56 of the 180 seats in the State House, giving Republicans the two-thirds majority necessary to pass constitutional amendments just as their Confederate predecessors had done when they reentered the Union and destroyed Reconstruction after the Civil War. Stacey faced the facts of the Democrats' difficult position and crafted a surgical and focused plan that targeted ten districts, with the objective of picking up at least five seats, to get to sixty-one and thwart the two-thirds goal of the Republicans. For each of the ten targeted seats, she'd identified the exact percentage of votes Democrats had historically received in that district, as well as the specific percentage of the electorate composed of Black and Latino potential voters.

Her analysis of the Georgia electorate and electoral trends led her to assert on Slide 14 of her twenty-six-page PowerPoint deck that "Bottom Line: Georgia Is Blue." Remember, this was in 2012 and such a proclamation was a radical and, to many, ridiculous assertion. Slide 14 further spelled out that "in presidential contests, the Democratic growth from 2004 to 2008 (477,968) was 3.5 times larger than Republican growth (134,503)." Rather than make pie-in-the-sky pronouncements that might entice fickle donors, Stacey presented a sober plan offering steady and methodical gains—toward a total of sixty-one seats in 2012, seventy in 2014, seventy-seven in 2016. Sure enough, the number of Democrats grew over the decade to seventy-seven by 2021—the goal Stacey targeted a decade before. As of this writing, Georgia's House Democrats are just fourteen seats away from a majority, and picking up those seats will be a core component of the Liberation Battle Plan for the 2022 election, with Stacey Abrams at the head of the Democratic ticket.

One critical function of a plan is to help assess and inventory the capacity of your forces. What Stacey's landscape scan revealed was that Georgia needed a stronger civic engagement infrastructure, with an anchor organization capable of turning population trends and demographic potential into tangible votes and real political power. Through her work as the top Democrat in the state House of Representatives, Stacey had built one important piece of the infrastructure in terms of fortifying the political arm of House Democrats, but they needed more if they were going to truly transform the state. Recognizing the hole in the landscape, Stacey set about filling it by creating the New Georgia Project (NGP) in 2013. Again, a hallmark of the organization was a detailed, data-driven plan.

NGP's 2014 prospectus stated that its focus was "in six main areas of the state—the Greater Atlanta region and the counties that contain the smaller cities of Macon, Augusta, Savannah, Albany, and Columbus"—the places in the state where the reverse migration of African Americans was upending the traditional electoral balance of power. While the New Georgia Project is a nonpartisan 501(c)(3) organization, it just so happened that democratizing the electorate in a racist state and making the voting population look like the state's population created conditions where the racists didn't always win.[23] Over the next several years, NGP would play a pivotal role in turning demographic change into electoral power.

BUILD STRONG CIVIC ENGAGEMENT ORGANIZATIONS

I'll admit that I'd never heard of Mannie Fresh and Trae tha Truth, but it turns out that they helped to forestall fascism in America.

Maybe I'm showing my age, but, historically, when one thinks of voter registration and civic engagement work, what comes to mind are images of organizers, wearing comfortable shoes and going door-to-door carrying a clipboard, voter registration forms, a list of registered voters, and a ballpoint pen to make notes about the conversations they have with the various voters. The twenty-first-century civic engagement work in Georgia was far more contemporary, hip, and cutting-edge.

In 2020, NGP built a website called Twitch the Vote that tapped into Twitch—the YouTube–like online streaming platform for video game enthusiasts—for a twelve-hour stream featuring live gaming and performances by people such as hip-hop artists Mannie Fresh and Trae tha Truth, as well as commentary from such prominent figures as Black astronaut Dr. Mae Jemison, actress Rosie Perez, and comedian Felonious Munk. Partners in the project included *Spawn on Me* (a Black-run podcast), Latinx in Gaming, and Sugar Gamers, a network of women who describe themselves as "a diverse group of trendsetters and aficionados within the worlds of technology, gaming, and the arts." This was not your grandparent's voter registration endeavor (it probably wasn't even your parents' voter reg drive).

Twitch the Vote registered nine thousand Georgians to vote *in one day*, in a state where Joe Biden defeated Donald Trump by 11,779 votes.[24]

NGP had started out as an idea in Stacey Abrams's head in 2013. In the subsequent years, under the exemplary leadership of Nsé Ufot, another Level 5 leader, NGP grew into an anchor organization and a dominant force for turning Georgia into the kind of multiracial democracy that Confederates have worked so hard to squash.

Since 2014, NGP has opened seven offices across the state, hired and deployed more than three thousand organizers and canvassers, and registered half a million voters across the 159 counties in the state.[25] As Aldon Morris highlighted in *Origins of the Civil Rights Movement*, organizations with deep ties in the community are essential to success, and NGP sank roots in cities and counties across the state, working with church leaders and local nonprofit organizations to recruit volunteers and get the word out about how and where to vote.

With the electorate significantly enlarged and diversified, it is not surprising that in Stacey's 2018 campaign, she received more votes than any Democrat who had ever run for office in the history of the state to that point. That electoral foundation served as a springboard for the 2020 triumph of Joe Biden and Kamala Harris and then the 2021 victories of Warnock and Ossoff.

As has too often been the case for the past 403 years, the people of color doing the work have had to do so with little or no help from the progressive powers that be. In 2020, Biden made no real effort to contest Georgia and was shocked that he won, admitting in a post-election speech, "We're still in the game in Georgia, although that's not one we expected."[26]

While Georgia is one of the Blackest states in America (African Americans make up 33 percent of the state's population as of the 2020

Census), the recent electoral breakthroughs for Democrats would not have been possible without the full spectrum of the rainbow. In particular, over the past decade the state's Asian American and Latino populations grew significantly, creating the conditions for the electoral revolution of 2020 and 2021. The number of Latinos in Georgia increased by 31.6 percent, from 2010 to 2020, and they currently make up 10 percent of the state. Within that same decade, "the number of Asians in the state jumped by more than 200,000 people, a 54.8 percent increase," as explained in a *New York Times* article.[27] Asians now make up 4.4 percent of the state population.[28]

Not surprisingly, one person who, early on, recognized the electoral implications of this demographic revolution was Stacey Abrams. NBC News journalist Kimmy Yam described in a 2021 article how Stacey's work with the Asian American community "stretches back more than a decade. Organizers and leaders in the state recall how she would regularly show up to AAPI [Asian American and Pacific Islander] events and, as the state's House minority leader from 2011 to 2017, appear on Radio Korea to inform the state's Korean population of what was going on under the Gold Dome."[29] Stacey's leadership under the Gold Dome of the state Capitol was complemented by Asian American community organizing outside the dome and across the state. Groups such as Asian Americans Advancing Justice, Asian American Advocacy Fund, and National Asian Pacific American Women's Forum have reached out to potential Asian American voters in recent years and talked to tens of thousands of voters in multiple different languages.

The seeds planted in the prior decade bore fruit in 2020 when Asian American voters turned out in historic numbers. According to an analysis by two of the country's leading academic experts, UC Riverside professor Karthick Ramakrishnan and Pomona College professor Sara Sadhwani, the Asian American vote in Georgia increased by 84 percent over its 2016 levels, a leap of 61,000 people, nearly six times larger than Biden's margin of victory.[30]

A powerful testament to the diversity of the movement in Georgia is the fact that the person who replaced Stacey in the state legislature was a Vietnamese American woman—Bee Nguyen. Nguyen is running for the office of secretary of state in 2022, and may well be on a Democratic ballot with Stacey Abrams for governor and Senator Raphael Warnock (who is up for reelection in 2022).

As important as the Asian American community has been in Georgia politics, in terms of the sheer size of its numbers, the Latino population is even larger. There are four hundred thousand eligible Latino voters in Georgia, and the state's civic engagement groups have steadily worked to transform this potential into power. Groups such as Mijente PAC and the Georgia Latino Alliance for Human Rights reported that in the weeks leading up to the January 2021 runoff elections for the U.S. Senate seats, they contacted nearly every registered Latino voter in the state—more than three hundred thousand people—"knocking on more than 310,000 doors amid a pandemic, calling more than 257,000 cell phones and landlines, and sending more than 376,000 texts."[31] Additionally, the national voter registration organization Voto Latino registered 48,000 people in the state, mainly Latinos, to vote in 2020.[32]

In a January 2021 article, NBC reporter Suzanne Gamboa chronicled the work that resulted in such a large Latino voter turnout, writing that the "numbers left no doubt among local and national Latino activists—as well as their financial backers—that something important had happened in Georgia, and that the years-long struggle to turn out Latino voters for Democratic candidates yielded results." Gamboa went on to add, "Leaders of the many Latino groups that descended on the state, along with Georgia Latino community groups, said there was a concerted, cooperative and multicultural effort to mobilize the estimated 377,000 Latinos in Georgia that are eligible to vote."[33]

———

What facilitated the historic and transformative victories in Georgia was the organizational infrastructure built over six steady years by Stacey, Nse, Leslie Small of America Votes, Aisha Yaqoob Mahmood of the Asian American Advocacy Fund, Susi Durán and Christine Senteno of Poder Latinx, and many, many other activists and organizers. The strength and resilience of the Georgia operation was on display in late 2020 and early 2021 when it withstood the full force of Republican opposition—including a furious and frantic Donald Trump trying to

suppress and discard Democratic votes as well as deep-pocketed conservative donors dumping half a billion dollars into the state to support
the incumbent Republican senators—as control of the Senate hung in
the balance.

Stacey reflected on the groundwork that had been laid in an exten-
sive *New York Times* essay published in February 2021 (co-authored by
Lauren Groh-Wargo, her campaign manager and CEO of Fair Fight
Action):

> Organizing is the soul of this work. Building progressive gov-
> erning power requires organizing. At its most basic, organiz-
> ing is talking to people about important issues, plus moving
> them to take collective action. Labor unions and groups like the
> N.A.A.C.P. are among the oldest examples of institutional orga-
> nizing models. Grassroots organizing pulls in individuals who
> see their interests being served. The most effective organizing
> for political revolution answers the question, How do we make
> change? . . .
>
> We cultivated a new generation of political operatives, orga-
> nizers and fund-raisers from the very start. Stacey intention-
> ally hired staff that looked like the diverse state of Georgia, and
> we augmented their work with a robust internship program.
> Year-round staff members, interns and fellows worked on the
> legislative session, learning the policy issues that affected Geor-
> gians. And every two years, we hired even more young people
> for the election cycle, training them to run campaigns, guide
> communications and organize in the legislative districts where
> we knew we could one day win but also where losing was highly
> likely. This new class of operatives came from every region
> of the state, carrying the concerns of their communities with
> them.[34]

The seeds of the strong showings and success in 2018, 2020, and
2021 were planted years earlier as Stacey and others patiently plotted
and planned, playing a savvy and sophisticated political long game
that is still paying off for Liberators and continues to offer great promise for the future.

PLAY THE LONG GAME

DuBose Porter had no idea that his decision in 2013 would—eight years later—end up dealing a decisive blow to a white nationalist president and his enablers, unlocking the spigot for trillions of dollars that would benefit tens of millions of Americans. An unassuming, older white lawyer, businessman, and former Georgia state legislator who had served in the State House from 1982 to 2011, Porter is not who you'd send from central casting for a key leadership role during the Obama era in the state that was home to Martin Luther King, Reverend Joseph Lowery, Reverend C.T. Vivian, Ella Baker, John Lewis, and many, many more Black civil rights leaders.

But Stacey Abrams was playing the long game, and in 2013 she thought Porter should be the chair of the Georgia Democratic Party. She understood the importance of having a revived, engaged, and active state party if Democrats were going to build the kind of statewide infrastructure necessary to compete in and win elections in future years. The savvy and sophistication of the state's Democratic Party was also strategic for another very simple reason: there is no limit on the amount of money a donor could give to the party. In a world where those who hold the most wealth generally cling to conservative public policies that facilitate their clinging to their many millions of dollars, the role of the much smaller number of progressive millionaires is vital. For those handful of progressive donors who were willing to invest significant large sums in Georgia, having a smart and dependable partner in charge of the state party apparatus was critical to the long-term plan.

So, in 2013, while several of the state's Democratic power brokers backed a different candidate for the chair position, Abrams threw her support behind Porter, helping him win a surprising victory in an election that was described as "a rebuke of powerful party leaders." [35] Over the next several years, Porter and Abrams went to work bringing order and discipline to the Democratic Party in Georgia, a key vehicle for progressive power in the state. By 2018, the state party had indeed been revived, opening up fifteen field offices and hiring 150 staffers across the entire state, laying the foundation for Abrams's historical gubernatorial run. [36]

Nikema Williams *is* from central casting for a leading role in a Georgia political production. A smart, savvy, energetic, personable, warm and engaging Black woman, Nikema is now a U.S. congresswoman, having become the successor to John Lewis after his death in 2020. Prior to winning elected office, she had worked with Stacey as a nonprofit leader and a volunteer with the state party. With Stacey's encouragement, Nikema ran for and won a seat in the State Senate in 2017, and then, when Porter stepped aside, Nikema contended for chair of the Democratic Party of Georgia in 2019, prevailing and becoming the first woman and first person of color to head the state party. As chair, she was perfectly positioned to build on the foundation that was laid in Stacey's gubernatorial bid and had activated volunteers and supporters across the state.

The fact that Raphael Warnock is now a U.S. senator is also the result of the Georgia long game. The Warnock for Senate bandwagon was very, very, very late in formation. Very. When I tried to raise money for his candidacy in March of 2020 with my co-workers at Democracy in Color, it was difficult to generate interest for a little-known Black man in a seemingly red state, and we were only able to raise $391 for him. Later that year, in June 2020, I co-hosted a fundraiser for him and it was still a struggle to wrest $30,000 from major donors who were far more enamored with white candidates in whiter states. In the summer of 2020, some prominent San Francisco fundraisers went so far as to organize an event for a dozen Senate candidates across the country, but they left Warnock out (while including white Georgia Senate candidate Jon Ossoff). By July 1, 2020, Warnock had raised $4 million, and his team was glad to have scraped that much together. At the same time, white Democrat Amy McGrath, who was running for U.S. Senate in Kentucky, had raised $47 million—ten times Warnock's haul.[37]

Reverend Warnock is a minister, as are both of Stacey Abrams's parents, and as was my grandfather, Reverend A.R. Cochran. The Bible says that "faith is the substance of things hoped for, the evidence of things not seen." Stacey Abrams had faith in Reverend Warnock years before his barrier-busting win in January of 2021. When, as a new and unknown author, I was trying to corral people to lend their names and reputations to my first book in 2015, Stacey suggested I seek out Reverend Warnock, thinking that his endorsement might age well (and I was blessed that he obliged and provided a very generous blurb). Stacey saw the reverend's political potential early and urged him in 2015 to declare for the Senate seat coming up for election in 2016. Concluding that 2016 was not his year, he passed on that political bid and focused on his work preaching the gospel at Ebenezer Baptist Church, regularly reading from the Bible that says that good things come to those who wait. By 2020, Warnock was done waiting and jumped into the race. With his and Ossoff's victories, good things have come to all of us who waited.

––––––

While few in national politics saw the potential of or believed in the winnability of Georgia in 2020, Abrams, Williams, and their partners and allies rolled up their sleeves and continued to do the work that the people who controlled the biggest checkbooks wouldn't invest in. Because of that work, because of their keeping the eye on the prize of a long game that required thinking through who should chair the party eight years earlier, the Georgia Democratic machine defeated Donald Trump and flipped control of the Senate to the Democrats.

After the Census results came out in 2021 showing that Georgia is truly on the precipice of becoming a "majority-minority" state with people of color making up 48 percent of the state's population, Richard Fausset of the *New York Times* clearly grasped the historical and future significance of the trend. In an August 2021 article he wrote, "Georgia, a state where white supremacy was for decades enshrined in law and custom, has seen a dramatic boom in ethnic and racial diversity in the last decade, a trend that is already having a profound effect on the politics of both the state and the nation."[38]

––––––

Gone with the Wind is set in Georgia. The story's fictional plantation, Tara, is in Clayton County, near where the book's author Margaret Mitchell grew up. When Jesse Jackson ran for president in 1984, he liked to say that "the hands that once picked cotton can now pick presidents." The population of Clayton is now 73 percent Black, and they are all free Black people. In 2020, Joe Biden got 85 percent of the vote in Clayton, his strongest showing in the entire state and 17,246 more

votes than Hillary Clinton had received in that county in 2016. Biden
won Georgia by just 11,779 votes.[39] The hands that had once picked cotton had in fact picked a president.

In urging congressional passage of voting rights legislation in 1957,
Dr. King said, "Give us the ballot, and we will transform the South."
As King prophesied, securing the right to vote for people of color is
transforming the South and, by extension, the country. This reality is
unfolding not only in Georgia but across the South and Southwest, the
land that was once the Confederacy and the region that once belonged
to Mexico. One of the states that has had the most success in transforming a formerly Confederate-aligned region is a place that has gone
on a similar decade-long journey as Georgia—the state of Arizona.

8

Arizona: "You Tried to Bury Us. You Didn't Know We Were Seeds"

First there were seven. Then 50. Then thousands of people, mostly Latino and many undocumented, who held a vigil on the lawn outside of the Arizona State Capitol in the spring of 2010, praying that Gov. Jan Brewer would not sign an anti-immigrant bill, the most punitive in generations. . . . Arizona Republicans no doubt hoped the law would chase out every immigrant, documented or undocumented. Some did leave. But many more stayed, determined to turn their fear and anger into political power.
—Alejandra Gomez and Tomás Robles Jr., "How to Turn Anger and Fear into Political Power," *New York Times*, December 21, 2019

Before becoming Arizona's first governor in 1861, John Baylor was an editor of a newspaper called *The White Man*. Baylor came to the role of co-founding such a paper easily and logically, having spent much of his adult life organizing white men to shoot and kill Native Americans and any people who dared to threaten the institution of slavery.[1]

One particularly noteworthy accomplishment occurred in 1860, when Baylor and some of his friends killed several Comanche Indians, cut the hair and skin off the tops of the skulls of their victims, and carried the scalps back to town, where they were hung from clotheslines stretched between buildings. The townspeople then danced in celebration underneath the blood-stained ropes during festivities fondly referred to as a "scalp dance."[2]

In August 1861, four months into the Civil War, Baylor helped win a key military battle in the land west of Texas and promptly declared himself governor of Arizona. Historian Megan Kate Nelson affirmed the strategic significance of Baylor's actions, writing in her account of that period, "There was no question that Arizona Territory was essential to the Confederacy's plans to reach California, and John Baylor had just cleared the way. He was the vanguard of Confederate manifest destiny."[3]

So that was Arizona's first governor.

———

Arizona's seventeenth governor, Evan Mecham, was elected in 1986 and then promptly set about trying to ensure that the state would only observe holidays honoring white people. After decades of people's organizing and advocacy, the United States Congress had finally established a federal holiday honoring Martin Luther King in 1983, but Meacham did not think Arizona should comply. Although the previous governor had signed an executive order establishing King's birthday as an Arizona state holiday, one of Mecham's first acts as governor upon taking office in 1987 was to rescind that order. He explained to a group of African Americans that King did not "deserve" a holiday, adding, "You folks don't need another holiday. What you folks need are jobs."[4]

It turns out that the country had changed a bit since the Civil War, however, and Mecham's racist recalcitrance about honoring King set off a firestorm of controversy, resulting in a national boycott of Arizona and the cancellation of conferences and events, draining millions of dollars from the state's economy. The majority of Arizona voters were resolute in their racism, however, opting to reject a 1990 statewide referendum to establish a King holiday in the state.[5]

Ultimately, Arizonans proved to love football more than racism. In 1990, the National Football League had selected the city of Tempe, Arizona, to host the 1993 Super Bowl. But after Arizona failed to establish a King holiday, the NFL gave that honor to Pasadena, California, instead. In 1992, the majority of voters had a change of heart and finally decided, five years after Mecham's initial obstruction, they would be just fine not working and getting paid on the day Dr. King was born (and four years later, Arizona did host the Super Bowl).[6]

So that was Arizona's seventeenth governor.

———

Arizona's twenty-second governor, Republican Jan Brewer, signed the law that lit the flames that fueled the movement that toppled Trump.

Brewer's tenure as governor of Arizona, from 2009 to 2015, was dominated by right-wing Republican Russell Pearce, who was a powerful state senator when she took office. Pearce was a proud white American who wanted to preserve the blessings of America for white people. Early in his time in the state legislature, he fondly recalled the 1950s mass deportation program dubbed "Operation Wetback" and expressed his admiration for the government's actions at that time, which resulted in the deportation of more than a million people.[7] Most infamously, Pearce is known for Arizona Senate Bill 1070—the "Show Me Your Papers" law—which he sponsored and championed in 2010.

The United States has a long history of asking non-white people for their papers. In a country that, from its inception, restricted citizenship to "free white persons," everyone who was not free and white has been treated as suspect from the get-go. The Constitution itself codifies the requirement for Black people to show their papers to white people. Specifically, Article IV, Section 2, Clause 3—the Fugitive Slave Clause, passed in 1787—says, "No person held to Service or Labour in one State, under the Laws thereof, escaping into another, shall, in Consequence of any Law or Regulation therein, be discharged from such Service or Labour, but shall be delivered up on Claim of the Party to whom such Service or Labour may be due."

I'm a lawyer, so let me translate. What the clause says is that if you come across a runaway slave, you gotta return him or her to the white person who owned that Black body. That's what "shall be delivered up" means. To enforce that law, the police could at any point in time force any Black person to produce papers proving that they were free.

Except sometimes it didn't work out the way the white nationalists intended. One of the realities of American racism is that, to many white people, all Black people look alike. During slave days, this tendency came in handy to Black folks fleeing captivity.

When the great nineteenth-century leader Frederick Douglass escaped from slavery in 1838, he "borrowed papers from a retired black sailor identifying him as a free man," because "it was the custom in the State of Maryland to require the free colored people to have what were called free papers. In these papers the name, age, color, height, and form of the freeman were described, together with any scars or other marks upon his person which could assist in his identification." [8] During the period of the Underground Railroad—a network of routes and houses by which Harriet Tubman and others helped people flee slavery—Douglass made his way to freedom via an *overground* railroad of an actual train traveling from Baltimore to Philadelphia. In his book *My Escape from Slavery*, Douglass described the harrowing moment of truth when asked for his papers by the conductor of the train:

> The conductor came into the negro car to collect tickets and examine the papers of his black passengers. This was a critical moment in the drama. My whole future depended upon the decision of this conductor. Agitated though I was while this ceremony was proceeding, still, externally, at least, I was apparently calm and self-possessed. He went on with his duty— examining several colored passengers before reaching me. . . . I drew from my deep sailor's pocket my seaman's protection as before described. The merest glance at the paper satisfied him, and he took my fare and went on about his business. This moment of time was one of the most anxious I ever experienced. Had the conductor looked closely at the paper, he could not have failed to discover that it called for a very different-looking person from myself, and in that case it would have been his duty to arrest me on the instant.[9]

At the dawn of the twenty-first century, Russell Pearce thought crafting the type of "Show Me Your Papers" law used to control and corral Black people in the eighteenth and nineteenth centuries was a wonderful way to spend his time in the Arizona state legislature. Pearce held himself out as a religious person—a "devout Mormon"— and a "family man." [10] On Sundays, he would go to church to pray and commune with other religious people who embraced the values of neighborly love and family cohesion. During the week, he crafted legislation that put Arizona police in the position of going after people of color, mainly from Mexico, without "legal" immigration status. His proposed bill, SB 1070, was little more than a twenty-first-century

continuation of the practice of the police tracking down and appre-
hending Black people fleeing slavery—the "illegals" of their day.

Separated by centuries, the spirit was similar, and the practical effect was the same—putting the state's resources behind law enforcement so that police could stop people of color on the street, ask them
for their papers, and if their papers were not "in order," then arrest
them and ship them off, often breaking up families in the process.

SB 1070 fit squarely in the long line of laws—starting with the
Black Laws of the 1600s—that have been rooted in white fears of people of color. If one is afraid of people of color, in general, and of increasing numbers of people of color in one's state, in particular, then Pearce
and Arizona's twenty-first-century Confederates had every reason to
be fearful.

Over the two decades prior to the introduction of Pearce's bill, the
Latino population in Arizona had steadily increased, growing nearly
threefold from 688,338 people in 1990 to 1.3 million in 2000 and
1.9 million in 2010, fully 30 percent of the entire state population (the
2020 Census shows there are now nearly 2.2 million Latinos in Arizona, 30.7 percent of the total population). As the Latino numbers were
zooming up, the white numbers were tumbling down from 78 percent
of all Arizonans in 1990 to just 58 percent in 2010 (the 2020 Census
data shows whites are now 54 percent of the population).[11] So you can
see why they wanted to identify, round up, and deport as many non-
white people as possible.

To be clear, for all the attention Pearce's legislation paid to immigration status and the attendant paperwork, the real issue was whiteness, as has been the case since the Confederates started newspapers
called *The White Man* and launched a Civil War to defend the right of
white men and women to buy and sell people of color. The hypocrisy
of Pearce and his peers is laid bare by the fact that the third largest
racial grouping in the state is Native Americans.[12] There are more indigenous people in Arizona than African Americans or Asian Americans, and the state is home to one of the largest populations of Native
people in the country.[13] The concentration of Native Americans in the
western part of this continent is a direct consequence of the "manifest
destiny" policy justifying the westward expansion of the United States
that drove indigenous tribes farther and farther from their original

homelands. (This was the kind of work Arizona's first governor John Baylor carried out with such bloody gusto that it caught the attention and admiration of the leaders of the Confederacy, who wrote that Baylor was "deserving of high praise" for his work "securing to the Confederacy a portion of the territory formerly common to all the States but now forming a natural appendage to our Confederate states, opening a pathway to the Pacific.").[14]

One might think that the notably large concentration of Native Americans in Arizona would present a staggering logical and moral contradiction to politicians ostensibly concerned about what they call "illegal immigration." Taken to its logical conclusion, legislation such as the SB 1070 Show Me Your Papers law would actually empower Native Americans to demand that white Arizonans show *their* papers justifying their presence on land that was stolen from its original inhabitants. But such has not been the conduct of politics in Arizona (or America). From the scalp dances of the first governor to the seventeenth governor's efforts to restrict state holidays so that they only honor white people to Jan Brewer's signing of Pearce's SB 1070, Arizona's political leaders have consistently carried on the Confederate cause of championing and protecting the interest of white people.

Despite passionate pleas from people of color about the devastating impact SB 1070 would have on their families, the Arizona Legislature, at a point when Democrats had historically small numbers in both chambers, passed the punitive measure. On April 23, 2010, Governor Jan Brewer signed it into law.

But, once again, the oppressors underestimated the oppressed. In a similar fashion to how the civil rights movement called a generation of young people to action and activism with the rise of leaders like John Lewis, Jesse Jackson, Ella Baker, Fannie Lou Hamer, Dolores Huerta, Yuri Kochiyama, and many others, the attacks on Latinos and immigrants in Arizona in the twenty-first century catalyzed an entire generation of organizers, leaders, and public servants. The adoption of SB 1070 unleashed a national furor, galvanized a multiracial generation of activists and ultimately led to both Pearce's own political downfall and that of his ideological soulmate, Donald Trump. In large part because of SB 1070, Arizona became the first state to put the first nail in the political coffin of Trump's presidency on election night 2020.

That evening, after Arizona was called for Biden, Phoenix-area Democratic congressman Ruben Gallego tweeted, "The children of SB 1070 ten years later grew to change Arizona. You tried to bury us, you didn't know we were seeds and we would grow to fight for Arizona." [15]

INVEST IN LEVEL 5 LEADERS—JOHN LOREDO

On the day Joe Biden became president of the United States, he placed a bust of Cesar Chavez in a prominent position in the Oval Office. Chavez, the leader of the United Farm Workers union (UFW) from the 1960s until his death in 1993, was a civil rights movement legend and an iconic figure to Latinos across the country. UFW is an activist labor union that has been an anchor organization in the Latino struggle for justice and equality, especially in the 1960s and 1970s. Coretta Scott King, widow of Martin Luther King and a woman who knew a thing or two about civil rights leadership, said, "Cesar Chavez challenged the tyrants, organized the working poor, and became a threat. . . . He is a genius of his people, and their union, the farmworkers union, is a hero union." [16]

For Biden, winning Arizona had been critical to victory, and one of the key architects of the Arizona civic engagement operation that defeated Trump in Arizona was John Loredo—a Level 5 leader who was a student and mentee of Chavez.

When John's aunt Barbara was a high school student in 1972, she wanted to drop out of school and go join Chavez, Dolores Huerta, and the UFW movement. Barbara's father was having none of it, and, undaunted by Chavez's celebrity status, he summoned the legendary leader to their home. During the meeting, Barbara's dad said he was against his teenager leaving to join the cause, and that the only way he'd allow it was if Chavez became her legal guardian, thinking that would end the matter. A few days later, Chavez did indeed become her guardian, and Barbara went to live with the movement activists at the UFW headquarters in California. For many years, she was the only person allowed to cook for Chavez because of security concerns that someone would try to poison the controversial civil rights leader. [17]

As a child, John would go spend summers in the 1970s with his aunt Barbara, Chavez, and the movement leaders at the headquarters, located in the Tehachapi Mountains in Southern California (the site, Nuestra Señora Reina de la Paz—known as "La Paz"—is now a national monument, and Chavez is buried there).[18] John describes the experience as follows:

> We'd go to visit my aunt in my aunt's trailer. There would be Cesar working in his office, and Dolores, and everybody else, like a commune. They grew their own food. They had their own school. It was a beautiful place. So for me, those values really got instilled in me from a very early age through organized labor on the farm. I started organizing when I got into community college, working with the farmworkers union here in Arizona. We would organize actions and we were involved in the Bruce Church Lettuce boycott and doing a variety of different actions. I would do press for Cesar when he'd come to town and we would do all of these organizing activities.[19]

Imbued with movement values and politics at a young age, John went on to attend Phoenix College, where he became an activist and a leader in politics, social change, and racial justice. In college, he was elected president of the activist Latino student organization MEChA (Movimiento Estudiantil Chicano de Aztlán). He also became the president and founding member of the LULAC Young Adult Council (LULAC stands for League of United Latin American Citizens). As many community-based Latino activists did at the time, he gravitated toward the movement led by the UFW, organizing protests, rallies, and boycotts across Arizona and the Southwest.

Historically, civil rights and social justice advocates have organized marches *to* the state Capitol where, on the outside looking in, they make demands on the powers that be. John helped take the movement to the next level, applying his organizing skills to the challenge of winning elections. Just seven years out of college, he was able to march *inside* the Arizona State Capitol and occupy an office, not as a protester, but as a member of the state legislature.

Organizing is organizing, whatever the setting, and John applied the lessons learned from working with Chavez to building power in a government building where people had historically been hell-bent on keeping farmworkers, immigrants, and people of color from influencing public policy and priorities. His work in the state Capitol paid off in 2002 when he was elected house minority leader, becoming the leader of all the Arizona Democrats in the state House of Representatives.

Apparently there's something about being the top Democratic legislator in a red state that produces especially effective leaders. Some of it is certainly attributable to the creativity and ingenuity that comes from having to fight against bigger and better-resourced opponents. As Stacey Abrams likes to joke about her time as minority leader of the Georgia State House, "I've been a minority for a long time, and I'm very good at it." There is truth in the humor, however, and being in the political minority brings into sharp relief the necessity for a sophisticated plan to turn political dreams into reality.

During his tenure in the state legislature (from 1997 to 2004), John was exposed firsthand to what power looks like and what was required to attain and wield it. As an elected official with movement roots, he carefully cultivated an inside/outside strategy of ratcheting up the pressure with "street heat" from grassroots activists on the outside as a way of increasing the incentives and motivation for those inside the Capitol building to focus on the needs of people of color and low-income communities. In his final two years as minority leader, he had a rare opportunity to work with a Democratic governor, after Janet Napolitano won a surprising and exceedingly narrow victory in 2002 to become the first Democrat elected governor in Arizona in twenty years. John worked with Napolitano to make some headway on progressive issues, but it was clear that more was needed. Much more.

In the face of the ferocious—and quite popular—racism of Russell Pearce and others, John knew that the movement needed to do something different. In 2010, after Pearce had successfully jammed the SB 1070 "Show Me Your Papers" law through the legislature, John called together the leaders of several progressive organizations, sat them around a table, and bluntly asked, "Who's tired of getting your asses kicked?" From that meeting was born the coalition, organizations, and movements that would go on to transform Arizona politics over the next decade.

DEVELOP DETAILED, DATA-DRIVEN PLANS

What John was forcing the state's progressive leaders to do was to unflinchingly face the brutal facts of their powerless position. It turns out that such a "come to Jesus moment"—the realization that one is on the wrong path and must change direction—is a critical step in organizational development in many spheres of society, including the business world.

The concept of squarely facing up to a harsh and seemingly bleak predicament was popularized by Jim Collins's book *Good to Great*. In his research, Collins found that the most successful companies displayed a "distinctive form of disciplined thought in that they infused the entire process with the brutal facts of reality. You absolutely cannot make a series of good decisions without first confronting the brutal facts."[20] Collins called this "The Stockdale Paradox," the word "paradox" capturing the sense of optimism in the face of a dire situation. James Stockdale was a U.S. naval aviator who was captured and held as a prisoner of war for seven years during the Vietnam War. Collins describes how, when asked how he'd managed to endure the years of captivity, Stockdale began by talking about how those who were unrealistically optimistic did *not* make it out of the prison camp.

> They were the ones who said, "We're going to be out by Christmas." And Christmas would come, and Christmas would go. Then they'd say, "We're going to be out by Easter." And Easter would come, and Easter would go. And then Thanksgiving, and then it would be Christmas again. And they died of a broken heart. . . . This is a very important lesson. You must never confuse faith that you will prevail in the end—which you can never afford to lose—with the discipline to confront the most brutal facts of your current reality, whatever they might be.[21]

Collins had found that the most effective Level 5 leaders embodied this Stockdale paradox, confronted the brutal facts, and then developed detailed plans to transform the ugly reality in which they found themselves. That is exactly what John Loredo forced his fellow movement leaders to do. Here's how John described that initial 2010 meeting:

We kind of pulled everybody together and said, "Look, you know, raise your hands, I mean, literally raise a hand—who's tired of getting your asses kicked?" And everybody raised their hands. Then it's like, OK, then we've got to do something different. We have to pool our resources. We have to pool our money. We have to come up with, instead of having twenty-five different plans, we need to have one plan to win. And it needs to be based on a realistic assessment of what we can win based on the numbers and our capacity.[22]

John knew that Arizona progressives needed one unified, detailed, data-driven plan because he'd been to Arizona's neighboring state of Colorado and seen what was possible.

———

As occurred in California, where the browning of the populace created the conditions for the political transformation of a formerly red state (see chapter 10), Colorado's demographic revolution also paved the path for the journey from red to purple, if not blue. From 1990 to 2010, the size of Colorado's Latino population doubled, swelling by more than six hundred thousand people in a state where presidential contests were frequently decided by fewer than a hundred thousand votes.[23] As the Latino population in Colorado grew, the political power of the state's Confederate forces faded, and John Loredo was watching carefully.

Colorado's political transformation was accelerated by a compelling manifestation of the power of intersectionality. In Colorado in the 1990s, the fears that were stoked by Confederates had to do with sexual orientation. Similar to how many politicians throughout U.S. history sought to restrict citizenship to white people, politicians in the modern era have sought to restrict love to straight people. Multiple anti-gay propositions were placed on statewide ballots in Colorado by right-wing political leaders. One of those measures, 1992's Amendment 2, which prohibited cities from passing nondiscrimination policies to protect the LGBTQ+ community, made the wrong person mad, and as a result Colorado is now reliably blue.

Tim Gill is a gay man who got rich by inventing a desktop publishing software program in the 1980s. In 1992, he was content to write

computer code and stay out of politics, focusing on building his company, Quark. But when he saw employees in his own company proudly
displaying Amendment 2 bumper stickers, Gill took offense, and then
took action, creating the Gill Foundation. Over the past twenty-five
years, the Gill Foundation has directed nearly $400 million to gay
rights causes (Gill was one of the most important funders of the multiyear movement for marriage equality).[24]

By the early 2000s, Gill's political sophistication and expertise had
matured to the point where he understood the importance and possibility of transforming the composition of the state legislature that
supported so much anti-gay legislation. In 2004, he joined forces with
three other major Democratic donors (including now governor Jared
Polis), and, together, they developed a detailed, data-driven plan for
flipping the political balance of power in Colorado.

Their work was so successful that it captured significant national
media attention and became a model for other progressives across the
country. (My own foray to Colorado in 2006 to learn about their work
opened my eyes and inspired me to start talking to California donors
about creating what is now the California Donor Table.) In their 2010
book *The Blueprint: How the Democrats Won Colorado (and Why Republicans Everywhere Should Care)*, authors Adam Schrager and Rob
Witwer showed how "a network of united progressive organizations
helped make Colorado—until recently, a reliably Republican state—
a deep shade of blue."[25]

The same year that Arizona's progressive groups were trying to figure out how to best fight back against SB 1070, the Colorado model for
upending a state's political status quo was becoming well known. At
various national gatherings in 2010, John met some of the key leaders involved in the Colorado transformation. He listened closely, asked
questions, took notes, and learned a lot. What these leaders shared is
that they had identified three core components of success: (1) a nonprofit, nonpartisan coordinating coalition, or "table," where various
groups could sit together and align their respective civic engagement
efforts, avoiding duplication and maximizing synergy on voter registration and nonpartisan voter turnout work; (2) a more partisan advocacy table where groups could coordinate efforts to elect or defeat
specific candidates (people like the author of SB 1070); and (3) a donor

table where those with resources to spend could compare notes and align investments to make sure the right people and groups were being funded to do the work in the most important places.[26]

Another brutal fact facing the movement in Arizona was that they had little money. What the Colorado leaders told John was that Arizona activists had little money because they lacked a detailed plan—a data-driven analysis of the electoral landscape, an assessment of promising opportunities where progressives and Democrats could win races, and a methodical and realistic calendar and schedule showing which races to prioritize in which years. In short, Arizona's leaders lacked a roadmap that was sufficiently credible and inspiring to donors to attract the financial investment that could fuel the movement.

So when John summoned the movement leaders and activists to the "come to Jesus" meeting in 2010, "Jesus," in the Arizona situation, was a detailed, data-driven plan. They then set about developing just such a plan. Then they followed that plan. Then they began winning more and more elections. Then Donald Trump was no longer president, and Democrats were in control of the United States Senate.

What the data showed was that, just as was the case in Georgia, there were large numbers of people of color who did not participate in Arizona elections, and registering and mobilizing those people could have a significant impact on electoral outcomes.

The movement leaders identified where those pools of non-voters were and divvied up the responsibility of who would contact which voters in the various cities and counties. Maricopa County, where Phoenix is situated, is home to 62 percent of all the residents in the entire state of Arizona, and 1.4 million of the state's 2.3 million Latinos live in that county—which is a fancy way of saying that Maricopa is the motherlode.[27]

The plan the activists developed tasked the civic engagement groups with registering and staying in touch with Latinos in Maricopa and getting them out to vote. Another 14 percent of the state's population—and 16 percent of all Latinos—live in Pima County (home of Tucson). There, the movement organizations further extended the program of contacting and building relationships with eligible voters.

Armed with that information, the progressive leaders made biennial plans on which races made the most sense to target, given their available resources and the likelihood that the pool of non-voters could influence the election results if they were brought into the electoral mainstream.

In 2011, the anger at the "Show Me Your Papers" law met the analysis of a detailed, data-driven plan, and the incipient coalition trained its fire on its chief antagonist—State Senator Russell Pearce.

———

People keep underestimating the political popularity of white nationalism. In 1980, Ronald Reagan was thought to be too radical, but he won the White House. And as discussed at length in chapter 5, we are living through what is perhaps the apogee of white nationalism in the wake of the Trump Make America White Again movement. A similar underestimation occurred in Arizona in 2010 with Russell Pearce. Originally seen as an extremist gadfly who was far outside the mainstream, after the passage of SB 1070, Pearce was elevated to become president of the Arizona State Senate. No longer a fringe legislator, he was now the head man in charge, and progressives faced a moment of truth. Would they try to fight the powerful Pearce or would they shirk from the battle?

Martin Luther King described the mental calculus many establishment leaders engage in when deciding how to confront injustice and the leaders of a status quo that perpetuates that injustice:

> On some positions, cowardice asks the question, is it expedient? And then expedience comes along and asks the question, is it politic? Vanity asks the question, is it popular? Conscience asks the question, is it right? There comes a time when one must take the position that is neither safe nor politic nor popular, but he must do it because conscience tells him it is right.[28]

Faced with the growing political power of Pearce and his white nationalist movement, many cowards asked, "Is it expedient?" and then flinched and proceeded to "bend the knee" to Pearce, to use the *Game of Thrones* phrase for capitulating to a person in power. In a clear foreshadowing of her future role of refusing to fight for justice and equality in the U.S. Senate, Kyrsten Sinema, then a state senator, was a leader of the "don't rock the boat" approach to politics as far back as 2011. When activists began planning for how to fight back in the new climate, Sinema actively worked to stop the leaders who wanted to launch a recall election of Pearce. She even went so far as to threaten reprisals against the organizers of the recall.[29]

While Sinema was stepping into her role as the face and voice of cowardice, others on the front line of the fight realized that Pearce's ascendance was the perfect time to answer Dr. King's question, "Is it right?" In the words of movement leader Randy Parraz, architect of the Pearce recall:

> The term "threshold for injustice" refers to a tipping point, an accumulation of past injustices that cause someone to be outraged enough to shift from being a private citizen to a public actor. The threshold for injustice manifests the moment one feels compelled to stand up, speak out, or take action. In that moment, an internal transformation occurs that unleashes the courage, energy, and determination to pursue the pathway towards justice relentlessly. Each individual has their own threshold for injustice.
>
> Pearce's election as senate president was my "threshold for injustice" moment. In a matter of minutes, all my other professional interests faded. I knew I could not rest until Pearce was unseated.[30]

There is a reason movements are propelled by people who bear the brunt of injustice, as they usually have the least to lose. They are most equipped to simply ask, "Is it right?" Randy Parraz asked such a question, and then he did a detailed, deep data dive into how to most effectively fight back. In his book *Dignity by Fire*, he describes how he carefully examined voting patterns in Pearce's district and reached the conclusion that Pearce was far more vulnerable politically than people realized. Explaining how he went about developing a detailed, data-driven plan for securing the necessary signatures to initiate a recall election of Pearce, he wrote:

None of this seemed out of reach. I clicked on the voter registration counts to get a sense of the universe of voters by party.
As the numbers popped up on the screen, I about fell off my
chair. It read, "Registered Republicans—26,616. Registered
Democrats—18,345. Registered Other—21,616." I felt a jolt of
energy surge through my body. . . .

I could not believe that we had a universe of 39,961 registered Democrats and "Other" voters from which to collect 7,756
valid signatures. And because the voter file—a database accessible to the public that contains the voting history of each registered voter—could be easily purchased, we had access to the
names, addresses, and in some cases, phone numbers of close
to 40,000 registered voters in LD 18. We could take our petition
directly to voters' homes and avoid the awkwardness of standing out in front of stores and on street corners. If only one out
of every four voters we talked to signed the petition we'd easily
surpass 7,756 signatures.[31]

A meticulous analysis of past electoral results revealed that voter
turnout in Pearce's state legislative district was relatively low, and influencing a few thousand votes could tip an election outcome. The district was heavily Republican and there weren't enough Democrats in
it to win that legislative seat (a brutal fact), but it might be possible
to back a more moderate—less Confederate—Republican to take on
Pearce. The data, plan, and determination gave them the confidence to
tackle the challenge.

In *The Art of War*, Sun Tzu says, "The victorious army first realizes
the conditions for victory, and then seeks to engage in battle." That's
data analysis. Armed with the insight about the data in Pearce's district, the activists involved in the recall ended up gathering 18,315 signatures, and the recall was scheduled for November 8, 2011. In that
election the progressive movement helped a moderate Republican,
Jerry Lewis, run and defeat Pearce by a margin of just under three
thousand votes. It was the first recall of a state elected official in Arizona history.[32]

———

Social change entails an interplay between planning and products, dreams and results, inspiration and accomplishment, and that alchemy sprang to life after the defeat of Pearce. The progressive movement was energized; more groups and leaders signed up to participate; the ranks of those tired of getting their asses kicked grew as more and more people saw that the ass-kicking could be delivered, and not just received. As the activists who'd gotten their start fighting against SB 1070 gained experience and sophistication, they expanded their repertoire by incorporating spreadsheets, charts, and PowerPoint decks into their political arsenal. Using the tools of data analysis and strategic planning, they identified the path to power that they have carefully followed for the past decade.

By 2015, John Loredo was being asked to speak at the kinds of national donor conferences where he'd learned about the Colorado work, and this time, he had a detailed, data-rich plan of his own. By March of 2015, he was sharing a plan that analyzed and aggregated Census data on demographic trends, past election results, predictive partisanship scores of eligible voters, and statistical projections of future electoral behavior. And it was working. They found that their program—based on community-based canvassers knocking on doors and having conversations with potential voters, followed by phone calls to those households—increased the turnout of voters by 7 percent.

The planning the activists had done illuminated the path forward. They'd identified that early voting had increased in Arizona from 41 percent in 2004 to 77 percent by 2014.[33] Acting on that information, they continued to concentrate their efforts on encouraging more and more people to sign up for the Permanent Early Voter List, to the point where early voting numbers for Latinos increased fivefold to 450,000 by 2020.[34] The entire electoral apparatus was such a well-oiled machine that by the end of the decade, it could withstand both a global pandemic and an active assault on the electoral operations by the president of the United States.

By 2020, the commitment to refining and following a detailed, data-driven plan was so entrenched that the civic engagement organizations formed a specific entity, the Arizona Research Consortium, to focus dedicated time, energy, and resources on the critical task of planning and analysis. According to a report from Ian Danley, executive director of Arizona Wins and coordinator of a coalition of civic engagement groups in Arizona, the consortium is a "project years in the making." Danley further explained that the consortium served as a hub for much of the progressive movement by sharing the findings of research and studies about what forms of voter engagement were most effective, especially for Latinos and voters of color.[35]

Having a plan is necessary, but a plan alone is not sufficient. Just as in Georgia, the math highlighted the need for organizations and leaders to drive the movement down the road toward power and impact. Having the clearest and best directions for how to drive to your favorite destination means little unless you have a well-functioning vehicle to get you there. That is where another part of the Liberation Battle Plan comes into play. In Arizona, largely by necessity, they turned the keys to the civic engagement vehicles over to the young people.

BUILD STRONG CIVIC ENGAGEMENT ORGANIZATIONS— ONE ARIZONA AND LUCHA

High school students find their friends in different ways. Some of my closest friends were my basketball teammates (we actually "obtained" a key to our school gym and would head up there late at night to play fun but intense contests against each other that our sixteen-year-old selves called "a man's game," but I digress). Others discover shared interests such as performing and music. My wife met one of her lifelong friends, Tanya Shaffer, during the California Summer with Shakespeare program (Cal Shakes!). For other high school students, the stakes are much more intense and the environment much more dangerous. In Arizona in 2010, teenagers Montse (pronounced "Mohnt-say") and Alejandra became buddies by joining protests to keep their parents from being deported.

Montse Arredondo's mother, Belen Arredondo, was born and raised in Sinaloa, Mexico, and didn't have the kinds of citizenship papers that Russell Pearce wanted her to have. While pregnant and living in Tijuana, Belan unexpectedly ran into one of her uncles, who brought her to the United States to live. She settled in Phoenix, Arizona, and worked as a waitress and a domestic worker to make ends meet.[36]

In many ways, the Arredondo family was like a lot of other Latino families in Phoenix in the early 1990s. They quickly connected with their neighbors in the public housing complex where they lived as they all sought to make a way and raise families in a harsh and inhospitable state that didn't want them there in the first place. As Montse tells it, "We were a very tight-knit community, and we like to say we shared a backyard" (referring to the common area of the housing complex). The serenity of that community was shattered in 2010 by Pearce's attack on immigrants and the SB 1070 bill.

At a time when many of her classmates at Phoenix's North High School were joining clubs focused on activities such as photography, ceramics, and choir, Montse found her peer group among those fighting to keep their friends and family from being kicked out of the country. The place where they received their most meaningful education was not in any classroom at school, but rather the area surrounding the Arizona State Capitol building. As Montse became more and more of an activist, she moved from sharing a backyard with other residents of public housing in Phoenix to sharing the lawn outside the Capitol, where she registered people to vote as they gathered to appeal to the governor not to sign SB 1070.

After the state legislature passed the anti-immigrant measure in the spring, the bill went to the governor's desk, where Governor Brewer had to decide whether to sign or veto the controversial legislation. Seeking to connect with the Republican Brewer on a humanitarian level, a small group of activists went to the state Capitol building to stand outside and make a moral witness about the catastrophic impact that the law would have on them and their families. In the book *Prisms of the People*, authors Hahrie Han, Elizabeth McKenna, and Michelle Oyakawa describe what happened next:

> The vigil started with seven people. "By lunch [on Sunday, April 18], we were 30; by night 100. On Monday, 200; Tuesday, 300," Jeff [one of the organizers] remembered. . . . On April 22, the numbers swelled as local students staged mass walkouts to support the protest. Michele [another organizer] said, "[We knew that] if the vigil [was] not growing every twenty-four hours, it [was] dying. [So we had] to get [people] there. A whole

team of people was reaching out in the schools, in Latino businesses, and phone banking. . . .

Once the vigil began, they realized they could use it as a leadership training ground to build an immigrant rights movement in the state. They learned to ask more of the people who attended, instead of having them be just another body for a head count or media headline, as is often the case at protests. Through 114-degree heat, using ice cubes to cool their faces, young people and a group of undocumented women became the core of the vigil. . . . The three-month-long action became a crucible for learning, leadership development, organization building, and strategizing that laid the foundation for a broader immigrant rights movement in the state.[37]

Montse was one of the young people on that lawn in the 114-degree heat. When she was younger, Montse thought she might become a social worker, as she had been inspired by the example of the case worker who had helped her family when she was growing up. The SB 1070 experience opened her eyes to the need for structural change and the imperative to transform a system where so many people needed the help of social workers in the first place. The moral appeal of the vigil failed to influence the powers that be, and the young activists quickly came to understand that what they needed was real political power. "We realized," Montse said, "that we needed to get more young people activated, out there voting, and paying attention to what elected officials were doing."[38]

That realization led Montse to get involved with One Arizona, a coalition of groups working to transform Arizona's rapidly diversifying population into an influential electoral force. As the organization's website says, "In the wake of SB 1070, four immigrant rights organizations came together with the goal of registering 12,000 Latino voters. Shortly afterwards, One Arizona was born. Ten years later, One Arizona is made up of 23 organizations active all over Arizona."[39] Montse was present from the inception of One Arizona and went on to become the coalition's deputy director and, in 2018, executive director. In that role, Montse has provided leadership, support, and assistance to the burgeoning civic engagement ecosystem that has brought hundreds of thousands of people of color into an electorate that had historically been overwhelmingly white.

While protesting on the lawn of the Arizona State Capitol in 2010, eighteen-year-old Montse bonded with and learned from a young woman who then went on to help lead one of the largest and most effective organizations in the state.

———

A decade before meeting Montse, Alejandra Gomez's family felt the full fear that comes from being immigrants in a state where white leaders demonize and target immigrants of color. In response to California governor Pete Wilson's xenophobic, career-building policy spree in the early 1990s (see chapter 10), Alejandra's family had a difficult decision to make. As she describes the events that shaped her childhood, "I just remember my father bringing us into the living room and sharing with the family, 'I am going to be detained or deported if we do not leave California.' And as a child, listening to that and wondering what's going to happen to your hero, as a family, we decided that it was time to leave." [40]

The Gomez family concluded, in a cruel ironic twist, that the safest course of action was to move from California to Arizona to "escape" anti-immigrant politicians and policies. Little did they know they were going from the frying pan of the polite and soft-spoken xenophobia of Pete Wilson's California to the fire of the raw, fangs-bared racism of Russell Pearce's Arizona. Alejandra learned a lasting lesson—"You can't run from bad politicians, you can't run from bad policy," she says, adding, "You have to lean in and find your people, and fight." [41] One of the people Alejandra found was Montse. Another was Tomás Robles, with whom she partnered in creating an organization—Living United for Change in Arizona (LUCHA)—that is transforming Arizona politics and policy in dramatic fashion.

As Alejandra and Tomás explained in a 2019 *New York Times* piece, "How to Turn Anger and Fear into Political Power," the vigil "was a training ground for novice organizers like us who would stop by the snack table, gather clipboards and then head out to laundromats and convenience stores to register neighbors." Thousands of people were registered to vote by activists in the summer of 2010, and the activism did not stop there. "In the wake of the vigil," Alejandra and Tomás wrote, "we built an organization that serves as a political home for people of color. We talk to working-class families about the issues important to them and how to get involved in politics."[42]

LUCHA started with two employees: Alejandra and Tomás. By 2020, they had built the organization to forty-eight people with offices in three counties.[43] A marquee moment in Arizona's political evolution occurred in 2016 when LUCHA's leaders decided the time was right to run a statewide campaign to pass a ballot measure to raise the minimum wage, which was $8.05 an hour at the time, to $12 an hour. In their organizing and conversations in the community, that issue had risen to the top of the agenda, and they believed it was important to give people tangible reasons to vote as part of a voter mobilization strategy. As the LUCHA team described it, "We learned at listening sessions with our 2,600 members, whom we've cultivated through neighborhood teams and high school civics clubs, that they wanted us to fight for higher wages and paid family leave."[44]

Running statewide campaigns and ballot measures has historically been the province of white people. In *Brown Is the New White*, I devoted an entire chapter to the imperative of having "Fewer Smart-Ass White Boys" in charge of progressive political campaigns. I described the phenomenon at the time as follows:

> Even after eight years of a Black president, the Democratic Party is still largely dominated and controlled by White men. . . . The key people who decide how and where the Party's hundreds of millions of dollars are spent are White guys. . . . It matters because in order to get that kind of voter turnout and loyalty, you need to develop trust, and to develop trust you need profound insight into the hopes and dreams and conditions and concerns of the people you're trying to reach; generally, those who have the lived experience and shared culture with the people we want to vote and support our causes have deeper knowledge and understanding of the communities we need to engage. It matters because when we don't master the politics of race, we lose.[45]

Brown Is the New White came out in 2016, the same year that LUCHA decided to launch its minimum wage campaign (and, spoiler alert, the near-apartheid arrangement in terms of who runs and funds campaigns is little changed in the early years of the 2020s). Alejandra and Tomás ran directly into this cautious consultant mindset, as Arizona's smart-ass white boys belittled their idea of running a ballot measure. But these two had faced far greater threats and obstacles than contemptuous consultants, and they went ahead anyway. They described the opposition they faced to the authors of *Prism:*

> Tomás and Alex noted that some philanthropists, national network representatives, and even union leaders told them that raising the minimum wage in a statewide ballot measure was neither possible nor strategic. "People would tell us, like, this is not an issue in Arizona. 'Why don't you do an immigration one? Why aren't you doing criminalization, or voting?' Nobody cares, and nobody thinks in Arizona you could pass an initiative for $15 an hour, or raising the minimum wage, or whatever," Tomás said. . . .
>
> At every step of the campaign, Alex and Tomás were told that they should not work on minimum wage, that they could not win the campaign, and that they could not lead it. Alex and Tomás had to fight not only to run the campaign but also to do it on their terms, never certain about whether LUCHA would obtain the resources and support it needed in order for that to happen.[46]

Undaunted by the naysayers and proceeding with confidence from the steady success of several years of organizing in the early 2010s, they formed a formal ballot measure campaign organization, Arizonans for Fair Wages and Healthy Families, got the measure on the ballot, raised $4 million to support the campaign, and coordinated a full-fledged statewide campaign for the endeavor. Tomás and Alex served as campaign leadership for an entire statewide effort consisting of paid communications, voter mobilization, polling, and media relations. Just like the white boys had been doing for years. Except, unlike most of the campaigns run by Arizona's traditional consultants, this campaign won, garnering a full 58 percent of the vote in the same 2016 election and on the same ballot that Trump won the state's presidential contest.[47] As a result of their work, nearly 1 million people in Arizona saw their incomes increase.[48]

―――

Montse, Alejandra, Tomás, and a whole generation of activists who found each other during that 2010 vigil at the state Capitol continue to work hand in hand to this day. As Tomás and Alejandra wrote, "In less than a decade, many organizers who first cut their teeth fighting [SB 1070] are now lawmakers, campaign managers and directors of civic engagement groups like Mi Familia Vota and the Arizona Dream Act Coalition."[49] The One Arizona coalition headed by Montse does nonpartisan voter registration and education, expanding the pool of potential voters. A parallel, but legally separate, constellation, Arizona Wins, consists of advocacy organizations such as LUCHA, CASE Action Fund, and others who inform the people in the expanding voting universe about which candidates and issues are most likely to advance the cause of racial, economic, and social justice.

One Arizona began as an alliance of four organizations who came together in 2010 and set a goal of trying to register 12,000 people to vote. By 2018, the coalition had grown to two dozen groups that registered nearly 200,000 people to vote, and that expanded universe helped win a previously Republican-held U.S. Senate seat by just 56,000 votes. (Sadly, the winner of that seat, Democrat Kyrsten Sinema, has repeatedly betrayed the people who elected her, and LUCHA is spearheading efforts to find a better Democrat to run against her in 2024.)[50]

In 2020, the network of civic engagement groups encountered the existential threat of a global pandemic that required physical distancing at a time when face-to-face conversations were a cornerstone of civic engagement work. But the leaders were nothing if not resilient, turning first to scientists and epidemiologists and then to technology and digital tools to continue to connect and converse in a time of distance and disconnection. Together, they figured out how to safely continue organizing, and in 2020, they helped bring onto the voting rolls an additional 184,868 Arizonans.[51]

Over the past decade, many other young people in Arizona have answered the call of public service and decided that they should in fact be running the state that was trying to deport them and their families.

Raquel Terán also received her political baptism in the SB 1070 protest movement in 2010, where she learned "how important it was to vote, and to register my peers to elect people who wouldn't criminalize the migrant community." With a clear understanding of the importance of political power, Raquel first ran for State Senate in 2012, losing by just 113 votes. Undeterred, she continued to work with grassroots organizations, and ran again in 2018, this time winning her bid for a seat in the Arizona House of Representatives. In 2021, Raquel was elected chair of the Arizona Democratic Party.[52]

At the local level, Carlos Garcia, who founded Puente Human Rights Movement, an immigrant rights advocacy organization, ran for and won a seat on the Phoenix City Council in 2019.[53] Daniel Valenzuela had a similar journey, and his story is captured in Erin Mayo-Adam's book, *Queer Alliances*. Valenzuela's electoral story began in "2011, [when] one Latino youth group knocked on 72,000 doors in one district, increasing Latino turnout by 480 percent in the district—and elected Valenzuela to the Phoenix City Council in a seat never before held by a Latino person."[54]

A hallmark of the work of this new, vibrant, multiracial ecosystem of electoral activity is a level of cultural competence and expertise too often missing in progressive and Democratic politics. In recent years, the groups on the ground in Arizona and Georgia have shown the rest of the country how it's done. Or at least how it should be done. In 2020, while Georgia was holding "Twitch the Vote" parties with hip-hop stars, Arizona was organizing "Ridin' with Biden" car rally and parade events featuring mariachi bands and lowriders (and also attracting the participation of Julian Castro, the only Latino Democratic presidential candidate in 2020).

The Native American community in Arizona has also flexed its political muscles in meaningful ways. In addition to the moral authority that Native Americans wield, especially in a state spouting nonsense about illegal immigration, the Arizona Native community also has considerable political clout at the ballot box as a result of the development of strong civic engagement organizations. In 2020, organizations such as the Rural Arizona Project, the Inter Tribal Council of Arizona, One Arizona, Arizona Wins, All Voting is Local, and Instituto formed a Native Vote coalition to coordinate tribal outreach. New organizations such as Diné Citizens Against Ruining our Environment (CARE) and Diné Action were incubated and launched, and received support with running targeted ads, hiring and training staff, and sending 58,000 pieces of mail to Native households, including bilingual materials to members of the Navajo Nation. All of that organizing paid off. An Associated Press analysis of the 2020 election returns found that "voters in precincts on the Navajo and Hopi reservations in northeastern Arizona cast nearly 60,000 ballots in the Nov. 3 election, compared with just under 42,500 in 2016."[55] That's 17,500 additional Native votes cast in a presidential election decided by fewer than 11,000 votes.

The results of that decade of post–SB 1070 organizing and activism were on full display for the world to see on Election Day, November 3, 2020. These hundreds of thousands of Latinos *did* have papers. They had voter registration forms that gave them access to the ballot box. In 2020, they showed not only their papers, but their political power by casting their votes. In large numbers. By the hundreds of thousands. All told, in the 2020 election, organizations in the Arizona civic engagement ecosystem contacted 1.3 million voters and encouraged them to vote. When the votes were tabulated and exit poll data crunched, the picture that emerged showed that nearly 1 million people of color (915,000) cast ballots in Arizona in 2020, compared with 625,118 in 2016. Joe Biden received 154,265 more Latino votes in Arizona than Hillary Clinton received four years earlier.[56] Biden beat Trump in Arizona by 10,457 votes.

PLAY THE LONG GAME

On election night 2020, after Arizona was called for Biden, John Loredo took a moment to celebrate and posted his perspective on Facebook, writing:

> Sometimes you have to stand up and fight when all the odds are against you. This is year 10 of a 10 year plan to flip this state. It's been a very long and challenging road. Thank you to so many partners both locally and nationally who have been on this journey and in the fight with us. We couldn't have done it without you. The fight continues!

They had had to start small. Reflecting on the beginning of the journey, John said they realized back in 2010 that "it's going to take us a decade to get where we want to get, but we have to start small and really focus in on the areas we need to be—winning piece by piece by piece." [57] Just as the Georgia activists had a plan to methodically win seats in state legislative districts across the state, the Arizona activists followed their plan year by year, race by race, summing up and doubling down on what worked while discarding what didn't. As with many things in life, the dimensions of the plan and work are clearest in hindsight:

- 2011—Organize, run, and win the campaign to recall SB 1070 author Russell Pearce, the first recall in Arizona history.
- 2011—Shut down legislative progress of birthright citizenship bills as legislators see Pearce facing a recall election.
- 2012—Challenge racist Maricopa County sheriff Joe Arpaio, falling 80,000 votes short.
- 2014—Continue registering people to vote and signing them up for the Permanent Early Voter List, eventually expanding the number of Latinos signed up from 90,000 to 450,000.
- 2015—Defy experts and decide to put a proposition to raise the minimum wage on the 2016 ballot.
- 2016—Register 190,000 people to vote; run and win the statewide minimum wage campaign; challenge Sheriff Arpaio again, this time defeating him (by nearly 200,000 votes).
- 2018—Register 200,000 people to vote, provide the winning margin to flip a U.S. Senate seat to Democrats, and also pick up the previously Republican-held Arizona 2nd Congressional District, helping Democrats win control of the U.S. House.
- 2020—Turn out 300,000 more voters of color than in 2016, defeating Trump and electing Mark Kelly to a previously Republican-held U.S. Senate seat, helping Democrats take control of the U.S. Congress.

A core component of the long game is winning strategic elections that then make greater progress possible in the ensuing years. In 2018 the burgeoning movement infrastructure coalesced around the candidacy of Katie Hobbs to become Arizona's secretary of state, the person responsible for protecting access to the polls and the fair conduct of the democratic process. Hobbs won her race in a year where the progressive electoral operation powered historic levels of voter turnout, smashing records and eclipsing turnout totals, achieving a level not seen in nearly thirty years.[58] Seeing the potential of having the person who oversees elections be someone who champions the expansion of democracy, Arizona advocates played a long game.

The Arizona activists focused the electoral machinery on electing Hobbs because they saw the long-term potential. Because Hobbs won in 2018, she was in the perfect position, with all the authority and tools conferred by virtue of her position, to defend Arizona's electoral process from the onslaught of post-election attacks in 2020 when Trump tried to invalidate the election results.

Even with all the progress it has made thus far, Arizona still has *significant* upside. Latino turnout in Arizona was just 34 percent in 2016. By 2020, that number had jumped dramatically, but the comparative rate remains far below that of whites. In 2020, 45 percent of Latinos cast ballots, but the figure for whites was 76 percent.[59] While that is sobering in the immediate term, it's actually very promising in the medium to long term, as it means there are comparatively many more Latinos to be brought into the electorate than the more conservative Caucasian population. And this trend will only increase each year as more and more young people in Arizona turn eighteen and become eligible to vote (currently *62 percent* of Arizonans under the age of eighteen are people of color).[60] All of which suggests that for those progressives playing the long game, the future in Arizona looks very, very bright.

———

At the height of his activism, Cesar Chavez was not someone who generated praise from the White House and presidents of the United States. In fact, he was under constant FBI surveillance. As the *Los Angeles Times* reported after his death in 1993, "The shadowing of Chavez under the administrations of Lyndon B. Johnson and Richard Nixon would continue for more than seven years, involving hundreds of agents nationwide at extensive public cost. . . . This resulted in a 1,434-page FBI file."[61]

But Cesar was not in it for praise from powerful people. He was in it to build a movement that could acquire the power to change the conditions that affected his people's lives. One of the people who gravitated to the movement was a fifteen-year-old high school student who left home to work full-time for the cause. That student's nephew spent his summers at the UFW headquarters, soaking up the lessons and developing into a Level 5 leader who could convene the players and support the emerging young leaders who would drive the movement that would go from protest to power, garnering enough power to oust a white nationalist president of the United States. And now the current president has a bust of Cesar in the Oval Office, symbolically signaling the dawn of a new day and keeping a watchful eye on the occupant of the most powerful office in the world. *Si se puede* indeed.

9

Virginia: "Alone Among the States of the Confederacy"

Alone among the states of the former Confederacy, Virginia has become a voting rights bastion, increasingly encouraging its citizens—especially people of color—to exercise their democratic rights.
—Reid J. Epstein and Nick Corasaniti, "Virginia, the Old Confederacy's Heart, Becomes a Voting Rights Bastion," *New York Times*, April 2, 2021

Captain William Tucker perused the group of twenty dark-skinned people lined up at the dock in Jamestown, Virginia, and thought about which ones he wanted to buy. A leader among the whites in Virginia, he decided to purchase two human beings, a Black woman named Isabella and a Black man called Antony. As twentieth-century poet June Jordan wrote about another such shopping trip, "You don't buy a human being, you don't purchase a slave, without thinking ahead. So they had planned this excursion. They were dressed for the occasion." [1] We do not know how William Tucker was dressed, but to the best of our knowledge, it was on that August day in 1619, in that Virginia city, that slavery began in what would become the United States of America. [2]

It should come as no surprise, then, that Richmond, a major city in Virginia, was chosen as the capital of the Confederacy at the start of the Civil War in 1861. In an ornate state Capitol building in that city, plans were made for how to most efficiently and effectively kill as many Northerners as possible so that white human beings could continue to buy and sell Black bodies just as William Tucker and others had done since 1619.

At the beginning of the Civil War, the Confederate Congress that was assembled in the Capitol building in Richmond passed myriad laws to support the war being waged to preserve white nationalism and

Black slavery. One law, the Confederate Conscription Act, was adopted in response to the concern that drafting young Southern white men into the military took them away from the plantations, reducing the number of people available to control the Black folks down on the farm (especially given the prevalence of the disease causing Negroes to run away). To address this worry, the law exempted from military service one Southern white man for every twenty Black people he owned or had responsibility for controlling. That piece of legislation came to be known as the Twenty Nigger Law.[3]

One hundred sixty years later, in 2022, in that same white-columned Capitol building, twenty-one African Americans hold office as members of the state legislature. In 2021, two of the Black women state legislators, Jennifer McClellan and Marcia "Cia" Price, introduced pathbreaking legislation that would secure and protect voting rights for the descendants of those dark-skinned people sold at Jamestown. *New York Times* reporters Reid Epstein and Nick Corasaniti captured the historical significance of that legislation in an April 2021 article:

> As states across the South race to establish new voting restrictions, Virginia is bolting in the opposite direction. . . . Virginia, which for nearly 50 years had to submit changes to its elections to the federal government for approval under the Voting Rights Act's preclearance requirements, has now effectively imposed the same covenants on itself, an extraordinary step for a state with a long history of segregation and racially targeted voting laws.[4]

Although most of the current debate about immigration in America focuses on the states along the Mexican border, from a historical perspective, Virginia is actually the immigration epicenter of this country. Conveniently situated on the coast of the Atlantic Ocean, it was the first place that white immigrants from England—unauthorized and undocumented by the indigenous inhabitants of the land upon which they were settling—arrived in 1607. When those first white settlers realized how hard it was to work the land, they, like Captain Tucker, quickly adapted to buying Africans brought across the ocean to do the work the white settlers didn't want to do. The non-immigrants, the Native Americans, were killed, infected with diseases, and driven from the land, and as a result the bulk of the state's population consisted of whites and African Americans for the first two hundred years of American history.

Over the past thirty years, the arrival of immigrants from non-white countries has accelerated the racial makeover of Virginia's population, and, as a result, the state is not nearly as white as it used to be. Sixty-one percent of the residents are white, down from 77 percent in 1990.[5] Today more than 1 million immigrants call Virginia home and, collectively, they make up 12.5 percent of the state's population.[6] As a result of this demographic revolution, Virginia is not nearly as politically conservative as it used to be.

Progressives suffered a setback in the 2021 elections when Republican Glenn Youngkin defeated Democrat Terry McAuliffe in the gubernatorial election and Democrats lost their majority in the House of Delegates, but that speedbump needs to be placed in proper historical perspective to understand the road ahead. In the closing decades of the twentieth century, the state's voters backed the Republican presidential nominee in every single race since Lyndon Johnson's landslide election in 1964. Even the Democrats who were Southerners, Jimmy Carter and Bill Clinton, didn't win there. Since 2008, Democrats have won nine of ten statewide elections. In 2021, the Republicans did a better job of injecting urgency into the election and framing the electoral battle as a referendum on the racial identity of the state by sounding an alarm about the perceived threat of "critical race theory" (CRT), their code for attacking teaching about the state and country's history of racism. As I wrote in *The Nation* at the time, "The Virginia results show the folly of [the race neutral] approach. CRT doesn't even exist, and McAuliffe sure didn't campaign on it. But it did the trick of alarming white people about the state's changing racial composition, and McAuliffe's silence did nothing to rally progressives to turn out in commensurate fashion."[7]

The 2021 results were a failure of Democratic turnout and strategy. The composition of the state's population and its voters continues to trend in a progressive direction. Nearly half of all Virginians under the age of eighteen are people of color, and the electorate gets browner by the hour as 108,000 young people turn eighteen every year, becoming eligible to vote in a state where Democrats lost by 63,000 votes in 2021. The future in Virginia still looks bright: Democrats are poised to recapture control of the House of Delegates in 2023, Jennifer McClellan is a leading candidate to become governor in 2025, and the state's journey over the past decade remains an essential textbook in understanding how to turn a red state blue.

Virginia's political transformation from the capital of the Confederacy to a progressive state in the vanguard of the movement to make America a multiracial democracy is much more than a political bookend in the place where slavery started. The state's journey also offers a roadmap for how to win the war that has been waged in America since the day Captain Tucker purchased bread, clothes, and Isabella and Antony.

INVEST IN LEVEL 5 LEADERS—TRAM NGUYEN

A key part of Virginia's twenty-first-century political story begins in twentieth-century Vietnam. Toward the end of the Vietnam War, in 1975, Tai Nguyen was arrested, taken to a "reeducation" camp in Vietnam, and held in captivity for several years. (Mr. Nguyen had cast his lot with the U.S. military, escorting American ships up and down the Mekong River during the Vietnam War, which was why he was captured by the North Vietnamese and "re-educated.") While he was imprisoned, his wife, Kimtu Nguyen, struggled to raise her two daughters on her own in a country that had just endured years of war. Mrs. Nguyen did what she could to provide for her family, selling street food to make ends meet, not knowing when, or if, she would ever see her husband again as he languished in what was essentially a prison camp where torture and abuse were common.[8]

A grossly underappreciated aspect of war is what happens to the people who are left behind after the shooting stops. Hundreds of thousands of people in Vietnam fled the country in the 1970s and 1980s, many in overcrowded boats. In one year, 80 percent of the boats were stopped and attacked by pirates, and on nearly half of the boats that were attacked, many of the women on board were raped.[9] Human resilience is a powerful force, however, and people in dire situations often tap deep reservoirs of courage and ingenuity to persevere and overcome.

Desperate to build a better life for her daughters, Mrs. Nguyen confronted the risks and decided to leave Vietnam, climbing into a boat in 1980 with her young children and setting out on the dangerous journey. She survived the trek and arrived safely with her daughters at Songkhla Refugee Camp in Thailand.

Nearly five hundred miles away, her husband wanted not only to live, but to be reunited with his family again. Driven by his dream, Mr. Nguyen escaped from the reeducation camp and, like the enslaved Africans in America who followed the Underground Railroad to freedom a century earlier, managed to make his way out of captivity, traveling to Songkhla where he was reunited with his wife and daughters after years of separation.

The Nguyen family regrouped and rebuilt their life during the months they lived in the camp, from 1980 to 1981. It was there, in the refugee camp, that their daughter Tram was born. The family of five subsequently boarded an airplane in 1981 to travel across the ocean to the United States to start a new life, settling in America's original slave state of Virginia, where Mrs. Nguyen's older brother had arrived years before.

Twenty-six years later, Tram would throw herself into the work of politically transforming the state where Black folks had first been brought during the Middle Passage after a perilous journey across a different ocean, overcrowded, undernourished, and packed into cargo holds—a journey where many died in transit to Virginia in 1619 and in the years thereafter working the fields and building the wealth that made America rich.

————

Like Stacey Abrams and John Loredo, Tram is a Level 5 leader, eschewing accolades and fame for impact and effectiveness. Few people in national politics are simultaneously more impactful and less known than Tram. In a country where many leaders lavish resources and time on promoting their profiles, reputations, and "brands," Tram's main public profile is a 136-word bio on her organization's website. She has let the work speak for itself, and she has channeled her ambitions into the cause and the mission.

Tram's life experiences shaped her understanding of race and racism in America and steeled her resolve to do something about it. In the late 1980s, on their first family vacation in the United States, she and her sisters jumped into a swimming pool in Virginia, and everyone else immediately jumped out of the water shouting, "Chinks in the pool!"

That type of racism had infused Virginia's politics for centuries. By 2008, however, the demographic composition of the state was changing, as were its political prospects. One month after Barack Obama won the Iowa caucuses in 2008, telling an inspired nation, "They said this day would never come," Tram resolved to seize the day and started work as the first employee of New Virginia Majority (NVM), an organization created to increase civic participation in Virginia. NVM was a start-up operation with $50,000 in the bank and no guarantees of organizational survival beyond six months.[10]

That decision set her on a course to serve as one of the key progressive generals in the fight to win the modern-day Civil War—a battle she has continued to fight in the state where Jefferson Davis, the president of the Confederacy, had based his operations. Tram is now a regular presence in the state Capitol building Davis once occupied, working with legislators like McClellan and Price to draft bills to empower the kind of people Virginia had once enslaved.

Over the course of fourteen years, she has helped devise and execute a strategy and plan to transform the potential of Virginia's rapidly growing demographic diversity into actual political power. This included strengthening the organizations and coalition needed to implement the plan, and coordinating the work required to turn ideas into action.

Since the founding of NVM in 2008, every Democratic presidential nominee has won the state, and voter turnout in gubernatorial elections has increased by 72 percent. In addition, in 2019, for the first time in two decades, Democrats in Virginia secured majorities in the state legislature and took control of the entire state government, winning all top state seats: governor, lieutenant governor, and attorney general. As discussed above, despite the setback of the 2021 election, given the continued demographic transformation in the state, the prospects for Democrats retaking control of the state government over the next few years remain quite promising.

The reach of Tram's influence is vast. Over the past decade she has served as co-director of New Virginia Majority; point person on progressive legislation; coordinator of a statewide coalition consisting of more than a dozen partner organizations; a trusted resource for multiple state legislators; and a key adviser to donors and activists across the country.

When Stacey Abrams needed help, she called upon Tram, twice—first in the final weeks of Stacey's 2018 gubernatorial campaign and then during the month leading up to the pivotal January 2021 runoff election that lifted Raphael Warnock and Jon Ossoff into the U.S. Senate.

Not only has Tram modeled how to *build* power, but she is one of the most advanced leaders in the country on how to *wield* power. Having helped elect many people to office, she has brought that influence to bear on governing by crafting legislation and cajoling elected leaders at the local and state level to pass policies that improve people's lives. Because of the work of Tram and her allies, more than four hundred thousand low-income Virginians now have health care coverage as a result of expanded Medicaid eligibility in 2019.[11] Nearly eight hundred thousand people received an increase in their salary as a result of the minimum wage increase in 2021.[12] And 155 years after the end of the Civil War, in 2020, Virginia—the state with more Confederate monuments than any other state in the nation—finally removed many of the tributes to the traitors that mocked the sacrifices that ended slavery.

Ashley Kenneth, president of the state think tank The Commonwealth Institute for Fiscal Analysis, reflected on the changes in Virginia, writing in 2021, "We know the formula for transformational change because we have done it—people from diverse communities across the commonwealth coming together to demand it, committed advocates who are connected and listening to impacted communities, and lawmakers who are willing to make bold, anti-racist, and intentional decisions that will have lasting impact."[13]

Just as in Georgia and Arizona, all of that change did not happen by magic or by ad hoc loner protests. It took organization, discipline, dedication, and careful planning.

BUILD STRONG CIVIC ENGAGEMENT ORGANIZATIONS— NEW VIRGINIA MAJORITY

All of the components of the Liberation Battle Plan must be present in order to succeed, but the development of the respective pieces can unfold in different sequences in different states. In Georgia, Stacey Abrams started with the plan, then identified the need for stronger civic engagement organizations and set about creating that capacity. In Virginia, building the organization came first and then, from that work, and on a related and parallel track, the detailed, data-driven plan emerged.

Civic engagement organizations are most effective when individual experiences are channeled into collective action. At their best, these organizations are vehicles for connecting disparate and often disempowered people and turning them into a coordinated, synergistic, and powerful political force. They are the reason wars are fought with armies and not just angry individuals running around in a million different directions.

No U.S. state has been doling out white supremacy and nationalism longer than the Commonwealth of Virginia. It is that context and background that has made the civic engagement work of New Virginia Majority so important. Below, we'll consider just two examples in Prince William County, the Virginia county named after Prince William, the uncle of England's King George III who was the monarch at the time of the American Revolution (and who has more recently returned to fame in Lin-Manuel Miranda's epic play *Hamilton*, in which the King George character sings such toe-tapping satirical lyrics as, "And when push comes to shove / I will send a fully armed battalion to remind you of my love").[14]

———

Much of Prince William County's history with immigration began in the 1600s with a white man from England named John Smith. You might know of Smith from schoolbooks that described him as an explorer and early settler of Jamestown, Virginia, who arrived in 1607, and, when facing execution at the hands of the Powhatan tribe, was allegedly rescued by a Native American woman named Pocahontas.[15]

Stripped of its hoary veneer, however, Smith's story is actually one of an illegal immigrant coming to a land without permission and proceeding to commit crimes of theft and murder. When Smith arrived in Virginia in 1607, he did not have papers from the government of the indigenous people saying that he was authorized to be in the country. Not only did his lack of legal status *not* stop him from entering the country, but he felt completely free to get together with his comrades and traipse all over the surrounding area, exploring the interplay of rivers and land, and creating maps so that other illegal immigrants from Europe could easily identify locations they might like to occupy without permission from the people already living on the land. One of the areas that Smith identified on such an excursion was the territory that is now Prince William County.

Although there used to be no white people on that land, many whites followed in the footsteps of John Smith over the years, and the ranks of Caucasians subsequently swelled to the point that the white population genuinely believed that this land they had stolen now belonged to them. It is not surprising, then, that it was in Prince William County where large numbers of white people—full of self-righteousness and historical ignorance—grabbed their guns on July 21, 1861, and started killing their fellow Americans in order to protect and preserve the right to keep America as the kind of place where white people could own, buy, and sell Black human beings down on the dock of the bay. These events are more grandly known as the Battle of Bull Run, the first major battle of the Civil War. One hundred fifty-six years after that bloody battle, New Virginia Majority would help lead a political fight in that county that would defeat the ideological descendants of the Confederate Civil War leaders.

To appreciate the metamorphosis of the population composition of Prince William County, it helps to remember the words of humorist Calvin Trillin, who once joked that he won't eat at an ethnic restaurant in a city that doesn't have at least two people of that ethnicity on the City Council.[16] Many a truth is spoken in jest, and the underlying truth here is that, generally, as the relative size of a group in a city or county grows, so too does its political power and representation. In the decades preceding 2010, the number of people of color in Prince William County grew exponentially, expanding from 19 percent of the population in 1990 to a clear majority—56 percent—by 2010.[17] The restaurant landscape went from a place mainly dominated by establishments like Outback Steakhouse to one with a proliferation of Mexican restaurants, barbecue joints, and Chinese takeout options.

—————

The story of Hala Ayala shows what can happen when a highly disciplined civic engagement organization coordinates the energy and efforts of an expanse of individuals concerned about a common issue such as access to health care.

Access to quality health care has been one of the most important concerns of Virginians since the first settlers from England arrived in Jamestown in 1607. More than half of the initial population died from sickness, disease, malnutrition, and inadequate health care to treat that sickness, disease, and malnutrition.[18] In the early twenty-first century, many Virginians still needed access to quality health care. Responding to the intensity and urgency of that need was the focus of much of the early work of NVM as it worked to build a collective and coordinated political force capable of making the government address those needs. Chief among those needs was the expansion of Medicaid.

Medicaid saved the life of Ayala's son. In 1997, Ayala, a self-described Afro-Latina, Lebanese, and Irish woman, was twenty-four years old, working at a gas station on Old Bridge Road in Prince William County, and, like hundreds of thousands of people in Virginia, she was living paycheck to paycheck. When she got pregnant, she worried about the health and prospects of her unborn son, especially since her employer didn't provide health insurance. Her fears were confirmed when her son was born with complications that required urgent medical attention. Lacking employer-provided health care, her only recourse was Medicaid; fortunately she qualified, enabling her to afford the doctors who would save her son's life.[19]

After her son was born, Ayala participated in civic life the way many do—by becoming active in her son's school. She joined the PTA and regularly volunteered when she could. She began to get a glimpse of what larger change was possible in 2012 when she got involved in

Obama's reelection campaign. Her increased activism increased her confidence, and she began to engage with her neighbors and friends to get them more involved in civic life.

In 2014, Ayala was selected to lead the National Organization for Women's Prince William County chapter. In that role, she continued to highlight the challenges of working people who lacked access to health care. While her horizons were expanding from the gas station on Old Bridge Road to her son's elementary school to the county non-profit women's rights group, Ayala was still just learning about the role and impact of state government on people's lives. Then she met an organizer named Tram Nguyen, who introduced her to New Virginia Majority. She liked what she saw and soon thereafter joined NVM's Progressive Leadership Project. Through that program she learned not only that change is possible, but how to go about making it happen, and she gained even deeper knowledge, confidence, and encouragement.

All of this took place at a time when people of color were becoming the majority of the residents in Prince William County. Despite the change in the composition of the voting population, the attitudes and priorities of the region's elected officials did not keep pace. Ayala understood that this meant they needed to be replaced. Working with NVM and applying the lessons from its leadership development program, Ayala learned the mechanics of running for office, identifying voters, and executing campaign plans. And then, with NVM's backing, she put that knowledge to work in 2017, mounting a campaign for Prince William's seat in the state legislature—a seat held at that time by four-term Republican Rich Anderson.[20]

For his part, Anderson couldn't have cared less about people without health care. A retired Air Force colonel, he puffed and postured and lectured as he took pride in blaming poor people for their poverty, and he repeatedly blocked any efforts in the state legislature to expand Medicaid in Virginia. Remember that at that time, the federal government, through the Affordable Care Act, was giving *free money* to the states so that they could make health care services available to their residents. But rejecting that money was part of the Confederate resistance to America's Black president, and callous and calculating politicians figured they could score political points by picking on poor people as a way of sending a signal to less-poor voters that they were on their side. The message Anderson and others sought to send was that the conservatives would not capitulate to "those people" who were clamoring for outrageous benefits like being able to take their babies to see a doctor. Anderson called providing that kind of assistance "redistributionist arithmetic." [21]

In her 2017 campaign, Ayala and NVM applied their own arithmetic to determine the number of votes needed to oust Anderson from office and replace him with someone who cared about the needs of people in pain. Their effort marshaled the support of several dozen volunteers and staff who knocked on thousands of doors and made phone calls to voters across the district. On November 7, 2017, the work paid off as the civic engagement apparatus brought an additional 4,441 voters to the polls, and Ayala bested Anderson by 1,768 votes, winning a seat in the Virginia House of Delegates and becoming one of the first Latinas ever elected to the Virginia state legislature. [22]

Ayala was not alone. Her experience with the health care system would ultimately reverberate politically across the state as thousands of people banded together into an electoral force powerful enough to shake up state politics. In cities, counties, and districts across the state, volunteers, activists, and organizations plugged their energy into the plans that NVM had created. All told in 2017, NVM fielded a massive statewide army of volunteers and activists who conducted a major mobilization that turned out tens of thousands of voters in more than two dozen districts, flipping fifteen Republican-held seats in the legislature, bringing Democrats within one seat in each legislative chamber of controlling the entire state government (a feat they would accomplish two years later, in 2019).

The Democratic gains in 2017 were significant enough to prove the importance voters attached to the issue of Medicaid expansion, and that newfound awareness tipped the balance of power in the state Capitol. After being sworn into office, Ayala—and her fourteen new Democratic colleagues in the legislature—voted to extend Medicaid protection to four hundred thousand low-income people in the state (several Republicans, seeing that they could lose their seats by being on the wrong side of the issue, dropped their previous opposition and decided to support Medicaid expansion). Through strong and steady civic engagement organizing, nearly half a million Virginians became eligible for the kind of medical assistance that had saved Ayala's son's life.

Thanks to Medicaid expansion in 2019, Virginia's uninsured rate dropped to a historic low of 7.9 percent.[23] As Ashley Kenneth of The Commonwealth Institute described the impact in 2020, "This drop in the number of uninsured people in Virginia is the direct result of the decision to expand Medicaid. . . . Nearly 463,000 [more] adults currently have health coverage in Virginia due to Medicaid expansion."[24]

———

NVM's work was not limited to the state capital. Just as battles in a war are won city by city, so too do political revolutions spread from one locale to the next. Prince William County did not just replace its white male Republican state representative with Hala Ayala. The newly organized and empowered multiracial movement in that county changed the face of the entire local governmental constellation. One of those faces belonged to Kenny Boddye—a man whose ancestors had been brought to the same Virginia shores where Captain William Tucker purchased Isabella and Antony in 1619.[25]

Four hundred years after white illegal immigrants began buying and selling Black bodies, Boddye sought a seat on the Prince William County Board of Supervisors, a board whose chairman, Corey Stewart, had become famous and powerful by railing against what he called illegal immigration. Much of what you need to know about Stewart was distilled into the headline of the 2018 *New York Times* feature article on him—"White Nationalists Love Corey Stewart. He Keeps Them Close."[26] Just as Donald Trump would ride the wave of anti-immigrant racism to the highest heights of U.S. politics, Stewart, a decade earlier, trod a similar path to contesting for power in Virginia.

Like his Confederate predecessors, Stewart understood that scaring white people about the rising numbers of people of color could be good politics, particularly in a county where the Latino share of the population had doubled in just ten years. Given that it was one of the principal gateways for the unauthorized arrival of white people from England in the 1600s, it is with some cruel historical irony then that in 2010, Prince William County, under Stewart's leadership, became one of the first counties in the United States to aggressively target and work with federal law enforcement to capture and deport immigrants (centuries too late for the members of the Powhatan tribe who first encountered immigrant John Smith and his caravan of illegals). When Stewart became board chair in 2007, he pushed Prince William County to the front of the fight to preserve the white nationalist spirit of the Confederacy. Stewart urged the county to devote its resources to the effort to identify, capture, and incarcerate dark-skinned residents of the region through the 287(g) Program—a provision of U.S. immigration law that allows state and local law enforcement officers to collaborate with the federal government to enforce federal immigration laws, including deportation.[27] Under Stewart's leadership, Prince William County became what the *Washington Post* called "a national symbol of hard-line immigration enforcement."[28]

Kenny Boddye was nineteen years old when Stewart started his antics on the Board of Supervisors. As a young and budding activist, Boddye settled in Prince William County when Stewart was at the peak of his powers and preparing a gubernatorial bid that, like Trump's presidential campaigns, was predicated on hostility toward immigrants. It was in Prince William County that Boddye connected with New Virginia Majority, joining its leadership program and learning the art and science of winning elections.

Empowered with sharpened skills and infused with inspiration and encouragement, Boddye decided to run for a seat on the Board of Supervisors in 2019.[29] The organizing, training, and activism paid off. He and his NVM team prevailed in his election by 322 votes, helping to diversify a board that had previously served as a symbol of white racial resentment, reaction, and fear.[30] In large part, because of the work of NVM, the locale that had hosted the first big bloody battle of the white nationalist rebellion known as the Civil War is now governed by a board that has a majority of people of color.

In 2020, after a decade of organizing, activism, and winning elections, the new multiracial majority in Prince William County brought to an end the anti-immigrant actions of the Board of Supervisors, finally ending its pursuit of immigrants by withdrawing from the 287(g) Program that Stewart and his Confederate comrades had spearheaded.

Today, Calvin Trillin would feel just fine dining at Tacos Chinoz, Granddaddy's Skillet, New Hunan Restaurant, or any of the other restaurants run by people of color in the county. Individuals shar-ing the racial and ethnic backgrounds of the owners of those types of restaurants—Latinos, African Americans, Asian Americans—were running the region's governing board.

The success of Ayala and Boddye and many others is a result of the strong civic engagement abilities of NVM and the overall civic engage-ment infrastructure it has helped build over the past decade. In its first year of operation in 2008, NVM had $50,000 and one employee, Tram. By 2019, the NVM team was managing a $7 million budget, coordinating hundreds of volunteer activists in cities across the state, registering more than three hundred thousand voters, and knocking on more than 2.5 million doors.

In a 2019 *New York Times* op-ed explaining the secret to Virginia's success, Tram reflected on her decade of activism and impact:

> Local organizations like mine understood the political potential of Virginia when we got started 12 years ago. We are winning because we recognize the power of an electorate that includes and reflects the diversity of our state. We don't talk to voters only when campaign season rolls around. We try to reach vot-ers of all colors, women, low-income workers and young people where they are, which has made it possible for us to develop a robust base of support along Virginia's so-called Urban Cres-cent, from Northern Virginia to Hampton Roads. . . .
>
> That work is ingrained in our organization's DNA. And we talk to people, all year, about issues that are important to them: affordable health care, access to a good education, reforming the criminal justice system, protecting voting rights and mak-ing sure our communities have clean air, water and public lands. . . . Changes in the shape of the electorate and rising en-thusiasm among voters can only go so far, without campaign architecture that channels those changes into tangible political outcomes.[31]

New Virginia Majority has not only had an impact on election re-sults; it has also reshaped public policies as politicians shifted their political survival calculus to get on the correct side of issues affecting voters of color. Critical to all of this success was the ability to develop and follow a detailed, data-driven plan.

DEVELOP DETAILED, DATA-DRIVEN PLANS

When I asked Tram for a copy of one of her organization's plans, she sent me a spreadsheet. Actually, she sent me several spreadsheets. One of the sheets had 1,081 rows, 31 columns, and 33,511 cells. Oh, and that was just one tab in one spreadsheet that had five other tabs. Tram and NVM definitely subscribe to the same school of thinking as Martin Eakes and his team at the progressive nonprofit Self-Help Credit Union in North Carolina, who once told me, "To us, a work of art is a well-designed spreadsheet."

There is a lot of fascination in media and political circles with what's been called Big Data. A 2020 *Vox* article by Teddy Schleifer described the gold rush of groups scooping up money from donors on the promise of delivering Big Data magic. Schleifer wrote, "Four years after the Democratic Party's data was described by Hillary Clinton as 'bankrupt' and 'on the verge of insolvency,' tech billionaires are regrouping and pouring millions into the party's digital infrastructure." [32]

All of these big-dollar, Big Data, analytics-driven, Silicon Valley–initiated endeavors could learn a lot from the data prowess and expertise underlying and powering the political plans and work of NVM. That work has steadily propelled the political refashioning of a state that was recently purple, and before that was reliably red, and before that was the capital of the Confederacy, and before that was the place where prominent white businessmen first sauntered down to the docks to purchase Black people.

What the NVM spreadsheet and its 1,081 rows of data revealed— the story the "work of art" told—was the location of the votes necessary to win elections in Virginia. Like a Bob Ross painting and its happy little trees, NVM dotted its document with happy little precincts, door knocks, and voter IDs. The universe of voters was further broken down by month and demographic subgroup, with Asian American Pacific Islanders, Latinos, African Americans, and eighteen-to-twenty-four-year-olds all getting their own specific spot on the spreadsheet— and, by extension, their own place of respect and importance in the civic engagement universe, and, ultimately, on the state's political landscape.

———

Shelly Simonds is certainly grateful for the precision of the plans that guided NVM's electoral work in the 2019 election. Especially after her 2017 campaign ended in a tie. Literally.

In a race that should be the poster child for the mantra "every vote counts," Simonds, a parent, elementary school teacher, and school board member, mounted a spirited campaign to dislodge Republican incumbent state representative David Yancey. In that closely fought contest, Simonds received 11,608 votes. Yancey received . . . 11,608 votes.[33] The "winner" was decided by picking a name out of a fishbowl, and Republican Yancey's name was selected.

Two years later, Simonds sought a rematch, and the data-driven plan of NVM guided the work that won the race. Scarred by the experience of the tie two years earlier, NVM devised an even better plan in 2019. A detailed, Big Data plan for winning outright and escaping the fickleness of the fishbowl.

Not only did NVM have a plan, but its data was better than the polling data the Democratic Party paid hundreds of thousands of dollars to white-led polling firms to provide. NVM's data showed that the polls were inaccurate, and in order to win, it needed to adjust its strategy and redouble its efforts in support of Simonds so that they could avoid the heartache of 2017 and, more importantly, seize political power in the legislature. And so the data drove the work, and NVM followed it like clockwork. Here is how NVM described, in real time, the situation in a memo to its stakeholders:

> Based on our hard IDs, Simonds has 50.7% support which is lower than what poll figures show and tracks very closely with the 2017 elections outcome. Additionally, among those that are undecided in the district, 77.4% have a DLCC [Democratic Legislative Campaign Committee (the Democratic party group focused on state legislative races)] support score above 50, which means that these voters are more likely to support Democrats—for that high a percentage of voters to be undecided shows that we have more

work to do to convince them to support Simonds. This district was also affected by the redistricting court case, so Simonds has three new precincts in the district that weren't a part of the district in 2017, and more work needs to be done to introduce her to those new voters and help her build trust with them. . . .

We believe that we may need to make another "persuasion" pass to the undecided voters, while pivoting to a turnout conversation with the strong D and lean D voters.[34]

They made the adjustment and pivoted, performing the persuasion tasks and knocking on the doors of 27,925 homes, in which 39,292 voters resided.[35] This time Simonds won by 3,493 votes.[36] No fishbowl needed.

NVM had a plan for not only Simonds's race, but for twenty-five other races across the state. The work in each of the priority places was informed by a detailed plan identifying the number of votes needed to win, where those voters resided, and what it would take to bring them to the polls.

In 2019, the possibility of Democrats controlling the governorship and both houses of the legislature in Virginia was tantalizingly close, something that hadn't happened in nearly twenty years. At stake was the quality of life for hundreds of thousands of Virginians—low-wage workers struggling to provide for their families and in need of a higher minimum wage, immigrants needing driver's licenses to be able to safely get to and from work, formerly incarcerated people seeking to rejoin their communities as productive members of society. But first, Democrats needed to flip four seats in the state legislature, and helping Simonds win was just one part of the puzzle. They needed a plan for taking control of the entire legislative branch. That's why the NVM spreadsheets were so all-encompassing.

———

Whether in politics, business, or social change (such as protest campaigns like the Montgomery Bus Boycott), paying careful attention to logistics is critical to success. If you're going to get a group of people together to knock on doors to support your cause or candidate, there are a lot of questions to consider. First of all, where do you gather? A parking lot, the coffee shop, a street corner? And what if, like NVM, you're canvassing in twenty-five different districts spread across the 43,000 square miles of your entire state?

In election-speak, assembling your canvassers is called "staging." At staging locations, organizers bring packets with information on which doors to hit up, forms for how to have effective conversations, ways to capture the outcome of those conversations, and maps indicating the location of the respective homes. NVM's spreadsheet listed seventy-two different staging locations ranging from a volunteer's home to a business office to the local Democratic Party headquarters. For each staging location, the spreadsheet tracks important and often underappreciated logistical considerations such as available Wi-Fi, accessible parking, number of bathrooms, ADA compliance, and "anything else."

NVM's spreadsheet brought order, discipline, and focus that enabled the organization to harness and deploy the energy and efforts of its respective partners to the areas where they would make the most impact. The National Korean American Service & Education Consortium (NAKASEC), for example, focused its door-knocking on House District 40, which has more Asian Americans than almost any other district in the state.

All told, the coalition targeted 357,583 voters across twenty-five state legislative districts, and 88 percent of its target universe actually went on to cast ballots, an extraordinarily high rate of efficacy and impact.[37] Highly respected academic research studies have found that typically just 6 percent to 8 percent of those who are targeted by canvassers actually turn out and vote.[38]

In 2019, with all of the progressive civic engagement groups working in concert, coordinated through the beautifully constructed and maintained spreadsheet, the movement helped Democrats win eight seats, and flipped control of Virginia's government for the first time in two decades.

And because of those plans, that data, and all of that work, eight hundred thousand Virginians received an increase in wages as a result of the minimum-wage raise; three hundred thousand immigrants, after a decade-long battle, can now get driver's licenses, and seventy thousand formerly incarcerated people can now vote.[39] Even with the setback in 2021, Democrats still control the State Senate, giving them the power to protect the progressive policies put in place over the past several years as they regroup and dig in for winning back power in 2023 and 2025.

Elections have consequences. Winning elections requires plans. New Virginia Majority had a plan—and a spreadsheet—and now life is much, much better for many more Virginians. Getting to the point of Democratic control of all branches of government did not happen overnight. Far from it. And recapturing such control will not happen overnight. It takes patience, perseverance, and carefully playing the political long game.

PLAY THE LONG GAME

Tram knew she really only had one shot. In 2013, she and New Virginia Majority had played a pivotal role in boosting turnout of voters of color in the gubernatorial election—helping Democrat Terry McAuliffe win his first race for governor and wrest control of the Virginia executive branch from the Republicans. As one of the key players in the network of nonprofit community-based organizations that had driven the voter turnout that tipped the election, Tram was in the room where it happens, but it was a crowded room, filled with other people, organizations, leaders, and forces that had played a role in the election. McAuliffe had many interests to balance, but he couldn't just ignore Tram and the movement she represented. So she knew she had just the one shot, and she wasn't going to throw it away.

Virginia is a state of 8 million people, and its governor appoints fifteen public servants to work in the cabinet of a government that oversees a $67 billion budget. Competition over who gets appointed to what spots is intense, and other political players had their picks for various posts.

Keenly aware of the long-term strategic significance of expanding the size of the electorate and bringing more and more people of color into the process, Tram decided to use her influence to forcefully advocate for the selection of a voting rights champion to serve in the job of the state's top elections officer. She knew that the impact of the right person in that role would reverberate for years, and so she aggressively and successfully pushed McAuliffe to choose Edgardo Cortés as Virginia's commissioner of elections.

Cortés had devoted his professional life to public service, working in local government as an election official focused on making it easier to vote, and he brought that perspective and commitment to the role of state guardian of democracy. Once appointed to the top elections job, he quickly showed what's possible when government officials actually want to help people vote rather than work to block them from participating in elections. In his first few years in office, he instituted such reforms as integrating voter registration into the process for getting and renewing driver's licenses, creating an online absentee ballot request system, and simplifying the voter registration forms so that they were far more user-friendly.[40]

The results were swift and powerful, with the number of people in the state casting ballots steadily increasing during the time Cortés was in office. Tram's focus on the long game paid off, as the decision she made in 2013 helped bring about steady gains in 2015 and then in 2017, when Ayala and others won a sufficient number of seats to pass Medicaid expansion, and then in 2019, when Boddye and others won the races that transformed the Prince William County Board of Supervisors. From 2014, when Cortés was appointed commissioner of elections, to 2019, when Boddye was elected to the Board of Supervisors, voter turnout in Virginia steadily increased. The number of voters in 2019 was nearly 60 percent bigger than the turnout four years earlier.[41]

In her *New York Times* piece, Tram attributed the progress in her state to playing the long game:

> It took years of organizing and multiple election cycles that resulted in incremental progress for Virginia to reach the point where a Democratic sweep was possible. . . . States don't become battlegrounds overnight. Democrats and national progressive organizations have the resources to take their case to the people and win, but they have to start early and organize relentlessly. When they lose, they have to stay in place and keep fighting for every political inch they can get.[42]

Beyond the specific strategic decisions, the long game also involves simply staying in the struggle for the long haul. Tram is still a relatively young woman, and she has worked at NVM for fourteen years, nearly a third of her life. In that time, she has worked on more than seventy-five races in thirteen cities and counties across the state. By her calculations, she has supervised over five hundred staff, who have contacted more than 1 million voters.

Virginia has a long and inglorious history as a leader in the fight to preserve white nationalism in America. After the destruction of Reconstruction, the state's political leaders led the charge in ruthlessly rewriting the state constitution to implement widespread voter suppression of Black people as a way to reestablish Confederate control of the state.

One of the chief architects of that work, as discussed in chapter 1, was Virginia state legislator Carter Glass, who in 1901 crafted and enthusiastically championed legislation to codify white supremacy, in deed if not in word. Glass's gleeful declaration that he was out to "eliminate the darkey as a political factor" has echoed across the years.[43]

But nineteenth-century white nationalists such as Carter Glass—and his twenty-first-century Confederate heirs such as Rich Anderson and Corey Stewart—could not contemplate or calculate the endurance and effectiveness of those carrying on the struggle to eradicate white supremacy and build a true multiracial democracy. Tram Nguyen's family traveled across an ocean in 1981 to settle in the state where Jennifer McClellan and Cia Price's ancestors had been brought across a different ocean and held in slavery in Virginia.

In her poem "Still I Rise," Maya Angelou wrote, "I am the dream and the hope of the slave." In 2021, Jenn, Cia, Tram, and their colleagues worked to make that dream manifest by drafting and passing a new Voting Rights Act for Virginia. A law designed to fulfill the promise of democracy in the state where slavery started. The headline of the April 2, 2021, *New York Times* article captured the significance of the changes taking place: "Virginia, the Old Confederacy's Heart, Becomes a Voting Rights Bastion." Transitioning from the birthplace of slavery and site of the first battle of the Civil War to a bastion of voting rights is the kind of change that's possible with Level 5 leaders building strong civic engagement organizations and playing the long game, guided by a detailed and sophisticated plan.

10

San Diego: "Transformed Within Less Than a Generation"

There's a reason why Richard Nixon and Ronald Reagan adored San Diego so much that they called us their "Lucky City" and loved to hold rallies here: We lavished Republicans with votes. . . . The [2020] local numbers reveal just how much our local politics have transformed within less than a generation: Biden got a higher percentage of the vote here (60 percent) than any Democrat since FDR's 1936 landslide victory. . . . What happened?
— Randy Dotinga, "How San Diego Got So Blue in a
Relatively Short Amount of Time," December 17, 2020

California's experience in weathering and overcoming the politics of white racial grievance offers valuable instruction for the current Civil War raging in America in the 2020s. Mainstream politicians and pundits across the country continue to wring their hands and worry about the electoral implications of unapologetically standing on the side of people of color who are working to beat back racism and create a multiracial democracy. In the face of such doubts, California offers a story of hope and a roadmap for success. As I wrote in the conclusion of *Brown Is the New White*, "California has shown that rather than being something to fear, the demographic revolution can actually mark the beginning of a hopeful and exciting era of positive and progressive change. If we correctly respond to the demands of the day, we gon' be alright."[1]

It is difficult for most people to appreciate today, but when I first came of age in politics, California was essentially a red state (and I'm not *that* old). When it served as the political launching pad for future presidents Richard Nixon and Ronald Reagan in the 1950s and 1960s, the state's electorate was overwhelmingly white, and, for the most part, so was its political leadership. In 1970, the state population was 89 per-cent white.[2] As of the 2020 Census, people of color account for nearly two-thirds (64 percent) of the state's residents (Latinos are 39 percent of the population, Asian Americans 15.5 percent, African Americans 6.5 percent, Native Americans 1.6 percent).[3] This demographic revo-lution has been so sweeping that it's now damn near impossible for a Republican to win statewide office, as reflected in the pitiful failed attempt to recall Democratic governor Gavin Newsom in September 2021, which occasioned *Politico* to write a story titled "California's In-credible Shrinking Republican Party."[4]

The road to the current Democratic reign of dominance was not easy. I know because I've been on it since my college days at Stanford in the 1980s, when I worked with then assembly members (now con-gresswomen) Maxine Waters and Barbara Lee, became a member of the state Democratic Party's Central Committee in 1986, ran for lo-cal office in 1992, and later created the political action committee that helped boost Kamala Harris to her razor-thin win in her first bid for statewide office in 2010. What made the journey especially challeng-ing was not so much the deployment of attacks from the Confeder-ate Battle Plan, which was to be expected, but rather the reluctance of white progressive and Democratic leaders to acknowledge the nature of the fight we were in and then commit commensurate resources to translate the rapidly growing numbers of people of color in the state into an overwhelming electoral force.

The lessons learned for the challenges of the 2020s are profound and on point. In California, conservative attacks in the 1990s on racial justice policies backfired spectacularly, directly resulting in dramati-cally increased voting by Latinos and Asian Americans and thereby changing the political calculus and trajectory of the Golden State for decades to come.

Such an outcome can absolutely occur nationally if the California example is carefully studied and followed. No place in California has been more reflective of and important to the state's political metamor-phosis than the city and county that sits on the border of California and Mexico—San Diego.

———

California's early political leaders were not fans of people of color. One of the very first laws the state's elected officials passed after becoming a state in 1850 authorized $1 million ($36 million in today's dollars) to reimburse white people for expenses they incurred in killing Native Americans; these "Indian hunters" were clearing the way for the Caucasians coming to the state to prospect for gold.[5] The eighth person to become governor of the state, Leland Stanford, left no ambiguity about his racial sentiments when, in accepting the Republican Party's gubernatorial nomination in 1859, he said, "I am in favor of free white American citizens. I prefer free white citizens to any other class or race." Just in case the message wasn't getting through, he added, "I prefer the white man to the negro as an inhabitant of our country. I believe its greatest good has been derived by having all of the country settled by free white men."[6]

Apparently a lot of voters agreed with Stanford, as he was subsequently propelled into the governor's office at a time when the country was engaged in a civil war to determine whether free white men could continue to buy and sell Black men, women, and children. Once securely ensconced in the highest office in the state, Governor Stanford made clear that his anti-Black policies and preferences also extended to "yellow" people as well. In language copied almost verbatim by a certain twenty-first-century president of the United States, Stanford warned in 1862 about the dangers of immigrants of color:

> To my mind it is clear that the settlement among us of an inferior race is to be discouraged by every legitimate means. Asia, with her numberless millions, sends to our shores the dregs of her population. . . . There can be no doubt but that the presence among us of numbers of degraded and distinct people must exercise a deleterious influence upon the superior race, and to a certain extent, repel desirable immigration.[7]

Not content to limit his influence to just one state, Stanford then ran for and won election to the U.S. Senate, where he brought his unapologetic racist views with him. At a time when Washington politicians were handing the South—and the fate of Black people—back to the Confederates, white purity politics also flourished in the West. As historian Mae Ngai has written, "In the late 19th century, Jim Crow and Chinese exclusion were related projects of white supremacy, one in the South and one in the West."[8] Senator Stanford was a strong supporter of the 1882 Chinese Exclusion Act, and he explained the basis of his support by saying, "It would be better for the Pacific coast to supplant the Chinese with the whites. . . . The Chinaman is a disturbing element in our civilization. . . . We will be, on the whole, better off without him."[9]

In addition to championing racist public policies from coast to coast, this distinguished senator, businessman, and former governor opened what would become one of the world's preeminent institutions of higher education, Stanford University (an institution whose undergraduate student body today, in a bit of historical poetic justice, is now more than 60 percent people of color).[10] That university would subsequently serve as a training ground for the woman who would drive the political transformation of San Diego.

———

One hundred years after former governor Stanford opened his university, California would elect another governor who picked up the baton of fanning the flames of white racial fears by demonizing immigrants and people of color. That governor had himself benefited from the Confederate long game in general, and the Southern Strategy, in particular.

The Southern Strategy focus on building political power by stoking white racial resentment was not geographically confined to the South, and some of its chief practitioners were politicians in the West. As discussed in chapter 3, Ronald Reagan launched his presidential campaign in a Mississippi county famous for the murder of civil rights workers, and he then rode the wave of Confederate energy into the White House in 1980. Prior to entering politics, Reagan had become famous as an actor, and long before reaching the White House—for what biographer Lou Cannon called "The Role of a Lifetime"—he rehearsed his lines and learned the part of white fearmonger on the "off-Broadway" stage of California politics.

Reagan's victory in the 1966 California gubernatorial election took place in the context of escalating intensity in the country's struggle for racial justice and equality. A few months after the 1965 Selma to Montgomery voting rights march, the Watts neighborhood in Los Angeles erupted in massive protests after a routine traffic stop escalated into the latest in a long line of incidents of police using excessive force against unarmed Black people. The arrest lit a long-simmering fuse, and over the course of six days, thousands of people took to the streets in protest. The state responded by calling up fourteen thousand members of the National Guard, and nearly four thousand people were arrested. Thirty-four people were killed during those six days of rage.[11] Civil rights leader and movement strategist Bayard Rustin called the protests a "rebellion" and said that they were "carried on with the express purpose of asserting that they would no longer quietly submit to the deprivation of slum life."[12] Martin Luther King pointed out that "a riot is the language of the unheard."[13]

Where responsible leaders saw an urgent societal need resulting from conflict rooted in long-standing inequality and injustice, Ronald Reagan saw a political opportunity for personal advancement. Capitalizing on the fears of white people who had watched the Watts protests, he launched his 1966 gubernatorial campaign with the theme of law and order and the not-so-implicit message that he would protect white Californians from dangerous and scary people of color. One person who paid careful attention to that political approach and was swept into office along with Reagan in 1966 was a thirty-three-year-old San Diego lawyer named Pete Wilson.

After his election to the state legislature, Wilson went on to enjoy a successful political career serving as mayor of San Diego, United States senator, and, starting in 1991, governor of California. Although perceived as a moderate during his political climb up the ladder, he never forgot the lessons he learned about the electoral power of stoking the fire of white grievance. Facing a tough opponent and a challenging campaign during his gubernatorial reelection bid in 1994, Wilson quickly shed his moderate persona and turned to the "Distort Public Opinion" part of the Confederate Battle Plan that had worked so well for so many others. Echoing the same alarmism espoused by previous governors Stanford and Reagan, Wilson poured millions of dollars into television ads in 1994 warning white people about immigrants of color, ads stating, "They keep coming! Two million illegal immigrants in California."[14]

Much as Leland Stanford had championed pro-white public policies stemming from his preference for "free white citizens to any other class or race," Wilson enthusiastically embraced a slew of high-profile ballot measures and public policies squarely targeting the same kinds of racial discomfort and fear that had always influenced California's white voters. Specifically, he used his considerable clout to back referenda designed to eliminate bilingual education, restrict immigrants from receiving public services, and dramatically toughen criminal justice sentences and punishment. Not content with that litany of pro-white public policy initiatives, and with his eye on a presidential bid in 1996, Wilson threw his full support that year behind efforts to dismantle affirmative action programs across the state.

The political and cultural atmosphere that Wilson both benefited from and further inflamed was defined by the same sort of white panic that led to the creation and secession of the Confederacy in the first place. In their book *Preserving Privilege*, professors Jewelle Taylor Gibbs and Teiahsha Bankhead described the 1990s Wilson-backed initiatives as follows:

> Politicians and power brokers who were ambivalent about the emerging majority of people of color and unwilling to accept its inevitability launched a series of initiatives that would effectively turn back the clock on the socioeconomic progress of minorities and immigrants in the state by undermining their civil rights, eroding their civil liberties, and restricting their access to educational, employment, and entrepreneurial opportunities. . . . [These initiatives] represent a form of "bargaining" by their sponsors and supporters who hope to slow the rapid growth of people of color in California or, failing that result, intend to limit their socio-economic mobility and weaken their potential political power.[15]

Against this anti-immigrant backdrop, a young immigrant from Mexico made her way in 1988 to the university created by former governor Stanford. There, she gained knowledge and skills that would help her when she moved to Pete Wilson's San Diego County, a county that is far larger than most people realize. If it were a state, San Diego

County would be the thirty-first largest state in the country in terms of population. Home to 3.3 million people, it is the second most populous county in California (after Los Angeles). Today it is also one of the most diverse counties in the entire nation, with people of color making up 55 percent of the region's residents (35 percent are Latino, 13 percent are Asian, 6 percent are Black).[16]

It was there in San Diego, on land that was once part of Mexico and is now directly on the current border with Mexico, that the young immigrant Andrea Guerrero went to work, building the movement that would accelerate California's change into the kind of multiracial democracy that Leland Stanford, Ronald Reagan, Pete Wilson, and so many other Confederates worked so hard to stop.

INVEST IN LEVEL 5 LEADERS—ANDREA GUERRERO

Andrea is a testament to the power of transcending barriers, boundaries, and borders. Her parents, Javier Guerrero and Andrea Boardman, met and fell in love at an international gathering that united people from all over the world—the Olympic Games in Mexico in 1968 (the Olympics made famous when African American medal winners Tommie Smith and John Carlos raised their fists from the podium in an iconic Black Power moment). Her dad, a Mexican citizen, was an architect whose employer helped build the Olympic Village. Andrea's Scottish American mother was an interpreter for the multilingual assembly. That they gravitated toward a global celebration of solidarity was not accidental. As Andrea says of her parents, "They both looked beyond their national borders, their cultural borders, linguistic borders. Both had engaged in international exchanges. Both were learning other languages. So it was fitting that they were both working at the Olympics and that they then fell in love."[17]

After the Olympics, Andrea's parents got married in Mexico City, where Andrea and her brother were born. After five years in Mexico, the family immigrated to the United States, living in several different cities and ultimately settling in Dallas, Texas, in the early 1980s.

It was in Dallas that Andrea was first called a "spic." That kind of racist hostility was not uncommon at her high school, W.T. White High—a place that had a diverse student population as a result of mandatory busing that had brought together white students with Blacks, Latinos, and refugees from the Middle East and Vietnam. While the Dallas school district didn't shut down all the schools in racist defiance of the *Brown v. Board* decision, as happened in the South in the 1950s and 1960s, Andrea recalls that the town was still rife with racism in the 1980s, and Latino students were called racial slurs on the regular.

Tired of the racism, Andrea's thinking when it came to attending college was, "Get the hell out of Texas." Her father, then divorced and remarried, had moved to San Diego, California, and that factor heavily influenced her college choice. As she said after her father passed away in 2019, "Un buen padre vale por cien maestros" (A good father is worth more than a hundred teachers), and Andrea decided to go West to learn from college instructors and to be near her father, her best teacher of all.[18]

One hundred and three years after Stanford University was founded, Andrea walked onto its campus to gain knowledge and chart her course and career. It's safe to say that with his hostility to people of color and his fidelity to and belief in white men, Leland Stanford did not create his university for the benefit of people like Andrea (or for people like me, lol; sorry, not sorry). Andrea used the knowledge, growth, and development she gained at Stanford to become a force and the kind of Level 5 leader who would go on to catalyze the political transformation of the city and county of San Diego. She is in fact a Mexican immigrant who came across the border and then settled in San Diego—just the kind of person Pete Wilson, and Leland Stanford before him, had warned fearful whites about.

Andrea's voice, clarity, and courage showed through early. Shortly after graduating from Stanford, she stood up and spoke out about California's—and Governor Pete Wilson's—attacks on affirmative action programs designed to redress the ongoing racial inequality stemming from long-standing systemic, government-approved racism. In 1996, she was in the last class of students admitted to UC Berkeley's law school under the affirmative action criteria California developed in the 1970s to slow down the practice of regularly admitting overwhelmingly white groups of students into a publicly funded university, in a state where the white share of the population was plummeting.

Fresh out of law school, a phase in life when most recent law

school grads are contemplating their career paths and many graduates of color are modulating their voice so as not to rock the boat of a
legal establishment where, by and large, white folks hand out the jobs,
Andrea took the road less traveled. She wrote a book, titled *Silence at
Boalt Hall: The Dismantling of Affirmative Action,* in which she took
Wilson to task and persuasively made the argument for the public
policy and social change imperative of preserving race-conscious affirmative action programs, writing, "It is my hope that the reader will
use this story to rethink the dismantling of affirmative action and
help set the country on a path that will open wide the doors of higher
education for students of all racial backgrounds and not just the privileged few. In an increasingly diverse nation, we cannot afford to do
otherwise."[19]

Andrea is soft-spoken by nature and humble to an extreme. She
and I first met during the 2003 campaign to defeat what was then the
latest in a string of California anti–affirmative action ballot measures.
We bonded and became friends and colleagues. Her determination
to build progressive political power was evident early, and I asked her
to join the board of PowerPAC.org, the nonprofit I had helped found to
expand voter participation of people of color in a California whose racial composition was rapidly diversifying. We worked together on the
PowerPAC board for years, with her consistently attending meetings,
quietly watching and observing, asking thoughtful questions, and
making valuable suggestions.

I vaguely knew that she was starting her own civic engagement organization, Alliance San Diego, and that she was executing on the model of
bringing organizing skills and discipline to the task of getting more people of color to vote, but she never talked much about her work and didn't
bombard us with self-congratulatory announcements of how great she
and her work were. Impressed with her dedication, I helped her secure
one of her first grants—a $25,000 contribution to help get her work
off the ground. From there we remained in regular touch via quarterly
PowerPAC board meetings, occasional emails, and a conference every
year or so. While we stayed in consistent contact, I was not prepared for
what I saw when I went down to the city of San Diego in 2016.

As part of my book tour for *Brown Is the New White,* Andrea gra-
ciously offered to host an event for me, and I traveled to San Diego

where she gave me a tour of the Alliance San Diego office. When I'd met her years earlier, she was an immigration lawyer working in a small, three-person office helping individuals navigate the complex and hostile immigration system. On my visit in 2016, she brought me into a sprawling office with two dozen people spread out in various offices and departments doing a wide assortment of civic engagement work. A couple of people were in a dedicated phone room calling through a list of eligible voters, talking to them in Spanish and telling them about upcoming elections and asking what issues were most important to them. That information was all captured in the computer and fed into a master database. Another team of people was holding a planning meeting about the week's activities, and a third cluster was working on written materials to send to voters about the upcoming election.

As she took me from office to office, my eyes grew bigger and bigger in amazement. This was no embryonic, small shop–style law office anymore. "This is a whole voter turnout machine!" I said in disbelief. She'd taken that $25K grant and turned it into a voter contact and political participation powerhouse with a $3 million annual budget. I'd known Andrea for a decade, was in regular touch with her, and I had *no idea* about the scale and scope and significance of the enterprise she had created. And I was one of her friends. In my time in politics, I've seen people who've built far less get far more media coverage and donor adulation, largely because of their aggressive self-promotion. Meanwhile, Andrea had just been keeping her head down and doing the work, choosing to let the work speak for itself.

In describing her decision to start the Alliance, Andrea offers a description deserving of the same kinds of respect usually reserved for white guys launching a fancy new tech app:

I saw that communities of color were not at the decision-making tables, not here, not anywhere. I started to really think about strategically how you make change. I thought about what it would take to get people to the table, to the decision-making table. In San Diego, the organizing is very siloed, ethnically speaking. So I reached out to an African American friend of mine and said, "You're from this community. What would it take to bring the Latino and Black communities together to start to address some of these issues?" And she said, "Let's pull the leadership together and see what happens." She had some clout and I had some ideas. So we had an initial meeting. When people came into the room they filed in and they sat on separate sides of the room. These were the elders, these were the old guard Chicano/Latino leaders and Black leaders. I thought, "Oh, my. We've got work to do." I didn't see any organization in San Diego that was working across racial and cultural lines.

So that's when I thought: it's time to start a new organization. I don't know why I thought I could do it, but I had been forged by all of these experiences where I had to define myself for myself. I looked around and I saw others of my generation and younger who were looking for a place to do organizing work, a place to engage, a place to feel affirmed in all of their identities, which were multiple. I bought a book on how to start a nonprofit and followed steps one through ten and filed the paperwork with the state to create the organization. At the time I was a practicing attorney. So I filed the organization, and since we couldn't afford an office, I worked out of the closet in my house for a couple of years until it really got off the ground in 2010.[20]

A big part of the answer to journalist Randy Dotinga's question about the political metamorphosis of San Diego—"What happened?"— is that Andrea Guerrero happened. What Andrea has built and what she has done is nothing short of transformative. She has created the organization and nurtured the networks and driven the work over the past decade that has turned San Diego from the launching pad for politicians seeking to capitalize on white racial grievance into a cornerstone of progressive politics and power in California. And while she has done it without singing her own praises, politicians and political players across San Diego County can now certainly hear Andrea and Alliance San Diego coming.

BUILD STRONG CIVIC ENGAGEMENT ORGANIZATIONS—
ALLIANCE SAN DIEGO

Most people thought Scott Peters didn't really have a chance to win his congressional race. Although the San Diego city councilman was wealthy and white, Peters was a Democrat, which had historically meant electoral doom in local congressional contests. For twenty years in a row, every Democratic nominee for the 52nd congressional district had been crushed by the Republican candidate on the ballot, generally losing by 30 points, and sometimes as many as 50 points.[21] So, in 2012, when Peters announced his candidacy for the seat, most experts wrote him off. But, unknown even to himself, Peters had a secret weapon in the form of a young Black woman named Diamond.

Diamond Brandon came from an entirely different part of town than Scott Peters did. While Peters was establishing his network and nurturing ties with the city's financial elite as he did while serving on boards of well-endowed charities, Diamond was building a different kind of network. An energetic and enthusiastic nineteen-year-old African American woman with broad and deep ties in Southeast San Diego, where the median income is just half the city's overall average, Diamond found her way in 2011 to Alliance San Diego, where Andrea hired her as a canvasser.[22] A decade later, the pride still shines through when Andrea describes Diamond's work:

> Diamond began as a canvasser, and she did very well. She would go out and work in her own community, and she would come back every day and she'd say, "I knocked on my cousin's door, I knocked on my great aunt's door, and I knocked on my schoolmate's door." She seemed to know everybody in Southeast San Diego. She was moved by the experience and she saw personally that people started to vote. People she knew started to vote. So when there was a job opening here, she applied and she became a team leader and then she ultimately rose to manage the whole program. She then went on to work for the legislative office. She now works for Assembly Member Lorena Gonzalez [as of January 2022], and she is actively doing a lot of training for a lot of other folks.[23]

Diamond was a natural in the role of canvasser because her neighbors knew and trusted her from the years of shared activities with their children and families. One of the first races that she worked on was the 52nd congressional district race in 2012, for which she registered people to vote and encouraged them to turn out to the polls in the election where Scott Peters was on the ballot making his long-shot congressional bid.

Diamond had company in her canvassing efforts. In 2012, in an early test of their electoral muscle, Andrea and Alliance San Diego hired, trained, and deployed 250 volunteers and organizers across the county, contacting 24,234 voters and getting 18,939 of them to vote.[24] Scott Peters won the 52nd congressional district race by 6,992 votes.[25]

———

As she set out on her journey of building an electoral engagement operation, Andrea turned to Anthony Thigpenn, the architect of what many consider to be the gold-standard voter engagement operation in California. Over the course of twenty years, Thigpenn had built a powerful political force in Los Angeles that had helped to elect many progressive candidates. I wrote about his operation in *Brown Is the New White*:

Thigpenn describes his approach as Integrated Voter Engagement (IVE), and he has distilled the formula into the following elements: (1) a multiyear strategy to increase the voter participation of communities and constituencies traditionally underrepresented in the electorate; (2) engaging target voters year-round to build a relationship, educate on issues, motivate to increase voter participation, and become involved in advocacy and community organizing; (3) local, community-based organizations (CBOs) that are rooted in communities embrace IVE as an integrated part of their organizing strategy and ongoing work; (4) development of grassroots leaders in communities as the primary voter engagement organizers; (5) use of voter engagement technology to increase the capacities of CBOs to reach a new scale of engaging target constituencies; and

(6) systematic tracking of engagement and results through a living and growing voter database.[26]

Andrea and her team applied those lessons over multiple years in their work in San Diego. "Every time we went out, we did a civic engagement program, which would be three to four weeks, at least twenty canvassers, sometimes as many as a hundred canvassers," Andrea explained in my interview with her. She added, "Depending on our resources, we would be ID'ing people. And as we ID'ed them, we would put them into our database and then we would always take the newest addition to our database and do the one-on-one contact in the election."[27]

By methodically following that formula over the past decade, Alliance San Diego has become a civic engagement and political force to be reckoned with. In the years since Andrea was working out of her closet, she has steadily constructed a multimillion-dollar operation that helps coordinate the civic engagement activity of dozens of organizations spanning the demographic spectrum from the ACLU to Planned Parenthood to the LGBT Community Center to Viet Vote to local labor unions. In each of those organizations, there are leaders like Diamond—talented, energetic, optimistic, and disciplined activists who have the relationships and trust necessary to effectively convince their friends, neighbors, family, and colleagues to get out and vote.

Similar to the sure and steady expansion of the anchor civic engagement organizations in Georgia, Virginia, Arizona, Texas, and other cities and states, Alliance San Diego has grown consistently and effectively. Over the past decade, the staff has increased from a one-woman operation to twenty full-time staff who coordinate the work of more than 250 volunteers and canvassers come election time.

By the end of its first decade of work, in 2020, the Alliance was everywhere and a driving force in the region's politics. In 2018 (the most recent pre-pandemic election), the Alliance helped anchor the work of Engage San Diego, the countywide coalition of organizations that deployed 621 volunteers and organizers across the county.[28] Union organizers, Latino activists, Asian American canvassers, LGBTQ+ volunteers, Black community members, and others each took responsibility for communicating with their demographic piece of the area's population puzzle.

The data from the voter contact work of the constellation of groups was funneled back to the data center in the Alliance San Diego office that Andrea had shown me in 2016. There, the information from the door-to-door contacts was collected and analyzed and fed to the data analytics team, which used it to refine its message and targeting. People like Chris Wilson, deputy director of Alliance San Diego, understood how to use technology to identify the voters most likely to support progressive ballot measures. He pinpointed tens of thousands of voters and then helped craft targeted messages to reach them.

By 2020, the burgeoning civic engagement machine had flipped control of the City Council from Republican to Democratic, with Democrats now holding a commanding 8–1 majority on the council. At the county level, encompassing a more far-flung and populous terrain, conservative power had been even more entrenched as Republicans held sway for decades in the body that controlled and allocated the county's $7 billion budget. The powerful network of progressive political engagement organizations helped flip control of that body in 2020, with Democrats now holding a 3–2 majority. Alliance San Diego and its allies had also helped win a second Republican-held congressional seat, electing Mike Levin in 2018 and giving Scott Peters an additional Democratic colleague in the House of Representatives, a body few people thought Peters himself could ever join.

DEVELOP DETAILED, DATA-DRIVEN PLANS

Although she was not a math major, Andrea could count, and she could see the unfolding demographic transformation and what it could portend for a place like San Diego. In 2011, around the same time that Stacey Abrams was putting the finishing touches on the plan for Georgia that she would take around the country to share with prospective supporters, and Tram Nguyen was creating spreadsheets to begin to build multiracial, New American Majority power in Virginia, and John Loredo was studying the Colorado model of strategic plan development, Andrea and her team at Alliance San Diego were drafting a document called "Target San Diego: A Roadmap to

Winning a Social Justice Agenda in San Diego." It would indeed turn out to be a turn-by-turn guide for navigating the journey to a transformed city and county.

The roadmap that Andrea and her colleagues developed in 2011 was anchored in a deep data dive into San Diego's demographics and electoral history, and it highlighted the potential impact on public policy priorities that could result from increasing the civic participation of people of color. The following are some key excerpts from that 2011 report that illuminate the level of data analysis and sophistication:

- With over 8 percent of the registered voters in the state, San Diego County constitutes the third largest electorate in California [behind Los Angeles and, at that time, Orange County]. Although the county has long been considered a stronghold of conservative voters, changing demographics have put San Diego in play.
- The Alliance has identified three communities of opportunity that could constitute the difference in electoral battles around tax and fiscal reform and other social justice issues: (1) communities of color, (2) low-income communities, and (3) infrequent voters.
- Latinos have increased from 27 to 32 percent of the population and Asians have increased from 9 to 11 percent. Simultaneously, African Americans have decreased slightly from 6 to 4 percent and Whites have decreased from 55 to 48 percent. Though they are a diminishing percentage of the population, African American voters turn out at a higher rate than other voters of color and nearly doubled their vote share of all voters statewide from 5 to 9 percent between the 2006 and 2010 general election.
- Infrequent voters (occasional and new voters) represent an untapped resource for social justice advocates. These voters constitute the largest single portion of the county electorate (43 percent), but are normally not engaged by campaigns at any significant level and are left out of the electoral equation.
- The use of new voter engagement practices, such as values-based framing and voter education, in addition to technological advances (predictive dialing systems, voter information software, and robo-dialers) enable us to conduct targeted large-scale

civic engagement. It also allows us to combine grassroots coalition building with strategic outreach, education, and voting.
- Understanding that San Diego County is in play, we have a great opportunity to advance social justice reforms if we work together. The Alliance seeks regional partners to form the next level of relationships: long-term collaborations formed by organizations that agree on strategy, distribute the work, and share resources and tools to pursue the long-term goal of reviving the California Dream.[29]

———

Progressive political donors spend hundreds of millions of dollars every year on outdated and ineffective strategies, rooted in flawed assumptions and bad data. One such assumption is the mistaken belief that canvassing and voter mobilization are inordinately expensive and inefficient. Oddly, that logic never stops them from spending millions on TV ads where the profit margins for consultants are higher and the available data for effectiveness is almost nonexistent, as evidenced by the famous phrase that "everyone knows half of all advertising dollars are wasted; it's just that no one knows which half."

In addition to the implicit racial bias that leads many to overlook and underinvest in people of color, a big part of the problem among progressive donors and those who run and fund campaigns is the failure to apply the best practices of business to the world of social change. In stock market investing, donors expect and receive regular reports describing a company's results from the past quarter and plans for the future. In social change and politics, such data is rarely demanded or received. To its credit, Alliance San Diego went a different direction, and it applied high standards of science and rigor, contracting with Dr. Tom Wong, a political science professor at the University of California, San Diego, to conduct research and analysis of its work. What they discovered has truly revolutionary implications for U.S. politics.

What Professor Wong revealed and what Andrea and her team demonstrated was that a sustained, multiyear approach would become both increasingly politically impactful *and* cost-effective. Ample empirical data showed that once an infrequent voter participates in two election cycles, they are likely to vote in future elections without further reminders or prompting. This insight about political behavior correlates with similar findings from the field of behavioral science. In her book, *Good Habits, Bad Habits*, research psychologist Wendy Wood found that "the second time you do something takes less time and mental effort than the first. The third takes less than the second. And so on. This creates a favorable mental condition for a habit to come in and take over."[30]

The implications of this insight, if applied across the country, can lead to saving millions of dollars for the progressive movement. It does in fact cost money in terms of staff time and follow-up communications to get an infrequent or unregistered potential voter to become an *actual* voter. But once that person forms the habit of voting, the financial commitment required to get them to cast a ballot drops dramatically. The money that previously went to engaging that set of new voters can then be used to contact another set of potential voters. In this fashion, a consistent commitment of resources can steadily and exponentially increase the size of the progressive voting army. It's how progressives can build an affordable, ever-growing network of millions of voters.

Andrea and her San Diego colleagues have followed their 2011 roadmap for the past decade, arriving closer and closer to their destination of winning a social justice agenda, in both San Diego and the state as a whole. In every single election cycle over the past decade, they have implemented the plan, assessed its efficacy, made strategic adjustments, and updated the plan for the subsequent fights to come. In this fashion, they have grown their influence from having no list at all of identified progressive voters when they started out in 2010, to building a database that today contains records relating to more than one hundred thousand eligible voters across the county who have expressed support for progressive policy priorities. As Andrea puts it, "We just executed what the math told us to do. Our entire voter plan is an Excel formula."

PLAY THE LONG GAME

For most of the twentieth century, the San Diego political status quo was skewed toward white people. In the early twenty-first century, people of color officially became the majority of the city's residents, growing from 41 percent of the population in 1990 to 55 percent by 2010.[31] San Diego has its share of modern-day Confederates (Confederates can wear flip-flops and sunglasses too), and as they watched the white share of the population plunge, they responded by manipulating the electoral rules much as their ancestors did when faced with the prospect of losing their hold on power as more and more people of color entered the electorate after the Civil War. In San Diego that manipulation took the form of holding elections in off years, when voter interest and turnout were lower.

It has long been the case that people with the most money have the fewest impediments to participating in the electoral process. As discussed in chapter 6, without having to navigate child care, public transportation, multiple jobs with unpredictable hours, and the other everyday yet daunting realities of being a working-class person, wealthier voters are disproportionately overrepresented in lower-turnout elections. If you're seeking to preserve an unequal and unjust status quo, that voting disparity is a good thing, and year after year, San Diego's leaders placed the conservative policy proposals on the ballot in the lower-turnout elections in June.

For those laboring to foster greater justice and equality in San Diego, a savvy and strategic long game required finding a way to remove the obstacles to people of color who are fully manifesting their political power at the ballot box.

Just as Tram Nguyen understood the long-term implications of getting the right person selected to serve as Virginia's chief election officer, and just as Stacey Abrams immediately saw the significance of training her attention on combating voter suppression in the run-up to the 2020 election, Andrea recognized the imperative of making structural and systemic changes to the electoral process if their movement in San Diego was going make the biggest impact possible. Accordingly, Alliance San Diego and their allies focused their sights on a strategic structural reform—changing the law so that the most important elections would take place in the higher-turnout elections in the fall, where there were usually the advantages of greater voter participation, a more reflective electorate and better prospects of passing progressive policies and electing progressive candidates.

In 2016, with their eye on the long game of future policy and political payoffs, the San Diego progressive coalition proposed and passed a ballot measure to require that tax matters relating to the city and also runoff elections go on the November ballot (the same kind of runoff elections that Georgia's Denmark Groover had dreamed up to dilute the Black vote in Georgia in the 1960s). Two years later, in 2018, Alliance San Diego and its allies turned their attention to the county level and passed a similar initiative shifting the county elections to November, away from the low-participation, more conservative electorates of June. With the rules made more small-"d" democratic, political empowerment and better policies ensued. In 2018 and 2020, progressives flipped City Council and Board of Supervisors seats, giving Democrats control of both bodies for the first time in decades.[32] On the City Council, Democrats went from holding just four of the nine seats in 2014 to having a commanding 8–1 edge after the 2020 election.

San Diego's Pete Wilson rode to power demonizing immigrants, stoking white fears about people of color, and aggressively championing "preserving privilege" policies such as the anti-immigrant Proposition 187. At that time, in 1994, a young high school student named Terra Lawson-Remer participated in a student walkout protesting the ballot measure, causing her school administration to strip her of her class presidency title. Twenty-six years later, in 2020, Lawson-Remer was elected to the San Diego County Board of Supervisors, putting control of that previously conservative body in the hands of Democrats. As one of her first actions, she and the new board majority passed a multibillion-dollar budget that allocated hundreds of millions of additional dollars to mental health services, pandemic-related economic recovery, and other progressive priorities. Commenting on the budget, Supervisor Lawson-Remer said, "San Diego County has never seen a budget like this before. It represents a footprint on our journey toward a more responsive and effective county and gives us a roadmap to tackle sustainability and the inequities in our region."[33]

Since Andrea first set about trying to build capacity for change in San Diego in 2009, she has helped solidify a coalition, craft a plan, and chart a course for the political transformation of that region. The city that launched Pete Wilson to the position where he could champion anti-immigrant policies is now a cornerstone of a new, progressive multiracial political order in California with profoundly different poli-cies, politics, and priorities.

———

The popular conception of San Diego is that it is next to the ocean, which it is, giving rise to images of beaches and surfing. What gets much less attention is that San Diego is also next to Mexico, as it is situated directly on the U.S.-Mexico border—the border that has been center stage in twenty-first-century Confederate efforts to whip up white hysteria and fear about people of color. The substance and sym-bolism of San Diego's geographic location give it great political and moral standing in one of the longest-standing fights in this country, one that even predates the Civil War.

The longest of long games is the centuries-long struggle over who gets included in the opening words of the U.S. Constitution: "We the People." It is truly an existential question for a nation that came into existence as a white nationalist entity and has continued to fight for centuries to define "we" as "whites" (as demonstrated by the actions of past California governors Stanford, Reagan, and Wilson, among oth-ers). For Liberators, this issue of who belongs in "we" is not only a pro-found moral one, but also lies at the heart of an ongoing political fight, one whose outcome will reverberate for decades to come.

One of the current battlefields in this fight to expand the definition of "we" is taking place each day in the form of a raging political battle over the treatment of immigrants from Mexico. Andrea Guerrero is a key general in that battle. Like the many who have come before them in doing this work, she and countless others are working tirelessly to overhaul U.S. immigration policies and humanize practices along the U.S.-Mexico border.

Looking to the long game—to the definitional fights over who counts as American and over which people in which regions get to vote—winning the politics of the border will be critical. Like the civil rights leaders of the 1950s and 1960s joining forces with like-minded activists in cities facing similar discrimination, Andrea and Alliance San Diego have linked arms with other border organizers, creating the Southern Border Communities Coalition.

That coalition has already played a critical role in pushing the U.S.

government to stop harming and start helping immigrants who are simply looking for a better life. It is also a key player in the years-long campaign to finally pass immigration reform, advocating for a path to citizenship for the millions of people, mainly immigrants of color, who have had to live in the shadows in a nation that reserved citizenship for free white persons and then, through violence and bloodshed, moved the border south, stealing land that had once belonged to Mexico.

In terms of the political balance of power, some of the largest pools of non-voting people of color can be found on the border—from San Diego to Texas. As the movement of border activists grows, civic engagement and organizing resources can and should flow to the kinds of work done by organizations such as the Southern Border Communities Coalition. As immigration reform advances, and as the ranks of young people—the majority of whom are people of color—turn eighteen and move into the electorate, the overall complexion of the voting population will change.[34] And with it, the country's policies, priorities, and definition of "we" will have to change from white to multiracial. That is the long game. It is a game Andrea Guerrero, Alliance San Diego, and many, many partner organizations and leaders are playing, and the entire country is and will be better for their efforts.

11

Texas: "The Task at Hand Is Epic"

Let's not be coy with this: When Texas changes, the whole electoral map re-
sets. This is the last stronghold of power for conservatism, and if it goes, they
would have to rewrite their whole playbook, their whole everything, so they
are going to hold on and push back as hard as they can in the state of Texas.
—Crystal Zermeño, director of electoral strategy for Texas
Organizing Project, CNN.com, March 23, 2021

When Sam Houston died in 1863, his children cried, his friends sent tributes, and his attorney began to settle his affairs. Houston had lived a long and successful life as an important political and military leader in Texas's formative years. His tombstone bears the following inscription:

A Brave Soldier. A Fearless Statesman.
A Great Orator—A Pure Patriot.
A Faithful Friend, A Loyal Citizen.
A Devoted Husband and Father.
A Consistent Christian—An Honest Man.[1]

In addition to the praise and accomplishments he had garnered, Houston had also come to own a significant amount of property that needed to be inventoried and distributed. During his years as a lawyer, businessman, military leader, and the first United States senator from Texas, Houston had accumulated 17,873 acres of land, a house, five horses, four cows, a rifle, a pistol, and a sword. Oh, and in addition to the horses, cows, and sword, Sam Houston also listed among his property twelve Black human beings—"the oldest a 55-year-old man named Lewis, valued at $400, the youngest a four-year-old girl named Lotte, also valued at $400." The person worth the most money on the open market, according to twentieth-century Texas journalist Bill Porterfield, "was a 35-year-old man named Joshua. He sold for $2000" (the rough equivalent of $43,000 today).[2]

In addition to feeling fine about holding Black people in slavery, Houston was no fan of Mexicans, saying in an 1835 speech, "The vigor of the descendants of the sturdy north will never mix with the phlegm of the indolent Mexicans, no matter how long we may live among them."[3]

That's the consistent Christian and honest man for whom the city of Houston is named.

———

Many people don't realize the extent to which the history of Texas shapes its contemporary politics. The land we now call Texas used to belong to Mexico until the 1830s. At that time, the white people who lived in that region wanted to buy, sell, and own Black people, and they were mad that the Mexican government wouldn't sanction slavery. So, in 1835, Houston and others started shooting and killing Mexicans. This is known as the Texas Revolution. The success of that violent and bloody rampage resulted in the creation of the Republic of Texas in 1836, with Sam Houston serving as president of said Republic.[4]

The government over which Houston presided was bound by a constitution that codified citizenship for whites and slavery for Blacks. Drafted and adopted in 1836, the constitution was a very thorough and detailed document. Section 6 of the General Provisions held that after six months of residence, "free white persons . . . shall be entitled to all the privileges of citizenship." A few paragraphs later, in Section 9, it decreed, "All persons of color who were slaves for life previous to their emigration to Texas, and who are now held in bondage, shall remain in the like state of servitude." As for those Black folks who happened to have secured their freedom? They had to get out, with Houston's government maintaining that "no free person of African descent, either in whole or in part, shall be permitted to reside permanently in the Republic."[5]

Meanwhile, Mexico was still unhappy that a big chunk of the country had been stolen, and the breakaway Texas Republic sought

protection in the bigger bosom of the United States with its extensive array of weapons of war, violence, and bloodshed. The ensuing
Mexican-American War lasted for two years (1846–48), and after killing thousands of Mexicans, the United States prevailed and forced
Mexico to accept terms of surrender that reverberate to this day. The
Treaty of Guadalupe Hidalgo, which moved the U.S. border deeper
into territory that had recently been Mexico, formalized the expropria-
tion of 525,000 square miles of land—land that we now call Arizona,
California, New Mexico, Texas, Colorado, Nevada, and Utah. By the
end of the war, the United States had taken *the majority* of the landmass of Mexico for itself.[6]

That's how Texas came to be, and it is no small part of why the
politics of the state have been so conservative (and so racist) for so long.
The irony of Texas's current conservative leaders bemoaning the perils
of "illegal immigration" is that originally it was the white Texans who
were the illegal immigrants in a territory that belonged to Mexico.

———

In the twenty-first century, things have not turned out quite as Sam
Houston had hoped. In 2015, the people in the city named after
Houston elected as their mayor Democrat Sylvester Turner, an African American descended from people like Lewis, Lotte, Joshua, and
other unknown and unnamed Black people once held in bondage in
the Lone Star State.[7] Turner was reelected in 2019 to a term that runs
through 2023. In addition to a Black man having the top job in the
city, the woman who presides over the county that includes the city of
Houston is a young Latina named Lina Hidalgo, an immigrant who
used to live in Mexico among the progeny of the people Sam Houston
called "phlegm."

The descendants of the phlegm and the descendants of the slaves
are now the majority of people in Texas. According to the 2020 Census,
white people now account for just 39.8 percent of the state population,
and there are essentially as many Latinos (39.3 percent) as whites. Over
the past decade, Texas has gained nearly eleven Latino residents for
each additional white resident. Throw in African Americans (11.8 percent of the state population) and Asian Americans (5.4 percent) and

you start to see how Texas in the 2020s is becoming browner than at any time since the land was first taken from Mexico.[8]

Houston (the city, not the man) and Harris County are at the forefront of that change, and the story of how that change came to pass offers inspiration and instruction for how we win the Civil War in Texas and the rest of the United States in the decades to come.

INVEST IN LEVEL 5 LEADERS—MICHELLE TREMILLO AND GINNY GOLDMAN

Michelle Tremillo and Ginny Goldman are kind of a political Odd Couple. The original architects of much of the work that has propelled political change in Texas over the past decade, they are two women who, individually and collectively, exemplify Level 5 leadership. But at first, they didn't really get along. It was a clash of class and culture that is not uncommon in progressive politics.

Michelle is Mexican American and a fourth-generation Tejana whose maternal great-grandmother immigrated from Mexico to Brownsville, Texas, to help raise her grandchildren. Like many families of color trying to make their way in a country that was originally designed for white people, Michelle's mom, a single mother, struggled financially and endured significant housing insecurity that resulted in moving eight different times before Michelle was eight years old.

In a manifestation of the constructive and crucial role of public assistance programs, Michelle's family eventually secured government-subsidized housing in San Antonio, and their life stabilized. Michelle's mom found work as a janitor (in addition to regularly working a second job to make ends meet), and the family was able to stay in one place for the next eight years. A gifted student, Michelle did well in school and got a scholarship to attend Stanford, arriving on campus the year after the graduation of another important and impactful Texas Latina, Andrea Guerrero—the Level 5 leader in San Diego (see chapter 10).

After graduating from college in 1997, Michelle returned home to San Antonio, where she answered an ad from ACORN (Association of Community Organizations for Reform Now) that said, "Do you want to work for social justice?" Thinking, "Why, yes. Yes, I do," she went to work for the community organizing group, starting out as a can-vasser knocking on doors and registering people to vote. Once she'd demonstrated that she was efficient enough at canvassing to register ten voters per hour and a hundred people per day, she was promoted to higher levels of responsibility and fairly quickly rose to the position of head organizer for the organization's San Antonio chapter and then statewide deputy director.[9]

Ginny Goldman also came of political age as an ACORN organizer. Founded in 1970, ACORN had grown by the early 2000s to become one of the largest and most effective community-organizing and civic engagement networks in the country. At its height, in 2008, the or-ganization had "more than six hundred staff, thousands of low- and moderate-income members, dozens of coalition partners, and over a hundred chapters in forty-two states."[10]

Ginny's story started out with a fairly typical white suburban child-hood in Long Island, New York. She was raised by her father, "a pretty classic Jewish guy from Brooklyn who moved to Long Island when he was in high school," and mother, a Protestant Unitarian from upstate New York. Her father worked as a chemist before losing his job and go-ing to work for a life insurance company, while her mother worked as a physical therapist. In terms of their religious background and prac-tices, the family belonged to the Unitarian faith, and that led Ginny to make a fairly atypical life decision when she was In college at the State University of New York, Buffalo, in the mid-1990s.

The Unitarian religious tradition is very progressive, and leaders of the faith have created a "faith in action" philanthropic initiative, the Veatch Program, that provides financial support for social justice or-ganizing. As part of that program, students can apply for internships paid for by Veatch. As an undergraduate, Ginny decided to seek an internship with a community organization based in Mexico. The fund-ing from Veatch allowed her to go to Guadalajara, Mexico, to do com-munity organizing.

While living in Mexico, Ginny met and worked closely with a col-lege student who was from Chicago, and that friend told her about ACORN. Trying to decide between law school and community orga-nizing, Ginny chose to move to Chicago to give the organizing thing a shot "for one year." For the next six years, she settled in with ACORN and dug into the work in Chicago, where she "learned a ton" work-ing on a wide range of issues including bank redlining, environmen-tal racism, immigration, and labor and other workers' rights issues.[11] While in Illinois, she and the ACORN team worked closely with a young state senator named Barack Obama who, earlier in the 1990s, had done community organizing of his own with an ACORN-affiliated group, Project Vote.[12]

In 2003, ACORN's leaders asked Ginny to move to Houston. Eager to see if the Chicago model of organizing would translate to a South-ern state, she packed her bags and headed to Texas. As Ginny took the reins in Houston, she met and got to know Michelle, who was, at the time, the head organizer of ACORN in San Antonio, two hundred miles west of Houston.

The pairing did not take at first. In terms of personality, Michelle is more introverted, low-key, and very focused on the nuts and bolts. Ginny is more extroverted by nature, with a sort of stereotypical New York brashness in dealing with people. As Ginny tells it, "I just re-member we just did not hit it off because I'm sure Michelle was like, 'This woman comes in here from Chicago thinking she's like this bril-liant organizer,' and we just didn't get along well. We just didn't really see eye to eye on things." Michelle's version also acknowledges initial tension: "I would not say that Ginny and I particularly cared for each other. She was like the obnoxious New Yorker who'd organized in Chi-cago and who was, like, rude and didn't say 'bye' when she hung up the phone." Upon learning that Ginny was going to become the head organizer for ACORN in Texas, Michelle cried.

But there's something about being at the barricades together that bonds people. When you're fighting for the same people and against the same entrenched forces, differences can fade away as trust gets built. As James Baldwin wrote of his friendship with Lorraine Hans-berry, "We had that respect for each other which perhaps is only felt by people on the same side of the barricades, listening to the accumulat-ing thunder of the hooves of the horses."[13] Such was the situation with Ginny and Michelle. "Little by little," Ginny recalls, "we really became very close collaborators, initially through the fights around predatory lending campaigns. We just became really synced up around some of the bigger foreclosure fights that we wanted to do together. Then we became almost attached to the hip. We were just yin and yang and just balanced each other out really well."

In the subsequent years, the yin-and-yang pair would be severely tested, and the results of that test would help propel the political transformations that have occurred in Texas over the past decade. Michelle and Ginny were especially challenged when ACORN came under withering right-wing attack after the 2008 election because of its association with that former community organizer named Obama.

ACORN's effectiveness invited scrutiny and attacks in ways that were both an echo and a foreshadowing: an echo of Confederate attacks over the centuries and a foreshadowing of the more recent faux outrage by Republicans allegedly concerned about "voter fraud." The same claims they used to mask the 2021 wave of voter suppression legislation that swept through Texas and other states where the white population is shrinking.

While some of ACORN's wounds were self-inflicted (an embezzlement scandal by the brother of the founder that was not reported to stakeholders, for example), the death blows to the organization were mostly dealt by the right-wing, modern-day Confederates. Peter Dreier, professor of politics at Occidental College, described the saga in a 2009 *Los Angeles Times* op-ed:

> For 40 years, the community organizing group ACORN has been a strong and effective voice for low-income Americans. It has registered more than a million citizens to vote. It has provided counseling and other assistance to help Americans buy and keep homes. It has fought on behalf of working people for fair treatment by employers, banks, mortgage companies and payday lenders. . . .
>
> But few Americans had heard of ACORN until last fall, when Sen. John McCain and then-Gov. Sarah Palin began attacking the organization for "voter fraud." Soon, more than 80% of Americans knew about the group, according to polls. . . . The attack on ACORN is not really about bogus names on voter forms or about staffers encouraging people to lie on their tax forms. Rather, it is part of a broader conservative effort to attack

progressive organizations and discredit President Obama and his liberal agenda.[14]

In late 2008, the assault on ACORN leaped from the airwaves of Fox News to the halls of Congress, where Democrats allowed right-wing politicians to focus on and cut off funding for ACORN programs that had helped millions of people living in poverty. With Democrats complicit in the attack through their silence and inaction, one of the largest and longest-running organizations in the progressive movement was left to twist in the wind and ultimately die. In 2009 and 2010, ACORN succumbed to the multifront battle, and the majority of its state chapters—including the Texas chapter—disbanded and closed up shop.

As the organization that had been their political home and base of operations was collapsing around them, Michelle and Ginny faced an existential dilemma. They had devoted their professional lives to an entity that had ceased to exist, and it had dissolved in the very year that most of America was infused with the thrill and hope of having elected the first Black president. Individually and together, they decided to step into the breach. Ginny recalls the situation clearly:

> When ACORN got attacked, I remember calling Michelle and being like, look, this thing is going down. I moved to Texas because I was excited about organizing in Texas, not just because I was excited about building ACORN. And [I told Michelle], "Either we should just call it quits and fold it up or we should think about building something new that really is tailored for the context that we're in." I had a three-year-old and a nine-month-old at the time. But we were both like, "We're not going out like this."
>
> And so, I thought, "Why don't we do a little listening tour?" So Michelle and I literally just got in the car and drove around and met with all of our allies in cities across the state. Everywhere we went, people were saying, "We need you to start an organization. There's just not enough organizing in the state. You guys need to be able to figure out how to keep the assets that you have and build something new."

Encouraged by the mandate they sensed from their listening tour, they proceeded to create an organization that could take the best of what they had been building in the past and chart a course to make a difference in the future. And they decided to draw upon the respective strengths of their different personalities. Ginny says that she first proposed that Michelle be the executive director, and Ginny would be the organizing director. To which Michelle said, "No, that's a terrible idea. You be the executive director and raise the money. I'll set up the internal operations so that we don't go down like ACORN did." They decided to call their new organization the Texas Organizing Project (TOP).

Michelle and Ginny didn't fit the prototypical picture of start-up entrepreneurs, but they were entrepreneurs nonetheless. They were two young women in a beat-up car driving across the vast stretches of Texas, picking up the pieces of what was once a powerful progressive political organization, and building something new, organic, and focused on the needs associated with the imperatives of the hour. And they did all of this without venture capital or significant investments from donors hoping to one day get rich off their work.

In 2017, after seven years as TOP's executive director, and having just marked the personal milestone of turning forty, Ginny stepped aside from her position and went on to become an independent political strategist. Michelle then took on the role of executive director (which she continues to hold to this day), and brought on a new partner, Brianna Brown. Brianna, an African American woman who is also, like Michelle, a fourth-generation Tejana, first served as deputy director and is currently co-executive director. Like Ginny, Brianna is an extrovert, and she is frequently the face and voice of TOP's work, appearing in media interviews on networks such as CNN and MSNBC. Like Ginny and Michelle, Brianna is also a Level 5 leader well suited to the Texas-sized tasks of the 2020s.

TOP's leadership comes from and is connected to Texas's African American and Latino communities, which collectively make up 51 percent of the residents of the Lone Star State. They are the inheritors of the struggles, sacrifice, and hope of the communities Sam Houston thought he had vanquished through slavery and slaughter. Together, these Mexican American and African American women are bringing Level 5 leadership to the essential work of turning Texas's demographic potential and trends into meaningful political power. Building a strong civic engagement organization and ecosystem that could unleash the transformative power of the state's voters of color is the imperative of the moment (as is the case in Georgia, Virginia, San Diego, and Arizona), and that is the journey that these women are helping to lead.

BUILD STRONG CIVIC ENGAGEMENT ORGANIZATIONS

My dad lived in Houston in the 1990s, and the first time I went to visit him, I missed my exit on the freeway, and I could not believe how long and how far I was driving before I was able to properly turn around and get back on course. That was my introduction to just how large and sprawling Houston is. The Greater Houston area spans nearly ten thousand square miles, covering more land than any other city in the country, and its geographic sprawl is larger than many states.[15] The local boosters like to point out that Houston could fit New York City, Washington, DC, Boston, San Francisco, Seattle, Minneapolis, *and* Miami within its city limits.

Not only is its landmass large, but Houston's population is huge, numbering more than 2.3 million people, bigger than the population of fifteen states. While there are a lot of stereotypes about the demographic profile of Texans, the true picture of who lives in Houston (and Texas) is much different. Native Houstonian singers Beyoncé and Megan Thee Stallion fit the profile much better than a white man in cowboy hat and cowboy boots. Houston has been described as the "Most Diverse City in America," based on an analysis of socioeconomic, cultural, economic, household, and religious criteria.[16] People of color make up a majority (76 percent) of the city's residents, consisting of Latinos (45 percent of the population), African Americans (23 percent), and increasingly Asian Americans, who are now 7 percent of the city's residents. As of 2020, whites were just 24 percent of the city's population.[17]

Given the city's size, scope, and complexity, it is not easy to win elections in Houston. Doing so requires considerable resources to communicate with nearly 2 million voters in far-flung, disparate neighborhoods and districts. That is why, up until 2015, 98 percent of the people who had been elected mayor of Houston were white (the one exception being Lee Brown, whose tenure as Houston police chief for most of the 1980s apparently reassured enough white people to hand him, a Black man, the keys to City Hall in 1997).

White voters in the United States generally don't support Black candidates, and that's essentially been the case since about 1619 or so. Fewer than 1 percent of all Black candidates who have run for any office in U.S. history have ever received a majority of the white vote. That's taking into account every election that has taken place in every state over the entirety of the history of these United States of America.[18] Seeking to educate the country's lawmakers about this reality when Congress, in 2006, was debating the necessity of renewing the 1965 Voting Rights Act, political science professor David Canon broke down the stats, facts, and history in his testimony to members of the Senate Judiciary Committee. Canon explained that "in the 8,047 House elections in white-majority districts between 1966 and 2004 (including special elections), only 49 (0.61 percent) were won by Blacks."[19] In Texas, the situation was even more pronounced, and there is no record of any Black candidate ever receiving a majority of the white vote.

Despite the fact that Houstonians had historically reserved their top job for people of the Caucasian persuasion, Sylvester Turner was undeterred. In 2015, the African American longtime state legislator threw his hat into the ring and sought to become the leader of the expansive metropolis named after a proud Confederate general and slave owner.

Although Turner possessed the meaningful advantages of name recognition and a respected track record in public life, he was still a Black man running for mayor in a city and state that regularly chose white people to govern their affairs. So if he were to prevail, Turner was going to have to win the only way Black candidates have ever won—with large turnout of voters of color and the backing of the meaningful minority of whites who consistently vote Democratic. That is, the New American Majority—the coalition that elected and reelected a Black man as president and then ousted the white nationalist who succeeded him.

The challenge of assembling New American Majority electoral

coalitions is that it's hard work. As discussed in chapter 6, people of color face far more obstacles to participating in the electoral process than white people do. On top of that, Confederates do everything in their power to erect as many additional barriers as possible to make sure that the electorate does not reflect the racial diversity of the population as a whole. Case in point: the 2021 voter suppression legislation passed in Texas that surgically targeted all of the recent innovations and reforms that had made it easier to vote in 2018 and 2020.[20]

In Houston, the discrepancy between the demographics of the actual population and the voting population has been especially acute. Historically, whites in Houston made up 24 percent of the city's population, but 43 percent of the voting population.[21] As was the case in San Diego, until Alliance San Diego and its allies changed things (see chapter 10), high white voter participation in low-turnout off-year elections—when the city's mayoral contests are held—gave the city's white population far more influence than its numbers would normally dictate.

To overcome this disparity—to turn population shifts into political power—required organization, discipline, and tenacity. It required a strong network of civic engagement groups with an effective and focused entity at the core. If Sylvester Turner wanted to become Houston's sixty-second mayor, he would need lots of support. Fortunately for Turner, the organization created by Michelle Tremillo and Ginny Goldman was just starting to hit its stride when he launched his mayoral bid.

In the first years of existence after its founding in 2009, TOP grew from a small team consisting of Michelle, Ginny, and seven other core staffers to a membership of more than fifty thousand people by the time Turner decided to make his mayoral bid in 2015. Sensing the possibility for changes that could improve the lives of people of color and working people across Houston, TOP members put their organizational muscle behind Turner's candidacy. He would need every vote that they delivered.

In the 2015 Houston mayoral contest, TOP fielded sixty core organizers to work hand in hand with labor and faith groups to fan out across the city to identify and communicate with infrequent voters, mainly people of color, who were likely to support Turner. All told, the coalition knocked on more than 100,000 doors and made over 150,000 phone calls. In one of the closest mayoral contests in the history of Houston (or anywhere for that matter), *Turner won by just 586 votes.*[22]

Without that organized effort to overcome institutional and systemic barriers, Houston would likely still be governed by descendants of people who waged a bloody war to seize hundreds of thousands of miles of land from Mexico so that they could continue to hold Black people in slavery.

———

After the success of helping elect Turner, the leaders of TOP and the progressive movement had to figure out what was next. Specifically, what they were going to focus on and where they would next concentrate their efforts.

Michelle describes their work by saying that TOP "fights with two fists," deploying a one-two punch of political power and people power. The political power piece—electoral force in the form of voter mobilization—is what propelled Turner to victory. The people power piece—canvassing, organizing, building deep relationships with a wide range of people—helped to surface what issues mattered most to their members and the state's communities of color. High atop that list was the need for criminal justice reform, in general, and better district attorneys, in particular.

In her seminal best seller *The New Jim Crow,* author Michelle Alexander explains the repressive relationship of the law enforcement apparatus to communities of color. She also shows how the managers of the criminal justice system—the district attorneys and others—are carrying on what is essentially a Confederate tradition of racial oppression:

> Rather than rely on race, we use our criminal justice system to label people of color "criminals" and then engage in all the practices we supposedly left behind. . . . Today it is perfectly legal to discriminate against criminals in nearly all the ways that it was once legal to discriminate against African Americans. Once you're labeled a felon, the old forms of discrimination—employment discrimination, housing discrimination, denial of the right to vote, denial of educational opportunity, denial

of food stamps and other public benefits, and exclusion from jury service—are suddenly legal. As a criminal, you have scarcely more rights, and arguably less respect, than a black man living in Alabama at the height of Jim Crow. We have not ended racial caste in America; we have merely redesigned it.[23]

Having answered the question of *what* next fight to fight, TOP's leaders then turned their attention to *where* to wage that battle. To make that decision, they looked at key counties in the state where they could replicate the model that worked so well in the city of Houston. The logical place to start was the county in which Houston was the largest city.

Houston is the county seat of Harris County. If you thought the city of Houston was big—and it is—Harris County is even more massive, with close to 5 million residents, more than the populations of twenty-eight states.[24] It is the third-largest county in the United States in terms of population, trailing only Los Angeles County and Cook County (Chicago). Not surprisingly—and offering ample encouragement about progressive electoral possibilities—the demographics of the county very much resemble the diversity of the city. People of color make up 71 percent of the residents, and break down as 44 percent Latino, 20 percent Black, and 20 percent Asians. Whites are 29 percent of the county population.[25] All of which makes it very surprising that Democrats had had so little success at the county level, particularly in regard to the office of district attorney. But all of that was about to change as TOP expanded its gaze beyond the city's borders.

In 2016, the Harris County district attorney was Devon Anderson, and she had to go. Anderson had been appointed to the seat three years earlier to replace her late husband, Mike Anderson, who'd been elected DA in 2012 and was the latest in a long, uninterrupted line of Republicans to occupy the office over the course of four decades. In addition to the typical district attorney repertoire of oppressive law enforcement operations, Devon Anderson's tenure was notable for incarcerating a twenty-five-year-old rape *victim* for a month after she broke down on the witness stand during the trial of her rapist. Anderson's office was also responsible for holding a Black man in jail for eight months *after* the Supreme Court had concluded he was wrongfully convicted;

furthermore, she publicly—and completely without basis—blamed the Black Lives Matter movement for the killing of a white sheriff's deputy in 2015.[26]

The electoral operation that had boosted Turner into City Hall was more than ready to tackle the challenge of organizing countywide, and TOP turned its growing electoral clout to the 2016 county contest for district attorney, throwing its weight behind Democrat Kim Ogg's challenge to the incumbent Anderson. In that race, TOP and its partners contacted more than eight hundred thousand people through calls and home visits; they also provided 2,500 rides to the polls to make sure their supporters could vote, helping Ogg prevail and break the Republican stranglehold on that pivotal position. (In an important cautionary tale for the progressive movement, Ogg has turned out to be quite the disappointment to many progressives, as she's been far more focused on burnishing her "tough on crime" credentials than in pursuing social justice.)[27]

Notably, Ogg was not the only Democrat who won that night. An article in *Harper's Magazine* described the fruits of the 2016 Harris County electoral labors:

> [In 2016] Houston Democrats had a full-scale Republican rout to celebrate. The party had swept the polls in Harris County, the vast region encompassing Houston, arguably the nation's most diverse city (as locals never tire of repeating). With 4.5 million inhabitants, the county is more populous than half the states in America. Now Harris voters had elected a Democratic district attorney—a very powerful post in Texas law enforcement—for the first time in thirty-six years. The Democrats had also captured almost every other slot on the ballot, including the tax assessor's office, which oversees voter registration: a crucial win in an age of Republican voter suppression.[28]

By 2020, the electoral engine in Harris County was so powerful that Democrats won *all* the countywide races in Harris.[29] All twenty-nine of them.

While Harris is the largest county in Texas, it is not the only county, and TOP's leaders understand that transforming Texas's politics statewide will require replicating the success of Houston and Harris County in other large counties in the state. In 2018, clear-eyed about the importance of criminal justice reform to people of color (most of TOP's membership is Black and Latino), and armed with confidence and lessons from having helped defeat a conservative district attorney, TOP set its sights on another place that needed to replace its district attorney.

Two hundred miles west of Houston, in Bexar County—the county where San Antonio sits—people of color also faced a hostile and repressive district attorney, Nicolas "Nico" LaHood. LaHood, like many or most DAs, was also carrying on the most repressive traditions of law enforcement in America. In 2018, TOP's members targeted LaHood and championed the candidacy of a progressive defense attorney, Joe Gonzales, ultimately ousting the incumbent. *Mother Jones* magazine observed that the election had "sweeping ramifications for criminal justice reform in one of the nation's most populous counties."[30]

From its founding in 2009, TOP has grown from an entity with a budget of $800,000 to an operation nearly ten times bigger, with its revenues exceeding $8 million in 2019. The organization's reach, influence, and impact have expanded commensurately, and its membership has increased to nearly three hundred thousand people across the state.[31] In 2018, the TOP team showed its potential to impact statewide elections through its work in four key counties—Harris, Dallas, Bexar, and Fort Bend—where the various campaigns collectively ran an electoral program that contacted more than 900,000 people and mobilized 465,405 voters.[32]

As is the case in the other states making notable progressive political progress, TOP is part of and contributes to a larger network of civic engagement organizations working to pool their resources to maximize their collective clout. In Texas, TOP works with the Workers Defense Project, Texas Freedom Network, the Civil Rights Project, Planned Parenthood, Jolt, Battleground Texas, labor unions such as the Communications Workers of America, and other progressive allies.

This civic engagement infrastructure in these key parts of Texas is laying the foundation for the realignment of the entire state's politics, making it increasingly possible to win the governor's office and state legislature and upend the policies and priorities that have privileged white people since its founding. That infrastructure and transformed electorate will also bring Texas into play in future presidential elections, possibly as soon as 2024.

Precisely because these voter mobilization tactics were so effective, the Confederate-inspired, Republican-led Texas legislature took dead aim at them by passing legislation to reverse and roll back nearly all of the measures that had been taken to increase the number of people participating in the democratic process. Nonetheless, the work goes on.

None of this success occurred accidentally or by happenstance. To get from the rubble of the wreckage of political bombs dropped on ACORN to the establishment of a multimillion-dollar, well-oiled political machine that has completely transformed the politics of one of the country's largest regions required careful planning and a very deep data dive. Fortunately, the Texas Odd Couple of Michelle and Ginny had just the person in mind for that task.

DEVELOP DETAILED, DATA-DRIVEN PLANS

I've known Crystal Zermeño since she applied to a fellowship program that my wife and I helped to start in the 1990s. Crystal is Mexican American and Tejana to the core—to the extent that she chose to get married in her grandmother's hometown, Goliad, Texas, a tiny town of 7,012 people. Goliad is a two-hour drive from Houston, which I know because I drove there to attend Crystal's wedding, where one of her relatives grabbed the microphone during the reception to loudly proclaim, "We didn't cross the border, the border crossed us!" A thirteenth-generation Texan, Crystal grew up in Houston and is a lifelong Houston sports fan, once telling my nephew Chris, who lives in Houston but roots for some inexplicable reason for the Dallas Cowboys, "You can't be from Houston and root for the Cowboys. It's a rule."

Crystal is also a social change lifer and a data savant (*Harper's Magazine* described her as a "Tejana math whiz whose mother grew up sleeping on the floor").[33] In one of my first conversations with her when she was fresh out of college, her eyes lit up as she waxed eloquent about the database program Microsoft Access and how she just loved to build databases.

From the moment she graduated college in 1999, Crystal started talking about going back home to Texas to help shake things up politically there. In the early 2000s, she did in fact move to Houston, where she worked as a researcher and analyst for the Service Employees International Union. While Houston is big geographically, the social justice activist community is fairly small and tight-knit, and Crystal quickly got to meet and work with Ginny on several local advocacy campaigns. After doing labor organizing at the local level for a number of years, Crystal wanted to try to have an impact on statewide politics. She got her chance as Michelle and Ginny were working to rebuild from ACORN's ashes.

In 2010, a national foundation wanted to conduct an electoral analysis of Texas and its potential for increasing the power and influence of people of color. To carry out the work, it planned to hire an outside consultant who would then inform the foundation of the findings. When Crystal found out about this, she told Ginny, "That's an awful idea. Tell them to give you the money, and then you hire me, and I'll do the analysis. That way, what we learn will live with TOP and not with some consultant." Recognizing the wisdom of that approach and the truth that an outside consultant would not have the history, background, and insights that Crystal did, Ginny secured the funds from the foundation for TOP, and it hired Crystal to unleash her talents on the task of doing a deep data dive and drafting an analysis and roadmap for a progressive future in Texas.

For comparison purposes, consider that the detailed, data-driven plan that Stacey Abrams took around the country was twenty-six pages long. Texas is bigger than Georgia, and, fittingly, the plan Crystal developed was thirty-seven pages. What is notable about that Texas plan is not just its length, but its depth, including, for example, maps and color-coded analysis of electoral results and political potential on a county-by-county basis. For Harris County alone, Crystal put together a spreadsheet that compared data from twenty-five different cities in the county. She examined the number of registered voters and low-propensity voters by racial group. The plan also included GIS maps showing the precise geographic location of these infrequent voters.

There is a saying that "all politics is local," and that also applies to developing political plans. For example, sometimes Google Maps will give you directions that don't make sense. The app might tell you to take a street that's closed or limited to one lane for construction. The most useful roadmaps rely on both an abundant amount of quantitative data about roads and highways as well as a qualitative overlay of local knowledge from someone who intimately knows the particular terrain. That's why it was so genius to turn to a Texas native like Crystal to draft the Texas strategic plan.

The advantage of having strategic political plans developed by people who are from, grew up in, and worked in Texas is that the quality of the insights and recommendations are more in line with the realities of that state. People from Texas are the ones who know best just how big the state is, and that to properly conduct social change and political work in such a sizable state is very expensive. Simply getting around the state is a Herculean effort, as it takes ten hours (driving the speed limit, which is not a given for Texans) to drive from El Paso, near the western border of Texas, to Houston, perched on the state's eastern edge. In addition to the sheer geographic enormity is the complexity of the state's political subdivisions: there are 254 counties spread across the state's nearly 300,000 square miles. (Fifteen of the smallest U.S. states could all fit within Texas's borders—Kentucky, Virginia, Indiana, Maine, South Carolina, West Virginia, Maryland, Vermont, New Hampshire, Massachusetts, New Jersey, Hawaii, Connecticut, Delaware, and Rhode Island. Also, Texas is about the size of France, except slightly larger.)[34]

While the complexity and cost of conducting mobilization work in hundreds of counties is prohibitive for most if not all civic engagement groups, what Crystal revealed is that big things can happen by focusing on just a small number of counties. More than half of the state's Latinos—and more than 8 million people of color overall—live in just five counties: Harris, Bexar, Dallas, Hidalgo, and El Paso.[35]

What Michelle, Ginny, Crystal, and Brianna have learned from their exhaustive analysis into the state's demographic and electoral data is that the road to statewide political power runs through the state's largest counties. This county strategy is the cornerstone of their plan to politically transform Texas. As they wrote in their 2012 blueprint:

- Of the 3 million Latino and African American voters that did not turn out in 2010, two million are concentrated in the top

8 densest counties: Harris, Fort Bend, Dallas, Tarrant, Hidalgo, Cameron, Bexar and El Paso.

- In 2012, we will focus on Dallas, Harris and Hidalgo counties targeting 130,000 to 198,000 low-propensity Latino and African American voters that both get us to our statewide numbers but also overlap with key strategic county, state and federal district races.[36]

Pursuing statewide change through a county-focused strategic plan is smart for multiple reasons. First, it's simply cost-effective. Civic engagement organizations are always grossly underfunded, and they have to make tough decisions about how to intelligently allocate limited resources. Concentrating those resources on a smaller geographic and population universe increases the prospects for making an impact. I know this from my own experience in elected office when I ran for a seat on the San Francisco school board in 1992.

San Francisco is a city of nearly eight hundred thousand adults, and roughly four hundred thousand people turn out to vote in presidential election years.[37] In addition to seeking endorsements from Democratic clubs, unions, newspapers, and elected officials, my campaign sought a competitive advantage through direct voter contact. We had a team of twenty volunteers who fanned out across the city every weekend for several months to knock on doors and talk to voters. In that fashion, we were able to interact with more than twelve thousand voters, informing them of my plans, and leaving my literature at their doors (along with a handwritten note from "me," although actually written by the canvasser, saying, "Sorry I missed you!"). Come election night, I won my seat by a margin of 5,651 votes.

If I'd been running in a city two or three times larger, I'd have needed an operation that was two or three times bigger to achieve comparable reach. But by focusing the team I had on a manageable universe, we were able to win a seat on a board responsible for a $400 million budget, the education of 55,000 students, and the jobs of nearly 10,000 employees. From that platform, we passed trailblazing reforms in early childhood education and captured the attention of the nation with our proposal to diversify San Francisco's literature curriculum. That kind of statewide and national impact was only possible because we were able to focus on a geographic and demographic universe small enough to be organizable. That's the beauty and efficiency of a county-focused effort.

A second benefit of a county strategy is that it's the fastest way to improve lots of people's lives, especially in a red or purple state. As I learned in San Francisco, I could help pass policies that improved the quality of education for tens of thousands of students, with the benefits extending to the additional thousands of people in the families of those students as they utilized their education in subsequent years to get good jobs and pursue impactful work.

Although Texas is a state where the current statewide elected officials are contemptuous of the conditions facing the lives of poor people and people of color, TOP is nonetheless making a meaningful difference by electing people to local office and passing local ballot measures. In Dallas, for example, they have made a direct and immediate difference by helping to pass a local ballot measure in 2018 that moved $126 million into the school district, providing much-needed funds for improving the conditions of those who teach the district's 145,000 children. Funds were specifically allocated to "strategies proven to lift school performance—strategic staffing, instructional excellence, social and emotional support, [and] extended learning and supportive partnerships [in] 24 Dallas [Independent School District] middle schools."[38]

These policy wins further strengthen the civic engagement organizational infrastructure by enhancing the credibility of TOP in the eyes of community members who look to it for electoral guidance. Because of TOP's success on the Dallas education funding measure, for example, the next time a canvasser wearing a TOP teal-colored T-shirt (the organization's distinctive brand and color is teal) comes knocking, or a mailer comes from the organization, the recipient will take the recommendation seriously. That cycle of listening to the concerns from community members, then advocating for reforms that address those concerns and then communicating back the results of that advocacy is a process that regularly increases the group's electoral reach and influence.

Which leads to the third strategic benefit of a plan rooted in a county strategy. In many states, the largest pools of eligible, non-voting people of color are in just a handful of counties. Often there are enough non-voters in those regions alone to tip the outcome in statewide elections.

Consider Beto O'Rourke's near-miss in his 2018 U.S. Senate run. In the previous U.S. Senate race in a non-presidential year (which was held in 2014) Republican John Cornyn won in a landslide, trouncing his opponent by nearly 30 points and a margin of 1.2 million votes. Four years later, through the work of the civic engagement groups, as well as the Beto campaign's own organizing efforts (aided by the expert strategic advice of Ginny Goldman, who had gone on to serve as a political consultant), the Democratic vote in TOP's three counties swelled by nearly a million votes, cutting the statewide deficit for Democrats by 75 percent.[39] Beto came closer than any Democrat had in years to winning a statewide election in Texas, losing by just 2.6 percent—215,000 votes—far, far better than the shellacking Democrats received just four years earlier. You can see how continuing to increase turnout in the core counties is the key to flipping Texas in 2022 and turning the state blue in the 2024 presidential contest. O'Rourke himself will benefit from this county strategy in his 2022 gubernatorial bid.

In boiling down politics to its essence, I am often reminded of the words of Willie Brown, one of the most dominant, influential, and successful politicians in the twentieth century. Brown is a native of Mineola, Texas, who moved to California where he made his political mark and where I got to know him. A whip-smart, highly disciplined, and charismatic African American man, Brown revels in his ascendance from poverty in Texas to the highest ranks of national politics (he was chair of Jesse Jackson's 1988 presidential campaign and served as mayor of San Francisco from 1996 to 2004 after leaving the California Assembly). Brown is most known for serving as the longest-serving Speaker of the California Assembly in state history, holding power from 1980 until 1995, and he liked to refer to himself as the "Ayatollah of the Assembly." In the mid-1990s, a group of five renegade white Democratic state legislators tried to depose him from his perch atop the Assembly by aligning with the Republicans to secure the necessary number of votes to dethrone him and elect a Republican in his stead. Being the master politician that he is, Brown outfoxed his opposition, cut his own deal with a couple of Republicans, and retained his position of power. I happened to be in the State Assembly chambers on the day that he successfully squashed the "Gang of Five" attempted coup, and I'll never forget his words as he stepped to the podium to continue to lead the legislature. "The first rule of politics," he said with a gleam in his eye and a smile on his lips, "is that you have to learn to count."

As evidenced by the political transformation of Harris County, Crystal Zermeño's thirty-seven-page plan, and TOP's data-driven, laser-like focus on key counties, the progressive political leaders in Texas know how to count.

PLAY THE LONG GAME

Harris County is central to the Texas long game precisely because it combines the key elements of political power built on the demographic revolution, a strong civic engagement organization, and visionary political leadership with statewide potential. One of the people most involved in stirring those elements together is a young woman named Lina Hidalgo.

Harris County judge Lina Hidalgo isn't actually a judge at all. What she is is one of the most strategic and important elected officials in the United States. Texas uses unusual nomenclature for its public offices, and the title "county judge" is given to the person who is the top executive in a county. Given the enormous size of Harris County, Lina arguably holds a more important office than half of the governors in the United States.

Elected when she was just twenty-eight years old and swept into office as part of the wave of voter turnout organized by TOP and other organizations in 2018, Lina is an intelligent, inspirational, and compelling public official who is rightly seen as a rising star in Texas and national politics. Over the past four years, she has modeled how counties can be laboratories for policy innovation that highlight what public policy changes are possible and how those changes can inspire and attract greater support for the progressive policy agenda. The fact that she has been able to do all of that from the perch of a once-obscure and poorly understood governmental office shows the substantive and strategic significance of focusing social change work on the county level.

In her role as county judge, Hidalgo oversees a budget of $5 billion and nearly eighteen thousand employees who are responsible for building and maintaining county infrastructure such as roads and bridges, and overseeing services like courthouses, hospitals, libraries, and parks.[40] She is also heavily involved in the core exercise of a democracy: voting. Under her leadership, the county, in just two years, implemented multiple innovative measures to expand the number of people who could participate in the democratic process. A Houston Public Media article published just before the 2020 election described the impact of those reforms as follows:

> Ballots came through the mail. They were cast from cars, inside drive-thru voting stations. Some ballots were cast in the middle of the night. . . . Now early voting is complete, and ahead of Election Day, voters have already cast a record 1,435,221 ballots during its historic early voting period in Harris County, including 170,410 mail ballots, out of roughly 2.5 million registered voters in the county. Harris County managed to shatter its total 2016 voter turnout. . . .
>
> That's the result of unprecedented investment on the election this year, according to Harris County Clerk Chris Hollins. The county spent more than $30 million on things like increased voting locations and poll workers, COVID-19 precautions, and mail-in balloting. "From the opportunity to vote around the clock, to the opportunity to vote from the safety and comfort of your vehicle, we have brought Harris County to the leading edge of voter access in this country," Hollins said.[41]

The amalgamation of Lina's public policy track record, progressive governance vision, compelling leadership style, national fundraising network, and close working relationship with civic engagement groups such as TOP have elevated her to the ranks of promising candidates for future statewide office in 2026 and beyond.

―――

Transforming a state requires more than the force of civic engagement groups and engaging leaders who can be a face of the state's political promise. It also requires funding in the form of smart, sophisticated donors who understand the long game, are prepared to invest capital in methodical and sustained fashion over many years, and are willing to be patient. Not all donors get that.

About a decade ago, I had dinner with an executive from a large foundation that made grants for civic engagement. I asked her why her foundation wasn't investing in Texas, and she replied, "Well, Texas is a long-term proposition." To which I said, "Exactly! Which is why we have to start right away." Transforming Texas is indeed a long-term proposition, and fortunately several key state funders and investors *have* kept their eyes on the prize of long-term political change.

While the data-driven plans of TOP and others showed that the potential in the state was enormous, a sober assessment of the electoral data and political behavior of the critical constituent groups also revealed that the journey, while doable, would be long—kind of like a statewide Texas road trip.

I was part of a small group of people who came together in 2012 to create a donor collaborative—the Texas Future Project (TFP)—to try to raise and move money to strategic political empowerment work in the state. TFP's founding executive director, Tory Gavito, now president of the national progressive donor network Way to Win, rooted herself in data and analysis (frequently tapping Crystal's expertise and data prowess) and crafted a plan that called for steady progress, but with a realistic look at how long it would take. Politics has been described as war without bloodshed, and civic engagement work is akin to being on the battlefield, with ballots taking the place of bullets. To win over the long haul, other elements of the operation also have to be nurtured and developed. In Texas, over the past decade, TFP and Tory have helped tend to that critical task.

In 2013, Tory wrote a memo to the TFP board laying out the framework for what donors should invest in:

1. **Voter engagement:** These organizations educate, organize, and mobilize eligible voters to turn out to vote and hold elected officials accountable throughout the year.
2. **Infrastructure:** These organizations conduct opposition research, provide policy analysis, and engage in strategic electoral planning.

3. **Communications:** Develop media relationships and create media messages designed to educate and agitate the voting base and hold elected officials accountable.
4. **Leadership Development:** These organizations cultivate new leadership in the areas of community organizing, political campaigns, and holding elected office.[42]

And then, in a similar fashion to how Stacey Abrams scanned the Georgia electoral landscape to identify key gaps and needs and John Loredo looked to Colorado's progressive infrastructure to see what Arizona was missing, Tory meticulously mapped which key political and social change components existed in Texas and which didn't, what organizations were playing what roles where, and, in that context, where money should go in the short term to produce meaningful progress and results both in the near and long term.

One point Tory repeatedly drilled home to donors was that Texas is a big state with a long history of Confederate power, so the planning and analysis would need to be of commensurate scale and extended duration, writing, "Because the task at hand is epic and resources are limited, funds must be invested strategically and efficiently, which, in turn, requires specific and concrete long-term goals from which to judge short-term and medium-term plans."

To reach the goal of contesting for power in the 2020s, Tory helped sketch out a map that was geographically broad and temporally long. Geographically and organizationally, the plan that was put in place analyzed and incorporated the work of twenty-nine different organizations working in multiple counties across the state. For each of those organizations, the plan assessed what piece of the progressive infrastructure that specific group helped provide—leadership development, messaging, voter engagement, or voter registration—as well as what demographic constituency the group prioritized. With this map and matrix, Tory and TFP were able in their first years of operation in 2013 and 2014 to intelligently allocate $2 million to the right places, people, and groups, always with an eye on the long game.

2014 was a very, very bad year electorally for Democrats and progressives all across the country. After Obama's successful reelection in 2012, progressives thought that the job was done, turned their attention to other matters, and Democratic voter turnout plummeted, causing Democrats to lose control of the U.S. Senate and several state-wide contests across the country.

In Texas, the electoral carnage in 2014 was considerable. Hopes had been raised that State Senator Wendy Davis could galvanize progressive support after her heroic eleven-hour filibuster in 2013 to stop an attack on reproductive rights had inspired progressives across the country. But her campaign for governor was hobbled by the strategic myopia of cautious Caucasian consultants who prioritized the futile folly of trying to woo white Texans to back the non-Confederate candidate. Turnout was abysmal, Davis lost badly, and progressives licked their wounds. Tory helped the donor community take the long view, pick themselves up, dust themselves off and focus on the future. In the days and weeks after the 2014 election rout, Tory took a deep breath and cautioned donors to keep their eyes on the prize, writing:

> While few expected a win, the size of the loss was not insignificant. National headwinds, campaign message miscalculations, years of Texas progressive infrastructure atrophy, and the early phases of strategic donor investments were all factors too great for the expanding infrastructure to overcome.
>
> The Texas progressive infrastructure built in 2014 is rapidly maturing and set to expand to take advantage of Texas' changing demographic landscape, which over time will build a progressive majority. In short, Texas is becoming more competitive for progressives as Texas undergoes dramatic demographic changes, cultural and economic shifts accompanying new industries, a rapidly growing creative class, and the return of Democratic dominance in the state's major urban areas. . . . The ingredients already exist in target counties, which have a combination of progressive mayors and county judges to anchor this progressive shift and build an electoral base. . . . Taking back Texas is not impossible, but it will take time and effort.[43]

Because the key players stayed the course, playing the long game and hiking the hard path, the seeds of early intelligent investment in 2012 and 2013 began to bloom in the form of a transformed electorate and electoral progress in 2018 and 2020. Hidalgo's victory and O'Rourke's near-win both grew out of this early and sustained investment. O'Rourke was able to come so close to winning in 2018 because the Latino vote, as outlined in Tory's 2013 memo, had become pivotal, growing to 23 percent of all voters, up from 17 percent in 2014.[44]

———

By 2020 hopes were high in Texas, and the polls were promising for progressives heading into an election in which Democrats thought that they could not just capture control of the State House but also get more votes than Trump. Neither of those goals came to fruition, and the conventional wisdom and takeaway from political pundits regarding 2020 is that Democrats badly underperformed in Texas. Most 2020 Texas post-mortems, however, are profoundly and dangerously incorrect.

What happened in Texas in 2020 is equivalent to a situation where a marathon runner and her coach calculate, based on decades of data, that she needs to run the race within a certain amount of time—say, under three hours—to come in first place. In this hypothetical scenario, such a conclusion would have been based on looking at past results showing that the person who ran the race in under three hours won every single marathon ever held in that state. To continue the analogy, after years of training and exercise and preparation, she indeed runs the race and finishes in 2 hours and 59 minutes, achieving her goal and accomplishing a historic feat in terms of speed. But it just so happens that one of the other runners in the same race ingested performance-enhancing drugs that enabled him to complete the course in 2 hours and 50 minutes. In such a scenario, the correct conclusion is not that the first runner failed, especially since they did in fact hit their goal. The conclusion is that something unusual happened with the runner who was boosted by the drugs, and the smart course of action is to try to determine whether that scenario might repeat itself in the future.

In terms of U.S. politics, the rush that comes from defending Confederate culture and white supremacy is a helluva drug, and has historically driven its users to perform abnormal feats including giving their limbs and often their lives in the fight to preserve their racial heritage and privileges. It's the behavior-modifying substance that enabled Confederate leaders to attract hundreds of thousands of men to enlist in the doomed quest to preserve slavery in America. It's the logic-defying elixir that prompted God-fearing, church-going Christians to put on their Sunday best and take their children to witness Black men being hung from trees. And it's the fuel that drove historic Republican voter turnout in 2020. The untold story of the 2020 election is the unprecedented level of voter participation by Confederate supporters who had previously shunned elections, but turned out in historic numbers to defend their cherished white man in the White House.

The Confederate over-performance in Texas, however, should not obscure the significant progressive accomplishments that were achieved. More Latinos voted in Texas in 2020 than at any previous time in history (well, since 1836), with more than 2.6 million Latinos turning out. The total number of voters of color increased by 821,041 over the turnout from 2016.[45] Democratic control of the State House remains in reach if Democrats flip just nine Republican-held seats in 2022. For the most part, in the contests for those nine seats, Democrats received more votes in 2020 than they had in any previous period. Using the earlier analogy of the marathon runner, Democrats hit their three-hour marathon mark in 2020.

Clearly, the ultimate goal of flipping Texas blue has yet to be achieved, but the future actually looks quite promising. Although progressives fell short in the 2020 presidential election, the upside remains enormous. Biden lost Texas by 631,221 votes. In that same election, nearly 4 million eligible people of color did not vote. Staying the course, backing Level 5 leaders, and investing in strong civic engagement organizations that are following detailed, data-driven plans will increasingly pay off in the coming years. Nearly three hundred thousand people of color in Texas turn eighteen every year, with thirty-three new voters of color becoming eligible every single hour. Help is on the way.

———

The political transformation of Harris County is one of the most remarkable and underappreciated political stories of the past decade.

Imagine if Louisiana or Kentucky or Oregon—all states with fewer people than Harris County—had evolved to *only* electing Democrats. Republicans need not apply. There would be extensive articles and analyses about the phenomenon and its implications for the future of U.S. politics.

The date June 19th has long been noted in the Black community as the day when word that Lincoln had signed the Emancipation Proclamation reached the distant state of Texas in those pre-internet days. Upon learning that they were officially free, Black folks broke into celebration. A holiday to commemorate that day of celebration came to be called Juneteenth. In 2021, Congress and President Biden even made Juneteenth a federal holiday.

Today we are experiencing a sort of an inverse Juneteenth regarding Texas in comparison with the rest of the country. The Liberation Battle Plan is politically transforming the cornerstones of Texas by turning the state's largest counties blue. But outside of Texas, most progressives and Democrats have not yet received word of the political Emancipation Proclamations that have already liberated Harris, Dallas, and Bexar counties as multiracial progressive coalitions contend for and take greater power. Much of what we do hear, often from mainstream political media, is that we don't stand a chance in Texas. When word does finally reach the rest of us, especially when the work comes to fruition in the form of Lone Star statewide victory, as occurred in Arizona and Georgia, that will be cause for a celebration unlike anything we've seen before.

Crystal Zermeño is correct. Texas is indeed the ballgame. When Texas changes, the whole electoral map in America will reset. Given the size and strategic significance of the state to right-wing power in America, flipping Texas will ring the death knell for the Confederate cause, dealing a decisive blow in finally winning the Civil War.

EPILOGUE

Once We Win—Creating a New Social Contract

No one cherishes freedom more than those who have not had it. And to this day, black Americans, more than any other group, embrace the democratic ideals of a common good. . . . Our founding fathers may not have actually believed in the ideals they espoused, but black people did. . . . For generations, we have believed in this country with a faith it did not deserve. Black people have seen the worst of America, yet, somehow, we still believe in its best.

—Nikole Hannah-Jones, creator of *The 1619 Project*, August 14, 2019

Laura Kidd-Plummer is a strong, proud Black woman living in Stockton, California. After working for twenty-one years at the Oakland, California, basketball arena cleaning and pressing uniforms of the people who worked in the arena, she lost her job. Seeking to find a city where she could afford to live on her pension of $1,500/month, she moved to Stockton, seventy-two miles east of Oakland. Then a fire ravaged her apartment complex, and she was left homeless. Trying to keep her head above water and stay one step ahead of the bills, she lived in a motel for a couple months and then stayed with various friends as she tried to stay afloat. All this after a lifetime of working and raising a family, and now approaching seventy years of age. When she was selected at random to start receiving $500 deposited into her bank account every month, she couldn't believe it and couldn't have been more grateful. She used the money to pay for the deposit on a new apartment that helped her stabilize her life.[1]

Laura was one of 125 people selected in 2019 for the country's first experiment with universal basic income (UBI)—a concept championed by Martin Luther King Jr. in the late 1960s when he wrote, "The solution to poverty is to abolish it directly by a now widely discussed

measure: the guaranteed income." King went on to point out that conventional wisdom about public policy actually had things backwards,
writing, "We are likely to find that the problems of housing and education, instead of preceding the elimination of poverty, will themselves
be affected if poverty is first abolished." [2]

Although controversial in a society that demonizes and distrusts
people living in poverty—especially people of color living in poverty—
the idea of a guaranteed income has gained significant traction and
momentum in recent years, largely as a result of the efforts and leadership of Michael Tubbs. Elected mayor of Stockton, California, in
2016 at the age of twenty-six, Tubbs was the youngest mayor of a major
American city, and, more than anyone in national politics, he brought
King's dream to life in the form of a tangible program to pilot and
popularize the policy and vision of UBI.

New York magazine ran a lengthy profile of Laura and four other
recipients in 2019. In addition to Laura, there was Phyllis, who had
just been diagnosed with thyroid cancer. She used the money to off-
set a wide range of unexpected expenses associated with her cancer
surgery and being unemployed yet unable to qualify for the state dis-
ability program. And there was Danielle, who paid down her debts,
helped support her unemployed father as he looked for work, and began saving to buy a house for her, her husband, and their two young
girls. Independent researchers at Stanford tracked the program's impact, and the results were captured in a *San Francisco Chronicle* article
headlined, "Stockton's $500 Monthly Income Program Led to Better
Jobs and Lives, Study Concludes." [3] The *New York* magazine reporter
wrote, "Danielle gets teary-eyed saying how humbled she feels by the
opportunity. 'Maybe somebody would deserve it better,' she says. 'But
at the same time, maybe this is my chance. Maybe this is my moment
of hope.'" [4]

Stockton's UBI initiative was a small program with big promise,
and Tubbs summoned his colleagues across the country to the cause.
Over the past few years, sixty-five mayors in twenty-six states across
the country have come together to form a network called Mayors for a
Guaranteed Income. Those mayors have worked with progressive philanthropists to run similar programs to the one that Laura participated
in in Stockton. Between 2018 and 2020, more than thirteen thousand

people began receiving monthly checks deposited into their accounts, just like Laura. And, like her, they used the funds to secure their housing, feed their families, and pursue their dreams.[5]

Ending poverty was King's last campaign—he was organizing the Poor People's Campaign when he was assassinated. Recognizing that UBI is an extension of her father's work, King's daughter Bernice invited Tubbs to speak at Ebenezer Baptist Church for the 2022 MLK Day celebration in recognition of his efforts focusing on ending poverty. (Tubbs has launched a drive in California modeled on the 1930s initiative started by Upton Sinclair called End Poverty in California [EPIC], and is pushing to expand UBI across the state.)

Despite the annual mid-January universal expressions of admiration for Dr. King, the level of support for his signature cause of ending poverty is not nearly as widespread. Attitudes toward UBI track the country's long-standing racial divide. Huge majorities of Blacks and Latinos are in favor (73 percent and 64 percent, respectively). Among whites, the approval rate is just 35 percent—close to the percentage of whites who voted to reelect America's first Black president.[6] As UBI initiatives gained greater visibility and coverage in the media and among mainstream politicians, there was widespread grumbling, sniping, snickering, and opposition from those who possessed little empathy for their fellow human beings and blamed people living in poverty for the fact that they were poor.

And then the pandemic hit. Within a matter of weeks, the U.S. Senate voted 96–0 to send checks with no strings attached, just like the checks Laura received, to just about every single adult in the country. An estimated 159 million people received a $1,200 check.[7] Other aid poured in as well. Millions of renters were spared the threat of eviction through a federal eviction moratorium. For the tens of millions of people who suddenly lost their jobs, the government provided and extended unemployment benefits—monthly checks to people in need—to 46 million people.[8]

Corporations—and even entire industries—got in on the act too. Businesses could apply for help from a $500 billion fund, to be doled out at the discretion of the U.S. treasury secretary. Airlines received about $58 billion to help them withstand the financial fallout of the global cessation of air travel.[9]

The assumption underlying the outpouring of support at the outset of the pandemic was that people were hurting, needed assistance, and could be trusted to do the right thing if lent a helping hand. Within a matter of weeks, in the time it took an airborne disease to sweep across the planet, the country's social contract was reevaluated and redefined. Gone were the decades of skepticism and hostility toward people receiving government benefits. The fulminations about government overreach trailed off into silence. The social contract was clear—lots of people needed and deserved help, and society and our elected governmental representatives should respond in kind. The speed and scale of the national response showed what is possible when everyone buys into the same social contract.

———

The current social contract in America is not an expression of our deepest values, greatest hopes, and highest ideals. Quite the contrary, it is the result of a centuries-long series of compromises with white supremacists:

- In his original draft of the Declaration of Independence, Thomas Jefferson included a forceful denunciation of slavery and the slave trade, condemning the "execrable commerce" as "cruel war against human nature itself." The leaders of the states engaged in the buying and selling of Black bodies balked at the offending passage, and Jefferson explained the decision to compromise, writing, "The clause . . . was struck out in complaisance to South Carolina & Georgia who had never attempted to restrain the importation of slaves, and who on the contrary still wished to continue it. Our Northern brethren also I believe felt a little tender under those censures; for tho' their people have very few slaves themselves yet they had been pretty considerable carriers of them to others." [10]
- The Constitution itself, the governing document seeking to "establish justice" and "secure the blessings of liberty," is replete with compromises with white supremacists' demands that the nascent nation codify the inferior status of Black people. As discussed in chapter 8, the "Fugitive Slave Clause"—Article IV,

Section 2, Clause 3 of the Constitution—made it illegal for anyone to interfere with slave owners who were tracking drapetomaniacs fleeing slavery. And, of course, there was Article I, Section 2, Clause 3, which contains the quintessential compromise on how to enumerate the country's Black population, resulting in the decision to count individual human beings—the Black human beings—as three-fifths of a whole person.

- The whites-first mindset about citizenship and immigration policy that still roils American politics to this day is not even really the result of compromise. It is in essence a complete capitulation to the concept that America is and should primarily be a white country. The 1790 Naturalization Act—one of the country's very first laws—declared that to be a citizen one had to be a "free white person." That belief was sufficiently noncontroversial that no compromise was necessary, and the provision was quickly adopted. In a unanimous opinion in the 1922 *Ozawa v. United States* case, the Supreme Court ruled firmly and unapologetically that U.S. law restricted citizenship to white people because "the words 'white person' means a Caucasian," and Ozawa "is clearly of a race which is not Caucasian, and therefore belongs entirely outside the zone" of citizenship. The racial restriction was official law until 1952, and standard practice until adoption of the 1965 Immigration and Nationality Act. This centuries-long, whites-first framework for immigration policy was most recently eloquently articulated by Donald John Trump—the man for whom 74 million Americans voted in 2020—when he asked in 2018, "Why are we having all these people from shithole countries come here?"[11]

- The sweeping social programs of the New Deal were the result of compromises with Confederate congressmen working to preserve white power. In a Congress that prized seniority, many of the most senior and influential members came from the states that barred Black folks from voting. In his book *When Affirmative Action Was White*, Ira Katznelson breaks down how "the South used its legislative powers to transfer its priorities about race to Washington. Its leaders imposed them, with little resistance, on New Deal policies." Social Security is perhaps the signature policy of the New Deal era, but in deference to the white Southerners, the program explicitly excluded farmworkers and domestic workers. As Katznelson explains, "These groups—constituting more than 60 percent of the black labor force in the 1930s and nearly 75 percent of those who were employed in the South—were excluded from the legislation that created modern unions, from laws that set minimum wages and regulated the hours of work, and from Social Security until the 1950s."[12]

• Even the cornerstone of democracy—the right to vote—remains to this day the result of a creaky compromise with white nationalists. Most constitutional rights don't require regular legislation.to be renewed. There are no Freedom of Speech or Right to Privacy or Right to Bear Arms acts. We don't revisit those fundamental rights every ten or twenty years. When it comes to the Fifteenth Amendment, however, the right to vote has necessitated further legislation to guarantee enforcement, and the opposition has been so intractable and long-standing that the Voting Rights Act has to be regularly renewed by Congress, necessitating negotiation and compromise with those who fear the power-shifting implications of letting everyone of all races actually cast ballots.

Even after extracting a cavalcade of compromises over the centuries, Confederates have consistently demonstrated that they do not feel obligated to honor any agreements or democratic institutions if those agreements or institutions fail to adequately protect whiteness. From the Civil War itself to the January 2021 insurrection, the white nationalist response to democratic defeat has been to attempt to destroy American institutions and shred our national agreements.

When a devastating global pandemic tore through the world, killing millions of people including more than 1 million in the United States, those imbued with the Confederate mindset showed in shocking fashion how little regard they have for mutual obligations to the common good. Governors in former slaveholding states such as Texas, Georgia, and Florida launched an all-out attack on basic public health measures by overruling and undermining local laws requiring lifesaving steps such as masks and vaccine mandates.

Modern-day Confederates continually elect and reelect (and, when necessary to their cause, un-elect) representatives who are fundamentally hostile and opposed to making society work for everybody. As addressed in chapter 4, they have spent more than a decade trying to take away people's health insurance. The lack of empathy and human connection was so intense it drove West Virginia Republican senator Shelley Moore Capito to recoil and remark in 2017, "I didn't come here to hurt people."[13] Because, clearly her colleagues *did* go to Washington to hurt people. As one Trump supporter put it in 2019 when she thought her president wasn't being sufficiently savage, "He's not hurting the people he needs to be hurting."[14] Because there was clearly a grouping of people in our country he was *supposed* to hurt. And as discussed throughout this book, since the day Robert E. Lee supposedly surrendered in 1865, Confederates of past and present have relentlessly written laws to make it harder for people of color to vote—from the 1882 Eight Box Law to the 1923 Texas white primary to the 2021 Georgia law making it a crime to give water to people standing in line to vote.

This is not the behavior of people who think they are bound by a common commitment to democratic processes and norms. It is not the conduct of people who, as Nikole Hannah-Jones put it, "embrace the democratic ideals of a common good." These are not the actions of people who subscribe to the notion that all the members of the society have agreed to a set of laws and rules to govern our individual and collective actions and affairs of state.

This *is* the conduct of people who are waging an unrelenting, centuries-long war in defense of their cherished belief that America should be a white nation. A war in which they will not give an inch, will distort public opinion through big lies and misinformation, will ruthlessly rewrite local laws in defiance of constitutional amendments, and, where and when helpful, will silently and not so silently sanction violence—including bloody domestic terrorism. And this is who many Democrats want to compromise and find common ground with.

In a relationship, compromise is not just okay, but required. In a community bound together by common values and mutual respect, compromise can be the grease that makes the machinery of society function, but, with people who are waging war against you and everything you hold dear, compromise is suicide. The compromises throughout U.S. history have crippled progress toward creating a true multiracial democracy, and it is nonsensical to continue to act like our opponents are people of good faith.

In contract law, a contract becomes null and void if one party did not enter into it in good faith, or if one party breaches the agreement and walks away from its mutual commitments. Given the clear bad faith and contempt for any allegiance to the common good, why do we have to cling to the old frameworks?

The answer is we don't. We do not have to stifle our dreams and surrender our principles. We can now craft a new, fundamentally different social contract.

———

Once we win the Civil War, we can let our imaginations run wild and hearts soar. We can craft a social contract for the society we *want* to live in. A society that we would be happy to leave to our children and grandchildren. We can draw up a societal agreement based on our values, hopes, and dreams instead of whatever we can get passed over the opposition of people who want to destroy us. The possibilities are endless.

A contract is an agreement between two or more parties where they make mutually enforceable promises. For centuries, philosophers from Plato to Kant have discussed and debated the underlying principles for how societies should be organized. The modern-day understanding of the social contract was perhaps most influentially elevated by law professor John Rawls, who laid out the underpinnings in his seminal 1971 work *A Theory of Justice*:

> The guiding idea is that the principles of justice for the basic structure of society are the object of the original agreement. They are the principles that free and rational persons concerned to further their own interests would accept in an initial position of equality as defining the fundamental terms of their association. . . . Those who engage in social cooperation choose together, in one joint act, the principles which are to assign basic rights and duties and to determine the division of social benefits.[15]

Such multisyllabic explorations of notions of mutual obligation, rights, duties, and societal benefits have been, as frequently happens in this country, boiled down to their essence by the people bearing the brunt of oppression and inequality. The whole question of the social contract is really as simple as the 1992 question posed by Rodney King after he endured the beating by Los Angeles police that launched days of protests that some described as riots. As more and more people took to the streets, and the president and governor responded by deploying more and more troops and military might, King simply asked, "Can we all get along?"[16] The simplicity of the query echoed the straightforward yet revolutionary 1964 words of Mississippi voting rights activist Fannie Lou Hamer, who in riveting, nationally televised testimony asked a Democratic Party committee, "Is this America, the land of the free and the home of the brave, where we have to sleep with our telephones off the hooks because our lives be threatened daily, because we want to live as decent human beings?"[17]

We *can* all get along, but first, we have to agree we *want* to get along. Then those of us who do want to get along must, like Fannie Lou Hamer, summon America to its highest and best self and challenge the country to write a new social contract. A contract infused with morality and ethics and love.

What, then, does a post–Civil War world look like? I have written this book as a resource for those working to build a better world. The task for those defining and developing the new social contract is for those in the trenches and on the front lines in the 2020s. I do not have all the answers in great detail, but, like Rodney King and Fannie Lou Hamer, I can pose some questions that are generally ignored and yet are fundamental to forging a more just, equal, and humane society. A truly multiracial democracy.

"WHAT WAS BEING FOUGHT OVER IN THE FIRST PLACE, AND HAVE WE ACCOMPLISHED THAT OBJECTIVE?"

Harvard's Henry Louis Gates Jr. has highlighted how Reconstruction involved grappling with the elemental questions of drafting a new social contract. In *Stony the Road*, Gates wrote, "Think of the fundamental questions that the study of the period forces us to consider: Who is entitled to citizenship? Who should have the right to vote? What is the government's responsibility in dealing with terrorism? What is the relationship between political and economic democracy? These are all Reconstruction questions."[18] The historian Lerone Bennett Jr. had asked a similar question during the height of the civil rights movement, what some have called the country's Second Reconstruction. Bennett succinctly framed the issues, writing, "In 1876, as in 1963, the central questions were the unresolved issues of the original American Revolution. Did all mean All? Was America a government of white people for white people or a government of all the people for all the people?"[19]

In the years immediately after the Civil War, the specific solutions for building a better country out of the war's bloody wreckage centered on racial justice and democracy in a country that had grown rich and powerful on the backs of people who were not paid and could not vote.

In 2016, in *Brown Is the New White*, I devoted a chapter to asking the question, "What Is Justice?" In the intervening six years, we have witnessed multiple more murders of unarmed African Americans, including the transformative May 2020 moment when the entire world watched a white Minnesota police officer nonchalantly kneel on the neck of the unarmed and handcuffed George Floyd for nine minutes and twenty-nine seconds while the life left Floyd's body, the same way it had for thousands of people who died from lynching in this country over the past four hundred years.[20] The visceral outrage and anguish over Floyd's murder sparked a rare, if brief, racial reckoning in this country. For the first time in decades, you heard the words "systemic racism" and "systemic anti-Black racism." Even Walmart was compelled to proclaim that Black Lives Matter.

At the core of that reckoning is a fundamental question that is usually ignored by those in positions of power: "What is owed?" As Hannah-Jones framed the question in the weeks after the murder of Floyd, "The real obstacle, the obstacle that we have never overcome, is garnering the political will—convincing enough Americans that the centuries-long forced economic disadvantage of black Americans should be remedied, that restitution is owed to people who have never had an equal chance to take advantage of the bounty they played such a significant part in creating."[21] Hannah-Jones went on to connect the dots of what is possible when there is a societal consensus for action, noting, "The coronavirus pandemic has dispatched the familiar lament that even if it is the right thing to do, this nation simply cannot afford to make restitution to the 40 million descendants of American slavery. . . . When, then, will this nation pass a stimulus package to finally respond to the singularity of black suffering?"[22]

Answering the question of what is owed has, thus far, remained too hot to handle for the country's elected leaders and most of white America. Starting in 1989, the late congressman John Conyers introduced a bill into Congress calling for the creation of a commission to study the issue of reparations—the bill did not call for acting on or implementing any proposals, mind you; it simply sought to initiate study of the issue. For decades, Conyers couldn't get a single co-sponsor of the proposed legislation. In the 2010s, Congresswoman Sheila Jackson Lee took the baton and reintroduced the bill, and the measure did slowly gain additional momentum. But even during the period of mass marches around the world in solidarity with the Black Lives Matter movement in 2020, increased receptivity among whites to the question of what is owed, and bookstores selling out of books such as Ibram X. Kendi's *How to Be an Antiracist*, Democrats wouldn't even bring the bill to a vote in the chamber they controlled.

While the word "reparations" has been used to scare white people and reduce support for the social contract, the range of solutions that could be contemplated is vast and has been well researched and thought through, spanning the provocative to the practical. The late brilliant scholar and activist Derrick Bell continually challenged the country to break free from the mental shackles that constrained our public policy imaginations. I remember having my mind blown in the early 1990s when I heard him say that racism should be legal, but you should have to pay an expensive fee to obtain a license to be racist. And then the fees from that license could fund measures to address the racial wealth gap. He described his idea—the "Racial Preference Licensing Act"—in a futuristic visioning in his book *Faces at the Bottom of the Well*:

> All employers, proprietors of public facilities, and owners and managers of dwelling places, homes, and apartments could, on

application to the federal government, obtain a license authorizing the holders, their managers, agents, and employees to exclude or separate persons on the basis of race and color. The license itself was expensive, though not prohibitively so. Once obtained, it required payment to a government commission of a tax of 3 percent of the income derived from whites employed, whites served, or products sold to whites during each quarter in which a policy of "racial preference" was in effect. Congress based its authority for the act on the commerce clause, the taxing power, and the general welfare clause of the Constitution."[23]

In Bell's sci-fi/fantasy vision of a socially just world, the license fees and commissions paid by license holders would be placed in an "equality fund" used to underwrite Black businesses, to offer no-interest mortgage loans for Black home buyers, and to provide scholarships for Black students seeking college and vocational education.[24]

Nearly twenty years after the publication of Bell's book, Angela Glover Blackwell and Michael McAfee, leaders of PolicyLink—a national research and action institute dedicated to advancing racial and economic equity—carried on Bell's work and further broke down in very practical terms what reparations could look like in the banking industry. Writing in the *New York Times* in the days after Floyd's murder in 2020, Blackwell and McAfee spelled out a detailed prescription for how the financial industry could contribute to reparations. "The financial industry is a good place to start," they asserted, because, "banks have been underwriters of American racism—no industry has played a bigger or more enduring role in black oppression, exploitation and exclusion. Banks financed the slave trade and in some cases 'repossessed' humans in bondage."[25] In their essay Blackwell and McAfee identified several concrete and specific measures that are both doable and meaningful in terms of impact. Among the ideas they promoted were providing interest-free mortgages to Black customers, eliminating bank fees for Black customers, and providing interest-free loans to Black businesses.

One can agree or disagree on the specific policy solutions facing a country that has practiced, tolerated, and benefited from hundreds of years of racial exploitation and oppression, but those who reject particular proposals are certainly morally obligated to credibly respond to the question, "What is owed?" Answering that question will then open the door to finalizing the additional elements of a post–Civil War social contract.

DO WE WANT PEOPLE TO VOTE?

A second objective of Reconstruction was to expand democracy and take the first faltering steps toward becoming a multiracial democracy. Again, before even getting to specific policy proposals, we can and should step back and affirm the core values underlying our new social contract.

Do we *want* everyone to vote? Why, in a democracy, wouldn't we encourage as much participation as possible? Denial of democracy has become so commonplace over the centuries that we have lost our sense of outrage. The opponents of true democracy—the legislators ruthlessly rewriting and reinterpreting voting laws to this day—do not believe all means *all*. They do not see all segments of the population as part of the same societal family. They treat people of color as "other," "opponents," "illegals," the ones against whom an ongoing Civil War should be waged.

What would we do if we *really* wanted everyone to vote? What strategies have other states and countries used to increase civic participation? The United States ranks thirtieth out of thirty-five industrialized nations in terms of voter participation.[26] Universal absentee voting, preemptively mailing a ballot to every eligible person, automatically registering people to vote when they turn eighteen or renew their driver's license are just some of the measures we could implement.

San Diego's Andrea Guerrero, the Level 5 leader profiled in chapter 10, highlighted for me the dichotomy between attitudes toward voting in the United States and those in Mexico. In Mexico, the government, by law, requires radio stations to dedicate a minimum number of minutes per day to upcoming elections so that everyone is informed and encouraged to participate. San Diego sits on the Mexican border, and many San Diego radio stations have transmitters in Mexico, subjecting them to that country's rules and regulations. As a result, many people in San Diego hear regular messages about elections in Mexico, but literal radio silence about elections in San Diego itself.

And if you really want to get crazy, we could follow the lead of the twenty-one countries around the world that have compulsory voting. In Singapore, 97 percent of the eligible voters vote. Peru has mandatory elections, where you are fined by the government if you *don't* vote.[27] And if you step back and think about it, is requiring people to vote that much different than requiring people to pay taxes? Aren't both acts civic duties? We require drivers to have car insurance. Everyone is now required to have health insurance. Why shouldn't we require people to participate in the democratic process?

As Ari Berman points out in *Give Us the Ballot*, "The United States is the only advanced democracy that has ever enfranchised, disenfranchised, and then reenfranchised an entire segment of the population."[28] That's what happens when a civil war never ends and one group of people works relentlessly to keep this a white nation. Once we win the Civil War, then we can come to agreement that, in a democracy, we should do everything possible to facilitate people voting. Making that happen could actually be done as quickly and easily as sending UBI-like checks to 159 million Americans.

———

The beautiful, snow-capped mountains of the Himalayas contain Mount Everest and are the highest mountain range in the world. The city of Jalandhar, India, is 124 miles away from the mountains and, like much of India, has been affected for years by widespread pollution that clouds the skies. Twelve days after the Covid lockdown began in March of 2020, amateur photographer Anshul Chopra was excitedly called to the roof of his apartment building by his father. Suddenly visible in the distance were the majestic mountains. Chopra recounted the wonder of what he saw, "For the first time in a lifetime, we can see the Himalayas. I couldn't believe my eyes. The Himalayas have been right there behind the pollution all along."[29]

All over the planet, during the lockdown, our air quality improved dramatically, and we could see things previously obscured to view. Things we didn't even know were there. Both literally and symbolically, our field of vision expanded, and expanded in ways that could have dramatic implications for our social contract.

Necessity being the mother of invention, the global pandemic opened our eyes and raised fundamental and previously unthinkable questions about how our society and economy operate. Do we really need to get in cars and drive to big office buildings to work for eight hours a day? With the abundance of available technology, can't we connect and engage with colleagues and co-workers in ways that are much more family friendly and conducive to better mental and physical health? When the vaccines were rolled out, anyone could get the jab just by making an appointment and showing up, and the whole transaction was free. Why can't all of health care be like that? The pandemic-inspired moratorium on student debt raises the more fundamental question of why is there student debt at all, and why don't we just erase it? In a society where we value education sufficiently to the point that public school is publicly funded and free to the population, why isn't higher education also free? From a values and social contract standpoint, what could be created, discovered, and improved in our world if students are encouraged to reach their potential, invested in, and freed from crushing bills and debt?

Racial justice and multiracial democracy are just the starting points—the first few paragraphs—of a new social contract. Subsequent sections will address education, health care, public safety, clean air and water, and all of the other aspects of how we live, work, and grow together—of how we all get along.

All of this and more is possible—once we win the Civil War. What stands in the way of us attaining and realizing our highest aspirations, biggest dreams, and boldest and best vision is the opposition of those who continue to wage that war. Those determined to make America a white nationalist country instead of the multiracial democracy it aspires to be.

But, just as the original eleven Confederate states represented a minority of the country's population (and a *small* minority when you count just the white population), the enemies of the multiracial promise of America are also a minority today. And a shrinking minority, as every single day seven thousand more people of color are added to our population, as compared with just one thousand whites (and 35 percent to 40 percent of those whites are aligned with us and constitute an important component of the New American Majority).[30] Mathematically, we absolutely *should* win. We know *how* to win. Most importantly we know *who* knows how to win.

The people who can lead us to victory—indeed, who are in the process of taking us to that promised land—look different than the typical profile of people in power. Maya Angelou wrote in her iconic poem "Still I Rise" that "I am the dream and the hope of the slave." The current and rising Level 5 leaders who are building the movement that is transforming the country are the living manifestations of the dreams of people who picked cotton, braved refugee boats, and raised families in a hostile and unwelcoming country.

The United States of America inarguably has a multiracial population. The task of the moment, the urgency of the hour, the fight we are engaged in, is to win a centuries-old Civil War and forge a multiracial democracy in which everyone can thrive. It is a fight we can and should win. And once we win this Civil War, once we defeat white supremacy for good, we can write a new social contract for the kind of country we really want to live in. One that celebrates people from all backgrounds, proceeds from a place of love for humanity, and lavishes resources on unlocking human potential. Empowered and unleashed by a new social contract, the new society we build can exceed our wildest imaginations. It will be a place of beauty, creativity, and love. Once we win, what we build will be glorious.

ACKNOWLEDGMENTS

Welp, it's been quite a journey to get here. It was on April 21, 2020, that Marc Favreau of The New Press reached out to ask, "Would you be interested in talking about your next book?" Nearly two years later, I'm finally submitting the manuscript of this, my second book. So many people helped make this a reality, lifted me up, pushed and cheered me on, and pitched in to keep me moving to get this done and get us here. It is time to acknowledge and express my deep, profound, and lasting gratitude.

Let me begin by thanking Marc Favreau and the whole team at The New Press for setting me on this journey, believing in me as a writer and author, being a great partner as I stepped onto the stage with my first book *Brown Is the New White*, and helping to shape, focus, and refine this book. Books matter a great deal in our society, and publishers play a critical role in influencing public opinion and societal priorities and direction. There is an alchemy that can occur when a writer and publisher meld their talents to produce a book, and I am hopeful that we will achieve that effect. I am blessed to partner with a publisher who gets what I am trying to do and say in this world and blends our strengths to make the greatest impact possible. And I want to give a special shout-out to Brian Baughan for a truly exceptional—and exceptionally careful and caring—job of copyediting. I felt seen, and I felt my manuscript was in very good hands.

A long journey requires a co-pilot, and I am extremely lucky to have found someone with the talent, skills, sensibility, and personality to travel this road with me. Sharline Chiang and I connected back in 2014 when I set out to write *Brown Is the New White*, and her support and partnership these past eight (!) years have been invaluable. Her combination of being cheerleader, book coach, and editor has been immensely beneficial every step of the way. Sharline has a, shall we say, "enthusiasm" for editing and excellence that, in my case at least, is not always fully appreciated in the moment (especially when I would open a draft chapter file and see that there were more than three hundred edits. Literally). But, now that we are here, let me say for the record that this is a better book and I am a better writer because of Sharline's, ah, "attention to detail." Thank you.

For the past twenty-five years, I have had the insanely good luck to enjoy the partnership and friendship of Emi Gusukuma. From our days starting out as lawyers together to our walks, talks, and meals over the years to her current role of keeping all the trains running on time in our various political and social change endeavors, none of this would have been possible without her keeping things moving—cheering me on, giving me the space, and, when necessary, metaphorically kicking my ass to complete this manuscript (though was it really necessary to do so *that* frequently?). From start to finish, Emi did what she does best—quietly, efficiently, and effectively getting "stuff" done.

Several years ago, I told Dr. Julie Martinez Ortega that her PhD was a collective asset, and I wasn't lying. Her big-brained data expertise, research skill, profound knowledge, warm personality, and generous spirit are my secret weapon and a source of great joy.

I have had the extreme good fortune to work with an extraordinarily talented team of people at Democracy in Color who play such an important role in helping to get my voice and messages into the world (literally, with our podcast, and overall as well). Olivia Parker, Fola Onifade, Shirley Burke, and April Elkjer, thank you for being so supportive and also so understanding and picking up the slack when the demands of writing this book took my attention away. And now, for better or worse, I'm back!

As I found during the writing of the first book, the work is so overwhelming that you need the help of talented researchers, and the added benefit of that reality is that you get to meet amazing, wonderful, smart people. Cathy Schreiber helped find and connect us to Caitilin Damacion, who was an absolute lifesaver (as evidenced by my going back to her time and time again for more and more help with research, footnotes, fact-checking, and more). Caitilin is both a top-notch talent with an extraordinary work ethic and a delight to work with. Matt Hoover lent us his masterful copyediting and Microsoft Word navigation talents to turn a sprawling set of separate documents into one properly merged file. In the final stretches of completing this manuscript, we were fortunate to add Brittany Poff to the team as a virtual assistant (through the appropriately enough named website Zirtual). Brittany cheerfully tackled multiple research tasks, keeping me out of myriad rabbit holes while regularly bringing back the needed information. In the early days, Judy Wu lent her research insights and guidance and also connected us to Marketus Presswood, who helped us get the research ball rolling.

Viveka Chen has been my coach for most of the past decade, and I am deeply indebted to her for so many things. Her wisdom, insight, counsel, and support have made me better and more effective in myriad ways, and, most pertinent to this project, she teamed up with Emi to force me to shut everything else out and focus on finishing this book at a key point in September. That tough love was much needed.

My life circumstances in writing a book were different this time around with Susan now being a brain cancer survivor. The logistics of living with and fighting cancer are considerable, and I absolutely would not have had the space, bandwidth, or focus without an amazing care team. Nina Pflumm Herndon, Marissa Hollmann-Butz, Shari Schoenfeld, and all the folks at Sage Elder Care have coordinated an extremely complex logistical support network that has run the gamut from identifying in-home nurses to attending doctor meetings to checking in on home maintenance to helping Susan record and post videos of her reading Dr. Seuss books for children. I will forever be grateful to my running buddy Eileen Goldman for connecting me to the Sage team (and to my entire "Running Family" of Laura, Steph, and Natalie for sustaining and sticking with me through the pandemic and the many miles over the many years).

I literally could not have written this book without the confidence and comfort afforded by a remarkable team of in-home caregivers. Tania, Emelyn, Tomoko, Cecille, Shay, and Rexie are all talented, hardworking, and empathetic, and they wrapped us in a vital web of support.

I am particularly indebted to Ingelle Tancioco, who has not only provided in-home nursing services for me and Susan these past two years, but who has served as the logistical impresario of everything operational and logistical in our home life. She has been a rock of stability in our life, and I would not have had the energy or ability to write this long and this intensively had she not applied her energy and ability to tending to all the things. Ingelle has indeed been an angel in our lives.

I also want to thank my therapist Esther Ehrensaft—and to encourage everyone to get a therapist! Tending to your mental health is no joke, y'all. Esther has kept me grounded, focused, and moving forward through turbulent times, and some of her feedback actually opened my eyes on how to edit a section of the book! My yoga teacher, Kimberly Hu, has tended to my physical well-being over eight years, two books, and one pandemic during which we continued to work together through the miracles of modern technology.

In terms of living in the world of cancer, I cannot say enough about the extraordinary medical team at the University of California, San Francisco (UCSF) that has supported us on every step of this journey— from the moment we called from the emergency room of New York University's Langone Health Center immediately after the CT scan showed a tumor in September of 2016 to the second we stepped off the plane back in San Francisco and every day, week, and month since. Andy Josephson, Mitch Berger, Steve Hauser, and the entire team at the UCSF Brain Tumor Center and all of the doctors and nurses at Executive Health have been literal lifesavers. And we will always be grateful for the enthusiasm and brilliance of all the amazing professionals who came together to create the UCSF Glioblastoma Precision Medicine Program. And, of course, Jenny Clarke and Terrelea Wong possess a combination of talent, knowledge, caring, and compassion that is difficult to describe with mere words.

As the line in *Hamilton* goes, "Can we get back to politics?" Yes. Yes, we can. I first want to thank everyone I interviewed for this book, especially the Level 5 leaders who were so generous with their time and trusting of me to tell their stories. Tram Nguyen, John Loredo, Montse Arredondo, Michelle Tremillo, Ginny Goldman, and Andrea Guerrero all not only put up with me but also took time out from their busy lives changing the world to give me the background, documentation, and materials to try to tell their stories. To all the other leaders featured—most especially Stacey Abrams, Alejandra Gomez, and Tomás Robles—thank you for the work that you do and the change you have already made in this country. I am also indebted to Ashley

Robinson, who filled in gaps and added information about the essential work in Georgia.

Several scholars and friends lent their time and insight and suggestions. Deepak Bhargava participated in an early Zoom interview to help me hone the arguments and messages of the book, and Harry Hanbury is and has always been a fount of fast information and historical reference. I am enriched by their support, grateful for Harry's careful reading of the manuscript, and fortunate to have their friendship. Sherry Broder participated in an early interview, regularly pointed out key information, and directed me to an important resource illuminating the reach of *Birth of a Nation*. Her grace, warmth, and knowledge mean a lot to me and to Susan. Writing nonfiction makes you especially aware of the intellectual commons, and I am indebted to those who shared their own research and writing. Hahrie Han sent me an advanced copy of her excellent work *Prisms of the People*, and Amy Heyse sent me her dissertation on the catechisms of the UDC.

Families also get pulled into the writing of a book whether they want to or not. My dad's ongoing encouragement, and my uncle Lumumba and aunt Janis's consistent cheerleading and encouragement mean more than they know. I am continually sustained by the spirit of my now-departed mother and the love of my brothers Jeff and Jimmy and my Aunt Mildred and cousin Karen. That I am a writer is in no small part due to my late uncle Renzi, who was a pioneering journalist in the 1950s and 1960s before stepping away from his career to help raise me and my brothers.

My brother-in-law and sister-in-law, Jim and Gretchen, are both enthusiastic supporters and indispensable backstops to the support and care team in our lives, and my cousin Lulie provided critical organizational backbone to the launch of *Brown Is the New White* and consistent encouragement ever since. The younger generations of my family probably don't realize how much their energy, activism, and involvement inspire me. Seeing my nephews and nieces Chris, Christian, Dierra, and Courtney and my cousin Africa find their voices and place on stage, standing up and speaking out warms my soul and fuels my fire. As Leah and Elijah go through and get ready for college, it has been a delight to engage with them and hear them discuss how they see the world and want to change it.

Making the connection between Leah's attendance at Barnard and the 1980s June Jordan essay, "Notes of a Barnard Dropout"—and sending Leah the book with that essay—was a very important symbolic and substantive moment for me. It showed me the duration of the influence of good writing, and it focused my mind on trying to make this book a resource for students like Leah trying to understand the world and how to make it better. The footnotes are kind of for Leah, lol. I saw them as bread crumbs for students and future students trying to find their way. Leah's intellectual inquiry and passion to make a difference inspired me to make this as good a resource as possible for people like her—so thirty years from now someone might send it to their niece or nephew.

Writing this book has also been a surprisingly spiritual endeavor for me. For more than a year, I was seated next to a table with fifty-four books by authors whose research and writing I drew on. Behind my desk stands a bookcase with the more than two hundred books I read in college in the early days of my own intellectual journey. I regularly felt those writers looking down on me from the bookshelves, urging me on and inviting me to take my place on the shelves. When I needed inspiration, I frequently took a book down off the shelf, opened it up, and drank in its eloquence and insight. I would then put my fingers back on the keyboard and try to channel that spirit and those insights into my own work so that the cause could continue into a new period, era, decade, and century.

I had perhaps my deepest spiritual connection with Isabel Wilkerson and her book *Caste*. She is a brilliant writer with remarkable clarity and insight about this moment and the human condition. Time and again, I would crack open *Caste* for clarity and guidance about how to tell this story.

And of course, there is Susan, my life partner. Covid and cancer shrunk our worlds, but we still had each other (and the internet and amazing co-workers) and were able to focus on what matters most. Susan advised me a long time ago that including and telling stories made writing more interesting, and I've tried to follow that advice to the best of my ability. We have encountered and weathered a lot in our lives these past few years—losing parents and entering the world of living with cancer. I have learned so much from Susan about how to live, how to face the most difficult challenges, and how to make a way. Her love, support, insight, and courage lift me up and drive me forward every day.

And so, we have arrived at this latest stop on our journey—publishing my second book. We would not have gotten here without the assistance of everyone mentioned above and many more people as well. Walking with Susan in our changed reality has given me a new phrase that has more meaning than its simplicity suggests—*and on we go.*

NOTES

AUTHOR'S NOTE

1. Lori L. Tharps, "The Case for Black with a Capital B," *New York Times*, November 18, 2014.

2. Touré, *Who's Afraid of Post-Blackness?* (New York: Free Press, 2011), 21, Apple Books.

INTRODUCTION: A CHOICE BETWEEN DEMOCRACY AND WHITENESS

1. Laura Pullman, "Trump's Militias Say They Are Armed and Ready to Defend Their Freedoms," *Sunday Times*, January 10, 2021; Michael Braun and Andy Humbles, "Mother of 'Zip Tie Guy' Arrested; Both Have Significant Ties to Florida and Fort Myers," *Fort Myers News-Press*, January 17, 2021, www.news-press.com/story/news/2021/01/17/mother-zip -tie-guy-arrested-both-linked-fort-myers-area/4196587001; "Affidavit in Support of Criminal Complaint and Arrest Warrant," United States District Court for the District of Columbia: *United States of America v. Eric Gavelek Munchel*, January 10, 2021, www.justice .gov/usao-dc/press-release/file/1352221/download.

2. "Affidavit in Support of Criminal Complaint."

3. Adam Friedman, "New Capitol Riot Video Appears to Show Actions of Accused 'Zip Tie Guy,' Eric Munchel, and Mother," *The Tennessean*, October 13, 2021, www.ten nessean.com/story/news/local/2021/10/13/capitol-riot-video-shows-nashville-accused-zip -tie-guy-mother-jan-6/8443587002/.

4. Michael S. Schmidt and Luke Broadwater, "Officers' Injuries, Including Concussions, Show Scope of Violence at Capitol Riot," *New York Times*, February 11, 2021.

5. Zachary Cohen and Marshall Cohen, "The January 6 Select Committee Will Hear from 4 Police Officers Tuesday. Here Are Their Stories," CNN, July 26, 2021.

6. Ibid.

7. Ibid.

8. Schmidt and Broadwater, "Officers' Injuries."

9. Pullman, "Trump's Militias Say They Are Armed."

10. Schmidt and Broadwater, "Officers' Injuries."

11. Caroline Sutton, "Tactical Vests, Firearms, Ammunition Found During Search of Eric Munchel's Home, Court Records Say," Newschannel5 Nashville, January 21, 2021, www.newschannel5.com/news/tactical-vests-firearms-ammunition-found-during-search-of-eric-munchels-home-court-records-say.

12. "Insurrection Index," insurrectionindex.org.

13. Abigail Tracy, "A Private Jet of Rich Trumpers Wanted to "Stop the Steal"—but They Don't Want You to Read This," *Vanity Fair*, March 18, 2021.

14. Nicole Austin-Hillery and Victoria Strang, "Racism's Prominent Role in January 6 US Capitol Attack," Human Rights Watch, January 5, 2022, www.hrw.org/news/2022/01/05 /racisms-prominent-role-january-6-us-capitol-attack.

15. "Identifying Far-Right Symbols That Appeared at the U.S. Capitol Riot," *Washington Post*, January 15, 2022.

16. Harry A. Dunn, Testimony Before House Select Committee to Investigate the January 6th Attack on the United States Capitol, January 27, 2021, legacy.npr.org/assets /pdf/2021/07/dunn_testimony.pdf.

17. Brad Meltzer and Josh Mensch, *The Lincoln Conspiracy* (New York: Flatiron Books, 2020), 217, 220–21, Apple Books.

18. "Confederate States of America—Declaration of the Immediate Causes Which Induce and Justify the Secession of South Carolina from the Federal Union," The Avalon Project: Yale Law School, avalon.law.yale.edu/19th_century/csa_scarsec.asp.

19. " 'Cornerstone Speech' by Alexander Stephens in Savannah, Georgia, March 21, 1861," State Historical Society of Iowa, iowaculture.gov/history/education/educator-resources /primary-source-sets/civil-war/cornerstone-speech-alexander.

20. Guy Gugliotta, "New Estimate Raises Civil War Death Toll," *New York Times*, April 2, 2012.

21. Ann McFeatters, "Relax, Folks: Trump Won't Win, and America Will Remain Great," *Seattle Times*, December 6, 2015, www.seattletimes.com/opinion/relax-folks -trump-wont-win-and-america-will-remain-great.

22. Ta-Nehisi Coates, "The First White President," *We Were Eight Years in Power* (New York: One World, 2018), 362.

23. Ta-Nehisi Coates, "Donald Trump Is Out. Are We Ready to Talk About How He Got In?," *The Atlantic*, January 19, 2021.

24. Kabir Khanna and Anthony Salvanto, "Republicans Still Back Trump but Don't Want GOP to Punish Disloyalty—CBS News Poll," CBS News, February 15, 2022, www .cbsnews.com/news/trump-republicans-gop-opinion-poll-02-2022/.

25. Perry Bacon Jr., "The Problem with Performative Centrism," *Washington Post*, December 23, 2021.

26. Ezra Klein, "David Shor Is Telling Democrats What They Don't Want to Hear," *New York Times*, October 8, 2021.

27. "Republican Party Platform of 1864," June 7, 1864, The American Presidency Project, www.presidency.ucsb.edu/documents/republican-party-platform-1864.

28. J.J. Beck, "Charles S. Wainwright: The Development of Loyal Dissent from 1861–1865," *Gettysburg College Journal of the Civil War Era* 3 (2013), Article 5, cupola.gettysburg .edu/gcjcwe/vol3/iss1/5.

29. "The Negro on the Brain. [graphic].," Library Company of Philadelphia, ca. 1863, digital.librarycompany.org/islandora/object/Islandora%3A8082.

30. Hparkins, "Lincoln to Slaves: Go Somewhere Else," National Archives: Pieces of History, December 1, 2010, prologue.blogs.archives.gov/2010/12/01/lincoln-to-slaves-go -somewhere-else.

31. Clayborne Carson, ed., *The Autobiography of Martin Luther King, Jr.* (New York: Grand Central Publishing, 2001), 428, Apple Books.

32. OWN, "Stacey Abrams: I'm Not Trying to Fit Anyone Else's Image | Black Women OWN the Conversation," YouTube, August 25, 2019, www.youtube.com/watch ?v=82Z5U2uXNzY.

33. Donna Britt, " 'They Killed a White Woman': Fifty Years Later, Leroy Moton Looks Back at the Killing That Changed the Civil Rights Movement Forever," *Washington Post*, February 27, 2019.

1: THE CONFEDERACY: FROM SURRENDER TO SUCCESS

1. Doris Kearns Goodwin, "The Night Abraham Lincoln Was Assassinated," *Smithsonian*, April 8, 2015, www.smithsonianmag.com/history/abraham-lincoln-team-of-rivals -180954850/?no-ist=&.

2. *The Athenaeum*, no. 1777 (November 16, 1861): 659, accessed via Google Books, www .google.com/books/edition/The_Athenaeum/ybbNeZhMxooC.

3. Robert Viagas, "The Night Lincoln Was Shot," *Playbill*, April 11, 2015, www.playbill .com/article/the-night-lincoln-was-shot-minute-by-minute-backstage-with-john-wilkes -booth-at-fords-theatre-com-346483.

4. "The Murderer of Mr. Lincoln," *New York Times*, April 21, 1865, www.nytimes .com/1865/04/21/archives/the-murderer-of-mr-lincoln-extraordinary-letter-of-john-wilkes .html.

5. Christopher Hamner, "Booth's Reason for Assassination," Teachinghistory.org, teachinghistory.org/history-content/ask-a-historian/24242.

6. Kearns Goodwin, "The Night Abraham Lincoln Was Assassinated."

7. Jeffrey Wm. Hunt, *The Last Battle of the Civil War: Palmetto Ranch* (Austin: University of Texas Press, 2002), 41–43, Apple Books.

8. John Salmon Ford, *Rip Ford's Texas*, ed. Stephen B. Oates (Austin: University of Texas Press, 1987), 6959, Kindle.

9. Hunt, *Last Battle*, 354.

10. "Colonel John S. Ford," Texas State Troops, 2008, hallofhonors.frb.io/inductees /colonel-john-s-ford.

11. "November 6, 1865: The Final Confederate Surrender," Daily Dose, November 6, 2014, www.awb.com/dailydose/?p=637.

12. "Waddell (DDG-24)," Naval Heritage and History Command, May 10, 2016, www .history.navy.mil/research/histories/ship-histories/danfs/w/waddell.html.

13. "Commissioning of the United States Ship Waddell," event program, Puget Sound Naval Shipyard, Bremerton, Washington, August 28, 1964.

14. Cong. Globe, 38th Cong., 1st Sess. 2939 (1864), memory.loc.gov/cgi-bin /ampage?collId=llcg&fileName=067/llcg067.db&recNum=12.

15. Cong. Globe, 2939.

16. Henry Louis Gates Jr., *Stony the Road: Reconstruction, White Supremacy, and the Rise of Jim Crow* (New York: Penguin Press, 2019), 11.

17. Cong. Globe, 38th Cong., 1st Sess. 2995 (1864), memory.loc.gov/cgi-bin/ampage ?collId=llcg&fileName=067/llcg067.db&recNum=68.

18. Julie Zauzmer Weil, Adrian Blanco, and Leo Dominguez, "More Than 1,700 Congressmen Once Enslaved Black People. This Is Who They Were, and How They Shaped the Nation," *Washington Post*, January 10, 2022.

19. Stephanie Condon, "After 148 Years, Mississippi Finally Ratifies 13th Amendment, Which Banned Slavery," CBS News, February 18, 2013, www.cbsnews.com/news /after-148-years-mississippi-finally-ratifies-13th-amendment-which-banned-slavery/.

20. Brenda Wineapple, *The Impeachers: The Trial of Andrew Johnson and the Dream of a Just Nation* (New York: Random House, 2020), 24, Apple Books.

21. Eric Foner, *Reconstruction: America's Unfinished Revolution, 1863–1877*, updated ed. (1988; repr., New York: Harper, 2014), 250.

22. Ibid., 252–54.

23. Andrew Johnson, "Third Annual Message to Congress," December 3, 1867, Miller Center, University of Virginia, millercenter.org/the-presidency/presidential-speeches/december-3-1867-third-annual-message-congress.

24. Gates, *Stony the Road*, 27.

25. Foner, *Reconstruction*, 577.

26. Ibid., 199–200.

27. Michael Perman, *Struggle for Mastery: Disfranchisement in the South, 1888–1908* (Chapel Hill: University of North Carolina Press, 2003), 11.

28. Bennett, *Black Power U.S.A.: The Human Side of Reconstruction, 1867–1877* (Baltimore: Penguin Books, 1969), 38.

29. Foner, *Reconstruction*, 189.

30. Ibid., 198.

31. *13th*, directed by Ava DuVernay (2016; Los Gatos, CA: Netflix, 2020).

32. W.E.B. Du Bois, *Black Reconstruction in America, 1860–1880* (New York: Free Press, 1935), 179–80.

33. Nikole Hannah-Jones, "Our Democracy's Founding Ideals Were False When They Were Written. Black Americans Have Fought to Make Them True," *New York Times*.

34. Perman, *Struggle for Mastery*, 10.

35. Walter Edgar, " 'E' Is for Eight Box Law," South Carolina Public Radio, January 29, 2021, www.southcarolinapublicradio.org/show/south-carolina-from-a-to-z/2016-01-29/e-is-for-eight-box-law-1882.

36. Carol Anderson, *One Person, No Vote: How Voter Suppression Is Destroying Our Democracy* (New York: Bloomsbury, 2018), 3.

37. Gates, *Stony the Road*, 19.

38. Ibid., 18.

39. Jon Meacham, "The South's Fight for White Supremacy," *New York Times*, August 23, 2020, updated September 2, 2020.

40. David W. Blight, *Race and Reunion: The Civil War in American Memory* (Cambridge, MA: Harvard University Press, 2002), 259, Kindle.

41. James Loewen, "Why Do People Believe Myths About the Confederacy? Because Our Textbooks and Monuments Are Wrong," *Washington Post*, July 1, 2015.

42. Meacham, "South's Fight for White Supremacy."

43. Mark Twain, *Adventures of Huckleberry Finn* (New York: Charles Webster and Company, 1885), accessed via Project Gutenberg e-book, www.gutenberg.org/files/76/76-h/76-h.html.

44. Christian McWhirter, "The Birth of 'Dixie,' " *New York Times*, March 31, 2012.

45. Stanley F. Horn, *Invisible Empire: The Story of the Ku Klux Klan, 1866–1871* (Boston: Houghton Mifflin, 1939), 9, archive.org/details/ invisibleempires00hornrich/page/8/mode/2up; see also Elaine Frantz Parsons, *Ku-Klux: The Birth of the Klan During Reconstruction* (Chapel Hill: University of North Carolina Press, 2015).

46. Julian Street, *American Adventures: A Second Trip "Abroad at Home"* (New York: Century, 1917), 522, accessed via Project Gutenberg e-book, www.gutenberg.org /files/18304/18304-h/18304-h.htm#CHAPTER_XLIX.

47. John Cimprich, *Fort Pillow, a Civil War Massacre, and Public Memory* (Baton Rouge: Louisiana State University Press, 2005), 46, Kindle.

48. George S. Burkhardt, *Confederate Rage, Yankee Wrath: No Quarter in the Civil War* (Carbondale: Southern Illinois University Press, 2007), 110.

49. Alan Axelrod, *Generals South, Generals North* (Lanham, MD: Rowman & Littlefield, 2016), 357, Apple Books.

50. John C. Lester and D. L. Wilson, *Ku Klux Klan: Its Origin, Growth and Disbandment* (New York: Neale Publishing Co., 1905), 27–28, accessed via Project Gutenberg e-book, www.gutenberg.org/files/31819/31819-h/31819-h.htm.

51. Jonathan M. Bryant, "Ku Klux Klan in the Reconstruction Era," *New Georgia Encyclopedia*, www.georgiaencyclopedia.org/articles/history-archaeology/ku-klux-klan-re construction-era.

52. "Report of the Joint Select Committee to Inquire into the Condition of Affairs in the Late Insurrectionary States," vol. 11, 587, Online Books Page, University of Pennsylvania, onlinebooks.library.upenn.edu/webbin/metabook?id=insurrection1872.

53. Du Bois, *Black Reconstruction in America*, 681.

54. "Report of the Joint Select Committee," vol. 1 (Minority Report), 289.

55. For Francis Blair campaign slogan, see Jared Goldstein, "The Klan's Constitution," New York Public Library Digital Collections, docs.rwu.edu/cgi/viewcontent.cgi ?article=1276&context=law_fac_fs; for Blair House, see "Blair House," DC Historic Sites, historicsites.dcpreservation.org/items/show/865.

56. Lester and Wilson, *Ku Klux Klan*, 13.

57. For background on Gordon, see W. Todd Grace, "John B. Gordon," *New Georgia Encyclopedia*, June 8, 2017, www.georgiaencyclopedia.org/articles/government-politics/john -b-gordon-1832-1904; see also "Gov. John Brown Gordon," National Governors Association, www.ndga.org/governor/john-brown-gordon.

58. See Richard J. Ellis, *The Development of the American Presidency* (New York: Routledge, 2012), 42.

59. Haworth Paul Leland, *The Hayes-Tilden Disputed Presidential Election of 1876* (Cleveland: Burrows Brothers Company, 1906), books.google.com/books?id=NoKHAAAAMA AJ&hl=en, via Google Books; see also Ronald G. Shafer, "The Ugliest Presidential Election in History: Fraud, Voter Intimidation, and a Backroom Deal," *Washington Post*, November 24, 2020.

60. Foner, *Reconstruction*, 581.

61. Bennett, *Black Power U.S.A.*, 402.

62. Foner, *Reconstruction*, 598.

2: THE TWENTIETH CENTURY, PART ONE: 50 YEARS, ONE BATTLE PLAN

1. Samuel Cartwright, "Diseases and Peculiarities of the Negro Race," *De Bow's Review* 11 (1851), www.pbs.org/wgbh/aia/part4/4h3106t.html.

2. "Samuel A. Cartwright and Family Papers, 1826–1864," Mss. 2471, 2499, Louisiana and Lower Mississippi Valley Collections, Louisiana State University Library, revised in 2008, www.lib.lsu.edu/sites/default/files/sc/findaid/2471m.pdf.

3. Cartwright, "Diseases and Peculiarities of the Negro Race."

4. Catherine Clinton, *Harriet Tubman: The Road to Freedom* (New York: Little, Brown, 2004), 137, Apple Books.

5. James Baldwin, The Fire Next Time (New York: Dell, 1962), 23.

6. Fergus M. Bordewich, "How Lincoln Bested Douglas in Their Famous Debates," *Smithsonian*, September 2008, www.smithsonianmag.com/history/how-lincoln-bested -douglas-in-their-famous-debates-7558180/.

7. Isabel Wilkerson, *The Warmth of Other Suns: The Epic Story of America's Great Migration* (New York: Random House, 2010), 42–44, Apple Books.

8. William Berman, *The Politics of Civil Rights in the Truman Administration* (Columbus: Ohio State University Press, 1970), x.

9. "Harry S Truman and Civil Rights," Harry S Truman National Historic Site, National Park Service, last modified August 18, 2021, https://www.nps.gov/articles/000/harry-s -truman-and-civil-rights.htm.

10. Ibid.

11. After the release of a final report by the President's Committee on Civil Rights, established by Executive Order 9808, Truman addressed Congress on February 2, 1948, with demands to create a "permanent Commission on Civil Rights, a Joint Congressional Committee on Civil Rights, and a Civil Rights Division in the Department of Justice." Included in these demands were measures "providing Federal protection against lynching," "establishing a Fair Employment Practice Commission to prevent unfair discrimination in employment," and "settling the evacuation claims of Japanese-Americans," among other progressive acts. President Harry S. Truman, "Special Message to the Congress on Civil Rights," BlackPast, February 2, 1948, www.blackpast.org/african-american-history/1948 -harry-s-truman-special-message-congress-civil-rights-2. See also "The Rise and Fall of Jim Crow: Harry S. Truman Supports Civil Rights," Jim Crow Stories, 2002, www.thir teen.org/wnet/jimcrow/stories_events_truman.html.

12. Joseph Crespino, *Strom Thurmond's America* (New York: Hill and Wang, 2012), 62.

13. Ibid., 75–76.

14. Ibid., 306.

15. "Platform of the States Rights Democratic Party," American Presidency Project, UC Santa Barbara, August 14, 1948, www.presidency.ucsb.edu/node/273454.

16. Crespino, *Strom Thurmond's America*, 71.

17. "1948" (presidential election results, by state), American Presidency Project, UC Santa Barbara, www.presidency.ucsb.edu/statistics/elections/1948. The author's calculations of data focus only on the states were the Dixiecrats received more than 0% of the vote.

18. Crespino, *Strom Thurmond's America*, 84.

19. Anderson, *One Person, No Vote*, 11.

20. O. Douglas Weeks, "The White Primary: 1944–1948," *American Political Science Review* 42, no. 3 (1948), www.jstor.org/stable/194991, 503–5.

21. Anderson, *One Person, No Vote*, 13.

22. Ibid., 14.

23. Gillian Brockell, "Some Call Voting Restrictions Upheld by Supreme Court 'Jim Crow 2.0.' Here's the Ugly History Behind That Phrase," *Washington Post*, July 2, 2021.

24. Loyal White Knights of the Ku Klux Klan website, via the Internet Archive, web.archive.org/web/20210426202918/https://lwkkkk.com/wp; see also " 'I'm Not a Racist,' the Answer a KKK Leader Gave to Ilia Calderon," YouTube, August 21, 2017, www.youtube .com/watch?v=BfntD7vLWow.

25. "How a Rising Star of White Nationalism Broke Free from the Movement," interview by Terry Gross, *Fresh Air*, NPR, September 24, 2018, www.npr.org/transc ripts/651052970.

26. Ta-Nehisi Coates, "Playing the Racist Card: Ferraro's Comments About Obama Were Racist. Why Can't We Say That?," *Slate*, March 14, 2008.

27. "Why Americans Don't Learn About Tulsa, or Juneteenth," *Post Reports*, podcast, *Washington Post*, June 19, 2020.

28. Richard Corliss, "D.W. Griffith's The Birth of a Nation 100 Years Later: Still Great, Still Shameful," *Time*, March 3, 2015.

29. James Agee, "D.W. Griffith, Remembered," *The Nation*, February 17, 2009.

30. Bob Wolfe, " 'California's Early Battle with Birtherism': D.W Griffith, the NAACP, the Ku Klux Klan and the Courts," California Supreme Court Historical Society, *California Supreme Court Historical Society Review*, Fall/Winter 2021, www.cschs.org/wp-con tent/uploads/2021/12/2021-CSCHS-Review-Fall.pdf.

31. Diane Roberts, "Thomas Dixon Jr: The Great-Granddaddy of American White Nationalism," *Washington Post*, January 21, 2019.

32. Andrew Leiter, "Thomas Dixon, Jr.: Conflicts in History and Literature," Documenting the American South, 2004, docsouth.unc.edu/southlit/dixon_intro.html.

33. Sara Hines Martin, *Georgia's Remarkable Women: Daughters, Wives, Sisters, and Mothers Who Shaped History* (Guilford, CT: Globe Pequot, 2015), 195.

34. Therese Oneill, "20 Things You Might Not Have Known About Gone with the Wind," *Mental Floss*, November 3, 2015, www.mentalfloss.com/article/56085/20 -things-you-might-not-have-known-about-gone-wind.

35. Frank Pallotta, "How 'Gone with the Wind' Became America's Biggest Blockbuster," CNN Business, December 15, 2014.

36. Richard F. Shepard, "CBS Buys 'Gone with the Wind' for TV for $35 Million," *New York Times*, April, 6, 1978.

37. Brian Lyman, "Southern Schools' History Textbooks: A Long History of Deception, and What the Future Holds," *The Tennessean*, December 3, 2020, www .tennessean.com/story/news/education/2020/12/03/southern-history-textbooks-long-his tory-deception/6327359002/.

38. Karen L. Cox, *Dixie's Daughters: The United Daughters of the Confederacy and the Preservation of Confederate Culture* (Gainesville: University Press of Florida, 2003), 247, Apple Books.

39. Allen G. Breed, "Women's Group Behind Rebel Memorials Quietly Battles On," *US News & World Report*, August 10, 2018.

40. "Whose Heritage? Public Symbols of the Confederacy," Southern Poverty Law Center, February 1, 2019, www.splcenter.org/20190201/whose-heritage-public-sym bols-confederacy.

41. "Mitch Landrieu's Speech on the Removal of Confederate Monuments in New Orleans," *New York Times*, May 23, 2017.

42. Martin Mfg. Co., Lancaster, OH, ad in *The Fiery Cross*, Indianapolis, IN, June 20, 1924, p. 3, bl-libg-doghill.ads.iu.edu/gpd-web/fierycross/1924/1924620.pdf.

43. Roland G. Fryer Jr. and Steven D. Levitt, "Hatred and Profits: Under the Hood of the Ku Klux Klan," *Quarterly Journal of Economics* 127, no. 4 (November 2012), doi .org/10.1093/qje/qjs028.

44. Ibid.

45. Linda Gordon, *The Second Coming of the KKK: The Ku Klux Klan of the 1920s and the American Political Tradition* (New York: Liveright, 2017), 164.

46. Jennifer Mendelsohn and Peter A. Shulman, "How Social Media Spread a Historical Lie," *Washington Post*, March 15, 2018.

47. Maria Cramer, "A Brokered Convention? Here's What's Happened Before," *New York Times*, February 27, 2020, updated March 3, 2020.

48. See Robert K. Murray, *The 103rd Ballot: The Legendary 1924 Democratic Convention That Forever Changed Politics* (New York: Harper, 2016), Apple Books.

49. Gordon, *Second Coming of the KKK*, 167–68.

50. William Robinson Pattangall, *The Meddybemps Letters: Reproduced from the Machias Union of 1903–1904; Maine's Hall of Fame, Reproduced from the Maine Democrat of 1909–1910; Memorial Addresses* (Lewiston, ME: Lewiston Journal Company, 1924), 51, accessed via Google Books, www.google.com/books/edition/The_Meddybemps_Letters /YClNAAAAYAAJ.

51. Gordon, *Second Coming of the KKK*, 169.

52. Elmer Davis, "Convention, by One Vote, Defeats Plank Naming Klan, Bryan, in Bitter Debate, Pleading for Party Unity; Proposal for League Referendum Wins, Despite Baker," *New York Times*, June 29, 1924.

53. Ibid.

54. Kristina DuRocher, *Raising Racists: The Socialization of White Children in the Jim Crow South* (Lexington: University Press of Kentucky, 2011), 12, Apple Books.

55. Ibid., 13–14.

56. Arthur F. Raper, *The Tragedy of Lynching* (1933; repr., Mineola, NY: Dover, 2003), 1, Kindle.

57. "Racial Terror Lynchings," Equal Justice Initiative, lynchinginamerica.eji.org /explore.

58. Carol Anderson, *Eyes off the Prize: The United Nations and the African American Struggle for Human Rights, 1944–1955* (New York: Cambridge University Press, 2003), 64.

59. Anderson, *One Person, No Vote*, 14–16.

60. "A Senator Refuses to Apologize for Joking About 'Public Hanging' in a State Known for Lynchings," *Washington Post*, November 12, 2018.

61. David Oshinsky, *Worse Than Slavery: Parchman Farm and the Ordeal of Jim Crow Justice* (New York: Free Press, 1997), 105–6.

62. Raper, *The Tragedy of Lynching*, 13, Kindle.

63. Dr. Martin Luther King, "Letter from a Birmingham Jail," August 1963, kinginsti tute.stanford.edu/sites/mlk/files/letterfrombirmingham_wwcw_o.pdf.

3: THE TWENTIETH CENTURY, PART TWO: 50 MORE YEARS, SAME BATTLE PLAN

1. Roxanne Dunbar-Ortiz. *An Indigenous Peoples' History of the United States* (Boston: Beacon Press, 2014), 326, Apple Books.

2. Bernice J. Reagon, "A Borning Struggle," *New Directions* 7, no. 3 (1980), article 3, dh.howard.edu/newdirections/vol7/iss3/3.

3. "The Southern Manifesto and 'Massive Resistance' to Brown," NAACP Legal Defense Fund, www.naacpldf.org/ldf-celebrates-60th-anniversary-brown-v-board-education /southern-manifesto-massive-resistance-brown.

4. Dan T. Carter, *The Politics of Rage: George Wallace, the Origins of the New Conservatism, and the Transformation of American Politics* (Baton Rouge: Louisiana State University Press, 1995), 86.

5. Ibid., 86.

6. Kristen Green, *Something Must Be Done About Prince Edward County: A Family, a Virginia Town, a Civil Rights Battle* (New York: HarperCollins, 2015), 127, Apple Books.

7. Glenn Frankel, "When a Va. County Closed Its Schools Rather Than Admit Black Students," *Washington Post*, July 1, 2015.

8. Emily Richmond, "The Forgotten School in *Brown vs. Board of Education*," *The Atlantic*, May 16, 2014.

9. Green, *Something Must Be Done About Prince Edward County*, 43.

10. Carter, *The Politics of Rage*, 109.

11. Bruce Weber, "J.L. Chestnut Jr., Early Leader in Civil Rights Movement, Is Dead at 77," *New York Times*, September 30, 2008.

12. Stephan Lesher, *George Wallace: American Populist* (Boston: Da Capo, 1995), 126.

13. Carter, *The Politics of Rage*, 96.

14. Alabama Audiovisual Collection, "Inaugural Address of Governor George Wallace in Montgomery, Alabama," YouTube, digital.archives.alabama.gov/digital/collection/rec ords/id/468/rec/2; see also "Confederate States of America—Inaugural Address of the President of the Provisional Government," Avalon Project, Yale Law School, February 18, 1861, avalon.law.yale.edu/19th_century/csa_csainau.asp.

15. Carter, *The Politics of Rage*, 358.

16. John J. Dunphy, "Dunphy: Time to Rewrite Jefferson's Words," *The Telegraph*, January 23, 2018.

17. Carter, *The Politics of Rage*, 471.

18. Jeff Stein, "Trump and the Racist Ghost of George Wallace," *Newsweek*, March 1, 2016.

19. Greg Huffman, "Twisted Sources: How Confederate Propaganda Ended Up in the South's Schoolbooks," *Facing South*, April 10, 2019, www.facingsouth.org/2019/04 /twisted-sources-how-confederate-propaganda-ended-souths-schoolbooks.

20. Kathleen Sheetz, "Catechism," *Encyclopedia Britannica* Online, www.britannica .com/topic/catechism.

21. Thomas L. Kinkead, *Baltimore Catechism, No. 4: An Explanation of the Baltimore Catechism of Christian Doctrine for the Use of Sunday-School Teachers and Advanced Classes* (1891: repr., Hard Press Publishing, 2006), Kindle.

22. Cox, *Dixie's Daughters*, 252.

23. Ibid., 278.

24. Amy Heyse, "Teachers of the Lost Cause: The United Daughters of the Confederacy and the Rhetoric of Their Catechisms" (PhD dissertation, University of Maryland, 2006), 275, drum.lib.umd.edu/bitstream/handle/1903/4060/umi-umd-3800.pdf.

25. Heyse, "Teachers of the Lost Cause," 43–44.

26. Heyse, "Teachers of the Lost Cause," 312.

27. "Catechisms," United Daughters of the Confederacy, hqudc.org/cofc-catechisms.

28. Frank B. Powell III, "From the Editor," *Confederate Veteran*, March/April 2021.

29. " 'The Lost Cause': The Women's Group Fighting for Confederate Monuments," *The Guardian*, August 10, 2018.

30. "United Daughters of the Confederacy, Form 990, 2019," ProPublica Nonprofit Explorer, projects.propublica.org/nonprofits/display_990/540631483/04_2021_prefixes _54-55%2F540631483_202008_990_2021040617898205.

31. "Sons of Confederate Veterans Inc., Form 990, 2018," ProPublica Nonprofit Explorer, projects.propublica.org/nonprofits/organizations/581825423.

32. "SCV Store," Sons of Confederate Veterans, scv.org/shop.

33. *Confederate Veteran*, November/December 2021, page 71.

34. Karen L. Cox, "The Confederacy's 'Living Monuments,' " *New York Times*, June 10, 2017.

35. In 2020, after the racial justice protests in the wake of the killing of George Floyd, the facility changed its name to "Travellers Rest Historic House Museum." Up until 2019, it was still going by its original name—Travellers Rest Plantation—and its URL was "travellersrest plantation.org." See "Historic Travellers Rest: The 1799 Home of Judge John Overton," Internet Archive, web.archive.org/web/20190921035553/https://travellersrestplantation.org.

36. Joel Ebert, "Nathan Bedford Forrest Bust at the Tennessee Capitol: What You Need to Know," *The Tennessean*, August 18, 2017, www.tennessean.com/story/news/2017/08/18/nathan-bedford-forrest-bust-tennessee-capitol-what-you-need-know/578112001.

37. "Lieutenant General Nathan Bedford Forrest, C.S.A.," Sons of Confederate Veterans, www.tennessee-scv.org/camp28/Forrest_Print.html.

38. Senate Joint Resolution No. 54, Tennessee, April 13, 1973, www.scribd.com/document/356566755/Nathan-Bedford-Forrest-Resolution.

39. Ebert, "Nathan Bedford Forrest Bust at the Tennessee Capitol."

40. Johnny Diaz, "Bust of Klan Leader Removed from Tennessee State Capitol," *New York Times*, July 23, 2021.

41. Kyle Horan, "Bill Would Remove All Members of the Historical Commission," Newschannel5 Nashville, March 17, 2021, www.newschannel5.com/news/bill-would-remove-all-members-of-the-historical-commission.

42. "General Forrest Homemade Soap," Sons of Confederate Veterans, scv.org/product/general-forrest-homemade-soap.

43. Nicholas Fandos, "House Votes to Purge Confederate Statues from the Capitol," *New York Times*, June 29, 2021, updated Sept. 28, 2021.

44. Ari Berman, *Give Us the Ballot: The Modern Struggle for Voting Rights in America* (New York: Picador, 2016), 146.

45. Bryan Greene, "Created 150 Years Ago, the Justice Department's First Mission Was to Protect Black Rights," *Smithsonian*, July 1, 2020, www.smithsonianmag.com/history/created-150-years-ago-justice-departments-first-mission-was-protect-black-rights-180975232/.

46. Jim Rutenberg, "A Dream Undone: Inside the 50-Year Campaign to Roll Back the Voting Rights Act," *New York Times Magazine*, July 29, 2015.

47. Tova Andrea Wang, "The Politics of Voter Suppression: Defending and Expanding Americans' Right to Vote," Demos, August 18, 2012, www.demos.org/publication/politics-voter-suppression-defending-and-expanding-americans-right-vote.

48. Berman, *Give Us the Ballot*, 149.

49. Ibid., 149.

50. Rutenberg, "A Dream Undone."

51. "QuickFacts: Mississippi," U.S. Census Bureau, July 1, 2021, www.census.gov/quickfacts/MS.

52. Sven Beckert, *Empire of Cotton: A Global History* (New York: Vintage, 2014), 343, Apple Books.

53. "Population of the United States in 1860: Mississippi," U.S. Census Bureau, www2.census.gov/library/publications/decennial/1860/population/1860a-22.pdf.

54. "Race of the Population of the United States, by States: 1960," U.S. Census Bureau, www2.census.gov/library/publications/decennial/1960/pc-s1-supplementary-reports/pc-s1-10.pdf.

55. "Interview with Sam H. Bowers Jr.," Oral Histories, Mississippi Department of Archives and History, October 24, 1983, da.mdah.ms.gov/bowers /transcript.php? page=3.

56. Edwin Du Bois Shurter, *Oratory of the South: From the Civil War to the Present Time* (New York: Neale Publishing Company, 1908), 258, viewed via Internet Archive, archive .org/details/bub_gb_UYQLAAAAMAAJ/page/n261/mode/2up.

57. "Sam Bowers: Nearing the Day of Judgment?," *Washington Post*, August 11, 1968, viewed via the Harold Weisberg Digital Archive Collection, Hood College, http://jfk.hood .edu/Collection/Weisberg%20Subject%20Index%20Files/N%20Disk/National%20States %20Rights%20Party/Item%20004.pdf.

58. Taylor Branch, *Pillar of Fire: America in the King Years, 1963–1965* (New York: Simon & Schuster, 1990), 1332, Apple Books

59. Jennifer 8. Lee, "Samuel Bowers, 82, Klan Leader Convicted in Fatal Bombing, Dies," *New York Times*, November 6, 2006.

60. Douglas O. Linder, "The 'Mississippi Burning' Trial: An Account," Famous Trials, updated June 2016, famous-trials.com/mississippiburning/1955-home.

61. Lee, "Samuel Bowers."

62. Bob Herbert, "Righting Reagan's Wrongs?," *New York Times*, November 13, 2007.

63. Margaret Mitchell, *Gone with the Wind* (New York: Macmillan, 1936), 9, Apple Books.

64. Kim Kimzey, "Daughter's Book Offers Tribute to Politician Dad," *Spartanburg Herald-Journal*, January 1, 2011, www.goupstate.com/story/news/2011/01/01 /daughters-book-offers-tribute-to-politician-dad/29848640007.

65. Crespino, *Strom Thurmond's America*, 209–10; see also David Stout, "Harry Dent, an Architect of Nixon's 'Southern Strategy,' Dies at 77," *New York Times*, October 7, 2007.

66. Crespino, *Strom Thurmond's America*, 209.

67. Ibid., 219, 226.

68. Angie Maxwell and Todd Shields, *The Long Southern Strategy: How Chasing White Voters in the South Changed American Politics* (New York: Oxford University Press, 2019), 5–6.

69. Carter, *The Politics of Rage*, 455.

70. "How Groups Voted in 1976," Roper Center, Cornell University, ropercenter.cornell .edu/how-groups-voted-1976.

71. Herbert, "Righting Reagan's Wrongs?"

72. "How Groups Voted in 1980," Roper Center, Cornell University, ropercenter.cornell .edu/how-groups-voted-1980.

73. Maxwell and Shields, *The Long Southern Strategy*, 2, 8, 9.

4: FEAR OF A BLACK PRESIDENT

1. A. Leon Higginbotham, *In the Matter of Color: Race and the American Legal Process: The Colonial Period* (Oxford: Oxford University Press, 1978), 167.

2. "The Preamble to the South Carolina Slave Code of 1712," in *Statutes at Large of South Carolina*, vol. 7 (Columbia, SC: A.H. Pemberton State Printer, 1840), 352.

3. James Shepherd Pike, *The Prostrate State: South Carolina Under Negro Government* (New York: D. Appleton and Company, 1874), name.umdl.umich.edu/AFK4119.0001.001.

4. Pike, *The Prostrate State*, 15, 12.

5. Michael B. Preston, "The Election of Harold Washington: Black Voting Patterns in the 1983 Chicago Mayoral Race," *Political Science and Politics* 16, no. 3 (Summer 1983): 486–88.

6. "History of Chicago's Mayoral Office," Ballotpedia, ballotpedia.org/History_of _Chicago%27s_mayoral_office.

7. Leanita McClain, "How Chicago Taught Me How to Hate Whites," *Washington Post*, July 24, 1983.

8. Kevin Klose, "A Tormented Black Rising Star, Dead By Her Own Hand. Leanita McClain: A Pioneer at the Racial Frontier Who Lost Her Way," *Washington Post*, August 5, 1984.

9. Isabel Wilkerson, *Caste: The Origins of Our Discontents* (New York: Random House, 2020), 311.

10. Pike, *The Prostrate State*, 12.

11. James McPherson, *Battle Cry of Freedom: The Civil War Era* (New York: Oxford University Press, 2003), 2063, Apple Books. See also James Lee McDonough and Thomas L. Connelly, *Five Tragic Hours: The Battle of Franklin* (Knoxville: University of Tennessee Press, 1983), 179, Kindle.

12. Jonathan M. Metzl, *Dying of Whiteness: How the Politics of Racial Resentment Is Killing America's Heartland* (New York: Basic Books, 2019), 16. Apple Books.

13. Ibid., 17.

14. Jennifer Tolbert, Kendal Orgera, and Anthony Damico, "Key Facts About the Uninsured Population," Kaiser Family Foundation, November 6, 2020, www.kff.org /uninsured/issue-brief/key-facts-about-the-uninsured-population/.

15. Jonathan Cohn, *The Ten Year War: Obamacare and the Unfinished Crusade for Universal Coverage* (New York: St. Martin's Press, 2021), 327.

16. Ibid., 214.

17. Abbe R. Gluck, Mark Regan, and Erica Turret, "The Affordable Care Act's Litigation Decade," *Georgetown Law Review* 108, no. 6 (June 2020), www.law.georgetown.edu /georgetown-law-journal/wp-content/uploads/sites/26/2020/06/Gluck-Reagan-Turret_ The-Affordable-Care-Act%E2%80%99s-Litigation-Decade.pdf.

18. Gluck, Regan, and Turret, "The Affordable Care Act's Litigation Decade."

19. Chris Riotta, "GOP Aims to Kill Obamacare Yet Again After Failing 70 Times," *Newsweek*, July 29, 2017.

20. David Axelrod, *Believer: My Forty Years in Politics* (New York: Penguin Books, 2016), 730, Apple Books.

21. Cohn, *The Ten Year War*, 332.

22. Thomas Edge, "Southern Strategy 2.0: Conservatives, White Voters, and the Election of Barack Obama," *Journal of Black Studies* 40, no. 3 (January 2010), doi.org/10.1177 %2F0021934709352979.

23. Aaron Blake, "Everything You Need to Know About the Pennsylvania Voter ID Fight," *Washington Post*, October 2, 2012.

24. Berman, *Give Us the Ballot*, 10.

25. Matea Gold, "In N.C., Conservative Donor Art Pope Sits at Heart of Government He Helped Transform," *Washington Post*, July 19, 2014.

26. Maydha Devarajan and Suzannah Claire Perry, "N.C. Senate Appoints Art Pope, Conservative Political Figure and Businessman, to UNC BOG," *Daily Tar Heel*, June 25, 2020, www.dailytarheel.com/article/2020/06/art-pope-0626.

27. Chris Kromm, "Art Pope's Big Day: Republican Benefactor Fueled GOP Capture of NC Legislature," *Facing South*, November 9, 2010, www.facingsouth.org/2010/11/art -popes-big-day-republican-benefactor-fueled-gop.html.

28. Jane Mayer, "State for Sale: A Conservative Multimillionaire Has Taken Control in North Carolina, One of 2012's Top Battlegrounds," *New Yorker*, October 10, 2011.

29. Erin Mizelle, "Loretta Biggs Becomes U.S. Judge," *Winston-Salem Chronicle*, March 12, 2015, wschronicle.com/loretta-biggs-becomes-u-s-judge.

30. *N.C. State Conference of NAACP v. Cooper*, 1:18 CV1034, M.D. N.C., November 7, 2019, casetext.com/case/nc-state-conference-of-naacp-v-cooper-1.

31. "#Selma50: What the Media and Hollywood Got Wrong About 'Bloody Sunday,' " NBC News, March 8, 2015, www.nbcnews.com/news/nbcblk/media-studies-selma -n319436; see also Taylor Branch, *At Canaan's Edge: America in the King Years, 1965–68* (New York: Simon & Schuster, 2007), 166, Apple Books.

32. Branch, *At Canaan's Edge*, 169.

33. Josh Clinton and Carrie Roush, "Poll: Persistent Partisan Divide over 'Birther' Question," NBC News, August 10, 2016, www.nbcnews.com/politics/2016-election /poll-persistent-partisan-divide-over-birther-question-n627446.

34. "Growing Number of Americans Say Obama Is a Muslim," Pew Research Center, August 18, 2010, www.pewforum.org/2010/08/18/growing-number-of-americans -say-obama-is-a-muslim.

35. Phillips, *Brown Is the New White: How the Demographic Revolution Has Created a New American Majority* (New York: The New Press, 2016), 35.

36. Adam Serwer, "Birtherism of a Nation," *The Atlantic*, May 13, 2020.

37. Mary Harris and Daryl Johnson, "He Saw the Storm Coming," January 11, 2021, in *What Next*, podcast, produced by *Slate*, slate.com/podcasts/what-next/2021/01/the -capitol-was-just-the-beginning.

38. David Neiwert, "Far-Right Extremists Have Hatched Far More Terror Plots Than Anyone Else in Recent Years," *Reveal*, June 22, 2017, revealnews.org/article / home-is-where-the-hate-is.

39. Sahil Kapur, " 'This Isn't the Final Chapter': Analyst Warns, Again, About Rise of Right-Wing Extremists," NBC News, January 13, 2021, www.nbcnews.com/politics /politics-news/isn-t-final-chapter-analyst-warns-again-about-rise-right-n1253950.

40. Katie Brenner, "Inside the Government, Addressing Domestic Terrorism Has Been Fraught," *New York Times*, August 11, 2019.

41. Office of Intelligence and Analysis, Extremism and Radicalization Branch, Homeland Environment Threat Analysis Division, in coordination with the FBI, *Rightwing Extremism: Current Economic and Political Climate Fueling Resurgence in Radicalization and Recruitment*, IA-0257-09, U.S. Department of Homeland Security, Washington, D.C., April 7, 2009, irp.fas.org/eprint/rightwing.pdf.

42. For background on the Congressional attacks on DHS, see H.R. 404, 111th Cong. (2009), www.congress.gov/bill/111th-congress /house-resolution/404; see also Teddy Davis and Ferdous Al-Farque, "Napolitano Facing Republican Calls for Her Ouster," ABC

News, April 23, 2009, abcnews.go.com/Politics/story?id=7412992&page=; and Daryl Johnson, "I Warned of Right-Wing Violence in 2009. Republicans Objected. I Was Right," Washington Post, August 21, 2017.

43. Katie Brenner, "Inside the Government, Addressing Domestic Terrorism Has Been Fraught," New York Times, August 11, 2019.

44. Jeff Nesbit, Poison Tea: How Big Oil and Big Tobacco Invented the Tea Party and Captured the GOP (New York: Thomas Dunne Books, 2016), 5–6.

45. Forbes Staff, "In Pictures: The 20 Richest Americans," Forbes, September 17, 2008

46. Shane Goldmacher, "How David Koch and His Brother Shaped American Politics," New York Times, August 23, 2019.

47. Jane Mayer, Dark Money: The Hidden History of the Billionaires Behind the Rise of the Radical Right (New York: Anchor, 2017), 49.

48. Crespino, Strom Thurmond's America, 84.

49. Alex Isenstadt, "Town Halls Gone Wild," Politico, updated August 3, 2009.

50. Sheryl Gay Stolberg and Mike McIntire, "A Federal Budget Crisis Months in the Planning," New York Times, October 5, 2013.

51. Algernon Austin, America Is Not Post-Racial: Xenophobia, Islamophobia, Racism, and the 44th President (Santa Barbara, CA: Praeger, 2015), xi.

52. Charles G. Koch with Brian Hooks, Believe in People: Bottom-Up Solutions for a Top-Down World (New York: St. Martin's, 2020), 407, Apple Books.

5: MAKE AMERICA WHITE AGAIN

1. Tim Naftali, "The Worst President in History," The Atlantic, January 19, 2021.

2. Aaron Rupar, " 'They Are Dying. That's True. It Is What It Is.' Trump's Axios Interview Was a Disaster," Vox, August 4, 2020.

3. Naftali, "The Worst President in History."

4. "The Trump Administration's Record of Racism, Part Two, October 2018–July 2020," Democracy in Color, democracyincolor.com/recordofracism2.

5. Ta-Nehisi Coates, "The First White President," The Atlantic, October 2017.

6. Wilkerson, Caste, 4.

7. Michael J. Kline, The Baltimore Plot: The First Conspiracy to Assassinate Abraham Lincoln (Yardley, PA: Westholme, 2008), 18–20, 24, Apple Books.

8. Jim Rutenberg et al., "77 Days: Trump's Campaign to Subvert the Election," New York Times, updated June 15, 2021.

9. Hilary George-Parkin, "Insurrection Merch Shows Just How Mainstream Extremism Has Become," Vox, January 12, 2021.

10. Olivia Nuzzi, "The Full(est Possible) Story of the Four Seasons Total Landscaping Press Conference," New York, December 21, 2020; see also Rachelle Hampton, "An Interview with the Owner of the Sex Shop Next to Four Seasons Landscaping," Slate, November 9, 2020.

11. "Four Seasons Campaign Crewneck Sweatshirt," Four Seasons Total Landscaping, www.fstl1992.com.

12. Gates, Stony the Road, 102–3.

13. "Trump Lambastes Detroit in Ballot Counting Criticism, Calling It Corrupt," Fox 2 Detroit, November 5, 2020, updated November 6, 2020, www.fox2detroit.com/news /trump-lambastes-detroit-in-ballot-counting-criticism-calling-it-corrupt.

14. "Quick Facts: Detroit City, Michigan; Philadelphia, Pennsylvania," U.S. Census Bureau, July 1, 2021, www.census.gov/quickfacts/fact/table/detroitcitymichigan,philadelphia citypennsylvania/PST045221.

15. Tiffany Hsu and John Koblin, "Fox News Meets Trump's Fraud Claims with Skepticism," *New York Times*, November 5, 2020, updated November 7, 2020.

16. "Quick Facts: Milwaukee City, Wisconsin; Atlanta City, Georgia; United States," U.S. Census Bureau, July 1, 2021, www.census.gov/quickfacts/fact/table/milwaukeecity wisconsin,atlantacity georgia,US/PST045221.

17. *King et al. v. Whitmer, E.D. Mich.*, No. 20-13134, December 7, 2020, www.mied .uscourts.gov/PDFFIles/20-13134Opn.pdf.

18. Alan Feuer, "Judge Orders Sanctions Against Pro-Trump Lawyers over Election Lawsuit," *New York Times*, August 25, 2021.

19. Michelle Ye Hee Lee and Toluse Olorunnipa, "Trump's Lie That the Election Was Stolen Has Lost $519 Million (and Counting) as Taxpayers Fund Enhanced Security, Legal Fees, Property Repairs, and More," *Washington Post*, February 6, 2021, updated June 15, 2021.

20. Jill Colvin, "Capitol Mob Built Gallows and Chanted 'Hang Mike Pence,'" *Our Quad Cities*, January 9, 2021, www.ourquadcities.com/news/national-news /capitol-mob-built-gallows-and-chanted-hang-mike-pence.

21. Larry Buchanan, Denise Lu, and Karen Yourish, "The 147 Republicans Who Voted to Overturn Election Results," *New York Times*, updated January 7, 2021, www.nytimes .com/interactive/2021/01/07/us/elections/electoral-college-biden-objectors.html.

22. "Voting Laws Roundup," Brennan Center, May 28, 2021, updated June 21, 2021, www.brennancenter.org/our-work/research-reports/voting-laws-roundup-may-2021.

23. Ibid.

24. Ibid.

25. Nick Corasaniti and Reid J. Epstein, "What Georgia's Voting Law Really Does," *New York Times*, April 2, 2021, updated June 25, 2021.

26. Alex Ura, "The Hard-Fought Texas Voting Bill Is Poised to Become Law. Here's What It Does," *Texas Tribune*, August 30, 2021, www.texastribune.org/2021/08/30 /texas-voting-restrictions-bill.

27. Ronald Brownstein, "Why Republican Voter Restrictions Are a Race Against Time," CNN, March 23, 2021, www.cnn.com/2021/03/23/politics/voting-rights-republicans-bills-demographics/index.html.

28. Ibid.

29. Mike Argento and Dylan Segelbaum, "Witness in Pa. Election Fraud Suit from York Is a Ghost Hunter with a Long Criminal Record," *York Daily Record*, December 8, 2020, www.ydr.com/story/news/2020/12/08/witness-pa-election-fraud-suit-ghost-hunter -long-criminal-record/6496500002.

30. "The Shadows Amongst Us This Is a Documentary on a Family Haunted by Paranormal Events Despite Living in Different Parts of the Country," iCrowdNewswire, December 30, 2019, icrowdnewswire.com/2019/12/30/the-shadows-amongst-us-this-is -a-documentary-on-a-family-haunted-by-paranormal-events-despite-living-in-different -parts-of-the-country.

31. Jesse Richard Morgan, "Affidavit of Jesse Richard Morgan," Commonwealth Court of Pennsylvania, 2020, www.pacourts.us/Storage/media/pdfs/20210603/212420-file -10836.pdf.

32. Khaya Himmelman, "Fact Check: Explaining the Claims Made by 'Whistleblower' Jesse Morgan," *The Dispatch*, January 5, 2021, factcheck.thedispatch.com/p/fact-check-explaining-the-claims.

33. Rutenberg et al., "77 Days: Trump's Campaign to Subvert the Election."

34. Adolf Hitler, *Mein Kampf*, trans. James Murphy, accessed via Project Gutenberg e-book, gutenberg.net.au/ebooks02/0200601.txt.

35. "Trump Made 30,573 False or Misleading Claims as President. Nearly Half Came in His Final Year," *Washington Post*, January 23, 2021, updated January 24, 2021.

36. Nuzzi, "The Full(est Possible) Story of the Four Seasons Total Landscaping Press Conference."

37. Julia Carrie Wong, "Facebook to Suspend Trump's Account for Two Years," *The Guardian*, June 4, 2021.

38. Frank Figliuzzi, "White Nationalist Domestic Terrorism Is Rising—Rethinking How We Label It Can Help the FBI Stop It," NBC News, August 10, 2019, www.nbcnews.com/think/opinion/white-nationalist-domestic-terrorism-rising-rethinking-how-we-label-it-ncna1040876.

39. "A Timeline of the Deadly Weekend in Charlottesville, Virginia," ABC30, August 10, 2018, abc30.com/charlottesville-virginia-violence-timeline/2305769.

40. Adam Gabbatt, " 'Jews Will Not Replace Us': Vice Film Lays Bare Horror of Neo-Nazis in America," *The Guardian*, August 16, 2017.

41. Emma Bowman and Wynne Davis, "Charlottesville Victim Heather Heyer 'Stood Up' Against What She Felt Was Wrong," NPR, August 13, 2017, www.npr.org/sections/thetwo-way/2017/08/13/543175919/violence-in-charlottesville-claims-3-victims.

42. "James Alex Fields, Driver in Deadly Car Attack at Charlottesville Rally, Sentenced to Life in Prison," NBC News, June 28, 2019, www.nbcnews.com/news/us-news/james-alex-fields-driver-deadly-car-attack-charlottesville-rally-sentenced-n1024436.

43. Rosie Gray, "Trump Defends White-Nationalist Protesters: 'Some Very Fine People on Both Sides,' " *The Atlantic*, August 15, 2017.

44. Glenn Kessler, "The 'Very Fine People' at Charlottesville: Who Were They?," *Washington Post*, May 8, 2020.

45. Christopher Cadelago and Ted Hesson, "Why Trump Is Talking Nonstop About the Migrant Caravan," *Politico*, October 23, 2018.

46. Ibid.

47. Annie Correal and Megan Specia, "The Migrant Caravan: What to Know About the Thousands Traveling North," *New York Times*, October 26, 2018.

48. Rowaida Abdelaziz, "Trump's 'Unknown Middle Easterners' Tweet Is Both False and Racist," *HuffPost*, October 23, 2018.

49. DHS Spokesperson (@SpoxDHS), ".@DHSgov can confirm that there are individuals within the caravan who are gang members or have significant criminal histories," Twitter, October 23, 2018, twitter.com/SpoxDHS/status/1054832882307530753.

50. Rebecca Kheel, "Mattis to Order 800 Troops to US-Mexico Border: Reports," *The Hill*, October 25, 2018.

51. Jason Silverstein, "Robert Bowers, Pittsburgh Shooting Suspect, Was Avid Poster of Anti-Semitic Content on Gab," CBS News, October 28, 2018, www.cbsnews.com/news/robert-bowers-gab-pittsburgh-shooting-suspect-today-live-updates-2018-10-27.

52. Jarrett Renshaw, "Who Is Robert Bowers, the Pittsburgh Synagogue Shooting Suspect?," Reuters, October 27, 2018.

53. Faith Karimi, "5 Days, 14 Potential Bombs and Lots of Questions. Here's What We Know," CNN, October 27, 2018, www.cnn.com/2018/10/26/politics/pipe-bombs-suspicious-packages-what-we-know/index.html.

54. Luke Mullins, "Inside the Mind of the MAGA Bomber, the Trump Superfan Who Tried to Wreak Havoc on the Last National Election," *The Washingtonian*, August 13, 2020, www.washingtonian.com/2020/08/13/inside-the-mind-of-the-maga- bomber-the-trump-superfan-who-tried-to-wreak-havoc-on-the-last-national-election.

55. Cedar Attanasio, Jake Bleiberg, and Paul J. Weber, "Police: El Paso Shooting Suspect Said He Targeted Mexicans," Associated Press, August 9, 2019.

56. Yasmeen Abutaleb, "What's Inside the Hate-Filled Manifesto Linked to the Alleged El Paso Shooter," *Washington Post*, August 4, 2019.

57. Del Quentin Wilber, "FBI director Says Capitol Riot Was 'Domestic Terrorism,' " *Los Angeles Times*, March 2, 2021.

58. Ryan J. Reilly, "Feds: Trump Supporter with Pipe Bombs Discussed Targeting Twitter, Democrats," *HuffPost*, January 27, 2021.

59. "White Privilege Card Trumps, 10pcs, Anti Democrat Deposit Romantic Card, Symbolizing Happiness and Success, A Life-Changing Gift to Ensure Peaceful Coexistence," Amazon, www.amazon.com/dp/B093CXWJY5/ref=cm_sw_em_r_mt_dp_E229 JTCW1FTH8G1QSCDV.

60. Julia Ioffe, "How Much Responsibility Does Trump Bear for the Synagogue Shooting in Pittsburgh?," *Washington Post*, October 28, 2018.

61. Glenn Thrush and Zolan Kanno-Youngs, "Refusing to Categorically Denounce White Supremacists, Trump Falsely Says Extremist Violence Is 'Not a Right-Wing Problem,' " *New York Times*, September 29, 2020, updated Jan 20, 2021.

62. "Proud Boys," Anti-Defamation League, www.adl.org/proudboys.

63. Tom Dreisbach, "Conspiracy Charges Bring Proud Boys' History of Violence into Spotlight," NPR, April 9, 2021 www.npr.org/2021/04/09/985104612/con spiracy-charges-bring-proud-boys-history-of-violence-into-spotlight.

64. Alyssa Lukpat, "Proud Boys Member Pleads Guilty and Will Cooperate in Jan. 6 Riot Inquiry," *New York Times*, December 22, 2021.

65. Sheera Frenkel and Annie Karni, "Proud Boys Celebrate Trump's 'Stand By' Remark About Them at the Debate," *New York Times*, September 29, 2020, updated January 20, 2021.

66. Bennie G. Thompson et al. v. Donald Trump et al, District Court for District of Columbia, No. 21-cv-00400-APM, February 18, 2022 storage.courtlistener.com/recap/gov .uscourts.dcd.227536/gov.uscourts.dcd.227536.66.0_6.pdf.

67. "Oath Keepers," Anti-Defamation League, www.adl.org/resources/backgrounders /oath-keepers.

68. Erin Donaghue, "Racially-Motivated Violent Extremists Elevated to 'National Threat Priority,' FBI Says," KUTV, February 6, 2020, kutv.com/news/nation-world /racially-motivated-violent-extremists-elevated-to-national-threat-priority-fbi-says.

69. Shaila Dewan and Robbie Brown, "All Her Life, Nikki Haley Was the Different One," *New York Times*, June 13, 2010.

70. "Charleston County Council 3," Our Campaigns, www.ourcampaigns.com/Race Detail.html?RaceID=782163; see also "November 2008 General Elections Voting Results, Charleston County, SC," Charleston County, www.charlestoncounty.org/departments /bevr/files/08gene.htm.

71. Aaron Blake, "The Case for Tim Scott," *Washington Post*, December 6, 2012.

72. Bill Barrow, Jake Bleiberg, and Brian Slodysko, "As Herschel Walker Eyes Senate Run, a Turbulent Past Emerges," Associated Press, July 23, 2021.

73. Jordan Fabian, "Republican Party: Get Diverse or Face Extinction," ABC News, March 17, 2013, abcnews.go.com/ABC_Univision/Politics/republican-party-diverse-face-extinction /story?id=18752174.

74. Henry Barbour et al., "The Growth & Opportunity Project," Republican National Committee, 2013, s3.documentcloud.org/documents/3111160/GOPAutopsy.pdf.

75. McKay Coppins, *The Wilderness: Deep Inside the Republican Party's Combative, Contentious, Chaotic Quest to Take Back the White House* (Boston: Little, Brown, 2015), 172, Apple Books.

76. Kyle Cheney, "Trump Kills GOP Autopsy," *Politico*, March 4, 2016.

77. Stuart Rothenberg, "Will 2020 Be the Year That the RNC's 'Autopsy' Was Right?," *Roll Call*, May 11, 2020, www.rollcall.com/2020/05/11/will-2020-be-the-year-the-rncs -autopsy -was-right.

78. Steven Levitsky and Daniel Ziblatt, "The Biggest Threat to Democracy Is the GOP Stealing the Next Election," *The Atlantic*, July 9, 2021.

79. Phillips, *Brown Is the New White*, 164.

6: THE LIBERATION BATTLE PLAN

1. Jim Collins, *Good to Great: Why Some Companies Make the Leap . . . and Others Don't* (New York: HarperCollins), 21.

2. Jim Collins, "Level 5 Leadership," Jim Collins website, www.jimcollins.com/concepts /level-five-leadership.html#:~:text=Level%205%20leaders%20display%20a,and%20its %20purpose%2C%20not%20themselves.

3. Michael Polzin, "Charles R. Walgreen III, Former Walgreen Co. Chairman and CEO, Dies at Age 80," Walgreens Newsroom, September 26, 2016, news.walgreens.com /press-center/news/charles-r-walgreen-iii-former-walgreen-co-chairman-and-ceo-dies-at -age-80.htm.

4. "United States Segment," Walgreens Boots Alliance, August 31, 2021, www.wal greensbootsalliance.com/our-business/united-states-segment.

5. "Poplawski, Stephen J. 1885–1956," Wisconsin Historical Society, www.wisconsinhis tory.org/Records/Article/CS11926.

6. Juliette Garside, "Walgreens: A Short History," *The Guardian*, June 19, 2012.

7. Collins, *Good to Great*, 32, 33.

8. Ibid., 30.

9. Aldon Morris, *Origins of the Civil Rights Movement* (New York: Free Press, 1986), vi.

10. Ibid., 285.

11. James Baldwin, "Sweet Lorraine," *Esquire*, November 1, 1969.

12. David Plouffe, *The Audacity to Win* (New York: Viking Press, 2009), 131, 162, Apple Books.

13. June Jordan, "Declaration of an Independence I Would Just as Soon Not Have," in *Civil Wars* (New York: Touchstone, 1995).

14. Hahrie Han, Elizabeth McKenna, and Michelle Oyakawa, *Prisms of the People: Power and Organizing in Twenty-First-Century America* (Chicago: University of Chicago Press, 2021), 1.

15. Ibid., 4.

16. Ibid., 157.

17. Morris, *Origins of the Civil Rights Movement*, 283.

18. Phillips, *Brown Is the New White*, 127–28.

19. Neil Bhutta et al., "Disparities in Wealth by Race and Ethnicity in the 2019 Survey of Consumer Finances," Federal Reserve, September 28, 2020, www.federalreserve.gov /econres/notes/feds-notes/disparities-in-wealth-by-race-and-ethnicity-in-the-2019-survey -of-consumer-finances-20200928.htm. See also my discussion of the racial wealth gap in Brown Is the New White, 118–25.

20. Elizabeth McKenna and Hahrie Han, *Groundbreakers: How Obama's 2.2 Million Volunteers Transformed Campaigning in America* (Oxford: Oxford University Press, 2014).

21. Jo Ann Gibson Robinson, *The Montgomery Bus Boycott and the Women Who Started It: The Memoir of Jo Ann Gibson Robinson* (Knoxville: University of Tennessee Press, 1987), 50, Kindle.

22. Taylor Branch, *Parting the Waters: America in the King Years, 1954–63* (New York: Simon & Schuster, 1988), 444. Apple Books.

23. Robinson, *The Montgomery Bus Boycott*, 92.

24. Greg Niemann, *Big Brown: The Untold Story of UPS* (San Francisco: Jossey-Bass, 2007), 86.

25. Ibid. *Big Brown*, 86.

26. Ibid., 184.

27. "The World's Largest Package Delivery Company," UPS, February 1, 2022, investors .ups.com.

7: GEORGIA: "THAT'S NOT ONE WE EXPECTED"

1. Alexander J. Azarian and Eden Fesshazion, The State Flag of Georgia: The 1956 Change in Its Historical Context, State Senate Research Office, Atlanta, Georgia, www .senate.ga.gov/sro/documents/studycommrpts/00stateflag.pdf; see also Joshua Holzer, "A Brief History of Georgia's Runoff Voting—and Its Racist Roots," *The Conversation*, November 23, 2020, theconversation.com/a-brief-history-of-georgias-runoff-voting-and-its -racist-roots-15035.

2. Holzer, "A Brief History of Georgia's Runoff Voting." See also Susan Cianci Salvatore, *Civil Rights in America: Racial Voting Rights*, National Park Service, www.nps.gov/sub jects/tellingallamericansstories/upload/CivilRights_VotingRights.pdf.

3. Tamar Hallerman, "Georgia's Unique Runoff System Shaped by Long, Complicated History," *Atlanta Journal-Constitution*, December 31, 2020, www.ajc.com /politics/election/georgias-unique-runoff-system-shaped-by-long-complicated-history/MN GES3JMXVERJKA4IRPXMCET4M.

4. "Primary Runoffs," National Conference of State Legislators, May 8, 2017, www.ncsl .org/research/elections-and-campaigns/primary-runoffs.aspx.

5. Timothy Bella and Tim Elfrink, "Warnock, Georgia's First Black Senator, Honors Mother and 'the 82-Year-Old Hands That Used to Pick Somebody Else's Cotton,' " *Washington Post*, January 6, 2021.

6. Center on Poverty and Social Policy at Columbia University, "Monthly Poverty Data," www.povertycenter.columbia.edu/forecasting-monthly-poverty-data.

7. Neely Young, "Embattled Battle Flag," *Georgia Trend*, February 1, 2004, www.geor giatrend.com/2004/02/01/embattled-battle-flag.

8. Correspondence with the author, December 16, 2010.

9. Emma Rothberg, "Stacey Abrams," National Women's History Museum, www.womens history.org/education-resources/biographies/stacey-abrams.

10. Stacey Abrams, "3 Questions to Ask Yourself About Everything You Do," TED, November 2018, www.ted.com/talks/stacey_abrams_3_questions_to_ask_yourself_about _everything_you_do.

11. Wilkerson, *Caste*, 40.

12. Paramount Plus, "Star Trek: Discovery | Stacey Abrams On Joining The Star Trek Universe | Paramount+," YouTube, March 19, 2022, https://www.youtube.com /watch?v=U3ihj9CvngM&t=20s.

13. Gwladys Fouche and Terje Solsvik, "U.S. Voting Rights Activist Stacey Abrams Nominated for Nobel Peace Prize," Reuters, February 1, 2021, www.reuters.com/article /us-nobel-prize-peace-usa/u-s-voting-rights-activist-stacey-abrams-nominated-for-nobel -peace-prize-idUSKBN2A12HY.

14. Collins, *Good to Great*, 25.

15. " 'Believe in Those You Serve': Stacey Abrams Urges Teachers Colleges' 2021 Graduates to Heed 'the Deeper Calling of Obligation,' " Teachers College Newsroom, Columbia University, April 30, 2021, www.tc.columbia.edu/articles/2021/april /stacey-abrams-urges-tcs-2021-grads-to-heed-the-deeper-calling-of-obligation.

16. Erin Durkin, "GOP Candidate Improperly Purged 340,000 from Georgia Voter Rolls, Investigation Claims," *The Guardian*, October 19, 2018. See also "Greg Palast for Salon TV: How to Steal Georgia in 7 Minutes," YouTube, October 28, 2018, www.youtube .com/watch?v=0SrV7tN23XA.

17. Alexis Okeowo, "Can Stacey Abrams Save American Democracy?," *Vogue*, August 12, 2019.

18. Stacey Abrams, *Lead from the Outside: How to Build Your Future and Make Real Change* (New York: Picador, 2019), 37–38.

19. Campbell Gibson and Kay Jung, *Population Division: Historical Census Statistics on Population Totals by Race, 1790 to 1990, and by Hispanic Origin, 1970 to 1990, for the United States, Regions, Divisions, and States*, Working Paper No. 56, U.S. Census Bureau, September 2002, www.census.gov/content/dam/Census/library/working-papers/2002 /demo/POP-twps0056.pdf.

20. Tim Henderson, "A Change in Politics with More Black Voters in the Deep South," Pew Charitable Trusts, August 12, 2019, www.pewtrusts.org/en/research-and-analysis /blogs/stateline/2019/08/12/a-change-in-politics-with-more-black-voters-in-the-deep- south. See also Alana Semuels, "Reverse Migration Might Turn Georgia Blue," *The Atlantic*, May 23, 2018.

21. "Current and Past Election Results," Georgia Secretary of State, sos.ga.gov/index. php/Elections/current_and_past_elections_results; se also "Table 4b: Reported Voting and Registration by Sex, Race and Hispanic Origin, for States," U.S. Census Bureau, revised November 2021, www.census.gov/data/tables/2012/demo/voting-and-registration /p20-568.html; and "Voting and Registration Tables, 2006, 2008, and 2010," U.S. Census Bureau, May 2013, www.census.gov/topics/public-sector/voting/data/tables.html.

22. NowThis News, "Rev. Jesse Jackson's Iconic 'David And Goliath' Speech Still Matters Today," YouTube, February 13, 2020, www.youtube.com/watch?v=BtL8QU_5-3s.

23. In recent years, NGP has created a sister organization, New Georgia Project Action Fund, that is a 501c(4) advocacy organization and legally able to participate in some partisan activities within the scope of its primary purpose.

24. "Georgia: What Winning Looks Like," *Democracy in Color,* podcast, season 4, ep. 2, December 10, 2020, democracyincolor.com/podepisodes/2020/12/9/georgia-what -winning-looks-like.

25. Ibid.

26. Kate Brumback and Sudhin Thanawala, "Georgia in the Spotlight as Vote Count Continues," Associated Press, November 5, 2020, apnews.com/article/election-2020-joe -biden-donald-trump-georgia-elections-3e4a91201f3d4f269d7b961e310ed2fe.

27. Richard Fausset, "Diversity Rises in Georgia, with Whites Making Up Only Half the State," *New York Times,* August 12, 2021.

28. "Quick Facts: Georgia," U.S. Census Bureau, www.census.gov/quickfacts/GA.

29. Kimmy Yam, "Asian American Voter Rates in Georgia Hit Record High. How Voting Bill Threatens Progress," NBC News, March 31, 2021, www.nbcnews.com /news/asian-america/asian-american-voter-rates-georgia-hit-record-high-how-voting-n 1262682.

30. Karthick Ramakrishnan and Sara Sadhwani, "Media Guide to the 2020 Asian American Vote," AAPI Data, March 2021, aapidata.com/blog/2020-vote-media-guide -march25.

31. Suzanne Gamboa, " 'Ready to Take Power': Progressives Mobilized Latino Voters in Georgia, and Here Are the Lessons," NBC News, January 29, 2021, www.nbcnews .com/news/latino/ready-take-power-progressives-mobilized-latino-voters-georgia-here-are -n1255856; see also Rachel Hatzipanagos, "How Grass-Roots Efforts by Georgia's Latinos Helped Tip the Senate Races," *Washington Post,* February 3, 2021.

32. Hatzipanagos, "How Grass-Roots Efforts."

33. Gamboa, " 'Ready to Take Power.' "

34. Abrams and Groh-Wargo, "How to Turn Your Red State Blue," *New York Times,* February 11, 2021.

35. Greg Bluestein, "Democrats Try to Move Forward with New Chair, Candidate for Governor," *Atlanta Journal-Constitution,* August 31, 2013, www.ajc.com/news/demo crats-try-move-forward-with-new-chair-candidate-for-governor/6HzCdloqNItIIjltHY UGCO.

36. Joan Walsh, "Stacey Abrams Always Knew They'd Try to Cheat," *The Nation,* October 18, 2018.

37. Bruce Schreiner, "McGrath Outpaces McConnell in Fundraising for Senate Seat," *Washington Post,* July 16, 2020.

38. Fausset, "Diversity Rises in Georgia."

39. "Quick Facts: Clayton County, Georgia," U.S. Census Bureau, July 1, 2021, www.cen sus.gov/quickfacts/claytoncountygeorgia; see also "Election Summary Report, Clayton County, State of Georgia General Election, November 8, 2016," November 15, 2016, www .claytoncountyga.gov/home/showpublisheddocument/1242/636491224224770000; and "November 3, 2020, Presidential Recount Results," Georgia Secretary of State, last updated December 7, 2020, results.enr.clarityelections.com/GA/107231/web.264614/# /summary.

8: ARIZONA: "YOU TRIED TO BURY US. YOU DIDN'T KNOW WE WERE SEEDS"

1. Megan Kate Nelson, *The Three-Cornered War: The Union, the Confederacy, and Native Peoples in the Fight for the West* (New York: Scribner, 2020), 245.

2. Ibid., 248.

3. Ibid., 60.

4. Michael Lacey, "The Good Fight," *Phoenix New Times*, May 24, 1989.

5. "State of Arizona Official Canvass, General Election, November 6, 1990," Arizona Secretary of State, November 26, 1990, azsos.gov/sites/default/files/canvass1990ge.pdf.

6. Rhiannon Walker, "When Arizona Lost the Super Bowl Because the State Didn't Recognize Martin Luther King Jr. Day," *The Undefeated*, March 22, 2017, theundefeated.com /features/when-arizona-lost-the-super-bowl-because-the-state-didnt-recognize-martin-luther-king-jr-day.

7. Sarah Lynch, "Pearce Calls on 'Operation Wetback' for Illegals," *East Valley Tribune*, September 29, 2006.

8. Eric Foner, *Gateway to Freedom: The Hidden History of the Underground Railroad* (W.W. Norton, 2015), 14, Apple Books. See also Frederick Douglass, "My Escape from Slavery (1881)," in *The Collected Works of Frederick Douglass* (Chicago: e-artnow, 2013), 2612, Kindle.

9. Douglass, "My Escape from Slavery," 2612–13.

10. Ted Robbins, "The Man Behind Arizona's Toughest Immigrant Laws," NPR, March 12, 2008; see also Jeremiah Stettler, "LDS on Illegal Immigration: Don't Split Families," *Salt Lake Tribune*, December 3, 2010.

11. "1990 Census of Population: General Population Characteristics of Arizona," U.S. Census Bureau, April 1992, www2.census.gov/library/publications/decennial/1990/cp-1 /cp-1-4.pdf.; see also "Arizona: 2000, U.S. Census Profile," U.S. Census Bureau, August 2002, www.census.gov/prod/2002pubs/c2kprof00-az.pdf; and "2010 Arizona Census Data," U.S. Census Bureau, www.ncsl.org/documents/redistricting/arizona_census _data_2010.pdf.

12. "Quick Facts: Arizona," U.S. Census Bureau, www.census.gov/quickfacts/AZ.

13. "Native American Population 2022," World Population Review, worldpopulationre view.com/state-rankings/native-american-population.

14. Nelson, *The Three-Cornered War*, 61.

15. Ruben Gallego (@RubenGallego), Twitter, November 11, 2020, twitter.com /RubenGallego/status/1326755305649180674.

16. Miriam Pawel, *The Crusades of Cesar Chavez: A Biography* (New York: Bloomsbury, 2014), 589–90, Apple Books.

17. Conversation with the author, February 19, 2021.

18. "Cesar E. Chavez National Monument," National Park Service, www.nps.gov/nr /travel/american_latino_heritage/Chavez_National_Monument_Nuestra_Senora_Reina _de_la_Paz.html.

19. Conversation with the author.

20. Jim Collins, *Good to Great*, 69–70.

21. Ibid., 85.

22. Conversation with the author.

23. "Quick Facts: Colorado, 2010," U.S. Census Bureau, www.census.gov/quickfacts /fact/table/CO/POP010210; see also "1990 Census of Population, Social and Economic

Characteristics, Colorado: Table 4. Race and Hispanic Origin," U.S. Census Bureau, www2.census.gov/library/publications/decennial/1990/cp-2/cp-2-7.pdf.

24. Jay Bouchard, "Who Is Tim Gill?," *5280*, December 2019, www.5280.com/2019/12/who-is-tim-gill.

25. Adam Schrager and Rob Witwer, *The Blueprint: How the Democrats Won Colorado (and Why Republicans Everywhere Should Care)* (Golden, CO: Speaker's Corner, 2010), 24, Apple Books.

26. Adam Schrager and Rob Witwer, "How the Dems Won Colorado," *Denver Post*, April 8, 2010.

27. "QuickFacts: Maricopa County, Arizona," U.S. Census Bureau, July 1, 2021, www.census.gov/quickfacts/maricopacountyarizona.

28. Martin Luther King Jr., *A Proper Sense of Priorities* (sermon, delivered in Washington, DC, February 6, 1968), pnhp.org/news/martin-luther-king-jr-a-proper-sense-of-priorities.

29. See Randy Parraz, *Dignity by Fire: Dismantling Arizona's Anti-Immigrant Machine* (Phoenix: Organizing Institute for Democracy, 2021), Kindle.

30. Parraz, *Dignity by Fire*, 29–30, Kindle.

31. Parraz, 28–29.

32. "Russell Pearce Recall, Arizona State Legislature (2011)," Ballotpedia, ballotpedia.org/Russell_Pearce_recall,_Arizona_State_Legislature_(2011).

33. Arizona Donor Collaborative, internal document shared with the author, March 2015.

34. Ian Danley (Arizona Wins executive director), email report shared with the author, November 17, 2020.

35. Danley email.

36. Correspondence with the author, September 1, 2021.

37. Han, McKenna, and Oyakawa, *Prisms of the People*, 6–7. The names that appear in the account are not the actual names of the community organizers and activists, who remained anonymous, the authors explain, "to protect our respondents from unpredictable political consequences."

38. Montserrat Arredondo and A'shanti Gholar, "Montserrat Arredondo: 'Always Start Within Your Community,' " June 15, 2020, on *The Brown Girls Guide to Politics*, podcast, produced by Wonder Media Network, the-brown-girls-guide-to-politics.simplecast.com/episodes/montserrat-arredondo-always-start-within-your-community-jzigCkyS.

39. "About Us," One Arizona, onearizona.org/about.

40. Elizabeth McKenna and Michelle Oyakawa, featuring Alejandra Gomez and Tomás Robles, moderated by Tova Wang, "Book Talk—Prisms of the People: Power & Organizing in Twenty-First Century America," May 4, 2021, YouTube, www.youtube.com/watch?v=oRS29dMfs2E.

41. Alejandra Gomez, "Book Talk."

42. Alejandra Gomez and Tomás Robles Jr., "How to Turn Anger and Fear into Political Power," *New York Times*, December 21, 2019.

43. Suzanne Gamboa and Anita Hassan, " 'Years in the Making': Established Latino Groups Helped Biden in Arizona, Nevada," NBC News, November 13, 2020.

44. Gomez and Robles Jr., "How to Turn Anger."

45. Phillips, *Brown Is the New White*, 80, 83.

46. Han, McKenna, and Oyakawa, *Prisms of the People*, 15.

47. "Arizona Minimum Wage and Paid Time Off, Proposition 206 (2016)," Ballotpedia, ballotpedia.org/Arizona_Minimum_Wage_and_Paid_Time_Off,_Proposition_206_(2016).

48. Jonathan Stall and Hans Olofsson, "Ballot Proposition 206: Fiscal Analysis" (report), www.azleg.gov/jlbc/16novprop206fn.pdf.

49. Gomez and Robles Jr., "How to Turn Anger."

50. Rachel Leingang, "Huge Increase in Number of Voters Registered in Arizona as Midterm Election Nears," *Arizona Republic*, October 17, 2018.

51. Cesar Aguilar, "One Arizona Reaches 184,868 New Voter Registrations Despite COVID-19 Limitations," Arizona Students Association, October 16, 2020, www.az students.org/one_arizona_reaches_184_868_new_voter_registrations_despite_covid_19 _limitations.

52. Raquel Tera?n, "Guest Blog: Building Community and Latinx Political Power with Arizona State Representative Raquel Terán," HECHO, November 24, 2020, www.hechoon line.org/blog/building-community-and-latinx-political-power-with-representative-raquel -tern; see also "Raquel Terán," Ballotpedia, ballotpedia.org/Raquel_Ter%C3%A1n.

53. Laura Gómez, "New Phoenix Council Members 'Unapologetic' About Who They Are," *Arizona Mirror*, June 11, 2019.

54. Erin Mayo-Adam, *Queer Alliances: How Power Shapes Political Movement Formation* (Stanford, CA: Stanford University Press, 2020), 80–81

55. Felicia Fonseca and Angeliki Kastanis, "Native American Votes Helped Secure Biden's Win in Arizona," Associated Press, November 19, 2020.

56. Li Zhou, "Young Latinx Voters Could Be the Ones Who Finally Flip Arizona," *Vox*, October 29, 2020. Author's calculations based on 2016 and 2020 exit poll data.

57. Conversation with the author.

58. Agnel Philip, "Congratulations, Arizona! Turnout in the 2018 Midterms Smashed Records," *AZ Central*, November 16, 2018.

59. "Voting and Registration in the Election of November 2016," U.S. Census Bureau, May 2017; "Voting and Registration in the Election of November 2020," U.S. Census Bureau, April 2021, www.census.gov/data/tables/time-series/demo/voting-and-registration /p20-585.html.

60. "Child Population by Race in Arizona," Kids Count Data Center, Annie E. Casey Foundation, datacenter.kidscount.org/data/tables/103-child-population-by-race?loc=4 &loct=2#detailed/2/4/fa lse/574,1729,37,871,870,573,869,36,868,867/68,69,67,12,70,66,71,72/423,424.

61. Alan C. Miller, "FBI Spied on Cesar Chavez for Years, Files Reveal," *Los Angeles Times*, May 30, 1995.

9: VIRGINIA: "ALONE AMONG THE STATES OF THE CONFEDERACY"

1. June Jordan, "The Difficult Miracle of Black Poetry in America or Something like a Sonnet for Phillis Wheatley," *On Call: Political Essays* (South End Press, Boston, 1985), 88.

2. Lerone Bennett Jr., *Before the Mayflower: A History of the Negro in America, 1619–1962* (Baltimore: Penguin Books, 2018), 29–30; Deborah Barfield Berry and Kelley Benham French, "Hundreds of Thousands of Africans Were Enslaved in America. Wanda Tucker Believes Her Relatives Were the First," *USA Today*, August 21, 2019; E.R. Shipp, "1619: 400 Years Ago, a Ship Arrived in Virginia, Bearing Human Cargo," *USA Today*, February 8,

2019; Deborah Barfield Berry and Rick Hampson, "The Founding Family You've Never Heard of: The Black Tuckers of Hampton, Virginia," *USA Today*, August 21, 2019.

3. James W. Loewen, *Lies My Teacher Told Me: Everything Your American History Textbook Got Wrong* (New York: The New Press, 2018), 194, Kindle; "Twenty Slave Law," *Encyclopedia Virginia*, encyclopediavirginia.org/entries/twenty-slave-law/#start_entry.

4. Reid J. Epstein and Nick Corasaniti, "Virginia, the Old Confederacy's Heart, Becomes a Voting Rights Bastion," *New York Times*, April 2, 2021.

5. "QuickFacts: Virginia," U.S. Census Bureau, July 1, 2021, www.census.gov/quick facts/fact/table/VA/PST045221; "1990 Census of Population General Population Characteristics: Virginia," U.S. Census Bureau, 1990, www2.census.gov/library/publications /decennial/1990/cp-1/cp-1-48.pdf.

6. "Immigrants in Virginia," American Immigration Council, August 6, 2020, www .americanimmigrationcouncil.org/research/immigrants-in-virginia.

7. Steve Phillips, "Lessons from Virginia: You Can't Ignore the Civil War," *The Nation*, November 3, 2021.

8. "Investing in Communities of Color to Make Progressive Change with New Virginia Majority's Tram Nguyen," *The Great Battlefield*, podcast, ep. 212, October 17, 2018, www.resistancedashboard.com/node/471; "Tram Nguyen on How Virginia Turned Blue," *Democracy in Color*, podcast, season 4, ep. 4, May 27, 2021, democracyincolor.com /podepisodes/2021/5/26/tram-nguyen-on-how-virginia-turned-blue.

9. Colin Campbell, "Fewer Vietnamese Reach Thai Coast," *New York Times*, April 26, 1982.

10. "Investing in Communities of Color," *The Great Battlefield* podcast.

11. "Virginia and the ACA's Medicaid Expansion," healthinsurance.org, December 2, 2020, www.healthinsurance.org/medicaid/virginia.

12. "Virginia Charts a Path to a $15 Minimum Wage," *The Half Sheet* (blog), The Commonwealth Institute, March 11, 2020, thehalfsheet.org/post/612326515149094912 /virginia-charts-a-path-to-a-15-minimum-wage.

13. Ashley Kenneth, "More Than Recovery: Reflecting on a Stronger Future for the Commonwealth," The Commonwealth Institute, May 18, 2021, thecommonwealthinsti tute.org/the-half-sheet/more-than-recovery-reflecting-on-a-stronger-future-for-the-com monwealth.

14. Lin-Manuel Miranda, "You'll Be Back," track 7 on *Hamilton: An American Musical*, 2016.

15. "Captain John Smith," National Park Service, updated February 26, 2015, www.nps .gov/jame/learn/historyculture/life-of-john-smith.htm.

16. Phyllis C. Richman, "Calvin Trillin Ruminates on 'Little Vietnam,' " *Washington Post*, May 18, 1983.

17. "1990 Census of Population General Population Characteristics: Virginia," U.S. Census Bureau, 1990, www2.census.gov/library/publications/decennial/1990/cp-1 /cp-1-48.pdf; "QuickFacts: Prince William County, Virginia," U.S. Census Bureau, April 1, 2010, www.census.gov/quickfacts/fact/table/princewilliamcountyvirginia,US /POP010210#POP010210.

18. Tee Loftin Snell, *The Wild Shores: America's Beginnings* (Washington, DC: National Geographic Society [U.S.], Special Publications Division, 1974), 82, archive.org/details /wildshoresamericoosnel.

19. Alex Koma, "Ayala Doubles Down in Support of ACA," *Inside Nova*, September 22, 2017; Jill Palermo, "Former Prince William NOW President Launches Bid for State Delegate," *Fauquier Times*, April 4, 2017.

20. Palermo, "Former Prince William NOW President Launches Bid for State Delegate."

21. Koma, "Ayala Doubles Down in Support of ACA."

22. "2017 November General: Official Results," Virginia Department of Elections, November 13, 2017, results.elections.virginia.gov/vaelections/2017%20November%20General/Site/GeneralAssembly.html. The Department of Elections website also has data for the previous contested race in District 51, in 2013 (actually it has election data going back go 1789!). Subtracting the turnout in 2013 from the turnout in 2017 gets you the increase in turnout when Ayala and NVM executed on their electoral program.

23. Shawna De La Rosa, "Virginia Only State to See Decrease in Uninsured After Medicaid Expansion," State of Reform, December 31, 2020, stateofreform.com/featured/2020/12/virginia-only-state-to-see-decrease-in-uninsured-after-medicaid-expansion.

24. Ibid.

25. "Biography," Kenny Boddye for Supervisor website, kennyforsupervisor.com/biography.

26. Danny Hakim and Stephanie Saul, "White Nationalists Love Corey Stewart. He Keeps Them Close," *New York Times*, August 5, 2018.

27. "The 287(g) Program: An Overview," American Immigration Council, July 8, 2021, www.americanimmigrationcouncil.org/research/287g-program-immigration.

28. Antonio Olivo, "Large Virginia County Ends Immigration Enforcement Agreement," *Washington Post*, June 18, 2020.

29. Kenny Boddye, "Beyond Our Dreams," *Visible Magazine*, August 16, 2019, www.visiblemagazine.com/beyond-our-dreams.

30. "Kenny Boddye," (Virginia Public Access Project) vpap.org, November 5, 2019, www.vpap.org/candidates/284783-kenny-boddye.

31. Tram Nguyen, "Democrats Could Learn a Lot from What Happened in Virginia," *New York Times*, November 6, 2019.

32. Theodore Schleifer, "Tech Billionaires Are Plotting Sweeping, Secret Plans to Boost Joe Biden," *Vox*, May 27, 2020.

33. Jordan Pascale, "Republican David Yancey Wins Tiebreaker in 94th House District Race," *Virginian Pilot*, January 4, 2018.

34. New Virginia Majority, "2019 Civic Engagement—Additional Persuasion," internal memo, 2019.

35. New Virginia Majority, internal spreadsheet, 2019.

36. "Virginia Elections Database," Virginia Department of Elections, historical.elections.virginia.gov/elections/search/year_from:2019/year_to:2019/office_id:8/district_id:27396.

37. New Virginia Majority, internal spreadsheet, 2019.

38. Donald P. Green and Alan S. Gerber, *Get Out the Vote: How to Increase Voter Turnout*, 4th ed. (Washington, DC: Brookings Institution Press, 2019), 301, Apple Books.

39. "Virginia Law Will Allow Undocumented Immigrants to Drive Legally," NBC Washington, December 15, 2020; Fredreka Schouten, "Virginia Gov. Northam Restores Voting Rights to 69,000 Former Felons with New Policy," CNN, March 16, 2021.

40. "Edgardo Cortés," Brennan Center for Justice, www.brennancenter.org/experts/edgardo-cortes.

41. "Summary of Virginia Registration & Turnout Statistics," Virginia Department of Elections, www.elections.virginia.gov/resultsreports/registrationturnout-statistics.

42. Nguyen, "Democrats Could Learn a Lot from What Happened in Virginia."

43. Anderson, *One Person, No Vote*, 3.

10: SAN DIEGO: "TRANSFORMED WITHIN LESS THAN A GENERATION"

1. Phillips, *Brown Is the New White*, 169.

2. Campbell Gibson and Kay Jung, "Population Division: Historical Census Statistics on Population Totals by Race, 1790 to 1990, and by Hispanic Origin, 1970 to 1990, for the United States, Regions, Divisions, and States—Working Paper No. 56," U.S. Census Bureau, September 2002, www.census.gov/content/dam/Census/library/working-papers /2002/demo/POP-twps0056.pdf.

3. "QuickFacts: California," U.S. Census Bureau, July 1, 2021, www.census.gov /quickfacts/CA.

4. David Siders, "California's Incredible Shrinking Republican Party," *Politico*, September 27, 2021.

5. James Rawls, "Native Americans in the Gold Rush," *PBS: The American Experience: The Gold Rush*, www.shoppbs.pbs.org/wgbh/amex/goldrush/sfeature/natives_03 .html.

6. George T. Clark, *Leland Stanford* (Stanford, CA: Stanford University Press, 1931), 8.

7. Leland Stanford, "Inaugural Address," January 10, 1862, governors.library.ca.gov /addresses/08-Stanford.html.

8. Mae Ngai, "Racism Has Always Been Part of the Asian American Experience," *The Atlantic*, April 21, 2021.

9. "Leland Stanford on Chinese Exclusion, 1889," *Sacramento Record-Union*, January 7, 1889, www.newspapers.com/clip/20518780/leland-stanford-on-chinese-exclusion.

10. "Undergraduate Student Profile," Stanford University, facts.stanford.edu /academics/undergraduate-profile.

11. Branch, *At Canaan's Edge*, 778.

12. Bayard Rustin, "The Watts," *Commentary*, March 1966, www.commentary.org /articles/bayard-rustin-2/the-watts.

13. Martin Luther King Jr., "The Other America," Stanford University, April 14, 1967, YouTube, www.youtube.com/watch?v=dOWDtDUKz-U&t=7s.

14. "Pete Wilson 1994 Campaign Ad on Illegal Immigration," PeteWilsonCA, February 15, 2010, www.youtube.com/watch?v=lLIzzs2HHgY.

15. Jewelle Taylor Gibbs and Teiahsha Bankhead, *Preserving Privilege: California Politics, Propositions, and People of Color* (Westport, CT: Praeger, 2001), ix–x.

16. "QuickFacts: San Diego County, California," U.S. Census Bureau, July 1, 2021, www .census.gov/quickfacts/fact/table/sandiegocountycalifornia,CA/POP815219.

17. Conversation with the author, February 17, 2021.

18. Conversation with the author, February 17, 2021.

19. Andrea Guerrero, *Silence at Boalt Hall: The Dismantling of Affirmative Action* (Berkeley: University of California Press, 2002), xiii.

20. Conversation with the author, February 17, 2021.

21. For election results since 1992, see "California's 52nd Congressional District," Ballotpedia, ballotpedia.org/California%27s_52nd_Congressional_District.

22. "San Diego County Top 25 Census Tracts: Lowest Median Household Income," Advancement Project California, 2019, www.advancementprojectca.org/wp-content/up loads/2019/03/SD_HHincome.pdf.

23. Conversation with the author, February 17, 2021.

24. "Electoral Impact 2012," Alliance San Diego, March 26, 2013.

25. "General Election—Statement of Vote, November 6, 2012," California Secretary of State, www.sos.ca.gov/elections/prior-elections/statewide-election-results/general-elec tion-november-6-2012/statement-vote. For any Confederates or other enemies of progress looking for fodder to attack the work of Alliance San Diego on the basis of its tax status, let me make clear here—for the record—that Diamond's work in 2012 was non-partisan civic engagement work, and she did not advocate for or against any candidate. It nonetheless remains a fact that the electorate expanded, got more diverse, and Peters won.

26. Phillips, *Brown Is the New White*, 113.

27. Conversation with the author, February 17, 2021.

28. "About," Engage San Diego, www.engagesandiego.org/about.

29. Equality Alliance of San Diego County, "Target San Diego: A Roadmap to Winning a Social Justice Agenda in San Diego," Winter 2011.

30. Wendy Wood, *Good Habits, Bad Habits: The Science of Making Positive Changes That Stick* (New York: Farrar, Straus and Giroux, 2019), 206, Apple Books.

31. "Table 5. California—Race and Hispanic Origin for Selected Large Cities and Other Places: Earliest Census to 1990," U.S. Census Bureau, February 2005, www.census.gov /content/dam/Census/library/working-papers/2005/demo/POP-twps0076.pdf, p. 35; "Quick Facts: San Diego County, California, 2010," U.S. Census Bureau, www.census .gov/quickfacts/fact/table/sandiegocountycalifornia,US/POP010210.

32. Jesse Marx and Maya Srikrishnan, "Welcome to a Dem-Controlled County," *Voice of San Diego*, November 4, 2020, www.voiceofsandiego.org/topics/politics /welcome-to-a-dem-controlled-county.

33. Deborah Sullivan Brennan, "County Approves $7.2 Billion Budget with Big Investments in Mental Health, Public Safety," *Del Mar Times* (*San Diego Union-Tribune*), July 1, 2021.

34. William H. Frey, "People of Color Comprise over Half of the Nation's Youth," August 13, 2021, Brookings Institution, www.brookings.edu/research/new-2020-cen sus-results-show-increased-diversity-countering-decade-long-declines-in-americas-white -and-youth-populations.

11: TEXAS: "THE TASK AT HAND IS EPIC"

1. Madge Thornall Roberts, *Star of Destiny: The Private Life of Sam and Margaret Houston* (Denton, Texas: University of North Texas Press, 1993), 359.

2. Bill Porterfield, "Sam Houston, Warts and All," *Texas Monthly*, July 1973; "Inflation Calculator," U.S. Official Inflation Data, Alioth Finance, January 12, 2022, www.official data.org.

3. Arnoldo de León, *They Called Them Greasers: Anglo Attitudes Toward Mexicans in Texas, 1821–1900* (Austin: University of Texas Press, 1983), 41, Apple Books.

4. Randolph B. Campbell, *Gone to Texas: A History of the Lone Star State* (New York?: Oxford University Press, 2003), chap. 7, Kindle; John Hoyt Williams, *Sam Houston: A Biography of the Father of Texas* (New York: Simon & Schuster, 1993), chap. 8, Apple Books.

5. "Constitution of the Republic of Texas (1836)," Gen. Prov. § 9, University of Texas, Tarlton Law Library, tarlton.law.utexas.edu/c.php?g=815580&p=5820525.

6. "The Treaty of Guadalupe Hidalgo," National Archives, www.archives.gov/education /lessons/guadalupe-hidalgo#background.

7. Sylvester Turner (@SylvesterTurner), "It's a proud moment today as several locations in Houston are designated Sites of Memory Associated with the Slave Route Project by @UNESCO . . . ," Twitter, May 9, 2019, twitter.com/sylvesterturner/status /1126589226890534912.

8. "QuickFacts: Texas," U.S. Census Bureau, July 1, 2021, www.census.gov/quickfacts /TX.

9. Conversation with the author, September 7, 2021. (All subsequent quotes from Michelle are from this same conversation.)

10. John Atlas, *Seeds of Change: The Story of ACORN, America's Most Controversial Antipoverty Community Organizing Group* (Nashville: Vanderbilt University Press, 2010), 165, Kindle.

11. Conversation with the author, June 29, 2021. (All subsequent quotes from Ginny are from this same conversation.)

12. Stephanie Strom, "On Obama, Acorn and Voter Registration," *New York Times*, October 10, 2008.

13. Baldwin, "Sweet Lorraine."

14. Peter Dreier, "The War on ACORN," *Los Angeles Times*, October 22, 2009.

15. "About Houston," City of Houston, Texas, www.houstontx.gov/abouthouston/hous tonfacts.html.

16. Catherine Wendlandt, "Houston Is the Most Diverse City in America," *Houstonia*, April 21, 2021.

17. "QuickFacts: Houston City, Texas," U.S. Census Bureau, July 1, 2021, www.census .gov/quickfacts/fact/table/houstoncitytexas/PST045219.

18. Author's extrapolation from David Canon's data (see the next endnote).

19. "David Canon's U.S. Senate Testimony on the Voting Rights Act," University of Wisconsin–Madison, June 21, 2006, news.wisc.edu/david-canons-u-s-senate -testimony-on-the-voting-rights-act.

20. For the latest on the attacks on voting rights and the litigation to fight it, see Democracy Docket, www.democracydocket.com, founded by Marc Elias.

21. Analysis of the Catalist voter file, by Julie Martinez Ortega, PhD, February 2022.

22. "Cumulative Report—Harris County, Texas, Joint Runoff Election, December 12, 2015," Harris County Elections Administrator, www.harrisvotes.com/HIS TORY/20151212/cumulative/cumulative.pdf.

23. Michelle Alexander, *The New Jim Crow: Mass Incarceration in the Age of Colorblindness* (New York: The New Press, 2010), 27–28.

24. "Annual Estimates of the Resident Population for the United States, Regions, States, District of Columbia, and Puerto Rico: April 1, 2020 to July 1, 2021," U.S. Census Bureau, July 1, 2021, www.census.gov/data/tables/time-series/demo/popest/2020s-state-total .html#par_textimage_1574439295.

25. "QuickFacts: Harris County, Texas," U.S. Census Bureau, July 1, 2021, www.census .gov/quickfacts/harriscountytexas.

26. Michael Hardy, "A Hard Look at the Harris County District Attorney's Office," *Texas Monthly*, September 12, 2016.

27. Robyn Ross, "Michelle Tremillo and Brianna Brown Are Waking the 'Sleeping Giant' of Texas Politics," *Texas Monthly*, December 2018.

28. Andrew Cockburn, "Texas Is the Future," *Harper's Magazine*, March 2017.

29. Author's analysis of Harris County election data and communication with county elections officials.

30. Tim Murphy, "One of Texas' Most Notorious Prosecutors Was Just Voted Out of Office. Expect More of That," *Mother Jones*, March 7, 2018.

31. "Texas Organizing Project Education Fund, IRS Form 990, 2019," ProPublica Nonprofit Explorer, projects.propublica.org/nonprofits/organizations/271481855.

32. "TOP PAC Bending History Together," Texas Organizing Project, 2020.

33. Cockburn, "Texas Is the Future."

34. Cassidy Lackey, "How Big Is Texas? You Won't Believe How Huge It Is!," Texas Proud, texasproud.com/how-big-is-texas-its-huge/#:~:text=How%20many%20states%20can%20fit,%2C%20Delaware%2C%20and%20Rhode%20Island.

35. Alexa Ura and Anna Novak, "Texas' Hispanic Population Grew by 2 Million in the Past Decade, on Pace to Be Largest Share of State by 2021," *Texas Tribune*, June 25, 2020; see also the U.S. Census Bureau's American Community Survey, 2011–2019, in particular "Table CP05, Comparative Demographic Estimates," which is customizable: data.census.gov/cedsci/table?tid=ACSCP1Y2019.CP05&hidePreview=true.

36. Texas Organizing Project, "Analysis of Voter Participation in Texas" internal memo, 2011.

37. "Historical Voter Turnout," San Francisco Department of Elections, sfelections.sfgov.org/historical-voter-turnout.

38. "Approved Dallas ISD 2019–2020 Budget Includes $57.6 Million in Annual Compensation Raises," Dallas ISD News Hub, June 28, 2019, thehub.dallasisd.org/2019/06/28/approved-dallas-isd-2019-2020-budget-includes-57-6-million-in-annual-compensation-raises.

39. "Race Summary Report, 2018 General Election," Texas Office of the Secretary of State, elections.sos.state.tx.us/elchist331_state.htm; "Race Summary Report, 2014 General Election," elections.sos.state.tx.us/elchist175_state.htm.

40. "About," Harris County, Texas, cjo.harriscountytx.gov/About.

41. Jen Rice, "Ahead of Election Day, Midnight Hours and Drive-Thru Lines Boost Historic Houston Early Voting Period," Houston Public Media, November 2, 2020.

42. Victoria Gavito, "Donor Cultivation and Investment Strategy," internal memo, Texas Future Project, April 9, 2013.

43. "2014 Election," Texas Future Project, internal white paper.

44. "Texas: Exit Poll for Governor Race," CBS News, 2014, www.cbsnews.com/elections/2014/governor/texas/exit.

45. "Voting and Registration in the Election of November 2020," U.S. Census Bureau, April 2021, www.census.gov/data/tables/time-series/demo/voting-and-registration/p20-585.html.

EPILOGUE: ONCE WE WIN—CREATING A NEW SOCIAL CONTRACT

1. Linnea Feldman Emison, "The Promising Results of a Citywide Basic-Income Experiment," *New Yorker*, July 15, 2020; Bliss Broyard, "What Would You Do with an Extra $500 a Month? A Financial Experiment in Five True Stories, *New York*, October 12, 2019.

2. Martin Luther King Jr., *Where Do We Go from Here: Chaos or Community?* (Boston: Beacon Press, 2010), 310, 312, Apple Books.

3. Alexei Koseff, "Stockton's $500 Monthly Income Program Led to Better Jobs and Lives, Study Concludes," *San Francisco Chronicle*, March 5, 2021.

4. Broyard, "What Would You Do?"

5. Mayors for a Guaranteed Income, www.mayorsforagi.org.

6. Hannah Gilberstadt, "More Americans Oppose Than Favor the Government Providing a Universal Basic Income for All Adult Citizens," Pew Research Center, August 19, 2020, (accessed February 21, 2022), www.pewresearch.org/fact-tank/2020/08/19/more-americans-oppose-than-favor-the-government-providing-a-universal-basic-income-for-all-adult-citizens.

7. Thesia I. Garner, Adam Safir, and Jake Schild, "Receipt and Use of Stimulus Payments in the Time of the Covid-19 Pandemic," *Beyond the Numbers*, US Bureau of Labor Statistics, August 2020, www.bls.gov/opub/btn/volume-9/receipt-and-use-of-stimulus-payments-in-the-time-of-the-covid-19-pandemic.htm.

8. Andrew Stettner and Elizabeth Pancotti, "1 in 4 Workers Relied on Unemployment Aid During the Pandemic," The Century Foundation, March 17, 2021, tcf.org/content/commentary/1-in-4-workers-relied-on-unemployment-aid-during-the-pandemic/?session=1.

9. Kelsey Snell, "What's Inside the Senate's $2 Trillion Coronavirus Aid Package," NPR, March 26, 2020.

10. Thomas Jefferson, *Autobiography of Thomas Jefferson* (1821; repr., Hoboken, NJ: Start Publishing, 2012), 47–48.

11. Josh Dawsey, "Trump Derides Protections for Immigrants from 'Shithole' Countries," *Washington Post*, January 12, 2018.

12. Ira Katznelson, *When Affirmative Action Was White* (New York: Norton, 2005), 21–22, Apple Books.

13. MSNBC, "Senator Shelley Moore Capito: 'I Didn't Come Here to Hurt People' | Morning Joe | CNBC," YouTube, June 29, 2017, www.youtube.com/watch?v=RyyI3dJPBxk&t=336s.

14. Patricia Mazzei, " 'It's Just Too Much': A Florida Town Grapples with a Shutdown After a Hurricane," *New York Times*, January 7, 2019.

15. John Rawls, *A Theory of Justice* (1971; repr., Cambridge, MA: Belknap Press, 1999), 48, Apple Books.

16. Anjuli Sastry Krbechek and Karen Grigsby Bates, "When LA Erupted in Anger: A Look Back at the Rodney King Riots," NPR, April 26, 2017.

17. "Fannie Lou Hamer's America | Is This America?," *America Reframed*, PBS, www.pbs.org/video/america-reframed-fannie-lou-hamers-america-is-this-america.

18. Gates, *Stony the Road*, 5–6.

19. Bennett, *Black Power U.S.A.*, 404.

20. Nicholas Bogel-Burroughs, "Prosecutors Say Derek Chauvin Knelt on George Floyd for 9 Minutes 29 Seconds, Longer Than Initially Reported.," *New York Times*, March 30, 2021.

21. Nikole Hannah-Jones, "What Is Owed," *New York Times*, June 30, 2020.

22. Ibid.

23. Derrick Bell, *Faces at the Bottom of the Well: The Permanence of Racism* (New York: Basic Books, 1992), chap 3, Apple Books.

24. Ibid.

25. Angela Glover Blackwell and Michael McAfee, "Banks Should Face History and Pay Reparations," *New York Times*, June 26, 2020.

26. Drew DeSilver, "In Past Elections, U.S. Trailed Most Developed Countries in Voter Turnout," Pew Research Center, November 3, 2020, www.pewresearch.org/fact-tank/2020/11/03/in-past-elections-u-s-trailed-most-developed-countries-in-voter-turnout.

27. Frieda Wallison, "Voting in Peru," Aspen Public Radio, March 5, 2014, www.aspenpublicradio.org/xyour-ideas/2014-03-05/voting-in-peru.

28. Berman, *Give Us the Ballot*, 11.

29. *The Year Earth Changed*, directed by Tom Beard (AppleTV+, 2021).

30. Figures based on author analyses of data from U.S. Census Bureau's "U.S. and World Population Clock," U.S. Centers for Disease Control and Prevention's "Number of Deaths and Percent Distribution by Specified Hispanic Origin and Race for Non-Hispanic Population: United States and Each State, 1999–2007," U.S. Department of Homeland Security's "2013 Yearbook of Immigration Statistics," and U.S. Census Bureau's Population Estimates Program (PEP) estimates of population for the United States by age, sex, race, and Hispanic origin released July 1, 2014.

ABOUT THE AUTHOR

Steve Phillips is the author of the 2016 *New York Times* bestseller *Brown Is the New White*. A national political leader and civil rights lawyer, he is a columnist for *The Guardian* and *The Nation* and the host of the podcast *Democracy in Color with Steve Phillips*. His writing has appeared in the *New York Times*, the *Los Angeles Times*, and the *San Francisco Chronicle*, and he has appeared on multiple national radio and television networks, including NBC, CNN, MSNBC, Fox News, the BBC, and C-SPAN. A graduate of Stanford University and Hastings College of the Law, Phillips is the founder of Democracy in Color, a political media organization focused on political strategy and analysis at the intersection of race and politics.

www.stevephillips.com

PUBLISHING IN THE PUBLIC INTEREST

Thank you for reading this book published by The New Press. The New Press is a nonprofit, public interest publisher. New Press books and authors play a crucial role in sparking conversations about the key political and social issues of our day.

We hope you enjoyed this book and that you will stay in touch with The New Press. Here are a few ways to stay up to date with our books, events, and the issues we cover:

- Sign up at www.thenewpress.com/subscribe to receive updates on New Press authors and issues and to be notified about local events
- Like us on Facebook: www.facebook.com/newpressbooks
- Follow us on Twitter: www.twitter.com/thenewpress

Please consider buying New Press books for yourself; for friends and family; or to donate to schools, libraries, community centers, prison libraries, and other organizations involved with the issues our authors write about.

The New Press is a 501(c)(3) nonprofit organization. You can also support our work with a tax-deductible gift by visiting www.thenewpress.com/donate.